TAKING SIDES

Clashing Views on Controversial

Issues in Management

TAKING⟳SIDES

Clashing Views on Controversial
Issues in Management

Selected, Edited, and with Introductions by

Marc Street
University of South Florida

McGraw-Hill/Dushkin
A Division of The McGraw-Hill Companies

To my most magnificent wife, Vera.
You are my reason, my inspiration, my motivation

Photo Acknowledgment
Cover image: Montage photos by Corbis/Royalty Free,
Getty Images, Photos.com, Punchstock

Cover Acknowledgment
Maggie Lytle

Taking Sides ® is a registered trademark of McGraw-Hill/Dushkin

Manufactured in the United States of America

First edition

1234567890DOCDOC0987654

0-07-248058-0
ISSN: 1552-4477

Printed on Recycled Paper

Preface

> He who knows only his side of the case knows little of that. His reasons
> may have been good, and no one may have been able to refute them. But
> if he is equally unable to refute the reasons on the opposite side he has no
> ground for preferring either opinion.
>
> —John Stuart Mill[1]

The U.S. criminal system is adversarial in nature. Two sides with incompatible goals meet in front of a judge and jury in order to determine the fate of an individual charged with a crime. Underlying this process is the presupposition that truth can be reached through the presentation of conflicting viewpoints. This book, the first edition of *Taking Sides: Clashing Views on Controversial Issues in Management,* is predicated on this very same presupposition. Each of the debates presented here mimics the courtroom: There are two opposing sides, each vigorously presenting its evidence and questioning their opponents case. There is a judge, the reader, who considers the relative merits of each side, hopefully maintaining objectivity while searching for truth. And there is a verdict, signaling victory for one side and conviction for the other.

This text consists of 17 debates on controversial issues in the field of business management. Each issue consists of opposing viewpoints presented in a pro and con format. It is your role as judge to give each side a fair and unbiased hearing. This will be a difficult task, because each of the authors of the 34 articles is an expert and defends his or her position with great vigor. To help in your task, we suggest that you ask difficult questions, make notes on troubling points, and interact with the material. Most importantly, if you have a preconceived opinion about an issue, force yourself to look critically at the side you support. This, too, is difficult to do; it's much easier to find the weaknesses in the opposing side than in your own. But doing so helps protect against self-deception and, frequently, strengthens your original belief. And, perhaps most importantly, it makes you think!

Organization of this book. Each issue starts with an *introduction*, which sets the stage for the debate as it is argued in the yes and no selections. The *postscript* follows the selections and provides some final observations and comments about the topic. The postscript also contains *suggestions for further reading* on the topic that should prove beneficial in the event you are still undecided. Keep in mind that the selections represent only two possible viewpoints on a topic; there may well be other positions on these subjects beyond the two in the book. Relevant Internet site addresses (URLs) have been provided for your benefit and can be found on the page immediately preceding the part openers. Finally, at the back of the book is a list of all the *contributors to this volume.* Biographical information on the philosophers, economists, social commentators,

---

[1]M. Neil Browne and Stuart M. Keeley, *Asking the Right Questions,* 6th edition. Prentice Hall, 2001.

educators, political analysts and other experts who contributed articles can be found here.

Acknowledgments.   I would like to thank several of my USF students for their help: Tommy Shepard, Robin Ashby, Angela Gay, Christina Harmeyer, and Rosanna Homb. I would also like to extend a special thanks to my tremendous editor at McGraw-Hill/Dushkin, Jill Peter. Without her patience, calmness, and flexibility, this book would never have been completed on time. Thanks Jill! Finally, I want to thank my wife, Vera, for her unflinching support and constant encouragement.

Marc Street
University of South Florida

Contents In Brief

Contents

Ethics scholar Chris Provis examines bluffing within the context of labor negotiations and concludes that it does indeed constitute unethical behavior. Bluffing, he argues, is deception and therefore unethical, regardless of whether it occurs in or out of the negotiation process. University of California, Santa Barbara philosopher Fritz Allhoff presents a clever and unique defense of bluffing in business negotiations. The central tenet in Allhoff's position is that certain roles that we are required to assume allow us to morally justify behaviors that might otherwise be considered immoral.

Justice Joyce Kennard, writing for the majority, argues that Nike's public response to charges they operated sweatshops overseas constituted "commercial" speech and, therefore, is not protected by the First Amendment of the U.S. Constitution. Justice Janice Brown contends that the U.S. Supreme Court has not provided the courts with an unambiguous definition of commercial speech and, consequently, part of the foundation of the majority's position is undermined. She also calls into question whether there should be a distinction between commercial and non-commerical speech in the first place.

Legal scholar Robert B. Thompson presents Manne's argument on insider regulation. Thompson then provides us with an analysis of the status and relevance of Manne's position three decades after the publication of his seminal text. UCLA professor of law Stephen Bainbridge does not accept Manne's arguments. Bainbridge believes that insider trading ultimately causes inefficiency in the markets and, therefore, must be subject to regulation.

Cato Institute research fellow Dr. Walter Williams argues that affirmative action is no longer useful in the workplace. He likens affirmative action to a "zero-sum" game where one group benefits at the expense of all other groups. Dr. Wilbert Jenkins presents, and then rebuts, the major points critics of affirmative action typically raise. He also provides a discussion on the relationship between affirmative action and diversity in the workplace. He argues that since diversity is good business, and affirmative action encourages diversity, then affirmative action is good business.

Michael Verespej notes that for many employees, it is the drug users who are problematic, not the testing. He points out that both employees and managers are becoming increasingly intolerant of drugs in the workplace and, as a result, actually welcome drug testing. Scholar Jennifer Moore presents a philosophical discussion of why the individual rights of the employee trump the corporation's right to protect itself. In so doing, she reaches the conclusion that drug testing cannot be justified as a legitimate corporate policy.

Mary Salomon and Joan Schork answered "yes" and provided a detailed argument built on the idea that there is a business case for diversity. During the course of their article, the authors consider several commonly accepted arguments supportive of workplace diversity. Researcher Thomas Kochan and his colleagues reported findings from their complex, sophisticated research project. Despite their initial expectations, the researchers failed to find support for the effects of diversity on performance and, thus, provided this issue with its "no" response.

Stephen J. Rose and Heidi I. Hartmann, scholars at the Institute for Women's Policy Research, argue in their 2004 study that discrimination is still the main reason for the persistence in the gender gap. Naomi Lopez, director of the Center for Enterprise and Opportunity at the Pacific Research Institute in San Francisco, provides evidence that the wage gap is a function of several different variables beyond gender discrimination. She concludes her analysis with the observation that we may never reduce the wage gap entirely and that such an outcome is not necessarily undesirable.

In presenting her view that whistle-blowing is usually a form of disloyalty, business ethics scholar Sissela Bok examines the nature of the whistle-blowing act itself as well as the motives of the individual exposing the wrongdoing. In contrast with Bok, University of New Brunswick philosophy professor Robert Larmer argues that it is not a breach of trust and, therefore, not an act of disloyalty.

PART 3   STRATEGIC MANAGEMENT

Sarah Anderson and John Cavanagh argue that outsourcing is a real threat to the economic health of the United States and provide several suggestions as to the types of governmental actions necessary to keep American jobs from moving overseas. Included in their discussion is an analysis of the views of the two 2004 presidential candidates, John Kerry and George W. Bush. Dr. Daniel Drezner argues that the controversy surrounding outsourcing is not new and that its current form is more hype than substance. He shows how outsourcing is actually economically beneficial to America, despite the warnings of critics. Dr. Drezner also asserts that the concept of outsourcing is consistent with a solid understanding of free-market capitalism and an appreciation of traditional American principles and values.

Hazard materials managers Raymond Patchak and William Smith believe that corporations, under the right set of circumstances, will willingly engage in self-regulatory environmental behavior. Environmental scholars Linda Greer and Christopher van Löben Sels present the results of a case study involving Dow Chemical in which expected cost savings were not enough incentive for Dow top management to adopt a voluntary pollution reduction plan.

Issue 16. Is Economic Globalization Good for Humankind? 306

Foreign policy expert Murray Weidenbaum, in a reprint of a speech he delivered in 2001, promotes his "yes" response by systematically presenting, and then debunking, the most common "myths" surrounding globalization. He believes that globalization is a force for positive change. Professor Herman Daly feels that increasing globalization requires increases in political, social, and cultural integration across borders as well. The outcome is a loss of national identity for the countries involved as power is transferred from traditional domestic sources—i.e., governments, domestic businesses, local enterprises—to transnational corporations.

Issue 17. Are Global Sweatshops Exploitative? 324

The first article, written by scholars Richard Appelbaum and Peter Dreier, chronicles the rise of the grassroots, college campus, anti-global sweatshops movement in the late 1990s. Columnist and social commentator Radley Balko argues that sweatshops are not exploitative. His article presents several additional points frequently offered in defense of globalization in general, and sweatshops in particular.

Introduction

Controversial Issues in Management

This introduction consists of four sections, each of which briefly discusses a different area of business management and sets the stage for the debate topics that comprise the book. This essay is organized in a manner paralleling the presentation of the debate topics in the text: Business ethics is discussed in the first section, organizational behavior and human resource management in the second, strategic management in the third, and environmental and international management in the final section.

Ethical Issues for Managers

Many business ethics scholars analyze this complex management topic at two levels. The macro-level involves issues broad in nature and relevant for analysis at the organizational level. In this text, we limit our discussion to a specific macro-level issue, albeit a critically important issue. This topic concerns the degree of moral responsibility an organization has to the society in which it functions. At the micro-level of analysis, business ethics is concerned primarily with the ethical decision-making process of individuals in the workplace. Both of these levels of analysis are expanded on briefly below.

Macro-level Analysis: Corporate Social Responsibility vs. Profit Maximization

Twenty-five years ago, corporate America measured success by the creation of shareholder wealth. Companies that increased shareholders' wealth were successful, and those that didn't, were not. In the early years of the new century, determining corporate success is a much more complicated affair. The traditional *shareholder theory* of profit maximization has been replaced with a new method of defining corporate success known as *stakeholder theory*.

Stakeholder theory and social responsibility.   This approach to defining corporate success differs dramatically from the traditional shareholder approach. In this view, a stakeholder is any entity that contributes resources to the firm and therefore, has a "stake" in the firm's survival. A typical list of an organization's stakeholders includes customers, employees, management, suppliers, shareholders, partners, governments, and society at large. Each stakeholder determines organizational performance independent of the others and, since each stakeholder has contributed different resources, each is likely to use different criteria by which to evaluate performance. This can lead to situations where one set of stakeholders is pleased with firm performance while another feels the firm has performed very poorly.

An important implication of stakeholder theory is that managers have obligations that go beyond profit maximization since they are concerned with satisfying the needs of all of its stakeholders. Thus, those firms that do not place the interests of one set of stakeholders above the rest are acting in a *socially responsible* manner, whereas firms that stick to the traditional emphasis of maximizing profit with disregard of other stakeholder interests are irresponsible and immoral.

Shareholder theory and profit maximization.   Standing in complete contrast to the current trend toward stakeholder-driven social responsibility is the traditional economic advocacy of shareholder theory. Advocates of free-market capitalism believe that the only responsibility an organization has is to maximize profits for its shareholders. They point out, correctly, that shareholders own the companies in which they invest, not employees, customers, suppliers, or other stakeholders. Their investment subjects them to the risks and rewards associated with ownership and also entitles them to expect management to act in accordance with their wishes. If, for example, management acts against shareholder interests by spending profits for a social program rather than increasing dividends, they have, in effect, stolen from the owners of the firm. Given this, we can see how advocates of this perspective view shareholder theory as both illegal and immoral. In this view, managers are morally obligated to maximize shareholder wealth.

Micro-level Analysis: Ethical Decision Making

At the micro-level of analysis, business ethics is the study of the influences and processes involved in individual ethical decision making (EDM). The primary focus is to identify those factors that affect an individual's decision to act morally (or not) at the workplace. Understanding these factors is of prime importance for managers, not only to understand their own ethical behavior, but that of their employees as well. Over the years, EDM scholars have developed many different models of ethical behavior but, despite these efforts, there is currently no dominant model accepted by all. However, scholars have managed to identify several factors that appear to be predictive of ethical behavior. We briefly discuss these next.

Personal characteristics.   Research has shown that individuals who score high on *Machiavellianism* are more likely to act unethically than those who score low. Machiavellianism is a personality trait best described with the adage, "the ends justify the means." High Machs, as they are known, are more concerned with reaching their goals than in the manner in which they achieved them. *Locus of control* measures the extent to which an individual feels that luck, fate, or forces beyond his control are primarily responsible for what happens to him in life. Individuals who strongly believe this to be the case (known as externals) are much more likely to engage in unethical behavior than are individuals who strongly disagree with this view (known as internals). *Gender* has also been shown to predict ethical behavior. All things equal, females are much more likely to act ethically than are males.

Situational characteristics.   EDM scholars have noted that several characteristics of the ethical decision situation play a role in whether an individual acts morally or not. One of the strongest predictors is the *likelihood of getting caught*; the greater it is, the lower the probability of unethical behavior. Peer behavior also plays a significant role in ethical behavior. An individual is more likely to act unethically if his/her peers are acting unethically. This is known as *differential association*—basically we tend to do what our peers do. Finally, the probability of unethical behavior increases if the *costs* of getting caught acting unethically are perceived as being less than the *benefits* from doing so.

Business Ethics and Taking Sides

Part 1 of this book consists of five debates, two at the macro and three at the micro-levels of analysis. We have already looked at background information about the corporate social responsibility vs. profit maximization controversy; Issue 1 frames this topic in a debate format and presents articles supportive of each side. Issue 4 concerns Nike Corporation's public response to allegations that it had knowingly employed sweatshop labor in the overseas production of its products. The question posed in this debate is whether or not Nike's response should have been protected by the First Amendment of the U.S. Constitution.

Issue 2 in Part 1 involves the popular corporate strategy of downsizing. Increasingly, U.S. firms are adopting the view that reducing costs through labor force reductions—downsizing—should not be reserved only for desperate firms on the edge of bankruptcy. But what about the human element involved?

Issue 3 examines an old, but still relevant, business behavior: bluffing. It's an age-old question—is it morally acceptable to bluff during negotiations? We present contrasting responses to this interesting topic.

Issue 5 presents a debate that has simmered beneath the surface of corporate America for two decades but is now enjoying a resurrection of sorts. Thanks to the Martha Stewart affair, the topic of insider trading has received renewed attention, both in the popular press and in academic circles. Our concern here is with its legality; specifically, we ask if insider trading should be illegal in the first place.

Organizational Behavior and Human Resource Management

Organizational Behavior Basics

According to a leading introductory textbook, organizational behavior (OB) is concerned with the "study of what people do in an organization and how that behavior affects the performance of the organization" (Stephen P. Robbins, *Organizational Behavior*, Prentice Hall, 2001). Some business scholars (including the author of this introduction) refer to OB as "psychology in the workplace," an apt description given that much of what we know about human behavior at work is based on the application of knowledge generated by the psychological sciences. This is really not surprising considering that the main goal of OB is to generate knowledge about human behavior as a means to improving organizational effectiveness.

The value of OB to the practicing manager. The field of organizational behavior has value for managers to the extent that it can positively affect important organizational outcomes. And although OB scholars study many different aspects of workplace behavior, a core group of four critically important outcomes has received the most research attention over the years.

U.S. corporations lose billions of dollars each year as a result of employees failing to report to work. Loss of labor hours is only part of the cost; *absenteeism* frequently upsets the flow of work and results in operational inefficiencies. Fortunately, OB scholars know quite a bit about what causes absenteeism and how it can be reduced. For example, research consistently shows that females tend to be absent more frequently than males, primarily because of family-related concerns (pregnancy, raising children, etc.). As a result of this finding, many managers reduce the impact of absenteeism by allowing female employees greater flexibility in their work schedules.

Turnover occurs when an employee, voluntarily or not, permanently leaves the organization. Like absenteeism, turnover is extremely costly to employers, affecting productivity and upsetting the flow of work. By some conservative accounts, turnover costs can run as high as $15–20,000 per employee. Understanding why an employee leaves an organization is a terrifically complicated process; nevertheless, OB scholars have made inroads here as well. For example, research shows that the more an employee is committed to the organization and its goals, the less likely he/she is to leave.

A third important outcome is *job satisfaction*. This is one of the most studied variables in organizational behavior, a fact attesting to its importance in the workplace. OB scholars have established, for example, that organizations with highly satisfied workers have lower absenteeism and turnover rates and higher levels of productivity than do organizations whose employees are less satisfied with their jobs. So, what can managers do to increase job satisfaction? Research suggests four ways: provide mentally challenging work, fair and equitable rewards, supportive working conditions, and supportive colleagues.

The fourth important outcome is *productivity*. OB scholars have studied this variable from the perspective of the organization as well as the employee. We've already seen that at the organizational level, job satisfaction, absenteeism, and turnover have been shown to impact organizational productivity. At the individual level, the belief is that the more motivated an individual is, the more productive he or she is likely to be. The OB literature contains many different models of workplace motivation, each offering managers various suggestions as to how they can motivate their employees.

Other OB topics of interest to managers. Organizational behavior has much to say about other issues of interest to managers beyond those discussed above.

Personality researchers are concerned with, among other things, identifying the various components of personality and exploring whether some personality traits are predictive of success on the job. Another important area of research involves *decision making*. This multifaceted field offers many different theories about how humans make decisions and offers managers much insight into the factors that lead to poor decision making and how to avoid them. Over the last 20 years, *work teams* have become an important work unit at most major corporations in America. As a result, many OB scholars study work group dynamics and processes and have learned much about what differentiates an effective work team from an ineffective one. One of the oldest areas of OB research concerns *leadership and the use of power and politics* in the workplace. Despite the large body of research on this topic, OB scholars have a less than impressive record of providing useful insights and suggestions to practicing managers about how to develop, identify, or create effective leaders in the workplace.

Human Resource Management Basics

Human resource management (HRM) is the design and implementation of formal systems that utilize human resources to accomplish organizational goals (Mathis and Jackson, *Human Resource Management*, South-Western Thompson, 2003). Although the fields of organizational behavior and human resource management are both conducted primarily at the individual level of analysis, HRM is a much more practical area of management than is OB. It is only a slight stretch to describe OB as a field characterized by theories and concepts, while laws, regulations, and formal systems characterize HRM.

Typical HRM functions.   Virtually every major U.S. corporation has an HR department that is in charge of managing several interlinked activities concerning the firms' employees. Although it varies from firm to firm, in general HR managers are responsible for at least seven different human resource functions: HR planning, equal employment opportunity compliance, staffing, human resource development, compensation, health and safety concerns, and employee/management relations.

Human resource planning involves anticipating and responding to the forces that will affect the supply of and demand for employees. For example, firms that are growing usually have a need for more employees; HR managers are responsible for determining how many are needed, where they are needed, and when they are needed. *Equal employment opportunity (EEO)* compliance affects every aspect of HR management and has become the single most important area of HR management over the last two decades. It is absolutely imperative that managers are aware of the requirements of affirmative action and the necessity of developing a diverse workforce. Firms that are oblivious—or worse, ignore—the dictates of EEO risk severe damage to their reputations and will likely face costly legal proceedings.

Staffing consists of three HR functions: job analysis, recruiting, and selecting. Job analysis tells HR managers what workers do and provides the basis for recruiting qualified applicants to apply for open positions. Selecting is the process of choosing from among the group of qualified applicants. *Human resource development* is concerned with such activities as new employee orientation, skills training, career development, career planning, and evaluating employee performance. *Compensation* is another crucial HR function and, along with pay and incentives for good performance, includes the distribution of employee benefits. HR managers help develop wage and salary systems, incentive and bonus plans, and competitive benefits packages.

Complying with federal safety regulations, dealing with drug-related issues, and managing workplace security—particularly in a post-9/11 America—are a few of the challenges involved in the *health and safety* HR function. Last, but certainly not least, is the HR function that monitors the *relationship between employees and management.* There has been a dramatic increase in the number of lawsuits brought by disgruntled employees who believe their rights to privacy, for example, have been violated by inappropriate corporate policies. Courts have been very receptive to such accusations; consequently, it is critical that the HR department develops, updates, and communicates organizational policies so that all parties involved know what is expected.

OB, HRM, and Taking Sides

Two of the five debates in this section involve the topic of discrimination: Issue 6 wonders if affirmative action has outlived its usefulness, while Issue 9 asks if the persistent wage gap between men and women is due to discrimination or to some other factors. Issue 7 involves a clash of rights: Does an employee's right to privacy supercede the employer's right to a drug-free workplace? In today's EEO-driven work environment, much is made about the productive benefits of maintaining a diversified workforce. Issue 8 takes this topic head-on and questions whether firms that embrace workplace diversity are more productive than those that do not. The final debate in this section, Issue 10, speculates as to whether or not individuals who go public with damaging information about corporate practices are being disloyal.

Strategic Management

Strategic Management Basics

While OB and HRM are primarily concerned with understanding, motivating, and managing individual employees in the workplace, the focus of strategic management is on the organization as a whole. As you might expect, the basic unit of strategic management is a *strategy.* At its most basic, a strategy is a plan designed to achieve a specific goal. In the business world, strategic management refers to the process of effectively developing and executing the collection of plans designed to achieve the organization's goals. Typically, the goals of the organization reflect the overall purpose of the company as spelled out in the firm's mission statement. In most large companies, top-level executives and managers are responsible for the development of the organization's strategies, while mid-level managers and supervisors are typically in charge of making sure the strategies are implemented successfully. Thus, the executives are involved in *strategy formulation,* while the managers and supervisors are concerned with *strategy implementation.*

SWOT Analysis as a source of strategy formulation.   So far so good, but where do the strategies come from in the first place? Perhaps the most frequent method used by executives to develop strategies is a SWOT analysis. In this procedure, the organization identifies its strengths, weaknesses, opportunities, and threats (SWOT). Once this information has been gathered, top management develops plans of attack that (1) capitalize on the firm's strengths and (2) allow the organization to take advantage of available opportunities. Management must also be careful, however, to (1) try and counter potential threats from the external environment (such as competitors), (2) while also avoiding spending excessive resources on weak areas. Thus, the most effective strategies are those that support the mission of the organization by taking advantage of the firm's strengths and opportunities and minimizing the effects of threats and weaknesses. In an ideal world, the firm can turn its strengths into a *sustained competitive advantage*. This occurs when an organization is able to consistently outperform its competitors even though the competitors have tried to reduce its advantage by duplicating the firm's sources of strength.

Levels of strategies.   Many corporations in the United States and abroad conduct business in more than one industry and/or in more than one market. Consequently, they have a need for more than one level of strategy. When top management develops plans and sets goals for the overall corporation, it is engaging in *corporate-level strategy* development. When top management chooses a specific set of strategies for a particular business or market, it is engaging in *business-level strategy* development.

Types of strategies.   There are several different models for identifying the major strategic approaches available to organizations when conducting business-level strategy development. One of the most popular approaches is Michael Porter's three generic strategies framework. Firms that attempt to distinguish themselves from competitors by virtue of the quality of their products or services are using a *differentiation* strategy. Other firms try to achieve success by keeping costs of production lower than their competitors, thus employing a *cost leadership strategy*. Still other firms will concentrate their efforts on a specific geographic region or market, employing what Porter calls a *focus strategy* approach.

    At the corporate-level of strategic development, perhaps the most important question concerns the extent and nature of *diversification*. Diversification refers to the number of distinct businesses an organization is involved in and the degree to which they are related to each other. Some companies, such as WD-40, make just one product and are not concerned with strategic issues of diversification—theirs is a single-product strategy. Others, like General Motors, are involved in literally hundreds of businesses. Firms such as GM need to make corporate-level strategic decisions about the nature and type of diversification they should employ. *Related diversification* occurs when the organization runs several different businesses that are linked to each other in some manner. RJR Nabisco, for example, has numerous different businesses that share the same distribution mechanism—your local grocery store. The main advantage of implementing a related diversification strategy is that it reduces the firm's dependence on a specific business, thereby lowering its economic risk. *Unrelated diversification* is a strategy in which the organization's multiple businesses do not share any obvious links. During the 1980s, this was a favored approach of many large non-financial corporations interested in establishing themselves in the securities industry. Sears, for example, adopted an unrelated diversification strategy when it bought Dean Witter, as did GE when it purchased Kidder Peabody. Interestingly, research strongly suggests that unrelated diversification is not a sure road to success, which probably accounts for why its popularity as a corporate-level strategy has waned in recent years.

Strategic Management and Taking Sides

Part 3 of this text contains issues particularly relevant to the topic of strategic management. For many U.S. firms, an increasingly popular and effective cost-control method is outsourcing. While moving domestically expensive operational functions to a country with lower wage rates may reduce costs, many have argued that it is an unpatriotic strategy and should not be condoned. You can decide for yourself when you read Issue 11.

In recent years, the business and news media have portrayed numerous examples of U.S. CEOs receiving millions of dollars in salary and benefits while their organizations were posting losses, laying off workers and, in some instances, declaring bankruptcy. As a result of the public outrage generated by these accounts, the question of top-level management compensation has taken on greater importance in the field of strategic management. We address this topic in Issue 12, where we ask, are U.S. CEOs overpaid?

The final issue in Part 3 concerns the Sarbanes-Oxley Act of 2002. This legislation was designed to address the numerous violations of corporate governance rules and procedures top-level executives committed during the wave of scandals that affected corporate America over the last half-decade. Like the question of CEO pay, this too is a "hot" topic in strategic management and provides us with Issue 13, "Corporate Governance Reform: Is Sarbanes-Oxley the Answer?"

Environmental and International Management

Over the last quarter-century, two managerial challenges have grown in importance so dramatically that executives in corporate America have no alternative but to take them into account when formulating organizational strategy. The first of these challenges originates in the conflict between an organization's need to be financially successful and society's expectations that it conduct its business in a socially responsible manner. More specifically, U.S. organizations now face the difficult challenge of maintaining financial success while recognizing obligations to protect and maintain the world's physical environment. The second major challenge also involves competitive pressures. U.S. firms need to develop successful responses to the threats and opportunities resulting from the tremendous increase in international competition and the expansion of global markets that has occurred over the last twenty-five years.

The Environmental Challenge

As noted in the ethics section of this introduction, the corporate social responsibility (CSR) doctrine holds that organizations have obligations to society that extend beyond merely maximizing profit for their shareholders. For example, an important obligation of every firm, according to the CSR perspective, is to conduct business in a way that, at a minimum, is respectful of the natural environment. The history of business in America is full of stories of companies carelessly polluting rivers and streams, pumping tons of soot and chemicals into the air, cutting down and destroying millions of acres of forest and wetlands, and causing ecological disasters such as the Exxon *Valdez* oil spill. Not surprisingly, CSR advocates—primarily environmentalist groups—have applied tremendous public pressure on U.S. corporations to act responsibly toward the environment. The federal government has responded to the decades of environmental neglect by passing numerous laws forcing corporations to regulate their environmentally damaging behaviors. And although many major corporations have responded to the challenge, the constant stream of ominous reports on the decline of the earth's environment indicate that there is still much to be done.

For managers, the problem is that complying with all the laws and regulations, as well as conducting their business operations in a socially responsible manner, can be very costly. Firms often spend millions of dollars bringing their operations into compliance with federal laws and regulations, thus diverting funds that would normally go to profitable projects. Clearly, then, twenty-first century managers in corporate America face a difficult challenge: conducting their business operations in a manner respectful of the environment while successfully responding to the rapidly increasing levels of competition both domestically and abroad.

The International Challenge

In the early 1980s, the U.S. lighting industry was dominated by the General Electric corporation. GE's reign as the major player in the field came under serious attack, however, when Westinghouse, its major domestic competitor, sold its lamp operations to the huge Dutch conglomerate, Phillips Electronics. Virtually overnight, GE's competitive picture changed, and they found themselves suddenly on the defensive. In response, GE went global; they bought a Hungarian electronics firm and entered into a joint venture with Hitachi in order to break into the Asian markets. In 1990, GE generated less than 20 percent of its lighting sales from abroad; today the number is closer to 50 percent.

GE's experiences are not uncommon, nor are they unique to American firms. In response to the tremendous growth of competition from international firms, corporations all over the world have embraced the idea of globalization by extending sales and/or production operations to markets abroad. Globalization offers firms many advantages: access to new sources of cheap labor, access to new sources of highly skilled labor, access to established markets, and access to emerging markets (China, Russia, and India, for example). These advantages come with a cost, however: globalization, by its very definition, means greater competition. Thus, a second critical challenge facing U.S. managers is responding successfully to the tremendous growth of competition from international firms, both here and abroad.

Environmental Management, International Management, and Taking Sides

Part 4 in this text contains four debate topics. Issues 14 and 15 deal with environmental questions important for managers, while Issues 16 and 17 are primarily concerned with the topic of globalization.

An underlying assumption of the environmental movement in the United States and abroad is that the health of the planet is deteriorating and that business activity is primarily responsible. But is this assumption true? Issue 14 provides two different responses to this important question.

Issue 15 is concerned with controlling environmentally harmful corporate behavior. Free-market advocates typically argue that potential economic gains provide incentive for managers to act in a responsible manner toward the environment. Consequently, they argue, there is no need for governmental regulation. Skeptics of this view contend that the only time most corporations act responsibly is when they are compelled by law to do so.

A growing number of countries around the world have embraced the idea of globalization as a means of raising the standard of living for their citizens. But despite the fact that much evidence attests to the economic benefits that accrue as a result of globalization, there are those who question whether globalization on the whole is a positive occurrence. Issue 16 provides two competing answers to the question, is economic globalization good for humankind?

The final issue in this book concerns a specific outcome of the globalization movement, the emergence of global sweatshops. For many Third World countries, an abundance of cheap labor is the only competitive resource they have to offer. Numerous multinational firms have moved some of their domestic production operations overseas in order to take advantage of the lower labor costs. To globalization advocates, "sweatshops" are a natural step in the economic growth of the country; to members of the anti-globalization movement, it's exploitation. One thing is certain—the question, are global sweatshops exploitative?, inspires passionate answers on both sides of the debate.

On the Internet . . .

The W. Maurice Young Centre for Applied Ethics

The mission of the Centre is to bring moral philosophy into the public domain by advancing research in applied ethics, supporting courses with a significant ethical component and acting as a community resource.

http://www.ethics.ubc.ca/about.htm

U.S. Securities and Exchange Commission

The primary mission of the U.S. Securities and Exchange Commission (SEC) is to protect investors and maintain the integrity of the securities markets. This site has information on all things related to securities investing, including the following link on the SEC's stance on insider trading.

http://www.sec.gov/investor/pubs/
insidertradingguide.htm

Politics1.com

This Web site calls itself "The Most Comprehensive Online Guide to American Politics" and has numerous links to organizations and Web sites covering all aspects of the political spectrum. Topics covered include First Amendment and Affirmative Action concern.

http://www.politics1.com/index.htm

The Adam Smith Institute

The Adam Smith Institute is the UK's leading innovator of market economic policies. Named after the great Scottish economist and author of *The Wealth of Nations,* its guiding principles are free markets and a free society. Many social issues, such as downsizing, are covered here.

http://www.adamsmith.org/about/

PART 1

Ethical Issues for Managers

*A*n old saying holds that business ethics is an oxymoron. For years, the generally accepted view on morality and business was that they don't mix—that business is a game played by a different set of rules. To act morally was to act weakly. And in the business arena, weak firms were dead firms.

   Well, things certainly change. In today's business arena, firms are finding that immoral behavior can prove fatal. Thanks to the plethora of scandals on Wall Street in the 1980s and the massive, corporate scandals of the past 10 years, the field of business ethics is enjoying unprecedented influence and popularity. The issues in this section of the book involve ethical questions that are important to many managers in corporate America.

- Do Corporations Have a Responsibility to Society that Extends Beyond Merely Maximizing Profit?

- Is the Corporate Strategy of Downsizing Unethical?

- Is Bluffing During Negotiations Unethical?

- Are Corporations Accused of Wrongdoing Protected by the First Amendment?

- Should Insider Trading Be Legalized?

ISSUE 1

Do Corporations Have a Responsibility to Society That Extends Beyond Merely Maximizing Profit?

YES: Robert D. Hay and Edmund R. Gray, from "Introduction to Social Responsibility," in David Keller, man. ed., *Ethics and Values: Basic Readings in Theory and Practice* (Pearson Custom Publishing, 2002)

NO: Alexei M. Marcoux, from "Business Ethics Gone Wrong," Cato Institute (July 24, 2000)

ISSUE SUMMARY

YES: Robert D. Hay and Edmund R. Gray believe that corporations should be held accountable for more than profit maximization. Their argument is based on stakeholder theory and is presented in the form of an historical account of the evolution of managerial thinking on this important topic.

NO: In answering "no" to this question, Alexei Marcoux presents a frontal attack on stakeholder theory. Consistent with the views of Nobel Laureate Milton Friedman, Marcoux argues that the very nature of stakeholder theory is immoral and can only lead to disastrous results for all involved.

Today business students are taught that organizations have responsibilities that extend beyond merely trying to maximize profits for their shareholders. The traditional "shareholder" theory of profit maximization has been replaced with a new perspective: stakeholder theory. This theory asserts that organizations have responsibilities to all groups that are affected by the ultimate success and survival of the firm. An organization is responsible not only to its shareholders, but to its employees, customers, suppliers, community, local governments, and all other stakeholders who are affected by its existence. On the surface, this approach seems to be for the better; after all, wouldn't concern for the interests of those impacted by the organization cause the company to act in a manner that makes each better off? Well, as is often the case in management, the answer is not clear-cut. Many business scholars and successful business leaders argue that stakeholder theory is both immoral in its premises and damaging in its practice. Thus, we have a controversy for you to consider: Do corporations have a responsibility to society that goes beyond maximizing profit?

Those who answer in the affirmative usually provide a two-pronged response—the first based on stakeholder theory and the second on practical observations and assertions. Stakeholder theory argues that the manager's job is to balance interests among the various groups with a stake in the company's survival. Consequently, management's obligations have been expanded beyond focusing primarily on financial gain for shareholders to include satisfying the needs and concerns of all of its stakeholders. Organizations that recognize this expansion and act on it accordingly are said to be acting in a socially responsible manner, whereas firms that stick to the traditional emphasis of increasing share price as priority one are deemed irresponsible and immoral. The second prong in the "yes" response consists of more practical arguments. One point often raised is that since corporations are the source of many problems in society—pollution, corruption, discrimination, etc.—they should be required to resolve those problems. After all, the community in which the corporation resides is a legitimate stakeholder of the firm. Another argument holds that organizations frequently have financial resources and, therefore, are in position to use the money for social good and not only for increasing the power and wealth of the firm.

On the other side of the debate, the strongest and most consistent defender of shareholder theory has been economist and Nobel Laureate Milton Friedman. In his anti-stakeholder approach, Friedman argues that shareholders—not employees, customers, or suppliers—own the companies in which they invest and, consequently, have the legal right to expect management to comply with their desires (which is usually to maximize the value of their investments). Consider the example of a corporation whose management, without shareholder consent, wants to use some of the company's profits on its local community by contributing to the creation of a park project. If management chooses to reduce profit distribution to its shareholders and spend it on the project, they have acted both immorally and illegally since they have, in effect, stolen from the shareholders. If they choose to pay shareholders out of profit and instead finance the project by reducing labor costs, the employees will suffer. If they choose to avoid antagonizing shareholders and employees and contribute to the park by raising product prices, they will hurt their customers and possibly price themselves out of the market. Thus, according to Friedman, doing anything other than increasing shareholder wealth is tantamount to theft, is immoral, and is ultimately self-defeating for the organization.

In the "yes" selection that follows, Robert D. Hay and Edmund R. Gray argue for the stakeholder theory that is presented in the form of an historical account of the evolution of managerial thinking on this important topic. The "no" article is written by Alexei Marcoux and represents a frontal attack on stakeholder theory. Consistent with Friedman's views, he attempts to show that the very nature of stakeholder theory is immoral and can only lead to disastrous results for all involved.

Robert D. Hay and
Edmund R. Gray

 **YES**

Introduction to Social Responsibility

It was Jeremy Bentham, late eighteenth century English philosopher, who espoused the social, political, and economic goal of society to be "the greatest happiness for the greatest number." His cardinal principle was written into the Declaration of Independence as "the pursuit of happiness," which became a societal goal of the American colonists. Bentham's principle was also incorporated into the Constitution of the United States in the preamble where the goal was stated "to promote the general welfare."

The economic-political system through which we in America strive to achieve this societal goal emphasizes the economic and political freedom to pursue individual interests. Adam Smith, another English political economist of the late eighteenth century, stated that the best way to achieve social goals was as follows:

> Every individual is continually exerting himself to find out the most advantageous employment for whatever capital he can command. It is his own advantage, indeed, and not that of the society, which he has in view. But the study of his own advantage naturally, or rather necessarily, leads him to prefer that employment which is most advantageous to the society. . . .
>
> As every individual, therefore, endeavors as much as he can both to employ his capital in the support of domestic industry, and so to direct that industry that its produce may be of the greatest value, every individual necessarily labours to render the annual revenue of the society as great as he can. He generally, indeed, neither intends to promote the public interest, nor knows how much he is promoting it. By preferring the support of domestic to that of foreign industry, he intends only his own security; and by directing that industry in such a manner as its produce may be of the greatest value, he intends only his own gain, and he is in this, as in many other cases, led by an invisible hand to promote an end which was not part of his intention. Nor is it always the worse for the society that it was no part of it. By pursuing his own interest he frequently promotes that of the society more effectually than when he really intends to promote it. I have never known much good done by those who affected to trade for the public good. It is an affectation, indeed, not very common among merchants, and very few words need be employed in dissuading them from it.

Adam Smith's economic values have had an important influence on American business thinking. As a result, most business people for the first hundred and fifty years of our history embraced the theory that social goals could be achieved by pursuing individual interests.

By 1930 American values were beginning to change from that of the individual owner ethic to that of the group or social ethic. As part of this changing mood, it was felt that Smith's emphasis on owner's interests was too predominant at the expense of other contributors to a business organization. Consequently, a new philosophy of management took shape which stated that the social goals could be achieved by balancing the interests of several groups of people who had an interest in a business. It was stated by Charles H. Percy, then president of Bell and Howell, in the 1950s as follows:

> There are over 64 million gainfully employed people in the United States. One half of these work directly for American corporations, and the other half are vitally affected by business directly or indirectly. Our entire economy, therefore, is dependent upon the type of business management we have. Business management is therefore in many respects a public trust charged with the responsibility of keeping America economically sound. We at Bell & Howell can best do this by keeping our own company's program on a firm foundation and by having a growing group of management leaders to direct the activities of the company.
>
> Management's role in a free society is, among other things, to prove that the real principles of a free society can work within a business organization.
>
> Our basic objective is the development of individuals. In our own present program we are doing everything conceivable to encourage, guide, and assist, and provide an opportunity to everyone to improve their abilities and skills, thus becoming more valuable to the company and enabling the company to improve the rewards paid to the individual for such additional efforts.
>
> Our company has based its entire program for the future on the development of the individual and also upon the building of an outstanding management group. This is why we have emphasized so strongly the supervisory training program recently completed by all Bell & Howell supervisors, and why we are now offering this program to others in the organization training for future management responsibilities.
>
> But a company must also have a creed to which its management is dedicated. I hope that we can all agree to the following:
>
> We believe that our company must develop and produce outstanding products that will perform a great service or fill a need for our customers.
>
> We believe that our business must be run at an adequate profit and that the services and products that we offer must be better than those offered by competitors.
>
> We believe that management must serve employees, stockholders, and customers, but that we cannot serve the interests of any one group at the undue expense of the other two. A proper and fair balance must be preserved.
>
> We believe that our business must provide stability of employment and job security for all those who depend on our company for their livelihood.
>
> We believe that we are failing in our responsibility if our wages are not sufficiently high to not only meet the necessities of life but provide some of the luxuries as well. Wherever possible, we also believe that bonus earning should be paid for performance and output "beyond the call of duty."

We believe that every individual in the company should have an opportunity for advancement and growth with the organization. There should be no dead-end streets any place in an organization.

We believe in the necessity for constantly increasing productivity and output. Higher wages and greater benefits can never be "given" by management. Management can only see that they are paid out when "earned."

We believe in labor-saving machinery. We do not think human beings should perform operations that can be done by mechanical or electronic means. We believe in this because we believe in the human dignity and creative ability of the individual. We are more interested in the intellect, goodwill, initiative, enthusiasm, and cooperativeness of the individual than we are in his muscular energy.

We believe that every person in the company has a right to be treated with the respect and courtesy that is due a human being. It is for this reason that we have individual merit ratings, individual pay increases, job evaluation, and incentive pay; and it is why we keep every individual fully informed—through The Finder, through our annual report, through Family Night, and through individual letters—about the present program of the company and also about our future objectives.

We believe that our business must be conducted with the utmost integrity. We may fight the principle of confiscatory taxation, but we will pay our full share. We will observe every governmental law and regulation, local, state, and national. We will deal fairly with our customers, we will advertise our product truthfully, and we will make every attempt to maintain a friendly relationship with our competitors while at the same time waging the battle of free competition.

Some business leaders, on the one hand, preach the virtues of the free enterprise, democratic system and, on the other hand, run their own business in accordance with autocratic principles—all authority stemming from the top with little delegation of responsibility to individuals within the organization. We believe in democracy—in government and in our business.

We hope that every principle we believe in is right and is actually being practiced throughout the company as it affects every individual.

Then in the late 1960s American business leaders began to take another look at the problems of society in light of the goal of "the greatest happiness for the greatest number." How could people be happy if they have to breathe foul air, drink polluted water, live in crowded cities, use very unsafe products, be misled by untruthful advertising, be deprived of a job because of race, and face many other problems? Thus, another philosophy of management emerged. It was voiced by several American business leaders:

Business must learn to look upon its social responsibilities as inseparable from its economic function. If it fails to do so, it leaves a void that will quickly be filled by others—usually by the government. (George Champion, Chase National Bank, 1966.)

I believe there is one basic principle that needs to be emphasized more than ever before. It is the recognition that business is successful in the long term only when it is directed toward the needs of the society. (Robert F. Hansberger, Boise Cascade, 1971.)

The actions of the great corporations have so profound an influence that the public has come to judge them not only by their profit-making record, but by the contribution of their work to society as a whole. Under a political democracy such as ours, if the corporation fails to perceive itself and govern its action in essentially the same manner as the public at large, it may find itself in serious trouble. (Louis B. Lundborg, Bank of America, 1971.)

With these remarks we can see that there has been a shift in managerial emphasis from owners' interests to group interests, and finally, to society's interests. Managers of some American businesses have come to recognize that they have a social responsibility.

Historical Perspective of Social Responsibility

The concept of the social responsibility of business managers has in recent years become a popular subject of discussion and debate within both business and academic circles. Although the term itself is of relatively recent origin, the underlying concept has existed as long as there have been business organizations. It rests on the logical assumption that because the firm is a creation of society, it has a responsibility to aid in the accomplishment of society's goals. In the United States concepts of social responsibility have moved from three distinct phases which may be labeled Phases I, II, and III.

Phase I—Profit Maximizing Management

The Phase I concept was based on the belief that business managers have but one single objective—maximize profits. The only constraint on this pursuit was the legal framework within which the firm operated. The origin of this view may be found in Adam Smith's *Wealth of Nations*. As previously noted, Smith believed that individual business people acting in their own selfish interest would be guided by an "invisible hand" to promote the public good. In other words, the individual's drive for maximum profits and the regulation of the competitive marketplace would interact to create the greatest aggregate wealth for a nation and therefore the maximum public good. In the United States this view was universally accepted throughout the nineteenth century and the early part of the twentieth century. Its acceptance rested not only on economic logic but also on the goals and values of society. America in the nineteenth and first half of the twentieth centuries was a society of economic scarcity; therefore, economic growth and the accumulation of aggregate wealth were primary goals. The business system with its emphasis on maximum profit was seen as a vehicle for eliminating economic scarcity. In the process employee abuses such as child labor, starvation wages, and unsafe working conditions could be tolerated. No questions were raised with regard to using up the natural resources and polluting streams and land. Nor was anyone really concerned about urban problems, unethical advertising, unsafe products, and poverty problems of minority groups.

The profit maximization view of social responsibility also complemented the Calvinistic philosophy which pervaded nineteenth and twentieth century

American thinking. Calvinism stressed that the road to salvation was through hard work and the accumulation of wealth. It then logically followed that a business person could demonstrate diligence (and thus godliness) and accumulate a maximum amount of wealth by adhering to the discipline of profit maximization.

Phase II—Trusteeship Management

Phase II, which may be labeled the "trusteeship" concept, emerged in the 1920s and 30s. It resulted from structural changes in both business institutions and in society. According to this concept, corporate managers were responsible not simply for maximizing the stockholders' wealth but rather for maintaining an equitable balance among the competing claims of customers, employees, suppliers, creditors, and the community. In this view the manager was seen as "trustee" for the various contributor groups to the firm rather than simply an agent of the owners.

The two structural trends largely responsible for the emergence of this newer view of social responsibility were: (1) the increasing diffusion of ownership of the shares of American corporations, and (2) the development of a pluralistic society. The extent of the diffusion of stock ownership may be highlighted by the fact that by the early 1930s the largest stockholders in corporations such as American Telephone and Telegraph, United States Steel, and the Pennsylvania Railroad owned less than one percent of the total shares outstanding of these companies. Similar dispersion of stock ownership existed in most other large corporations. In such situations management typically was firmly in control of the corporation. Except in rare circumstances, the top executives were able to perpetuate themselves in office through the proxy mechanism. If an individual shareholder was not satisfied with the performance of the firm, there was little recourse other than to sell the stock. Hence, although the stockholder's legal position was that of an owner—and thus a principal-agent relationship existed between the stockholder and the managers—the stockholder's actual position was more akin to bondholders and other creditors of the firm. Given such a situation it was only natural to ask, "To whom is management responsible?" The "trusteeship" concept provided an answer. Management was responsible to all the contributors to the firm—that is, stockholders, workers, customers, suppliers, creditors, and the community.

The emergence of a largely pluralistic society reinforced the logic of the "trusteeship" concept. A pluralistic society has been defined as "one which has many semi-autonomous and autonomous groups through which power is diffused. No one group has overwhelming power over all others, and each has direct or indirect impact on all others. From the perspective of business firms this translated into the fact that exogenous groups had considerable impact upon and influence over them. In the 1930s the major groups exerting significant pressure on business were labor unions and the federal government. Today the list has grown to include numerous minority, environmental, and consumer groups among others. Clearly, one logical approach to such a situation is to consider that the firm has a responsibility to each interested group and that management's task is to reconcile and balance the claims of the various groups.

Phase III—Quality of Life Management

Phase III, which may be called the "quality of life" concept of social responsibility, has become popular in recent years. The primary reason for the emergence of this concept is the very significant metamorphosis in societal goals which this nation is experiencing. Up to the middle part of this century, society's principal goal was to raise the standard of living of the American people, which could be achieved by producing more goods and services. The fact that the U.S. had become the wealthiest nation in the world was testimony to the success of business in meeting this expectation.

In this process, however, the U.S. has become what John Kenneth Galbraith calls an "affluent society" in which the aggregate scarcity of basic goods and services is no longer the fundamental problem. Other social problems have developed as direct and indirect results of economic success. Thus, there are pockets of poverty in a nation of plenty, deteriorating cities, air and water pollution, defacement of the landscape, and a disregard for consumers to mention only a few of the prominent social problems. The mood of the country seems to be that things have gotten out of balance—the economic abundance in the midst of a declining social and physical environment does not make sense. As a result, a new set of national priorities which stress the "Quality of life" appear to be emerging.

Concomitant with the new priorities, societal consensus seems to be demanding that business, with its technological and managerial skills and its financial resources, assume broader responsibilities—responsibilities that extend beyond the traditional economic realm of the Phase I concept or the mere balancing of the competing demands of the sundry contributors and pressure groups of the Phase II concept. The socially responsible firm under Phase III reasoning is one that becomes deeply involved in the solution of society's major problems.

Personal Values of the Three Styles of Managers

Values are the beliefs and attitudes which form one's frame of reference and help to determine the behavior which an individual displays. All managers have a set of values which affect their decisions, but the values are not the same for each manager; however, once values are ingrained in a manager, they do not change except over a period of time. It is possible to group these values into a general pattern of behavior which characterizes three styles of managers—the profit-maximizing style, the trusteeship style, and the "quality of life" style of management.

Phase I Managers

Phase I, profit-maximizing managers have a personal set of values which reflects their economic thinking. They believe that raw self-interest should prevail in society, and their values dictate that "What's good for me is good for my country." Therefore, Phase I managers rationalize that making as much profit as is possible would be good for society. They make every effort to become as efficient as possible and to make as much money as they can. To them money and wealth are the most important goals of their lives.

In the pursuit of maximum profit the actions of Phase I managers toward customers are reflected in a *caveat emptor* philosophy. "Let the buyer beware" characterizes decisions and actions in dealing with customers. They are not necessarily concerned with product quality or safety, or with sufficient and/or truthful information about products and services. A profit-maximizing manager's view toward employees can be stated as, "Labor is a commodity to be bought and sold in the marketplace." Thus, chief accountability lies with the owners of the business, and usually the Phase I manager is the owner or part owner of the organization.

To profit maximizers technology is very important. Machines and equipment rank high on their scale of values, therefore, materialism characterizes their philosophy.

Social values do not predominate the thinking of Phase I managers. In fact, they believe that employee problems should be left at home. Economics should be separate from societal or family concerns. A Phase I manager's leadership style is one of the rugged individualist—"I'm my own boss, and I'll manage my business as I please." Values about minority groups dictate that such groups are inferior, so they must be treated accordingly.

Political values are based on the doctrine of laissez faire. "That government is best which governs the least" characterizes the thinking of Phase I managers. As a result anything dealing with politicians and governments is foreign and distasteful to them.

Their beliefs about the environment can be stated, "The natural environment controls one's destiny; therefore, use it to protect your interests before it destroys you. Don't worry about the physical environment because there are plenty of natural resources which you can use."

Aesthetic values to the profit maximizer are minimal. In fact, Phase I managers would say, "Aesthetic values? What are they?" They have very little concern for the arts and cultural aspects of life. They hold musicians, artists, entertainers, and social scientists in low regard.

The values that a profit-maximizing manager holds were commonly accepted in the economic textbooks of the 1800s and early 1900s although they obviously did not apply to all managers of those times. It is easy to see how they conflict with the values of the other two styles of management.

Phase II Managers

Phase II, trusteeship managers have a somewhat different set of values. They recognize that self-interest plays a large role in their actions, but they also recognize the interests of those people who contribute to the organization—the customers, employees, suppliers, owners, creditors, government, and community. In other words, they operate with self-interest plus the interests of other groups. They believe that "What is good for my company is good for the country." They balance profits of the owners and the organization with wages for employees, taxes for the government, interest for the creditors, and so forth.

Money is important to them but so are people, because their values tells them that satisfying people's needs is a better goal than just making money.

In balancing the needs of the various contributors to the organization, Phase II managers deal with customers as the chief providers of revenue to the firm. Their values tell them not to cheat the customers because cheating is not good for the firm.

They are concerned with providing sufficient quantities of goods as well as sufficient quality for customer satisfaction. They view employees as having certain rights which must be recognized and that employees are more than mere commodities to be traded in the marketplace. Their accountability as managers is to owners as well as to customers, employees, suppliers, creditors, government, and the community.

To the trusteeship-style manager, technology is important, but so are people. Innovation of technology is to be commended because new machines, equipment, and products are useful to people to create a high standard of living. Materialism is important, but so is humanism.

The social values held by trusteeship managers are more liberal than those held by profit maximizers. They recognize that employees have several needs beyond their economic needs. Employees have a desire for security and a sense of belonging as well as recognition. Phase II managers see themselves as individualists, but they also appreciate the value of group participation in managing the business. They view minority groups as having their place in society. But, a trusteeship manager would add: "Their place is usually inferior to mine; they are usually not qualified to hold their jobs but that's not my fault."

The political values of Phase II managers are reflected in recognizing that government and politics are important, but they view government and politics as necessary evils. They distrust both, recognizing that government serves as a threat to their existence if their firms do not live up to the laws passed since the 1930s.

The environmental beliefs of trusteeship managers are stated as follows: "People can control and manipulate their environment. Therefore, let them do it for their own benefit and incidentally for society's benefit."

Aesthetic values are all right to the trusteeship manager, but "they are not for our firm although someone has to support the arts and cultural values."

Phase III Managers

In contrast to profit maximizers and trustee managers, "quality of life" managers believe in enlightened self-interest. They agree that selfishness and group interests are important, but that society's interests are also important in making decisions. "What's good for society is good for our company" is their opinion. They agree that profit is essential for the firm, but that profit in and of itself is not the end objective of the firm. As far as money and wealth are concerned, their set of values tells them that money is important but people are more important than money.

In sharp contrast to *caveat emptor* in dealings with customers, the philosophy of Phase II managers is *caveat venditor*, that is, let the seller beware. The company should bear the responsibility for producing and distributing products and services in sufficient quantities at the right time and place with the necessary quality, information, and services necessary to satisfy customers' needs. Their views about employees are to recognize the dignity of each, not treating them as a commodity to be bought and sold. Their accountability as managers is to the owners, to the other contributors of the business, and to society in general.

Technological values are important but people are held in higher esteem than machines, equipment, computers, and esoteric products. A "quality of life" manager is a humanist rather than a materialist.

The social values of "quality of life" managers dictate that a person cannot be separated into an economic being or family being. Their philosophy is, "We hire the whole person including any problems that person might have." Phase III managers recognize that group participation rather than rugged individualism is a determining factor in an organization's success. Their values about minority groups are different from the other managers. Their view is that "A member of a minority group needs support and guidance like any other person."

The political values of "quality of life" managers dictate that government and politicians are necessary contributors to a quality of life. Rather than resisting government, they believe that business and government must cooperate to solve society's problems.

Their environmental beliefs are stated as, "A person must preserve the environment, not for the environment's sake alone, but for the benefit of people who want to lead a quality life."

As far as aesthetic values are concerned, Phase III managers recognize that the arts and cultural values reflect the lives of people whom they hold in high regard. Their actions support aesthetic values by committing resources to their preservation and presentation.

NO

Alexei M. Marcoux

Business Ethics Gone Wrong

It arose from the scandals that plagued Wall Street during the 1980s: a growing public support for business ethics as an object of study and teaching in America's colleges and universities. Business ethics courses are offered (and often, for business majors, required) in ever-increasing numbers. The ranks of the academy swell with professors whose principal vocation is teaching and writing in business ethics. Philanthropists endow chairs in business ethics faster than universities can fill them.

Although deriving and explaining the ethical norms that support and lubricate a well-functioning market economy are worthwhile tasks, the intellectual fashion in business ethics is quite a different matter. For among business ethicists there is a consensus favoring the stakeholder theory of the firm—a theory that seeks to redefine and reorient the purpose and the activities of the firm. Far from providing an ethical foundation for capitalism, these business ethicists seek to change it dramatically.

Shareholders and Stakeholders

Stakeholder talk is rampant. In Great Britain, Tony Blair's Labour Party came to power promising Britons a "stakeholder society." Perhaps capitalizing on the trend, Yale law professors Bruce Ackerman and Anne Alstott argue for a far-reaching overhaul of the American tax and welfare systems in their recent book, The Stakeholder Society. But stakeholder theory, as it has emerged in business ethics, is different.

Stakeholder theory is most closely associated with R. Edward Freeman, Olsson Professor of Applied Ethics at the University of Virginia's Darden School. The theory holds that managers ought to serve the interests of all those who have a "stake" in (that is, affect or are affected by) the firm. Stakeholders include shareholders, employees, suppliers, customers, and the communities in which the firm operates—a collection that Freeman terms the "big five." The very purpose of the firm, according to this view, is to serve and coordinate the interests of its various stakeholders. It is the moral obligation of the firm's managers to strike an appropriate balance among the big five interests in directing the activities of the firm.

From *Cato Journal*, July 24, 2000. Copyright © 2000 by Cato Institute. Reprinted by permission.

This understanding of the firm's purpose and its management's obligations diverges sharply from the understanding advanced in the shareholder
theory of the firm. According to shareholder theorists such as Nobel laureate
economist Milton Friedman, managers ought to serve the interests of the firm's
owners, the shareholders. Social obligations of the firm are limited to making
good on contracts, obeying the law, and adhering to ordinary moral expectations. In short, obligations to nonshareholders stand as sideconstraints on the
pursuit of shareholder interests. This is the view that informs American corporate law and that Friedman defends in his 1970 New York Times Magazine
essay, "The Social Responsibility of Business Is to Increase Its Profits."

Corporate Social Responsibility and Stakeholder Theory

Stakeholder theory seeks to overthrow the shareholder orientation of the firm. It
is an outgrowth of the corporate social responsibility (CSR) movement to which
Friedman's essay responds. According to CSR, the firm is obligated to "give something back" to those that make its success possible. The image of the firm presented in CSR is that of a free rider, unjustly and uncooperatively enriching itself
to the detriment of the community. Socially responsible deeds (such as patroniz-
ing the arts or mitigating unemployment) are necessary to redeem firms and
transform them into good citizens.

One wonders, however, why firms are obligated to give something back
to those to whom they routinely give so much already. Rather than enslave
their employees, firms typically pay them wages and benefits in return for their
labor. Rather than steal from their customers, firms typically deliver goods and
services in return for the revenues that customers provide. Rather than free ride
on public provisions, firms typically pay taxes and obey the law. Moreover,
these compensations are ones to which the affected parties or (in the case of
communities and unionized employees) their agents freely agree. For what
reasons, then, is one to conclude that those compensations are inadequate or
unjust, necessitating that firms give something more to those whom they have
already compensated?

Stakeholder theory constitutes at least something of an advance over
CSR. Whereas CSR is fundamentally antagonistic to capitalist enterprise, viewing both firm and manager as social parasites in need of a strong reformative
hand, stakeholder theory takes a different tack. Rather than offer stakeholder
theory as a means of overthrowing capitalist enterprise, stakeholder theorists
profess to offer theirs as a strategy for improving it. As Robert Phillips of the
University of Pennsylvania's Wharton School writes, "One of the goals of the
stakeholder theory is to maintain the benefits of the free market while minimizing the potential ethical problems created by capitalism."

On the theory that "you'll catch more flies with honey than with vine-
gar," stakeholder theorists ostensibly praise corporate leaders and maintain
that firms are social institutions and their managers are community leaders.
Given appropriate latitude, firms and managers are disposed to serve the social

good. Corporate law and the market for corporate control, however, preclude firms and managers from following their inclinations and serving their social missions. Stakeholder theory seeks to free both firm and manager from their exclusive attention to the narrow, parochial concerns of shareholders so that they can focus on a broader set of interests.

But although the diagnosis of the problem with capitalist enterprise is (at least, on the face of it) different from that advanced in CSR, the stakeholder theorists' remedy is largely the same: the elevation of nonshareholding interests to the level of shareholder interests in formulating business strategy and policy. The stakeholder-oriented manager is admonished to weigh and balance stakeholder interests, trading off one against another in settling on a course of action. Stakeholder theorists seek a reorientation of the corporate law toward the interests of stakeholders and the insulation of managers from the market for corporate control.

Problems

Whatever the appeal of the stakeholder theory's inclusiveness of and sensitivity to the myriad interests that affect and are affected by firms, there are several powerful reasons to resist the theory's adoption and embodiment in a reformed corporate law.

Equity Capital.   Because it undermines shareholder property rights, stakeholder-oriented management denigrates and discourages equity investment. In the stakeholder-oriented firm, equity investors bear the same downside risks that they bear in the traditionally governed, shareholder-oriented firm. The upside potential of their investment, however, is diminished significantly; for in distributing the fruits of the firm's success, equity investor interests are only some among many to be considered and served. In short, when the firm loses, shareholders lose; when the firm wins, shareholders might lose anyway if other interests are deemed to be more weighty and important.

Stakeholder-oriented management effectively eliminates issuing shares as a means of financing the firm's growth and new ventures. By diminishing the orientation of the firm toward shareholder interests, stakeholder-oriented management will presumably lead investors to discount sharply the value they attach to shareholdings. So stakeholder-oriented management essentially entails a near-exclusive reliance on debt as the fuel of expansion.

But the problems do not stop there. Debtholders, whether banks or bondholders, typically use equity holdings, returns to equity, and appreciation in the market price for shares as signals of financial health, and hence as mechanisms for pricing debt capital. Widespread or legally mandatory adoption of stakeholder-oriented management threatens to undermine well-established, stable, and efficient market norms for pricing capital in favor of a regime under which capital is more costly for firms to acquire because investment (whether in the form of equity or debt) is an inherently riskier proposition. That, in turn, threatens prospects for economic growth, stable employment, and the liquidity of financial markets. In short, stakeholder-oriented management promises poorer, static, risk-averse firms and hence a poorer, static, risk-averse economy. Stakeholder-oriented management is contrary to the interests of the very stakeholders it is intended to help.

Managerial Accountability.   People recoil in horror at corporate officers' and directors' salaries, perks, and other bonuses that at times bear no relation to the performance of the firms they manage. This sorry state of affairs results from the confluence of a number of recent trends in corporate law that make it more difficult for shareholders to discipline self-serving managers:

The decline of the ultra vires doctrine (under which shareholders could sue managers for embarking on projects contrary to the corporate purpose).

The emergence of so-called corporate constituency statutes (which permit managers to consider and appeal to a broader range of interests in determining how and whether to fend off a takeover bid—and thereby hamper the smooth operation of the market for corporate control).

The expansive reading given to the business judgment rule (which shields some managerial actions from substantive review by courts) by the Supreme Court of Delaware—where many firms are incorporated.

But whatever the impediments to disciplining self-serving managers under current law and public policy, they pale in comparison with those promised by stakeholder-oriented management (and a stakeholder-oriented corporate law). Whereas under the current corporate law much self-serving managerial behavior is recognizably self-serving but shielded from substantive review, under stakeholder-oriented corporate law such behavior would be considerably more difficult even to detect, as well as to deter.

It would be more difficult to detect because all but the most egregious of self-serving managerial behavior will coincide with the interests of some stakeholding group, and hence the self-serving manager may point to the benefited and burdened stakeholders and argue that, in his estimation, this was the optimal way to balance competing stakeholder interests. Absent a powerful principle of balanced distribution of the benefits of the firm (something stakeholder theorists have been notoriously slow to sketch), stakeholder theorists must acquiesce in self-serving managerial action that can plausibly be said to accomplish some sort of balance among competing stakeholder interests. That point is made with admirable clarity by Frank Easterbrook and Daniel Fischel in their 1991 book, The Economic Structure of Corporate Law: "A manager told to serve two masters (a little for the equity holders, a little for the community) has been freed of both and is answerable to neither. Faced with a demand from either group, the manager can appeal to the interests of the other."

Self-serving managerial action would be more difficult to deter under stakeholder-oriented corporate law because stakeholder theory anticipates that good-faith stakeholder-oriented managerial actions will serve some interests and frustrate others in pursuit of an overall balance of interests. Therefore, stakeholder-oriented corporate law must provide protections to managers at least as extensive as those afforded under current business judgment rule doctrine— lest managers be the perpetual object of derivative lawsuits brought by shareholders, employees, customers, suppliers, or communities who believe that their interests were unfairly or improperly weighed and balanced. Between the ability of managers to justify their self-serving behavior in terms of the balanced pursuit of stakeholder interests, on the one hand, and the protections that a stakeholder-oriented corporate law must afford to managers if firms are to be managed at all, on the other hand, the accountability of managers for their actions must necessarily suffer.

Interest-Group Politics. Because stakeholder-oriented management anticipates the weighing and the balancing—and hence often the frustrating—of competing interests, it promises to make the boardroom (populated, per Freeman, by representatives of all stakeholding groups) the site of wasteful, inefficient interest-group politicking. That is, the corporate boardroom will be transformed from a forum in which economically rational strategies are adopted in pursuit of added value into one in which legislative and bureaucratic political maneuvering will be the order of the day. Surprisingly, stakeholder theorists recognize and, apparently, welcome this. In a 1998 issue of Business Ethics Quarterly, communitarian thinker Amitai Etzioni is comforted by the thought that there "is no reason to expect that the politics of corporate communities would be any different from other democratic systems."

One can scarcely imagine how firms, whose resources are far more limited than are those of governments (and unsupported by the taxing power), can remain viable if their decision procedures are characterized by the strategic bargaining, logrolling, and other wasteful tactics that are the hallmark of democratic politics. If a camel is a horse designed by a committee, then what misshapen beast is a firm shaped by the strategic interactions of its stakeholder representatives?

Small Victories

The market economy, the liberty it safeguards, and the prosperity it secures are threatened not, as in the recent past, by firebrands who seek to abolish it, but by more modest tinkerers who seek to "improve" it in the name of myriad social concerns. Defending the market economy from this attack requires more than cataloging the defects of alternative economic systems and the merits of markets. It requires a principled defense of the shareholder-oriented firm—the basic productive institution on which the market economy is constructed.

Despite its worrisome implications, stakeholder-oriented management and its accompanying rhetoric encounter little systematic opposition in philosophy departments, business schools, or boardrooms. The costs of complacency about that state of affairs are potentially high. For although they have so far failed to bring wholesale change to the corporation and the law that governs it, stakeholder-oriented activists have won important piecemeal victories. The passage of corporate constituency statutes in several states has weakened the market for corporate control and, hence, the property rights of shareholders. Federal plant-closing legislation has legitimized among policymakers the idea that firm managers ought to be responsive to a multiplicity of interests. Corporate mission statements in which stakeholders and their interests feature prominently—whether adopted earnestly or as cover for self-serving managers—serve to further legitimize the subordination of shareholder interests to other concerns. If the market economy and its cornerstone, the shareholder-oriented firm, are in no danger of being dealt a decisive blow, they at least risk death by a thousand cuts.

Business Ethics Reconsidered

Too often the free-market response to the changes sought by stakeholder-oriented business ethicists has been to denigrate the role of ethics in business—as if stakeholder-oriented reforms are the inevitable consequence of injecting concern for ethics into business. But the partisans of stakeholder theory are not spokespeople for ethics; they are spokespeople only for a particular conception of ethics—and a particularly flawed conception, at that. The manifold failings of stakeholder theory should not be taken to reflect poorly on the project of business ethics; rather, they reflect poorly on stakeholder theory itself.

Defenders of the free market, limited government, and the rule of law must articulate an alternative business ethics, one that recognizes and provides reasoned argument for the moral merit of the shareholder-oriented firm. Norms of honesty, integrity, and fair play, rather than an albatross around the neck of the free market, are a central, if neglected, part of the story of the success of the shareholder-oriented firm. In short, shareholder-oriented firms are not merely wealth-enhancing, they are good.

POSTSCRIPT

Do Corporations Have a Responsibility to Society That Extends Beyond Merely Maximizing Profit?

Advocates of the shareholder approach generally believe that free-market capitalism is the best mechanism for addressing social problems. They argue that the free market, guided by Adam Smith's invisible hand and based on the view that organizations exist to maximize shareholder wealth, will provide the necessary incentives for solving problems society considers important. Some organization, driven by the desire to maximize shareholder wealth first and foremost, will provide a solution and reap its just rewards. In this scenario, all parties involved are better off when the company concerns itself with trying to make as much money as it can for its shareholders and does not distract itself with the claims of other groups with which it interacts. Critics point out that this scenario fails to take into account the issue of time. Consider a situation where a community has a pollution problem that, for whatever reason, cannot be solved by current pollution-control technology. Free-market advocates would argue that someone (or company) will invent the necessary technology since doing so will result in large financial gains. Maybe so, say the critics. But what if it takes 10 years for the technology to be developed? What happens to the community in the meantime? The point is that situations occur where the time lag between the onset of a problem and its solution can be too long to let the corporations ignore the concerns of other stakeholders while they search for a profit-maximizing solution.

Alexei Marcoux provided a direct attack on stakeholder theory in his article. But even if you did not find his arguments convincing, there is much potential for trouble if corporations become too involved in the concerns of their stakeholders. One possible problem is conflict of interest: Managers could play one group of stakeholders against another. Another problem concerns the concentration of power that might result. Do we really want corporations making decisions and wielding even more power than they currently have in community affairs, for example?

We conclude, then, that both sides of this interesting and topical debate have powerful arguments on their side. Where do you stand on this issue? Should the only purpose of an organization be to maximize profit, or do other stakeholders have a legitimate claim to the fruits of the organizations' success?

Suggested Readings

Thomas Donaldson, Patricia H. Werhane, & Margaret Cording, *Ethical Issues in Business: A Philosophical Approach* (7th ed.). Prentice Hall, 2002.

R. Edward Freeman, Fixing the ethics crisis in corporate America. *Miller Center Report*, Fall 2002.

Milton Friedman, The social responsibility of business is to increase its profits. *The New York Times Magazine*, September 13, 1970.

Samuel Gregg, "Stakeholder" theory: What it means for corporate governance. *Policy*, Winter 2001, vol. 17, no. 2. The Center for Independent Studies. http://www.cis.org.au/Policy/winter01/polwin01-7.htm

David Henderson, The case against corporate social responsibility. *Policy*, Winter 2001, Vol. 17, No. 2. The Center for Independent Studies. http://www.cis.org.au/policy/winter01/polwin01-6.pdf

ISSUE 2

Is the Corporate Strategy
of Downsizing Unethical?

YES: Larry Gross, from "Downsizing: Are Employers Reneging on
Their Social Promise?" *CPCU Journal* (Summer 2001)

NO: Joseph T. Gilbert, from "Sorrow and Guilt: An Ethical Analysis
of Layoffs," *SAM Advanced Management Journal* (vol. 65, 2000)

ISSUE SUMMARY

YES: Larry Gross contends that downsizing violates the psychological
and social contracts implicit in the employer–employee relationship
since there is an implied sense of job security afforded the employee
as long as he or she is productively advancing the goals of the organization. Downsizing productive employees is a clear violation of this
contract and, therefore, immoral.

NO: Professor Joseph Gilbert analyzes the ethicality of downsizing
through the application of three prominent approaches to the study
of ethics: utilitarianism, rights and duties, and justice and fairness.
Gilbert concludes that, with one notable exception, downsizing is an
ethically valid and morally responsible corporate behavior.

$\mathbf{C}$orporate downsizing is the strategic action of reducing the size of an organization's workforce in the hope of achieving greater efficiency and productivity
through the reduction in labor costs. Although academic discussion of the concept can be traced back to the 1950s, it wasn't until the early 1980s that the idea
of downsizing as a strategic tool found expression in the marketplace of corporate America. The accelerated growth of international and global competition
during the decade of the 1980s forced American businesses to reduce costs and
focus on increasing organizational efficiency. An obvious way to quickly lower
costs and trim waste is to reduce the size of the workforce. This line of thinking,
coupled with the growing competitive pressures, proved irresistible to thousands of corporations of all size and financial condition. The result? Millions of
employees were laid off as corporate America embraced the notion of downsizing as a valuable managerial weapon. By the time the 1990s were over, the

acceptance of downsizing as an effective and dependable arrow in the corporate quiver was complete.

Although top management has expectations about the impact downsizing will have on their labor costs, they are typically much less concerned about the impact on the employees affected by the decision. An important moral question arises when we view downsizing from the perspective of the employee—namely, does the corporation have the moral right to downsize in the first place? In other words, is downsizing unethical? Most frequently, those answering "no" base their position on a stakeholder approach to business ethics. This approach argues that businesses have obligations that extend beyond merely maximizing shareholder wealth to include any entity or individual that is impacted by the organization's activities. Consider the following statement from Larry Gross, author of the "yes" position of this Taking Sides debate: "Downsizing is driving a breach in the corporation's social responsibility not only to the employees who lose their jobs, but also to the others who remain . . . That same breach of promise on the part of these companies also affects the society where they do business" (*CPCU Journal*, 2001, vol. 54, no. 2, p. 113). Gross also contends that downsizing violates the psychological and social contracts implicit in the employer–employee relationship since there is an implied sense of job security afforded the employee as long as he or she is productively advancing the goals of the organization. Downsizing productive employees is a clear violation of this contract and, therefore, immoral. As you read this article, ask yourself if you would feel the sense of violation Gross refers to if you were to fall victim to downsizing at your job.

Professor Joseph Gilbert, in the "no" selection for this debate, analyzes the ethicality of downsizing through the application of three prominent approaches to the study of business ethics: utilitarianism, rights and duties, and justice and fairness. According to Gilbert, an important element in this analysis involves understanding the motivation behind the decision to downsize. He argues, for example, that a moral analysis of an organization that reduces labor costs as a last-ditch effort to avoid bankruptcy and the resultant loss of all jobs will yield a different conclusion than an analysis of a highly successful organization that downsizes in a proactive, aggressive effort to increase its profits. Gilbert further suggests that it makes sense to view the motivations for downsizing as existing on a continuum: At one end is the corporation that lays off workers to avoid closing, at the other is the profitable organization that downsizes to further increase profits, and somewhere in the middle is the company that downsizes to forestall potential problems. To further complicate the matter, the results of the analysis may differ depending on which of the three approaches are used.

After conducting this analysis, Gilbert concludes that, with the exception of successful firms that lay off employees primarily to further increase profits, downsizing is an ethically valid and morally responsible corporate behavior. Keep Gilbert's conclusions in mind next time the media report that another major corporation has laid off thousands of its workforce. Was the company's survival in doubt, or was the downsizing the apparent effort of top management to make a good situation even better?

Larry Gross  **YES**

Downsizing: Are Employers Reneging on Their Social Promise?

. . . The phenomenon of downsizing, which is advertised to create financial and operational efficiencies in the modern corporate environment, has impacted millions of employees over the last several years. In the first half of 1996, the number of job cuts increased by 28 percent from the year before, resulting in 100,000 layoffs in January 1996 alone. The list of corporations that had made significant cuts included all types of industries including communications, technology, and manufacturing as well as insurance.

There was a resurgence in the number of job cuts in the last six months of 2000 due to companies looking to dilute the impact of a projected economic slowdown. In December 2000, U.S. corporations announced 133,173 layoffs, a 203 percent increase over November's total according to a report by Challenger, Gray, and Christmas, an international outplacement firm. This number of reductions represented the highest number of job cuts ever recorded since the survey began in 1993, and this was only the fourth time that the number of layoffs totaled more than 100,000 in one month. These job reductions crossed over all industry sectors, and included a major health insurer who cut 5,000 jobs as part of restructuring plan to improve profit.

The trend in the increase of downsizing activity is predicted to continue due to companies taking action to compensate for the loss of market share and sharp drops in profitability expected from a slowing economy, according to John Challenger, chief executive of Challenger, Gray, and Christmas. He observes, "Companies are jumping in to make decisions to get their costs in line now and not wait."

Many companies in the insurance community, both large and small, adopt downsizing as a business strategy. Downsizing, which may be proposed for any number of objectives, including cost management, always results in reduced staff. This is critical because reducing staff is downsizing's real objective, contrary to any of the stated objectives that attempt to rationalize it. One irony about the downsizing trend is that those released are not the newest employees. Long-term employees, especially middle managers who may have given 10 to 30 years in service to the company, are often discharged. Many of those who fall into that category are unable to find employment that allows them to use their current skill sets or to maintain their lifestyle. A study by the American Society for Training and Development indicated that onethird of the displaced managers over 35 years old find jobs that pay less than they previously earned. These victims of downsizing often need five years to get back to their former pay level.

Corporate downsizing has posed an even more serious dilemma than the individual situations suggest. Downsizing is driving a breach in the corporation's social responsibility not only to the employees who lose their jobs, but also to the others who remain either as an employee or with a vested interest in the company's future. That same breach of promise on the part of these companies also affects the society where they do business.

There is a fallacy inherent in downsizing. Organizations that undergo this type of change do not appear to be better off than they were before they implemented the process.

Downsizing does not appear to be in the best long-term interest of the corporation, its employees, or its shareholders. In fact, there is considerable evidence in this regard.

As a result, it is important to understand downsizing's key objectives in order to evaluate whether its stated goals are met. One definition states that downsizing is "a set of activities . . . undertaken on the part of management, designed to improve organizational efficiency, productivity, and or competitiveness. It represents a strategy that affects the size of the firm's workforce and its work processes."

Atwood cites that existing research describes the attributes of downsizing as intentional; it usually involves, although is not limited to, reductions in personnel; it focuses on improving efficiency of the organization; and it also affects work processes intentionally or unintentionally.

Reviewing the financial results for companies engaged in significant downsizing during the early 1990s, one study cited that the massive job cuts rarely lead to strong sustained gains in the affected company's stock over the long term. Where median share prices initially rose six months after downsizing by 8 percent, they slid to a 26 percent loss within three years. In another study, only 21 percent of the firms surveyed reported that they achieved satisfactory shareholder return on investment as a result of downsizing, and 46 percent found that reducing head count did not reduce expenses to the degree that had been anticipated. In the same study, only 32 percent increased profits to anticipated levels and only 22 percent of the downsized companies saw the increase in productivity they expected.

In some cases, no effective increase in stock prices occurred even in the short term. In 1995 the Times Mirror Company reported third and fourth quarter losses coincident with the elimination of more than 2,000 jobs. It blamed the losses on the cost of huge layoffs, downsizing, and closures aimed at saving money in the long run.

A report by the Wyatt Company, a national management consultant firm, stated that only 12 percent of downsized companies increased market share, 9 percent improved product quality, and just 7 percent increased innovation.

Despite various actions taken by management at these firms to downsize, the data indicated that many had experienced unexpected and undesirable outcomes.

In a four-year study examining 30 firms in the automotive industry, the data revealed "very few organizations in the study implemented downsizing in a way that improved their effectiveness. Most deteriorated in terms of predownsizing levels of quality, productivity, effectiveness, and the 'dirty dozen,' e.g., conflict, low morale, loss of trust, rigidity, scapegoating." Ellen Bayer, global human resources chief for the American Management Association, states, "We've found that in both the long and short term, growing companies tend to outperform downsized firms-especially in such areas as employee morale and turnover rates." These financial effects of downsizing are directly impacted by the fact that the downsizing process is the wrong choice from an ethical perspective. Downsizing is in direct conflict with the Stakeholder Approach to corporate social responsibility. This approach emphasizes accountability to a larger constituency that has significant interest in the corporation's well-being and long-term survival. This infers that purely market-driven ethical decision-making can only capture a short-term benefit without regard for the viability of the organization in the environment it operates.

In fact, the short-term advantages of downsizing only benefit a very small segment of the organization, if at all. The downsizing process indicates a rationalization of action based on a corporate application of psychological egoism. Employees are sacrificed for the apparent benefit or survival of the larger corporation, which is considered an entity in itself that is worthy and capable of self-interest. This "culture of narcissism" represents the acceptance of a business environment where corporations have only one objective, profit, which is in contrast to the need to keep the triangular interests of shareholders, management, and employees in balance.

In a 1999 case study of downsizing that was used by a hospital to address a $16 million budget shortfall, the report cited that within two years almost every reduced position was back in place. The study suggested that the organization never asked whether the projected cost saving was worth the turmoil and impact on productivity and whether better options should have been evaluated by the organization instead.

The fact that downsizing is a bad decision for all affected is coupled with a level of responsibility that the corporation has to two key environments—the employees affected and the society in which the corporation operates. People who are productive employees with years of tenure and education lose their jobs, with seemingly little regard for the disruption of their lives by the corporations that employed them. The financial impact is obvious, but what about the psychological and social implications this action caused?

Despite the absence of a written contract, employees have an implied agreement from their employers in return for their effort to advance the corporation's goals. This includes a promise of protection and safety through wages, benefits, and good working conditions. While the assumption of the implicit psychological contract that assured lifetime job security may no longer hold, a new contract in which employees are more autonomous and self-reliant has taken its place. In the new employment relationship, trust is established through this contract that represents the obligations between the employee and the organization and is based on a normative approach of trust. In this approach employees see trust as an ethical relationship explained in terms of shared ideals and values. This obligation matches Lawrence Kohlberg's Social Contract Legalistic Orientation, a stage of moral reasoning that creates a socio-legal obligation that exists without statutory support. Downsizing violates the promise this relationship creates.

Employees expect that all parties will honor their explicit and implicit obligations. Distrust occurs when these obligations are not met or when the parties have different expectations regarding the obligations. When downsizing is employed as an organizational strategy, it focuses on economic goals over the promotion of commitment, and, as a result, the employees view the strategy with distrust.

The further impact of this breach of the promise is evident anecdotally. John A. Challenger notes, "It may be unrealistic to expect intense loyalty on the part of the worker when in many instances the employer cannot promise in return. The current spate of mergers in the banking, media, utilities, and other industries, major re-engineering efforts, and downsizings all have weakened the ties that spur employee commitment and productivity."

The lack of the corporation's initiative to protect its employees causes the individual workers to suffer. Employees are devastated by the emotional aspect of downsizing, which rocks their self-esteem and self-confidence. They see themselves valued solely as an expense item of the corporation and believe that if that's the way it is, why bother? Frederick Reichheld, a corporate strategy consultant and expert in loyalty practice states, "The great betrayal of American workers is the failure of companies to let them know how much value they are creating, versus how much they are costing."

A 1996 survey commissioned by the American Management Association demonstrated the physical toll to employees by downsizing and restructuring through evidence that the number of both occupational and nonoccupational disability claims increased significantly during these periods. These increases were also found to occur not only to employees whose jobs were being eliminated but also among those who remained employed. These remaining employees suffered distress from several sources: threat of job loss, job description changes, added responsibility due to the layoff of co-workers, salary freezes or cutbacks, and forced relocation, among others. In a 1997 European study, the authors found a significant association between downsizing and medically certified sick leave where the rate of absenteeism was 2.3 times greater after major downsizing.

Downsizing also causes a conflict for those managers who are charged with the decisions of who to let go and the implementation of the downsizing process when they recognize the implied agreement exists. Based on the ethics standard that is applied, the individual manager is forced to decide between what is his or her responsibility to the corporation's will and survival and the promise of security that he or she offers on behalf of the corporation in return for the employee's productivity. Because downsizing often results in almost explosive change, there is little time for the manager to come to terms with this inconsistency or to distance him- or herself from the result. When faced with this task, many decide to leave the company rather than deal with the stress of the conflict. Other managers defer the dilemma to upper management instead of implicating themselves.

The breach of promise to society is perhaps the most serious implication of all because everyone is hurt as a result. The rationale that corporations use to describe the benefits of a particular "cost management" effort appear to be flawed-not only in terms of its return to the corporation, but to the society in which it operates as well. The continuous implementation of restructuring efforts that did not appear to have focus are evidence of this rationale, which continues to cause damage to employees' lives and the corporation itself. The reduction of the work force for the singular purpose of reduced costs/more profits breaches the integrity the corporation has in relation to the quality of its contribution to the overall health of society. A profit-oriented approach simply leads to a restriction of the corporation's definition of a goal and an indifference to the means by which these goals are pursued.

Loss of perspective hinders a corporation's ability to compete in the marketplace because it diminishes the corporation's sensitivity to the needs and preferences of customers. Nash writes, "One cannot achieve market sensitivity or organizational cooperation by working on the assumption that your own way of doing things and your profit are necessarily more compelling than anything else."

Feldman and Liou in their article "Downsizing Trust," indicate that the call for principled implementation of downsizing strategies has become a current theme in management literature. They state that the term leadership based on the ideals of trust and power has replaced the word management. Trust has become the new foundation of leadership, replacing authority, and focusing on the reciprocal relationship between leaders and followers. Reciprocity in this relationship refers to a mutual loyalty and commitment between leaders and followers based on truth and honesty. This accounts for the fact that organizational leaders acknowledge that the social contract exists between the employee and the organization and that the organization must honor the contract.

This concept points to new strategies for staff reduction based on organizations approaching it with a quality focus, which requires them to change their fundamental assumptions about people, organizations, and management. This strategy embodies the issue of trust between the employee and the organization. It recognizes the need for empowerment of the individuals who work there and their need to strive to maintain pride in their work and the continuous improvement of all aspects of work within the organization. In this scenario, the organization is responsible for providing training, opportunity, and responsibility for decision making in tandem with accountability, mutual respect, and trust.

In the future, companies must do everything in their power to provide training or placement for employees who may lose their jobs because of the normal dynamics of change that is inherent in any system that requires a destabilizing element to allow organizations to shift away from the status quo. Companies must also pay serious attention to the transition experienced by employees remaining within the organization. This is necessary to provide the protection factor that is implied in the employee/employer relationship.

A well-designed and consistent communications plan is key to any effort designed to successfully assist an organization through change. Communication must be provided, and it should be proactive so that information can be shared early in the process. In a 1995 survey, 65 percent of the responding organizations ranked "gaps in communication channels" as the number one negative factor experienced after restructuring. A well-designed communication plan breaks down barriers and helps people accept the change. An additional study found that insufficient communication from top management might result in middle managers not supporting or even sabotaging new initiatives.

T. Quinn Spitzer, CEO of Kepner-Tregoe, an international consulting firm, states, "There is no new social contract. The companies that always had one still do; the companies that never had one are more inclined to talk about it." Spitzer contends there are four dimensions to this responsibility that have been misapplied over the years:

1. Culture—Organizations will run their businesses with the idea that an employee is at least as important as the investor and the customer.
2. Skill building—Organizations will give employees the skill sets needed to do their jobs; workers have the reciprocal responsibility of self-reliance.
3. High performance work environment—Organizations will offer a hospitable workplace and reward systems that allow opportunity for excellence. For their part, workers must have some control over their destiny and must perform.
4. Employment security—This is considered as a paramount concern rather than employment for life. Organizations will be mindful of job security in decision making, instead of laying off as an initial strategic response to business downturns.

Recent management literature reviews the evolution of a work/life initiative, where action to benefit the individual is directly linked to business strategy such as flexible work scheduling. This results in a change in perspective from a human-cost to a human—investment approach when evaluating the benefit to the organization. Specifically, it allows a corporation to measure the value of a work/life procedure and balance it in terms of organizational efficiencies. As part of the process, the intervention and related investments are defined in terms of the broadest group of stakeholders and its measurable return in terms of the company's business strategy.

Lee Perry, professor of strategy and organizational behavior at the Marriott School of Management, believes that by using technology and redeploying people based on comprehensive process analysis, the reduction-in-staff aspect of restructuring may be mitigated. He states, "Managers are using a machete when they should be using a scalpel." He suggests, "If organizations could bring the goals of business and society together, what would it look like?"

There is a definite correlation between the need to do what is "right" and a successful business enterprise. From my observations about downsizing, I also see that the definition of that term is the result of a cooperative understanding of the employer, employee, and the other stakeholders to make sure all interests are addressed. The reality is that although we cannot escape the dynamics of change, we cannot allow it to serve as an excuse to act unethically. As Edward B. Rust Jr., chairman and CEO of State Farm Insurance Company, stated, "Mutuality of trust makes it far less difficult to go through the changes that the marketplace places on us." We must confirm our responsibility to each other through how we face these types of situations, whether we act as individuals or as the conscience of our corporations.

Joseph T. Gilbert

Sorrow and Guilt: An Ethical Analysis of Layoffs

Closing the office door, looking straight into an employee's face, and telling him that he no longer has a job is not an easy task. When that employee's performance has been satisfactory or even exemplary, it is even more difficult for a manager to terminate him or her. Yet, this happens hundreds of thousands of times when companies decide to reduce the size of their workforce by layoffs. From the stock market's point of view, such a decision is usually a good thing—a company's stock price often rises on the day that a layoff decision is announced. From top management's point of view, such a decision can seem to be the best, or even the only one, available to solve serious problems that the top manager must address. From the point of view of the managers or supervisors assigned to deliver the news to individuals about to be terminated, the decision often produces sorrow or guilt, or both. From the point of view of the terminated employees, shock, disbelief, and anger are among the typical reactions. . . .

Since layoffs cause suffering, sorrow is an appropriate emotion. Is guilt appropriate, and if so on whose part? In other words, is moral or ethical wrong involved in layoffs?

This article focuses on the decision to conduct layoffs and the subsequent decision about which employees will be laid off. . . . We will argue that in some circumstances, laying off some employees is the ethical thing to do, and managers who fail to do so are guilty of unethical conduct. In other circumstances, no ethical defense of layoffs can be found, and managers who decide on layoffs in these circumstances are guilty of unethical acts. In a wide range of circumstances in between, there are ethical arguments for and against layoffs. For these cases, we show how ethical reasoning can be applied to assist managers in determining the morally right thing to do.

One common definition of an act with ethical or moral consequences is that such an act involves decisions freely taken that will have positive or negative consequences for others. Layoff decisions clearly fall within this definition. Our analysis will employ the three major approaches often used in writing and teaching about managerial ethics: utilitarianism (the greatest good for the greatest number), rights and duties, and justice and fairness. . . .

From *SAM Advanced Management Journal*, Spring 2000, pp. 4–13. Copyright © 2000 by Society for Advancement of Management. Reprinted by permission.

Ethical Analysis: The Basic Tools

To determine whether a decision, such as downsizing, or an action, such as lay-ing off an employee, is ethical, managers have certain analytical techniques available to them. While these techniques are not as widely known as statistical analysis or flow charting, they are gradually becoming part of a manager's standard tool kit. Business schools are placing more emphasis on ethics, partly because of the large number of clearly unethical business practices exposed during the 1980s.

Most business school textbooks and courses on ethics take the same basic approach to analyzing the morality or ethics (we use the words interchange-ably in this article) of business decisions. The three most commonly accepted approaches draw on the work of moral philosophers dating back more than two thousand years to Plato and Aristotle. While these philosophers were not familiar with corporations or computers, they did think long and deeply about issues of morality. The fact that their writings are still read and discussed indi-cates that they have something worthwhile to say.

Ethics is the branch of philosophy that deals with the morality of human decisions and actions, and business ethics deals with them in a business set-ting. These dry-sounding definitions point to the link between the best work of some deep moral thinkers and particular decisions or actions taken by manag-ers in a contemporary business setting. . . .

Utilitarianism.   One approach to determining the morality of a decision or action is utilitarianism, which holds that a moral decision or action is one that results in the greatest good for the greatest number of people. The philosophers most commonly identified with this view are two nineteenth century English-men, Jeremy Bentham and John Stuart Mill. The assumption of this approach is that pleasure causes happiness and pain takes it away. Since pleasure and the happiness it causes are the ultimate good for humans, the act that causes the greatest pleasure or happiness for the greatest number of people is the morally good act. This view also assumes that people live in communities and must take this fact into account in deciding on the moral rightness of what they do. While this view may sound simplistic, it is often called upon in business settings to justify or condemn certain actions. We will examine the issue further, but it is common to justify layoff on the basis that terminating 500 people will save the company from bankruptcy and hence preserve the jobs of 2,500 others.

Rights and duties.   A second approach to ethical analysis is to examine the issues of rights and duties. The basic position here is that individuals have rights, either as humans, as citizens of a given country or state, or as occupants of a particular position. These right rights confer duties on others, and the morality of a given decision or act can be determined by an analysis of these rights and duties. The philosopher most commonly associated with this view is Immanuel Kant. While issues of rights and duties may sound more philosophical and less mathematical than that of determining the greatest good for the greatest number, it is not necessarily so. My right to personal comfort may be outweighed by your right to live. My duty to my family may be outweighed by my duty to serve my country in time of war. Once again, calculation enters into many, but not all, ethical decisions. Few people would question that humans have a basic right to life, and that random killing is morally wrong. A somewhat different question, related to layoffs, is whether workers have a right to their jobs, and therefore, managers have a duty not to lay them off.

Justice and fairness.   The third basic approach involves issues of justice and fairness. While some would treat justice and fairness as issues within the first two approaches, others maintain that they constitute a third approach. Both utilitarianism and rights and duties have been criticized for being unfair in certain cases. In some situations, you may not have a clear right to your job, and it may not be clear that maintaining your job serves the greatest good of the greatest number, but does not seem fair for you to be terminated when you have been performing well and earning both praises and raises. In the United States, we tend to equate justice with legality, but there are situations where an action that is legal does not seem fair or just. As with the previous two approaches, calculation sometimes enters into considerations of justice and fairness, because it may be impossible in a given situation to be fully fair to everyone involved. The philosopher whose work is most often cited on issues of justice and fairness is John Rawls, a professor at Harvard University.

With this brief summary of the three most common approaches to analyzing issues of managerial ethics, we now turn to the issue of layoffs. . . . There are a variety of reasons why managers may choose to layoff employees. An ethical or moral analysis of layoffs requires that we identify some of these reasons.

At one extreme is the situation where a company ceases operation, either at the choice of its owners or because of bankruptcy. In this case, obviously, all employees lost their jobs, but this is not usually referred to as a layoff. A similar situation, but not as drastic, occurs when a company is in serious danger of going out of business, and reducing labor costs through layoffs is the only apparent alternative. We will refer to such situations as layoffs to save the company. In other situations, layoffs are a preventative measure. In such cases, managers analyze their company's competitive situation, see that it is deteriorating and that labor costs are a significant factor, and move to reduce these costs before the company reaches the life or death stage. We will refer to this category as layoffs to improve the company.

In still other situations, layoffs are conducted to improve an already good situation. Here it is the judgment of managers that while the company is not deteriorating, greater profits could be achieved by reducing labor costs. Such layoffs may come about in mergers or acquisitions. Here two companies become one, and frequently plants or offices are closed and their employees laid off to reduce duplication. These layoffs are also conducted to reduce labor costs, but the motivating factor (or at least the precipitating factor) is the merger or acquisition.

Another circumstance in which layoffs are conducted to improve an already good situation involves outsourcing. The theory of core competency, popular in current strategy literature, suggests that a company can perform best by identifying its core competency, concentrating its efforts and its employees on performing core functions, and contracting with other companies to perform other functions. In practice, this can lead to layoffs if a company decides to stop performing certain functions and not to employ those people who formerly carried them out. We will categorize these situations (mergers, acquisitions, and outsourcing) as layoffs to change the company. The three categories of layoffs that we have identified (to save, to change, or to improve the company) are not mutually exclusive, but they are sufficiently different to provide a basis for further discussion.

Utilitarianism and Layoffs

On the face of it, deciding the morality of a decision or action by counting may seem strange. Yet it is an approach to decision-making that is frequent in everyday life and in the business world. . . .

When a manager terminates an employee who has done nothing wrong, it can scarcely be argued that this is good for the employee. Whether the action is called downsizing, rightsizing, outplacement, or some other term, the terminated employee had a job yesterday and now does not. . . .

The utilitarian argument focuses on obtaining the greatest happiness or good of the greatest number. Happiness is also the goal in other systems of ethics, dating back to Aristotle in the fourth century, B.C. This basis for deciding on moral acts makes some intuitive sense. Most people would probably agree that is morally better, in general, to make people happy than to make the unhappy, to being them pleasure rather than to bring them grief. What the utilitarian argument maintains is that it is not enough to consider the happiness or unhappiness of a single individual. Attention must be focused on the sum of happiness or grief resulting from a decision or action. Thus, the terminated employee receives pain rather than pleasure from his termination. The manager who conducts the face-to-face interview terminating the employee is likely to suffer grief rather than happiness as a result of the termination interview. If there is any moral justification for this action, it must lie in a greater sum of happiness coming to a larger number of others. An echo of this approach can be heard in the stakeholder analysis approach to issues of business strategy.

This line of reasoning is strengthened if the company, and hence the jobs of employees who are not laid off, can only be saved by reducing the labor force. If this is the case, then the happiness or pleasure of employment for all those who remain justifies the pain of those laid off and those managers who conduct the termination interviews. Further justification can be found in the happiness of stockholders, bondholders, and others who would be hurt by the company's bankruptcy. Given this situation, the utilitarian approach would clearly condone the layoffs as the moral thing to do. But how can we be sure that we are dealing with layoffs to save the company rather than to improve it.

Resolving this issue is not easy. When a company is in serious trouble, there is usually a perceived need to act quickly. Thoughtful consideration of all available alternatives is not likely to occur. Competing by price reductions only worsens a company's financial situation unless there are accompanying cost reductions. Competing by improving the present products or services, or introducing new and better ones, is often not a short-term possibility. Competing by greatly increased marketing efforts is costly, and if the company is already in financial trouble, costly solutions do not appear practical. Reducing staff can be done quickly, and there is ample precedent for such a decision. . . . While not an attractive alternative, a U.S. company in financial trouble can seek protecting by entering Chapter 11 bankruptcy, reorganizing its finances, and continuing as a going concern. As an alternative to layoffs, this solution may postpone the action, but often companies in Chapter 11 bankruptcy reduce staff as part of their reorganization before emerging from bankruptcy. So layoffs are still carried out, and the negative consequences of bankruptcy are added to the mix. In a utilitarian analysis, such a scenario is apt to result in greater unhappiness for more people (suppliers, creditors, shareholders) than would occur with layoffs alone.

In the final analysis, the only way to know for sure whether a company was in a situation of either conducting layoffs or going out of business is to wait and see. Yet it is cold comfort to managers or employees to find out after the fact that layoffs were needed to save the company and that, as a result of inaction, all jobs have been lost. Some uncertainty is inevitable regarding the question of whether the situation involves saving or improving the company. The luxury of waiting for definite answers is simply not available. Hence, we suggest a decision rule which says that if, in the judgment of senior management at the time the layoff decision is made, the situation was one of saving the company, it should be treated as such for purposes of ethical analysis.

Another possibility is that layoffs are not the only step between the present situation and a company's closing, but are seen as a way of dealing with deteriorating performance (layoffs to improve the company). In this case, it is more difficult to conclude that the unhappiness of those laid off and of managers who conduct the terminations is outweighed by a greater good for a greater number of people as a result of the company's improved performance. The unhappiness is clear, the greater good and those who benefit from it is less clear. In this category of layoffs, the further the situation deviates from a clearcut choice between layoffs and the company's closing, the less compelling the utilitarian argument becomes. However, top managers, by their positions, are charged with the future as well as the present well-being of the company. They are responsible for being proactive as well as reactive. In a situation where layoffs now can prevent a crisis later, choosing layoffs can be the best decision for the greatest number.

In the case of layoffs to improve already adequate performance (layoffs to change the company), the decision might bring happiness to managers whose compensation is tied to company performance through stock options or bonus plans, and to stockholders if the resulting improvements in performance cause the stock price to rise. However, in many cases companies conducting layoffs to improve performance do not attain the hoped-for results. Even if the results are achieved, unhappiness comes not only to the workers laid off and their managers, but also to many of the workers who remain. They face increased workloads and uncertainty about their own future with the company. Further, the families of those laid off also suffer pain. Workers at competing companies, observing the layoffs carried out by their rival may well suffer pain at the prospect that their own company will lay them off to maintain competitive. Thus, by a utilitarian analysis, it is by no means clear that layoffs to improve a company's position are always moral. . . .

The second question concerns how many and which employees are to be laid off. A utilitarian analysis emphasizes the impact of these choices (how many and who) on the results to be obtained. For the choices to be moral, the unhappiness caused must be offset by a greater sum of happiness for others resulting from the company's improved performance. . . .

If the reason for layoffs is to reduce labor costs, then it seems clear that laying off highly paid employees will reduce cost most. Older employees with greater seniority are normally more highly paid than newer and younger employees. A utilitarian analysis would note that older employees may suffer a greater degree of pain, since they often have a more difficult time finding new jobs than younger employees. Where negotiated contracts between labor and management prevail, unions typically negotiate as part of the contract that any layoffs occurring during the contract period will be based on reverse seniority, with the newest workers being laid off first. Another factor to be considered in a utilitarian analysis is that employees who perform their jobs best provide the most good to the company. Following this approach, the poorest performers should be laid off. However, many companies do not document performance in a way that can serve as a ground for determining layoffs on merit. Others do not choose to follow such an approach, even if they are able to.

A utilitarian approach concludes that layoffs are sometimes ethical, but some circumstances involving the desire to change a company, this approach finds that layoffs are not ethical. This approach emphasizes a consideration of human as well as financial factors and a concern for balancing the unhappiness which such actions bring to some participants with the benefits that result to others. The utilitarian approach does not assume that the company's financial situation is paramount, but does consider that greater good may come to a larger number of people, and that the unhappiness resulting from layoffs, might be morally justified by an analysis of the whole situation. It further considers that, if layoffs are to occur, the basis for deciding who will be laid off is also open to moral analysis.

Of the three approaches to ethical analysis used in this article, utilitarianism is the least abstract. Because major corporate decisions are so often based on impersonal analysis of financial considerations, the utilitarian approach adds an important perspective to those decisions.

Rights, Duties, and Layoffs

Much of philosophy deals with what it means to be human. There is general agreement that humans have a right to live, and that they have this right not because of their citizenship in one or another country, or because of their membership in a religion, or because of their occupation or position in life. If humans have a right to live, then they have a duty not to randomly take each other's lives. In general, rights imply duties. This is obvious with a little thought. If I have a right to privacy, you have a duty not to invade my privacy. If I have a right to free speech, you have a duty not to silence me.

In addition to rights that people may have simply by reason of being human, other rights are conveyed to all or some citizens of a country. In the United States, citizens who are at least 18 and are not felons have a right to vote. Not all humans have this right, but citizens of some countries have it. Rights can also be granted to citizens of a state or province. Citizens can also have duties by virtue of their status as citizens. . . .

A third group of rights consists of those a person may have by virtue of their positions in a company or agency. A supervisor may have the right to sign company checks for up to $5,000, while the chief financial officer may have the right to sign for up to $5 million. A police officer has the right to apprehend and jail a suspect, while ordinary citizens do not. These rights can be very powerful in practice. The central point is that a person has these rights not as a human or as a citizen, but by virtue of occupying a certain position.

It is important in conducting an ethical analysis to distinguish legal rights and duties from moral rights and duties. They often overlap: most people agree that random killing is both legally and morally wrong. However, they are not always identical. In the not-so-distant past, it was illegal to drive over 55 miles per hour in the U.S., but one could argue that it was not morally wrong. If legal and moral rights and duties are always identical, then a change in the legal speed limit results in a change in the moral rightness of driving at a certain speed. A further argument against identity of legal and moral rights and duties lies in the source of laws. In the U.S., federal laws that apply to all citizens are made by Congress. Many people are uneasy with the idea of Congress as their source of moral right and wrong.

The law in the U.S. as to whether an employer can terminate an employee at will (for any reason or no reason) varies from state to state. Federal law prohibits termination for some reasons (age, gender, disability). In cases where a labor-management contract determine wages and conditions of work, grounds for termination are usually specific and limited. Whatever rights to a job an employee has under such agreements come from the employee's membership in a group covered by the negotiated contract. Applying a rights and duties approach to the ethical analysis of layoffs, it appears that the central question is whether an employee has a moral right to his or her job, and whether supervisors then have a corresponding moral duty not to determinate that employee until he or she forfeits that right.

Upon reflection, it is clear that an employee does not have an absolute right to retain a job. An employee who shoots his boss or is caught embezzling large amounts of money does not have a right to keep a job. A more limited question involves the right of an employee to keep a job as long as he or she is performing it satisfactorily. It is difficult to see the basis of such a right. As indicated, some rights come from our status as humans. . . . With some few exceptions, U.S. employees do not have legal rights (rights as a citizen) to keep their jobs as long as they perform well. Some countries do provide such rights; others provide less legal job protection than the U.S. The third source of rights is from status in an organization, but the general status of employee does not in and of itself seem to confer the right to keep a job. . . .

The moral analysis of layoffs in terms of rights and duties requires an emphasis on the individual. What a manager may or may not morally do is determined by examining the rights of the individual employee. If the manager has a duty to retain the employee the duty results from the employee's right. If the manager is free to determine whether the employee keeps or loses a job, and can morally make either decision, in terms of this analysis the manager has that freedom because the employee does not have a right which constrains the manager's freedom. This part of the analysis, then, concludes that under a rights and duties approach, managers are not morally prohibited from conducting layoffs.

Managers have duties by virtue of their positions as manager. Top managers have a duty to act in the best interests of their company and its stakeholders; a wealth of literature on agency theory analyzes the manager's role as an agent for the owners or stockholders of a company. In the extreme case that characterizes our first category, where layoffs provide the only means to save the company, one could argue that top managers have a duty to do what is best for the company, and that in this case conducting layoffs is best. This approach leads to the conclusion that managers sometimes have a duty to conduct layoffs, and that failure to act on this duty would be unethical.

It is considerably less clear whether managers have a duty to conduct layoffs to improve or to change their company. Because such attempts in the past have often failed to improve performance, it makes sense to ask whether managers have a duty to take steps that might fail. The discussion of rights and duties leads to the conclusion that managers have a right to conduct layoffs in these situations (since employees do not have an overriding right to keep their jobs); it is much harder to prove that they have a duty to do so. If they have a right to conduct layoffs to improve or change the company, then under this method of analysis, it would not be unethical to do so. Particularly in the case of layoffs to change the company, when performance is already good, it does not appear that a credible arguments can be made for a managerial duty to conduct lay-offs. . . .

Fairness, Justice, and Layoffs

. . . A philosophical approach tries to remove the level of analysis from what an individual perceives to be fair and just, and to prescribe some rules and guidelines that can be applied across many situations. Many philosophers, beginning with Plato discuss justice as involving a sense of proportion. The just reward for a heroic deed is greater than for a minor, inconsequential action. The punishment for murder is greater than for petty theft. An unjust consequence (reward or punishment) is one that is out of proportion to the action that triggers it. Justice, in most philosophical analyses, also involves a sense of consistency. If certain actions are judged worthy of reward or punishment, each person who performs the action should, in justice, receive the same reward or punishment. This idea is sometimes expressed in the statement that those similarly situated should receive similar treatment. . . .

Applying this analysis to the question of layoffs, it appears that a central question is that of the fairness to the laid-off employee. Since the employee has, by our earlier definition of the situation, performed well and done nothing to trigger termination, it does not appear that there is a proportion between the action (termination) and the preceding behavior (satisfactory performance). It also does not appear that the principle of consistency is followed, since some employees who have performed well lost their jobs, while others who have performed similarly remain employed.

An approach that is sometimes taken in the name of fairness is to lay off a certain percentage of employees "across the board." In practice, this means that each division or department or region must lay off some percentage of its employees. This does not solve the problem of fairness or consistency but merely shifts it to a lower level of decision-maker. Under this approach, the head of each unit must still decide which employees will keep their jobs and which will lose them. A disadvantage of this approach is that it disconnects layoff decisions from improving the company's performance, since it is rare that all units are equally overstaffed or equally important in their contribution to the company's overall performance.

Viewed from the perspective of the social system or the whole company, the discussion of fairness changes. In the extreme case, where failure to reduce labor costs by conducting layoffs results in the company's closing, all employees lose their jobs. . . .

As the cause for layoffs deviates from the clearcut case where they represent the only way to avoid the company's closing, the argument from fairness when the system is viewed as a whole becomes weaker. Layoffs taken as a proactive step to forestall problems management foresees are less clearcut but still defensible. If layoffs are conducted to increase the profits of an already profitable firm, it is unlikely that a person behind Rawls' veil of ignorance would consider the system allowing this to be just.

Would it be fair and just if the employees laid off were those with the least seniority or those who, while performing adequately, did not perform as well as others who retain their jobs? From the point of view of the system, seniority or merit present arguably consistent bases for deciding who loses their job and who keeps it. We should note, however, that relative seniority is much easier to establish than relative merit in performance. From the point of view of the individual, although these approaches attain some consistency, the problem of lack of proportion remains. . . .

Of the two approaches, merit would appear to be more defensible, since it ties the goal of layoffs (improved company performance) to the judgment of which individuals should suffer layoffs (those who contribute least to the company's performance). Seniority might be defensible if there is not sufficient evidence to use merit. The defense of seniority would lie in the fact that it is measurable and might be seen as a proxy for individual performance in the sense that employees with more experience will, in general, contribute more to the company's performance than those with less experience. . . .

The fairness and justice approach requires an emphasis on more than just the individual, who is the center of the rights and duties approach. Questions of fairness and justice address issues of proportion and consistency, but within a narrower setting than that addressed by the utilitarian approach. Of the three methods for ethical analysis, then, utilitarianism takes the widest view, considering the greatest good of the greatest number, whoever and wherever they might be. A major criticism of this approach is that it neglects important individual concerns. The rights and duties approach, as we have noted, centers on the individual, and looks out from the individual's rights to those on whom these rights impose duties. The fairness and justice approach considers both the individual and the social system within which he or she operates. The major focus of this approach is limited to a company or agency or possibly a community.

Comments and Conclusion

We have applied the three basic theories commonly used in managerial ethics to analyze the issue of the morality of layoffs. The views of these three basic theories generally coincide. In the extreme case where layoffs are the only way to save a company, the utilitarian approach finds the decision to conduct layoffs to be moral, because the layoffs generate the greatest good for the greatest number. The rights and duties approach sees the action of layoffs in the same situation to be moral because employees do not have absolute rights to their jobs. However, this view also requires that layoffs be conducted in a fair and just manner, because employees do have a right to be treated fairly. Finally, the justice and fairness approach, does not find layoffs to be moral, because they lack proportionality between the individual's behavior (good performance) and the resulting action (termination of employment). However, when the focus is changed from fairness to each individual to fairness in the total system, layoffs are justified—at least when the alternative is that all employees lose their jobs. Since all the individuals involved are part of the system, a reasonable argument can be made that the system view is the more appropriate one to be used here. Given that layoffs are to be conducted, this approach finds seniority or merit to be moral bases for determining who will lose jobs and who will keep them.

In the opposite extreme case, where layoffs are proposed in an attempt to change a company that is already performing well and does not appear to be in danger, none of the three approaches supports the conclusion that such layoffs are ethical. In this situation, the greatest good for the greatest number is not achieved. While employees do not have rights to their jobs, managers do not have a duty to conduct such layoffs. Finally, justice and fairness are not served. . . .

POSTSCRIPT

Is the Corporate Strategy
of Downsizing Unethical?

Predicting the future is always difficult. However, when it comes to business, one thing seems certain: Global competition is here to stay and is likely to become even more intense in the foreseeable future. As a result, U.S. firms will continue to be exposed to intense competitive pressures from both domestic and international businesses. As a means of reacting to these pressures, we also expect downsizing to remain a popular strategic initiative for reducing labor costs and increasing organizational efficiency. But as the two articles in this debate make clear, the popularity of downsizing does nothing to address the basic moral question of whether or not downsizing is immoral.

Larry Gross argues that downsizing—under all conditions—is immoral. The basis of his view is that laying-off workers violates important aspects of the employer–employee relationship as well as ultimately harming society itself. There may be trouble with this view, however. Consider this observation by Frank Navran: "The truth is that unless an organization was designed expressly and overtly for the purpose, it is not in business to provide employment. Jobs are the by-product of successful organizational endeavors, not their intended output" ("The Ethics of Downsizing," *The Ethics Resource Center*, 1996). The first responsibility of an organization is, like that of an individual, to act in a manner that is life-sustaining. From this perspective, downsizing is not inherently unethical, despite Gross's protestations.

John Gilbert argues downsizing is not immoral in most instances, depending on the health of the organization at the time of the layoffs. According to Dr. Gilbert, the only time downsizing is unequivocally immoral is when the organization is profitable, its prospects for the future bright, and it chooses to reduce its workforce primarily to increase immediate profit levels. Critics might assert that this is the motivation behind the majority of layoffs by huge U.S. firms over the last twenty or so years. After all, giant corporations such as GE, IBM, and Merrill Lynch have never really been in danger of going out of business, but each has engaged in aggressive, large-scale downsizing initiatives. It's hard to believe that these actions were motivated by much more than keeping stock prices high and increasing overall shareholder wealth.

This is a topic that invites passionate responses on both sides of the debate. Hopefully, the articles presented here provided you with some insight about the topic and alternative ways in which to view and think about the morality of downsizing.

Suggested Readings

James K. Glassman, Thank you American business men. *American Enterprise Institute Magazine,* March 2000.

C. Jenkins, Downsizing or dumbsizing: The restructuring of corporate America. *Brigham Young Magazine,* 51, 1997.

V. Mabert and R. Schmenner, Assessing the roller coaster of down-sizing. *Business Horizons,* 1997, issue 49, volume 4: pp. 45–53.

Ian Maitland, The upside of downsizing. *The Star Tribune,* 1996. `www.startribune.com/stonline/html/special/leaky/mait07.html`

Frank J. Navran, The ethics of downsizing. *Ethics Resource Center,* 1996, article ID #17. `www.ethics.org`

John Orlando, The fourth wave: The ethics of corporate downsizing. *Business Ethics Quarterly,* April 1999.

ISSUE 3

Is Bluffing During Negotiations Unethical?

YES: Chris Provis, from "Ethics, Deception and Labor Negotiation," *Journal of Business Ethics* (Kluwar Academic Publishers, The Netherlands, 2000)

NO: Fritz Allhoff, from "Business Bluffing Reconsidered," *Journal of Business Ethics* (Kluwar Academic Publishers, The Netherlands, 2003)

ISSUE SUMMARY

YES: Ethics scholar Chris Provis examines bluffing within the context of labor negotiations and concludes that it does indeed constitute unethical behavior. Bluffing, he argues, is deception and therefore unethical, regardless of whether it occurs in or out of the negotiation process.

NO: University of California, Santa Barbara philosopher Fritz Allhoff presents a clever and unique defense of bluffing in business negotiations. The central tenet in Allhoff's position is that certain roles that we are required to assume allow us to morally justify behaviors that might otherwise be considered immoral.

In 1968, business scholar Albert Carr published an article in the *Harvard Business Review* entitled, "Is business bluffing ethical?" In this paper, now a classic of its kind in the field of business ethics, Carr argued that "most bluffing in business might be regarded simply as game strategy—much like bluffing in poker, which does not reflect on the morality of the bluffer." He noted that in other areas of life we expect people not to always be truthful, and we typically do not condemn them for doing so. In criminal trials, for example, no one expects the accused to tell the truth when he claims his innocence. "Everyone from the judge down takes it for granted that the job of the defendant's attorney is to get his client off, not to reveal the truth; and this is considered ethical practice" (Carr, 1968). The essence of Carr's argument is based on his view that ethics of business are different from the ethics of morality or religion. Carr's article both reflected, and supported, the dominant perspective on the relationship between business and ethics at that time; namely, that business exists outside the normal bounds of ethical scrutiny. Therefore, behaviors such as bluffing—immoral in non-business settings—are "fair game" and not immoral in the business world.

Much has changed in the study and practice of business ethics since the publication of Carr's seminal article. The view that business is a human activity exempt from moral considerations no longer holds sway. The business scandals of the 1980s and 1990s focused much attention on corporate malfeasance and contributed mightily to the current intensive scrutiny of the behavior of American executives. Now, in the early part of the twenty-first century, the dominant view holds that corporations—and the executives who run them—have moral obligations to society beyond their traditional financial obligations to shareholders. Given the dramatic shift in how society views its relationship with the business community, it makes sense to ask whether attitudes toward bluffing in business transactions have changed as well. So, with that background, we present two articles with different answers to the question, is bluffing during business negotiations unethical?

Ethics scholar Chris Provis examines bluffing within the context of labor negotiations and concludes that it does indeed constitute unethical behavior. The basis of his analysis is the assertion that "other things being equal, it is wrong to deceive others or conceal information from them if doing so is likely to affect their actions and harm their interests." Bluffing, he argues, is deception and therefore unethical, regardless of whether it occurs in or out of the negotiation process. Thus, we are subject to the same degree of moral scrutiny in negotiations as we are in any other social interaction. "Negotiation," he writes, "is not a world set apart from our usual interactions with one another." Despite its rather simplistic charm, Provis's argument is not new. Many scholars past and present have rejected this analysis. So, to further bolster his position, he examines, and then rejects, the traditional arguments that the negotiation process, by its very nature, is a unique activity and cannot be subject to the same moral constraints as other forms of human behavior.

University of California, Santa Barbara philosopher Fritz Allhoff presents a clever and unique defense of bluffing in business negotiations. His argument rests on two very important papers supporting the legitimacy of bluffing: the afore-mentioned work of Albert Carr and a 1993 article by Thomas Carson. He examines the papers one at a time, pointing out the important points of each. And although he feels that both papers make positive contributions, he too concludes that both fail to convince the reader of the moral legitimacy of bluffing. Thus, the stage is set for Allhoff to present his unique argument.

The central tenet in Allhoff's position is that certain roles that we are required to assume "make acts permissible [or impermissible, or obligatory] that would otherwise be impermissible." He provides various non-business examples to show the validity of this "role-differentiated morality" before turning his attention back to bluffing in negotiations. As you read this article, do you accept his concept of role-differentiated morality? And if so, do you agree with his conclusion that bluffing is ethical?

Chris Provis  **YES**

Ethics, Deception and
Labor Negotiation

. . . There has been widespread emphasis on the importance of trust amongst parties to the employment relationship. Trust seems to be bound up with ethical action, but there is some question about what is ethical in bargaining, particularly where deception and bluffing are concerned. Because it is possible for cooperative bargainers to be exploited, some writers suggest that deceptive behavior is an established practice that is ethical and appropriate. There are several problems about that view. It is questionable how clear and uniform such a practice has been, even amongst experienced negotiators; in many cases an appearance of bluffing can be explained as exchange of concessions where claims were genuine but parties make sacrifices in order to reach agreement. . . . Deception cannot be justified as self-defense on the basis of a presumption that others will try to deceive us, since it is not reasonable to make a general presumption to that effect, and it is questionable to what extent bluffing and deception are necessary for self-defense, since there other techniques available by which parties can guard themselves against exploitation. Several factors explain why some writers endorse deception, including failure to make some important distinctions amongst different types of strategies.

Clearly, the discussion requires some basic assumptions about what is ethical and what is not. In particular, it is assumed here that other things being equal it is wrong to deceive others or conceal information from them if doing so is likely to affect their actions and harm their interests. There is room for further discussion of that assumption, but the following analysis is intended to pursue some of its implications rather than to defend it. The intention here is to suggest that negotiation is not somehow different, that we are subject to the same ethical constraints in negotiation as we are in other social interaction. Claims that negotiation is different are often based on claims about conventions and accepted practices and the need for self-protection, but those claims will be called into question. The view put here is that even though deception may sometimes be ethical (to prevent harm to others, perhaps), it is not especially so in negotiation. Negotiation is not a world set apart from our usual interactions with one another. . . .

From *Journal of Business Ethics*, Vol. 28, 2000, pp. 145–158. Copyright © 2000 by Kluwer Academic Journals. Reprinted by permission.

Deception, Bluffing and the Practices of Negotiation

It has been contended by some authors that there is an accepted practice of parties' bluffing when they state their "reservation prices": the least they will accept or the most they will yield. An example is Carr's article "Is Business Bluffing Ethical?", where he suggested that

> Most executives from time to time are almost compelled, in the interests of their companies or themselves, to practice some form of deception when negotiating with customers, dealers, labor unions, government officials, or even other departments of their companies. By conscious misstatements, concealment of pertinent facts, or exaggeration—in short, by bluffing—they seek to persuade others to agree with them.

Carson and his colleagues have written similarly that

> There can be no doubt that bluffing is an important bargaining tool. It can be employed to create impressions of enhanced strength as well as to probe the other party to find out the level of its critical sticking points.

"Bluffing" may seem a relatively innocuous tactic. Sometimes, the term may be used to refer just to exaggerated claims. However, it often goes beyond this to the case where a negotiator tries to convince the other party falsely that no further concessions can be made. Then, bluffing involves deception about what a bargainer is able or willing to accept, and there seems to be no clear line between that case and simple exaggerated claims, since sometimes it is just by exaggerated claims that a negotiator tries to produce a false impression. As Carr's statement implies, general acceptance of bluffing may be taken to imply acceptance of "conscious misstatements," "concealment of pertinent facts," "exaggeration" and presumably of other similar tactics. Many negotiators would think twice about some of these maneuvers. Nevertheless, bluffing is widely defended in academic literature. In fact, however, I shall argue that negotiators may bluff less often than many writers suggest: an appearance of bluffing sometimes results from the dynamics of concession exchange.

There can be no doubt that deception and bluffing are tactics which negotiators sometimes use. However, there is a question about how often they do so. It has been suggested that this is related to the degree of experience and sophistication of the negotiators. In his 1993 paper, Carson suggests that it is amongst "hardened and cynical negotiators" that statements about intentions or settlement preferences are not warranted to be true. Friedman and Shapiro say that "experienced labor negotiators expect that opponents will hide information and try to build up false perceptions about their limits and determination." They imply that MGB trainers may need to refrain from advocating openness and honesty because doing so can make them appear naïve.

It is certainly plausible that experienced negotiators are attuned to nuances in statements of position, and allow for them in what they say. As an example, we may take Ann Douglas' transcript of the Atlas case, where the mediator comments at one point "see—if you went in there now and started to talk about a 35-hour week, you're dealing with experienced negotiators and they'd m—immediately read something that might not be there." It is also plausible to suggest that experienced negotiators are discreet at the outset of a negotiation. Earlier in that transcript, professionals show great mirth at the story of an error made by the president of a company in disclosing the company's real position in a negotiation.

However, it is questionable to what extent these examples confirm that negotiators generally practice "deception." Neither sensitivity to what other negotiators may infer, nor discretion at the outset of negotiation, amounts to deceptive conduct, and there are other accounts which paint pictures of honesty. Dufty recounts the comment of a union official who referred to employer representatives as "four honest men who called a spade a spade and laid their cards on the table and got down to business." Douglas' Atlas transcript elsewhere suggests that professional negotiators may condemn deception and concealment: for example, the union negotiator at one point expresses concern and anger that in a previous negotiation his management counterparts gained an advantage by such tactics:

> They gave us the same business last time in here—in this same room, cried the blues all over the place . . . And immediately after the reopening negotiations were over, decentralization announcement is made in November. (Pause) So they're—they're in no position to give us that, "We're playin' nice and fair and square with you boys and girls."

Some well-known historical figures and some recent writers with wide experience of negotiation in other areas have advocated honesty rather than deception. Nyerges says that "honesty is unconditional" and that "a good negotiator should resist the temptation to be dishonest when dealing with a partner whose honesty is questionable." Williams reports a research project on the negotiating behavior of attorneys. It found that a significant majority used a cooperative approach rather than a competitive approach with an exaggerated opening position. There is evidence that while experienced negotiators may do better than naïve negotiators, that results not from deception or bluffing, but by their making more different proposals that they would find satisfactory. Overall, the actual behavior of negotiators does not present a clear, uniform picture. However, the evidence does suggest that deception is less consistent than often contended.

People's beliefs that deceptive behavior is widespread may be partly the result of a self-fulfilling prophecy. By acting deceptively in anticipation of deceptive behavior by others, we tend to elicit the sort of deceptive behavior we anticipate. This dynamic has been documented for competitive behavior in Prisoners' Dilemma situations in general, and it seems likely to apply to deceptive behavior in particular. We have noted that some experienced negotiators advocate honesty rather than deception, and this suggests that there is not a general practice of deception. However, the possibility of a self-fulfilling prophecy could explain why some people think there is.

Conventions, Practices and Concession Exchange

Even though those points cast some doubt on it, the idea persists that it is both usual and ethical to use tactics like bluffing, exaggeration and distortion. The idea that tactics like these are ethical is supported with the claim that in such negotiation "some statements are *expected* to be untrue while others are not." On this view, a union statement that it will not settle for less than a 5% wage increase might be acceptable because the management negotiators know that the true figure is something less, and the union negotiators intend them to know. Carr suggested that there is no lying, or no deception, in negotiation, because people are interpreting one another's statements differently than usual. He quotes British statesman Henry Taylor's comment that "falsehood ceases to be falsehood when it is understood on all sides that the truth is not expected to be spoken." A series of writers about negotiation have suggested that much of the deception that occurs is ethically sound because the deceptive statements in question are not taken seriously and are not expected to be.

Now it is true that inferences may depend on context, as well as on the way the negotiator makes the statement. There may be some negotiations where all parties are aware that others are not committed to the positions they are stating, just as people may not be committed to what they say in many other situations, ranging from jokes to role plays. But a number of writers generalize beyond that. Carson says that "it is not expected that one will speak truthfully about one's negotiating position," while Strudler claims that "at the outset of the negotiation, both parties would know that they can expect lies." He says that "deception is a signaling and symbolic device," and that "the conventions of deception are often clear."

However, it seems too strong to say that the conventions are clear, in labor relations at least. If I bluff by saying that 10% is as high as I can go, then as Carson and his colleagues suggest, "even if I don't *expect* you to believe that 10% is my final position, I probably still *hope* or intend to deceive you into thinking that I am unwilling to offer as much as 12%." Still, it could be that there was at least an accepted norm which permitted deception in negotiation, so that listeners would not make all the same inferences they might outside of the negotiation context. Carr rests his argument on the analogy with games like poker, where bluffing and deception are sanctioned by the rules of the game. The implication is that even though each party may really be trying to deceive the other, each also knows that the other party is trying to do that. On this view, bluffing and similar tactics are genuine efforts to mislead, but they are not unethical since other negotiators can be expected to anticipate them and will be on their guard accordingly.

Perhaps this sort of idea lies behind the contention by Carson and his colleagues that "no one familiar with standard negotiating practices is likely to take at face value statements which a person makes about a 'final offer.'"

It could also be what Lewicki had in mind when he went so far as to suggest that

> In fact, bargainers are *expected* to bluff in negotiation; if they did not inflate their desired objective and make concessions toward that goal, they would be accused of bargaining "unfairly" . . .

Self-Defense, Fairness, and Alternatives to Deception

. . . The point can be stated as one about fairness. People commonly enter into games at which they have some capacity and skill. However, where wages and conditions are determined by negotiation, that is not a game that people can ignore. Haggling and bluffing in some voluntary bargaining over the price of a carpet in an oriental bazaar may be enjoyable and satisfying for both parties, particularly if they do have a shared understanding of what they are about, but the situation is different if they have no choice but to participate, if they are bargaining over their livelihood, and if one party has more skill or power than the other. In that situation, tactics of bluffing and deception may be quite unfair.

Dees and Cramton's point is too strong as a general proposition, that in the absence of trust and reciprocity one is entitled to use otherwise immoral practices. However, we may still be inclined to feel that because we expect bluffing and deceptive practices from others, we are entitled to protect ourselves, and that means trying to deceive them in turn. However, there remain two major difficulties with that view. First, it is not reasonable to presume that other negotiators always try to deceive us. Second, even where we are uncertain about others' honesty, there are other strategies for us to use in response than trying to deceive them.

As to the first point, we have already raised some questions about whether there is a general practice of attempted deception amongst negotiators, and those can be supplemented by some general considerations. There is evidence that "the disposition to employ deception as a tactic is influenced by a wide variety of factors." These factors include individual differences, the relationship between the parties, what is at stake, and so on. Since there are many factors that affect whether another party will try to deceive us, and since there are at least some occasions where the other party will try to be honest, it seems reasonable to suggest that there is an obligation on us to try to discern whether the other party is trying to deceive us on any particular occasion. There is evidence that individuals differ in their levels of generalized interpersonal trust, and at the same time it is clear that there are significant differences in negotiators' expectations of one another as a result of differences in linguistic background and cultural norms.

Since there are differences amongst individuals and situations, prudence suggests that we ought to take account of these detailed differences so far as we can, and ethical requirements point in the same direction. If we simply act on the basis of some blanket assumption that "people always do it," we run two risks: the risk of obtaining a less satisfactory agreement than we might otherwise, and the ethical risk that we may disadvantage another party who is being more frank and open than we realize. The overall implication is that we ought not act on any general assumption about others' lack of honesty or openness.

It is true, however, that we have only limited ability to detect others' attempts at deception. To decide quickly that the other is being honest can often carry significant risk. On the other hand, to be deceptive because of the mere possibility of deception by the other party may do them an injustice and may wreck any possibility of cooperation and trust. Is there a way out of that dilemma?

Fortunately, there are well-documented strategies that we can use to guard against deception by others without leaving ourselves too wide open. These tend to revolve around "indirect communication," including possibilities of fractional concessions and other indirect communication. Fractional concessions allow each party to take small initial risks which can grow into a process of reciprocal exchange resulting in agreement. A small concession may elicit one in return from the other party, by the process of 'reciprocity' mentioned above; this may allow another in response, and so on. Neither party risks a great deal more than the other at any particular point. Further, the concessions may have a communicative function. As well as inducing concessions in response, the willingness to make appropriate concessions can communicate willingness to cooperate, and information about one's interests and preferences. This can be supplemented by verbal interchange, and by other processes of indirect communication, which may include hints, non-verbal behavior and other "back-channel" communication. These can be used independently as well as in conjunction with concession exchange. Indirect communication allows each party to make offers or put suggestions which are ambiguous and therefore disavowable if the other does not respond, but which allow increasingly clear communication if both parties wish that to occur.

Conclusion

Indirect communication requires some experience and skill, and one implication is that for negotiation to be both ethical and effective parties may need to have appropriate skills as well as good intentions. The ability to send and comprehend quite subtle verbal and non-verbal messages may be an important part of the process, and lack of those skills can inhibit trust and cooperation just as much as dishonest intentions may. That fact may go together with others to help account for the idea that dishonesty and deception are widespread in negotiation. The theme of this paper is that deception and bluffing are less common in labor negotiations than is contended in some literature, that they ought to be considered less ethical than suggested by that literature, and that they are less necessary than implied in that literature.

In explaining why those views are held, the fact that a lack of communication skill can look like dissimulation goes part of the way to account for them. Processes of self-fulfilling prophecy may also help to explain those views: deceptive bargainers may elicit deceptive behavior in response to their own and so confirm their expectations. Another relevant factor is that the process of concession exchange can seem to be one in which parties move from false positions to real positions. A better account of the process recognizes that the parties are likely to have been making genuine exploratory claims which they then give up piece by piece in exchange for others doing so, in order to reach an agreement. Alternatively, it may be a process in which they clarify or revise their preferences. But in neither case need it involve deliberately misleading the other party.

Another part of the explanation why some writers report and endorse deceptive behavior may be a failure to make significant distinctions. "Bluffing," "concealment," "distortion," "deception," "conscious misstatements," "hiding information" and "lies" can be distinguished from actions that are often appropriate or necessary. If questioned by police, I may not lie to them, but I have a right to remain silent, and fundamentally the same distinction is available to negotiators. To decline to inform people about something is not necessarily to deceive them about it. How much a negotiator is obliged to tell another will depend on circumstances. For example, it may depend how the other party's interests are affected, and on their relative power. In many cases, we may be able to adopt the strategy Adler and Bigoness draw from Fisher and Ury, that "a principled negotiator need not disclose information or intentions so long as the negotiator makes clear that he or she is withholding information and is doing so for good reasons." Sometimes, there will be good reasons; sometimes, there will not. But there are much more likely to be good reasons for doing that than for lying or distortion.

There can be debate on how to apply some of the terms referred to above: for example, does "withholding information" amount to concealment? Does "bluffing" always involve deception, or only sometimes? It would be easy to become enmeshed in purely semantic disputes over matters like those. The answer may depend on details of the case. But it seems clear that not all of the dispute is a semantic one, and we can generalize to some extent. Strategies of "indirect communication" involve some withholding of information, but they do not involve "distortion," "deception" or "conscious misstatements." Negotiators who try deliberately to deceive others about their own intentions for the sake of pursuing their own advantage will generally be doing something unethical, even if they rationalize it as protecting themselves against possible exploitation, since there are usually other strategies of self-protection available. In practice there will be hard cases, as there are in many ethical matters. However, they can be made easier by taking care over detail, and not being misled by questionable ideas about how common deceptive practices are. Failure to analyze the various different sorts of tactics available can encourage behaviors which are unethical and which are inimical both to sound agreements and to good relationships between parties.

NO

Fritz Allhoff

Business Bluffing Reconsidered

1. Introduction

Imagine that I walk into a car dealership and tell the salesperson that I absolutely cannot pay more than $10,000 for the car that I want. And imagine further she tells me that she absolutely cannot sell the car for less than $12,000. Assuming that neither one of us is telling the truth, we are bluffing about our reservation prices, the price above or below which we will no longer be willing to make the transaction. This is certainly a common practice and, moreover, is most likely minimally prudent—whether our negotiating adversary is bluffing or not, it will always be in our interest to bluff. Discussions of bluffing in business commonly invoke reservation prices, but need not; one could misrepresent his position in any number of areas including the financial health of a company poised for merger, the authority that has been granted to him by the parties that he represents, or even one's enthusiasm about a project. The goal of bluffing is quite simple: to enhance the strength of one's position during negotiations.

Bluffing has long been a topic of considerable interest to business ethicists.[1] On the one hand, bluffing seems to bear a strong resemblance to lying, and therefore might be thought to be *prima facie* impermissible. On the other, many people have the intuition that bluffing is an appropriate and morally permissible negotiating tactic. Given this tension, what is the moral standing of bluffing in business? The dominant position has been that it is permissible and work has therefore been done to show why the apparent impermissibility is either mis-motivated or illusory. Two highly influential papers have taken different approaches to securing the moral legitimacy of bluffing. The first, by Albert Carr, argued that bluffing in business is analogous to bluffing in poker and therefore should not be thought to be impermissible insofar as it is part of the way that the game is played. The second, by Thomas Carson, presented a more subtle argument wherein the author reconstrued the concept of lying to require an implied warrantability of truth and, since business negotiations instantiate a context wherein claims are not warranted to be true, bluffing is not lying.

I think that both papers are on the right track to the solution to the problem, but that both authors' positions are problematic. In this paper, I will consider the arguments of both Carr and Carson, and I will present my criticisms

From *Journal of Business Ethics*, Vol. 45, 2003, pp. 283–289. Copyright © 2003 by Kluwer Academic Journals. Reprinted by permission.

of their ideas. Drawing off of their accounts, I will then develop my own argument as to why bluffing in business is morally permissible, which will be that bluffing is a practice that should be endorsed by all rational negotiators.

2. Albert Carr

Carr's article is somewhat informal and therefore lacks clear and rigorous argumentation. His thesis, however, is that business is a game, just like poker, and that bluffing is permitted under the rules of the game. To strengthen the analogy between business and poker, he points out that both business and poker have large elements of chance, that the winner is the one who plays with steady skill, and that ultimate victory in both requires knowledge of the rules, insight into the psychology of the other players, a bold front, self-discipline, and the ability to respond quickly and effectively to opportunities presented by chance.[2]

Even if we grant Carr that there are no morally relevant disanalogies between poker and business, which seems dubious, he still has a problem by trying to legitimize bluffing on the grounds that it is permitted by the rules of the game.[3] As Carson has pointed out, Carr seems somewhat confused as to how we determine the rules of the game.[4] In some passages, Carr seems to think that convention determines the rules, whereas in others he seems to think that the law delineates boundaries and all acts within those boundaries are permissible. Regardless, neither of these standards can help to establish the moral legitimacy of bluffing.

The reason is that either one of these moves would violate a long standing principle in moral philosophy, dating back to David Hume, that one cannot reason from what is the case to what ought to be the case.[5] There have been numerous conventions, such a discrimination, that have nevertheless been immoral. And there have also been numerous practices, such as slavery, that have been legally sanctioned but that are also immoral. Facts about the way that the society operates or about the way that the law is, can not be used to derive values. The two supports that Carr gives for the moral permissibility of bluffing are precisely the sorts of considerations that are patently disallowed in moral philosophy.

Carr hints at, but does not discuss, a potentially more promising notion, that of consent. Certainly bluffing in poker, and most likely bluffing in business, is a practice to which all involved parties consent, which is more than can be said for other conventions. But since the fact-value divide makes convention wholly irrelevant, consent would have to do the entirety of the work, and not merely be used to identify a special kind of convention. This is clearly not what Carr has in mind, and I do not propose to read it into his argument. Furthermore, I still do not think that consent alone establishes permissibility. Just as I may consensually enter a poker game knowing full well that bluffing might happen, I may consensually travel to a dangerous neighborhood knowing full well that a crime against me might happen. Since my consent in the latter case does not provide moral license for the act against me, consent can similarly not be used to legitimize bluffing in the former.

3. Thomas Carson

Carson approaches the problem from a different direction, though he arrives at more or less the same conclusion. His strategy is to deny that bluffing is a form of lying and, in order to make this argument, he takes issue with the conventional idea that lying is a false statement made with the intent to deceive and proposes instead that "a lie is a false statement which the 'speaker' does not believe to be true made in a context in which the speaker warrants the truth or what he says."[6] Bluffing is certainly lying on the traditional definition; the bluffer's statement is false and it is intended to deceive. But Carson thinks that his definition of lying excludes bluffing. Why? He argues that the second requirement, the warrantability of truth, is largely absent in negotiations. There are some claims made during negotiations that convention dictates to be warranted as true, such as claims to have another offer on the table. If I were to claim that I had another offer while I did not, this would be a lie because it would satisfy both parts of Carson's requirements. Claims about reservation prices, however, do not carry implied warrantability of truth—as a matter of fact, nobody *ever* takes such claims to be literally true. Carson therefore thinks that bluffing is not lying and should therefore not hold the moral disapprobations that we confer on lying.

There are, I think, two problems with Carson's defense of bluffing. The most obvious one is that, even if bluffing is not lying, it does not follow that it is morally permissible. It might be wrong for some other reason. For example, we might want to distinguish between lying and other kinds of deception which are still morally objectionable. Imagine that I leave my children home for the weekend and tell my oldest son that his girlfriend is not allowed in the house. If I call home to ask my younger son what my older son is doing and am told "he is talking to his friend Robert," this might be strictly and literally true only because his girlfriend is in the kitchen getting something to drink and is currently unavailable for conversation. The answer, though true and not a lie, is deceptive insofar as it masks a fact that my younger son knows to be salient. Or I might ask my older son directly whether his girlfriend is in the house and he truthfully answers no because she is still in transit to the house. Again, this answer is not a lie, but is deceptive. If we find such behavior morally objectionable, which many of us would, then the absence of lying alone does not secure moral license. And if it is not morally objectionable, some argument has to be given as to why; it certainly not intuitively obvious that all non-lying deceptions are morally permissible. Therefore, the most that Carson's argument can establish is that bluffing does not carry the same *prima facie* wrongness that lying does, not that it is morally permissible, which is his desired conclusion.

The second problem is that Carson's account still requires the same dependence convention that caused trouble for Carr. Carson admits that he will not pursue specific guidelines to determine whether a context involves implied warrantability of truth, but the examples that he gestures at are suggestive of conventionality playing a strong role.[7] For instance, he says that statements made in negotiations between experienced negotiators are understood to be not warranted as true. But this is only the case because it is a matter of convention;

we could easily imagine another society wherein negotiators do not bluff, but are honest about their reservation prices. We have already seen why convention alone cannot provide any reason to think that a practice is morally permissible.[8] To say it another way, we can meaningfully ask whether a practice is morally permissible *despite* its being conventional. A defense of bluffing must extend beyond mere conventionality and into the realm of moral philosophy, else it is doomed to violate the fact-value divide.

4. Bluffing, Role-Differentiated Morality, and Endorsement

I will now develop what I think is the correct solution to the problem of bluffing in business. As I said earlier, I think that both Carr and Carson start off on the right track, but then go wrong for the reasons that I have presented.[9] In particular, both authors appeal to games in order to argue for the permissibility of bluffing in business; Carr uses a poker analogy and Carson argues that claims made during bluffing are similar to claims made during the game of Risk. But the problem that both authors have is that they infer moral legitimacy from the rules of their games, and this inference cannot be made. What we need is not an appeal to convention, but rather a moral argument that legitimizes bluffing within those games and that can be extended to bluffing in business.

One way that we could get this is to invoke what has become known as role-differentiated morality. Conventional wisdom within ethics has held that ethical rules are universal, and that everyone should be bound by the exact same moral laws. But work in professional ethics has recently come to challenge this idea.[10] These applications have come most auspiciously in legal ethics, where legal ethicists have often sought to defend ethically objectionable practices of lawyers (such as discrediting known truthful witnesses and/or enabling perjurious testimonies) on the grounds that the lawyer's role, that of zealous advocate, carries different moral rules than non-lawyer roles.[11] Though the applications have certainly been controversial, the underlying idea, role-differentiated morality, has garnered wide support.

Put simply, role-differentiated morality suggests the following three claims:

1. Certain roles make acts permissible that would otherwise be impermissible.
2. Certain roles make acts impermissible that would otherwise be permissible.
3. Certain roles make acts obligatory that would otherwise not be obligatory.

In this paper, I do not wish to provide an extended defense of the plausibility of role-differentiated morality; this has been done by other authors (including the two I cited above), and I do not feel that I have anything of value to add. What I will say in defense of the idea here is that it has tremendous intuitive resonance, as I think can be clearly shown through examples. In support of the first claim, we might say that soldiers fighting a just war are morally permitted to kill, whereas ordinary civilians are not. In support of the second claim, we could suggest that college professors should not have sexual relationships with their students (nor bosses with their subordinates), regardless of the act being consensual. In support of the third claim, we might claim that parents have special obligations to their children, such as providing for them and caring for them, that non-parents would not have towards the same child. I think the self-evidence of these examples gives strong support for the notion of role-differentiated morality.

Now, we can return to bluffing and ask whether some roles should allow for its moral permissibility.[12] I think that it is pretty clear that yes, some roles do allow for bluffing, while others definitely do not (though it remains, for now, an open question under which one bluffing in business falls). Some roles clearly do not morally permit bluffing. For example, consider a relationship between a husband and a wife. They have duties to each other to be honest and not to manipulate each other to secure advantages in negotiation. We might even want to say that negotiating, which is a necessary precondition for bluffing, is not the sort of activity in which husbands and wives should partake. Negotiating assumes conflicting aims of the negotiators and pits them against each other as adversaries, whereas husbands and wives should, ideally, share the same goals and cooperate. When disagreements do occur (such as on how much to pay for a new house), they should not negotiate against each other to determine their collective reservation price but rather should debate the issue and build a consensus as a unified front. I think that husband or wife is a role in which bluffing is not morally permissible,[13] but there are others, such as any fiduciary role wherein one is morally bound to be fully open with another.

There are, on the other hand, roles under which bluffing *is* morally permitted. Both Carr and Carson suggested that bluffing is permitted in games, and I think that they are exactly right. But they got the reason wrong, convention alone cannot deliver moral permissibility. Whatever justifies bluffing in these cases needs to have moral, rather than merely descriptive, force. I think that the key to these cases is that the players involved in the game actually *endorse* the practice of bluffing; people play these games for fun, and bluffing makes the games much more fun. If bluffing did not exist in poker, and everyone's bet merely reflected the strength of their hands, there would be no game at all since the final results would all be made apparent. Thus, insofar as anyone even wants to play poker in a meaningful way, he is committed to endorsing the practice of bluffing. Bluffing in Risk is similarly explained; bluffing adds an exciting (though in this case non-essential) element to the game to which players are attracted. If this were not the case, we would certainly expect a proliferation in strategy games in which there were no bluffing via diplomacy, and this is certainly not what we see. Bluffing, in some games, is a welcome feature in which participants actually want to be involved.

Is endorsement a moral feature? Absolutely. Imagine that my son takes $20 out of my wallet. There could be two scenarios leading up to this act. In one, he asks me for the money and I endorse his taking it (to pay the deliveryperson for pizza, let's say) and, in the other, he does not ask and instead takes it without my permission. Obviously he acted permissibly in the first scenario and impermissibly in the second, and it was my approval, or endorsement, of his actions that is the *only* morally relevant difference. Therefore, endorsement carries with it the moral force to legitimize certain acts (or practices), and I think that it is precisely what is necessary to legitimize bluffing in games.[14]

I hope to have established both the plausibility of role-differentiated morality and that bluffing is permitted in some roles, but not in others. I can now return to my central aim and ask under which category bluffing in business falls. I think that bluffing in business is permissible for the same reason that it is permissible in games, namely that the participants endorse the practice. To explain why, let us return to the example with which I started. When I go to the car dealer with a reservation price of $12,000, what that means is that, all factors considered, that car has to me a utility marginally greater than the $12,000 does. *Ex hypothesi*, I am already willing to spend the $12,000; if that were the best that I could do, I would accept the offer. Any price that I can achieve below $12,000 would obviously be an improvement on the situation. Bluffing and negotiating are the mechanisms wherein I can achieve a final sale at a price beneath my reservation price and, insofar as any rational agent would welcome that end, he should also endorse its means.

Furthermore, other than bluffing, I cannot think of another reasonable procedure for the buyer to lower the sale price below my reservation price (or for the seller to raise the sale price above his reservation price). I might, for example, try to do so by force or threats, but these are obviously immoral. I might also make outright lies, such as to assert that the dealer across town has already guaranteed me a lower price. As Carson has already argued, this seems seriously immoral. So I think it is quite reasonable to suppose not only that the prospective buyer would endorse bluffing, but that there are no other reasonable alternatives.

One response to my position might be that bluffing does help the individual but that in negotiations there is not one, but two bluffers, and that the addition of the second cancels out all advantage to the first. Therefore, bluffing would should not actually be endorsed, since it yields no expected improvement, and maybe even eschewed on the grounds that it takes time and energy. However, I do not see how the addition of another bluffer really changes anything. If the car dealer will go as low as $10,000 and I will pay as high as $12,000, then we would both agree to (and, *ex hypothesi*, be happy with) any transaction at any price between and including $10,000 and $12,000. Assuming that the reservation price of the buyer is higher than the reservation price of the seller, the issue is not whether the two parties will come to mutually agreeable terms, the question is just what those terms will be. Ideally, each party would like to be able to bluff while having his opponent's position be transparent, but since that is obviously not a possibility, both should welcome bluffing as an opportunity to improve their positions.

It is also interesting to note that, without bluffing, the idea of negotiations itself almost (though not quite) becomes incoherent. Suppose that bluffing were not practiced, but that parties merely met and announced their respective reservation prices. I tell the car dealer that I will give him $12,000 for the car and she tells me that he will take as little as $10,000 for the car. Now what? I do not even know how to settle on a transaction price other than to do something arbitrary such as splitting the reservation window in half and settling at $11,000. This seems like the wrong answer for a number of reasons. Such resolutions could be inefficient (i.e. not Pareto optimal), not utilitarian, unfair to those who negotiate well, etc.[15] Negotiating is, I think, an essential part of business. To reach a transaction price, it makes the most sense for the buyer to start low and the seller high, and to reach some agreement in the middle. By announcing reservation prices, we would be creating a system that I find less attractive and, furthermore, would give the participants every reason to transgress and to bluff.

Finally, I think that there really is a lot of merit in the analogies between business negotiating and games (despite the criticisms by Koehn and others). But I would go further than claiming that it is *like* a game, it seems to me that it *is* a game. Perhaps this is not true in the sense that negotiators are drawn to their work because they find it amusing, this is false in a wide number of cases and I certainly do not mean to trivialize many serious negotiations. But if two parties come to the negotiating table and the reservation price of the buyer is higher than the reservation price of the seller, then we already know that, *ceteris paribus,* the transaction will occur and, furthermore, it will occur at a price to which both parties are amenable. It seems to me that the occurrence of the transaction and the satisfaction of the parties is what is really important, where the price falls within the reservation window just determines what each party gains (in terms of money not spent or extra money earned) *in addition to* a mutually beneficial transaction. Whether the stakes are millions of dollars or not, the parties are still merely trying to secure money that they would otherwise be satisfied without.

Notes

1. The first important paper was Albert Carr's "Is Business Bluffing Ethical?" *Harvard Business Review* January/February 1968, pp. 143–153. John Beach later reflects upon the treatment that the topic received in the years since Carr's publication (though Beach is somewhat critical of this response). See his "Bluffing: Its Demise as a Subject unto Itself," *Journal of Business Ethics* 4 (1985), pp. 191–196. Then, Thomas Carson reconsiders Carr's classic treatment of the subject and proposes an alternative conception of business bluffing; see "Second Thoughts about Bluffing," *Business Ethics Quarterly* 3(4) (1993), pp. 317–341. There are also numerous other examples within the literature, though I take these to be the most important.

2. Carr (1968), p. 72.

3. Daryl Koehn has, for example, argued that the analogy between business and poker is quite weak; he takes nine features that exist in games and argues that few, if any, of these exist in business. For the sake of argument, I am willing to grant Carr's analogy; I think that, even with this analogy, he is unable to secure the conclusion that he desires. See Koehn's "Business and Game-Playing: The False Analogy," *Journal of Business Ethics* 16 (1997), pp. 1447–1452. Norman Bowie also argued against the legitimacy of adversarial models (such as poker) as proper characterizations of bargaining and negotiating. See his "Should Collective Bargaining and Labor

Relations Be Less Adversarial?." *Journal of Business Ethics* **4** (1985) 283–291. Robert S. Adler and William J. Bigoness also challenge adversarial models in their work and find Carr's poker analogy to be flawed. See "Contemporary Ethical Issues in Labor-Management Issues in Labor-Management Relations," *Journal of Business Ethics* **11** (1992), pp. 351–360.

4. Carson (1993), 324–325.

5. *A Treatise of Human Nature,* ed. P. H. Nidditch, 2nd ed. (Oxford: Oxford University Press, 1978) III.I.i.

6. Carson (1993), p. 320. I assume that speaker is placed in scare quotes in order to allow for the possibility of non-verbal lying, such as when someone gives false directions by pointing in the wrong direction without saying anything. This definition results partly from earlier work by Carson and a criticism that he consequently received from Gary Jones. To trace through this, start with Thomas Carson, Richard Wokutch, and James Cox's "An Ethical Analysis of Deception in Advertising," *Journal of Business Ethics* **4** (1985), pp. 93–104. Jones's criticism can be found in "Lying and Intentions," *Journal of Business Ethics* **5** (1986) 347–349. And, finally, Carson's response is in "On the Definition of Lying: A reply to Jones and Revisions," *Journal of Business Ethics* **7** (1988), pp. 509–514.

7. Carson (1993), pp. 321–322.

8. And, in an interesting recent article, Chris Provis argues that bluffing (or, more precisely, deception) is not as ubiquitous in business as everyone often assumes; he thinks that the appearance of bluffing can often be accounted for by genuine concessions. If Provis is correct, then Carson's reliance on conventionality is empirically flawed. Or, as I argue, the reliance on convention is conceptually flawed (in order to secure moral permissibility). So, either way, the approach will not work. See Provis's "Ethics, Deception, and Labor Negotiation," *Journal of Business Ethics* **28**(2) (2000), pp. 145–158.

9. As I have indicated, other authors have also criticized the two approaches. What I have tried to do however, is be as charitable as possible: to grant all of their assumptions (the analogies, the adversarial nature of negotiating, Carson's definition of lying, etc.) and then aspired to show that they still cannot, even on their own terms, secure their desired conclusions.

10. An especially good and influential article is Richard Wassterstrom's "Lawyer's as Professionals: Some Moral Issues," *Human Rights Quarterly* **5**(1) (1975).

11. Monroc H. Freedman, "Professional Responsibility of the Criminal Defense Lawyer: The Three Hardest Questions," *Michigan Law Review* **27** (1966).

12. This step of my argument might be overly pedantic, and I might fare just as well if I skipped it and went directly to arguing for bluffing in business contexts specifically. However, I do think that it is an important part of the conceptual framework that I want to establish.

13. This is obviously not to say that husbands or wives cannot bluff in business situations, just that a husband cannot bluff *qua* husband nor a wife *qua* wife. The husband or wife who bluffs in business is not bluffing *qua* husband or *qua* wife, but rather *qua* businessperson.

14. John Rawls has argued that it is not morally permissible sell oneself into slavery (i.e., *even if* I endorsed the sale, it is still immoral). See his *Theory of Justice* (Cambridge: Harvard University Press, 1971). This poses an interesting objection to my idea that endorsement alone suggests *prima facie* permissibility. There are two ways that I could respond. First, I could disagree with Rawls and argue that any decision made by free and rational agents should be honored (so long as it did not harm others), that to do otherwise would show lack of respect for the being's rational nature. I am personally inclined towards this

view, though I know that many are not. The other way that I could go would be to argue that Rawls' point merely indicates that people cannot voluntarily give up their rights and that consenting to being bluffed is not problematic since we do not have the moral right to be told the truth. I think that either of these responses could be profitably developed, though I will not do so here.

15. The "Split-the-Difference" theory of negotiating is discussed by Roger Bowlby and William Schriver in their "Bluffing and the 'Split-the-Difference' Theory of Wage Bargaining," *Industrial and Labor Relations Review* **31**(2) (January 1978), pp. 161–171. Their discussion, however, is quite empirical and numerical rather than normative.

References

Adler, R. S. and W. J. Bigoness: 1992, 'Contemporary Ethical Issues in Labor-Management Relations,' *Journal of Business Ethics* **11**.

Beach, J.: 1985, '"Bluffing" its Demise as a Subject unto Itself,' *Journal of Business Ethics* **4**.

Bowie, N. E.: 1985, 'Should Collective Bargaining and Labor Relations Be Less Adversarial?,' *Journal of Business Ethics* **4**.

Bowlby, R. L. and W. R. Schriver: 1978, 'Bluffing and the "Split-the-Difference" Theory of Wage Bargaining,' *Industrial and Labor Relations Review* **31**(2).

Carr, A.: 1968, 'Is Business Bluffing Ethical?' *Harvard Business Review* (January/February).

Carson, T. L.: 1993, 'Second Thoughts about Bluffing,' *Journal of Business Ethics* **3**(4).

Carson, T. L.: 1988, 'On the Definitions of Lying: A Reply to Jones and Revisions,' *Journal of Business Ethics* **7**.

Carson, T. L., R. E. Wokutch and J. E. Cox, Jr.: 1985. 'An Ethical Analysis of Deception in Advertising,' *Journal of Business Ethics* **4**.

Freedman, M.: 1966, 'Professional Responsibility of the Criminal Defense Lawyer: The Three Hardest Questions,' *Michigan Law Review* **27**.

Hume, D.: 1978, *A Treatise of Human Nature* (2nd ed.). P. H. Nidditch (ed.). (Oxford University Press, Oxford).

Jones, G. E.: 1986, 'Lying and Intentions,' *Journal of Business Ethics* **5**.

Koehn, D.: 1997, 'Business and Game-Playing: The False Analogy,' *Journal of Business Ethics* **16**.

Post, F. R.: 1990. 'Collaborative Collective Bargaining: Toward an Ethically Defensible Approach to Labor Negotiations,' *Journal of Business Ethics* **9**.

Provis, C.: 2000. 'Ethics, Deception, and Labor Negotiation,' *Journal of Business Ethics* **28**.

Rawls, J.: 1971. *A Theory of Justice* (Harvard University Press, Cambridge).

Wasserstrom, R.: 1975, 'Lawyer's as Professionals: Some Moral Issues,' *Human Rights Quarterly* **5**(1).

POSTSCRIPT

Is Bluffing During Negotiations Unethical?

One of the central questions inherent in the business negotiation process concerns the morality of using deception (i.e., bluffing) as a means of achieving one's goals. The traditionally accepted view held that business is an activity akin to a game and, as such, is played according to its own set of rules. From this perspective, bluffing during negotiations not only falls within the rules of the game, but constitutes accepted, reasonable behavior as well. In recent years, however, the belief that business plays by a different set of rules from the rest of society has been overthrown and replaced with a new perspective. The dominant viewpoint now demands much greater corporate responsibility and accountability to society on the part of executives and their firms. Managerial behavior is subject to much greater moral scrutiny now than at any other time in American history. It's not surprising, then, that the moral legitimacy of bluffing as a common business behavior has come under question in recent years.

The first of the two articles presented here argued that the original justifications for the moral legitimacy of bluffing are deficient. Scholar Chris Provis, in his reassessment of the long-standing dominant viewpoint, rejects the suggestion that business is analogous to a game in which the rules not only allow, but encourage, bluffing as a legitimate behavior. He also rejects the contention that bluffing is necessary as a form of negotiating self-defense: If I don't bluff, I'll be at a major disadvantage since my opponents will. As you read Provis's article, did you find his arguments to be persuasive?

In the second article, philosopher Fritz Allhoff argues that bluffing is morally permissible when individuals are acting in certain roles, such as a negotiator. He also contends that reasonable people will want to allow for bluffing in the negotiation process. Indeed, he states that without bluffing, "the idea of negotiations itself almost (though not quite) becomes incoherent." How about Allhoff's clever attempt at justifying bluffing? Do you feel his argument is sound?

Suggested Readings

Albert Carr, Is business bluffing ethical? *Harvard Business Review,* January/February, 1968.

Thomas L. Carson, Second thoughts about bluffing. *Journal of Business Ethics,* vol. 3, no. 4, 1993.

T. L. Carson, R. E. Wokutch, and J. E. Cox Jr., An ethical analysis of deception in advertising. *Journal of Business Ethics,* vol. 4, 1985.

F. Flores and R. C. Solomon, Creating trust. *Business Ethics Quarterly*, vol. 8, no. 2, pp. 205–32, 1998.

F. R. Post, Collaborative collective bargaining: Toward an ethically defensible approach to labor negotiations. *Journal of Business Ethics*, vol. 9, 1990.

ISSUE 4

Are Corporations Accused of Wrongdoing Protected by the First Amendment?

YES: Joyce L. Kennard, from "Majority Opinion, *Marc Kasky v. Nike, Inc. et. al.*," California Supreme Court (May 2, 2002)

NO: Janice Brown, from "Dissenting Opinion, *Marc Kasky v. Nike, Inc. et. al.*," California Supreme Court (May 2, 2002)

ISSUE SUMMARY

YES: Justice Joyce Kennard, writing for the majority, argues that Nike's public response to charges they operated sweatshops overseas constituted "commercial" speech and, therefore, is not protected by the First Amendment of the U.S. Constitution.

NO: Justice Janice Brown contends that the U.S. Supreme Court has not provided the courts with an unambiguous definition of commercial speech and, consequently, part of the foundation of the majority's position is undermined. She also calls into question whether there should be a distinction between commercial and non-commerical speech in the first place.

In the late 1990s, press and media were awash with news stories about American corporations engaging in illegal and immoral labor practices overseas. Newspapers and television reported numerous cases of U.S. firms employing underaged children and forcing them to work excessive hours in horrid conditions for virtually no pay. And while the public was outraged to learn that many American firms condoned these sweatshop operations, it was the case involving the Nike Corporation that most captured the public's attention. In this issue, we examine whether or not Nike's First Amendment rights were violated by a lawsuit brought against them as a result of charges that the company was engaging in illegal labor practices overseas. But, before you turn to the two articles here, a little history on the case is necessary.

Public attention on Nike's overseas labor practices was the result, primarily, of a 1996 report by the television news program *48 Hours*. In the months that followed this broadcast, newspapers around the country published stories concerning the working conditions of overseas factories where Nike products were made. Typically, the reports alleged that employees working in Nike sanctioned factories were (1) required to work overtime, (2) paid less than required local wage rates, (3) routinely subjected to physical and mental abuse, and (4) exposed to unsafe working conditions. In response, Nike embarked on a well-orchestrated public relations campaign in which they vehemently denied any and all allegations of wrongdoing. The company took out ads in newspapers across the country, issued press releases to the television media, and wrote letters explaining its position to athletic directors at universities across the country.

In 1998, a social activist named Marc Kasky sued Nike for false advertising. And, although Kasky did not sustain personal damages as a result of Nike's rebuttal, as a state citizen he was entitled to sue under California's false advertising laws. Kasky's goal was not to receive monetary damages himself, but rather to have Nike pay the steep fines stipulated by the statutes governing corporate advertising violations.

The issue in this case centers on Nike's public response to the charges that they utilized sweatshops overseas. Specifically, the focus is on the nature of Nike's claims: If they constitute social or political comment, then they are afforded full protection under the First Amendment of the Constitution. Such a determination would thus protect them from Kasky's charges and represent a victory for Nike. If, however, they are deemed to be commercial speech, then Nike's statements would not protected by the First Amendment. In this instance, Kasky's false advertising charges would be supported, and Nike would be subject to substantial financial penalties (Katch and Rose, in *Taking Sides: Legal Issues*, McGraw-Hill Dushkin, 2004, p. 255).

Thus, the stage was set for a series of court battles. Two lower courts ruled that Nike's responses were social commentary and not commercial speech, thus handing Kasky two early losses. Not surprisingly, Kasky refused to quit, and the case ended up in the California Supreme Court.

In the first article, Justice Joyce L. Kennard, writing for the majority, argues that Nike's public statements represented commercial speech and, therefore, are not afforded protection under the First Amendment of the U.S. Constitution. In coming to this decision, the justices relied on previous U.S. Supreme Court rulings that attempted to draw a distinction between commercial and non-commerical speech. As you read this article, ask yourself if you agree with the "limited-purpose test" the majority used to reach its decision.

In the second article, Justice Janice Brown presents the dissenting viewpoint. Her argument consists basically of two points: First, she contends that the U.S. Supreme Court has not provided the courts with an unambiguous definition of commercial speech as the majority opinion would have us believe. Consequently, part of the foundation of the majority's position is undermined. Second, Justice Brown calls into question whether there should be a distinction between commercial and non-commerical speech in the first place. To the extent that there should be no distinction, all speech would be protected under the First Amendment. As you read this article, do you find yourself being persuaded by her argument?

YES

Majority Opinion

Kasky *v.* Nike

. . . Plaintiff alleged that defendant corporation, in response to public criticism, and to induce consumers to continue to buy its products, made false statements of fact about its labor practices and about working conditions in factories that make its products. . . .

The issue here is whether defendant corporation's false statements are commercial or noncommercial speech for purposes of constitutional free speech analysis under the state and federal Constitutions. Resolution of this issue is important because commercial speech receives a lesser degree of constitutional protection than many other forms of expression, and because governments may entirely prohibit commercial speech that is false or misleading.

Because the messages in question were directed by a commercial speaker to a commercial audience, and because they made representations of fact about the speaker's own business operations for the purpose of promoting sales of its products, we conclude that these messages are commercial speech for purposes of applying state laws barring false and misleading commercial messages. . . .

Our holding, based on decisions of the United States Supreme Court, in no way prohibits any business enterprise from speaking out on issues of public importance or from vigorously defending its own labor practices. It means only that when a business enterprise, to promote and defend its sales and profits, makes factual representations about its own products or its own operations, it must speak truthfully. Unlike our dissenting colleagues, we do not consider this a remarkable or intolerable burden to impose on the business community. . . .

Facts

This case comes before us after the superior court sustained defendants' demurrers to plaintiff's first amended complaint. We therefore begin by summarizing that complaint's allegations, accepting the truth of the allegations, as we must, for the limited purposes of reviewing the superior court's ruling.

Allegations of the First Amended Complaint

. . . Nike manufactures and sells athletic shoes and apparel. In 1997, it reported annual revenues of $9.2 billion, with annual expenditures for advertising and

California Supreme Court, May 2, 2002.

marketing of almost $1 billion. Most of Nike's products are manufactured by subcontractors in China, Vietnam, and Indonesia. Most of the workers who make Nike products are women under the age of 24. Since March 1993, under a memorandum of understanding with its subcontractors, Nike has assumed responsibility for its subcontractors' compliance with applicable local laws and regulations concerning minimum wage, overtime, occupational health and safety, and environmental protection.

Beginning at least in October 1996 with a report on the television news program *48 Hours,* and continuing at least through November and December of 1997 with the publication of articles in the Financial Times, the New York Times, the San Francisco Chronicle, the Buffalo News, the Oregonian, the Kansas City Star, and the Sporting News, various persons and organizations alleged that in the factories where Nike products are made workers were paid less than the applicable local minimum wage; required to work overtime; allowed and encouraged to work more overtime hours than applicable local law allowed; subjected to physical, verbal, and sexual abuse; and exposed to toxic chemicals, noise, heat, and dust without adequate safety equipment, in violation of applicable local occupational health and safety regulations.

In response to this adverse publicity, and for the purpose of maintaining and increasing its sales and profits, Nike and the individual defendants made statements to the California consuming public that plaintiff alleges were false and misleading. Specifically, Nike and the individual defendants said that workers who make Nike products are protected from physical and sexual abuse, that they are paid in accordance with applicable local laws and regulations governing wages and hours, that they are paid on average double the applicable local minimum wage, that they receive a "living wage," that they receive free meals and health care, and that their working conditions are in compliance with applicable local laws and regulations governing occupational health and safety. Nike and the individual defendants made these statements in press releases, in letters to newspapers, in a letter to university presidents and athletic directors, and in other documents distributed for public relations purposes. Nike also bought full-page advertisements in leading newspapers to publicize a report that GoodWorks International, LLC., had prepared under a contract with Nike. The report was based on an investigation by former United States Ambassador Andrew Young, and it found no evidence of illegal or unsafe working conditions at Nike factories in China, Vietnam, and Indonesia.

Plaintiff alleges that Nike and the individual defendants made these false and misleading statements because of their negligence and carelessness and "with knowledge or reckless disregard of the laws of California prohibiting false and misleading statements.". . .

The False Advertising Law

California's false advertising law (§ 17500 et seq.) makes it "unlawful for any person, . . . corporation . . . , or any employee thereof with intent directly or indirectly to dispose of real or personal property or to perform services . . . or to induce the public to enter into any obligation relating thereto, to make or disseminate . . . before the public in this state, . . . in any newspaper or other publication . . . or in any other manner or means whatever . . . any statement, concerning that real or personal property or those services . . . which is untrue or misleading, and which is known, or which by the exercise of reasonable care should be known, to be untrue or misleading. . . ." . . .

Constitutional Protections for Speech

Federal Constitution

Constitutional Text and Its Application to State Laws

The United States Constitution's First Amendment, part of the Bill of Rights, provides in part that "Congress shall make no law . . . abridging the freedom of speech. . . ." (U.S. Const., 1st Amend.) Although by its terms this provision limits only Congress, the United States Supreme Court has held that the Fourteenth Amendment's due process clause makes the freedom of speech provision operate to limit the authority of state and local governments as well.

Constitutional Protection of Commercial Speech

Although advertising has played an important role in our nation's culture since its early days, and although state regulation of commercial advertising and commercial transactions also has a long history, it was not until the 1970's that the United States Supreme Court extended First Amendment protection to commercial messages. In 1975, the court declared that it was error to assume "that advertising, as such, was entitled to no First Amendment protection." The next year, the court held that a state's complete ban on advertising prescription drug prices violated the First Amendment. The high court observed that "the free flow of commercial information is indispensable" not only "to the proper allocation of resources in a free enterprise system" but also "to the formation of intelligent opinions as to how that system ought to be regulated or altered."

Tests for Commercial and Noncommercial Speech Regulations

"[T]he [federal] Constitution accords less protection to commercial speech than to other constitutionally safeguarded forms of expression."

For noncommercial speech entitled to full First Amendment protection, a content-based regulation is valid under the First Amendment only if it can withstand strict scrutiny, which requires that the regulation be narrowly tailored (that is, the least restrictive means) to promote a compelling government interest.

"By contrast, regulation of commercial speech based on content is less problematic." To determine the validity of a content-based regulation of commercial speech, the United States Supreme Court has articulated an intermediate-scrutiny test. The court first articulated this test in *Central Hudson Gas & Elec. v. Public Serv. Comm'n* (1980) and has since referred to it as the *Central Hudson* test. The court explained the components of the test this way: "At the outset, we must determine whether the expression is protected by the First Amendment. *For commercial speech to come within that provision, it at least must concern lawful activity and not be misleading.* Next, we ask whether the asserted governmental interest is substantial. If both inquiries yield positive answers, we must determine whether the regulation directly advances the governmental interest asserted, and whether it is not more extensive than is necessary to serve that interest." The court has clarified that the last part of the test—determining whether the regulation is not more extensive than "necessary"—does not require the government to adopt the least restrictive means, but instead requires only a "reasonable fit" between the government's purpose and the means chosen to achieve it.

Regulation of False or Misleading Speech

"[T]here is no constitutional value in false statements of fact. Neither the intentional lie nor the careless error materially advances society's interest in 'uninhibited, robust, and wide-open debate on public issues.'" For this reason, "[u]ntruthful speech, commercial or otherwise, has never been protected for its own sake."

Nevertheless, in some instances the First Amendment imposes restraints on lawsuits seeking damages for injurious falsehoods. It does so "to eliminate the risk of undue self-censorship and the suppression of truthful material" and thereby to give freedom of expression the "'breathing space'" it needs to survive. Thus, "some false and misleading statements are entitled to First Amendment protection in the political realm."

But the United States Supreme Court has explained that the First Amendment's protection for false statements is not universal. ([S]tating that when speech "concerns no public issue" and is "wholly false and clearly damaging," it "warrants no special protection" under the First Amendment.) In particular, commercial speech that is false or misleading is not entitled to First Amendment protection and "may be prohibited entirely." (*In re R.M.J.* (1982). . . .

Reasons for the Distinction

The United States Supreme Court has given three reasons for the distinction between commercial and noncommercial speech in general and, more particularly, for withholding First Amendment protection from commercial speech that is false or actually or inherently misleading.

First, "[t]he truth of commercial speech . . . may be *more easily verifiable by its disseminator* than . . . news reporting or political commentary, in that ordinarily the advertiser seeks to disseminate information about a specific product or service that he himself provides and presumably knows more about than anyone else."

Second, commercial speech is *hardier* than noncommercial speech in the sense that commercial speakers, because they act from a profit motive, are less likely to experience a chilling effect from speech regulation.

Third, governmental authority to regulate commercial transactions to prevent commercial harms justifies a power to regulate speech that is "'linked inextricably' to those transactions." The high court has identified "preventing commercial harms" as "the typical reason why commercial speech can be subject to greater governmental regulation than noncommercial speech." . . .

Distinguishing Commercial From Noncommercial Speech

The United States Supreme Court has stated that the category of commercial speech consists at its core of "'speech proposing a commercial transaction.'"

Although in one case the court said that this description was "the test for identifying commercial speech," in other decisions the court has indicated that the category of commercial speech is not limited to this core segment. For example, the court has accepted as commercial speech a statement of alcohol content on the label of a beer bottle, as well as statements on an attorney's letterhead and business cards identifying the attorney as a CPA (certified public accountant) and CFP (certified financial planner).

Bolger, supra, 463 U.S. 60, presented the United States Supreme Court with the question whether a federal law prohibiting the mailing of unsolicited advertisements for contraceptives violated the federal Constitution's free speech provision as applied to certain mailings by a corporation that manufactured, sold, and distributed contraceptives. One category of mailings consisted of "informational pamphlets discussing the desirability and availability of prophylactics in general or [the corporation's] products in particular." The court noted that these pamphlets did not merely propose commercial transactions. Although the pamphlets were conceded to be advertisements, that fact alone did not make them commercial speech because paid advertisements are sometimes used to convey political or other messages unconnected to a product or service or commercial transaction. The court also found that references to specific products and the economic motivation of the speaker were each, considered in isolation, insufficient to make the pamphlets commercial speech. The court concluded, however, that the *combination* of these three factors—advertising format, product references, and commercial motivation—provided "strong support" for characterizing the pamphlets as commercial speech.

In two important footnotes, the high court provided additional insight into the distinction between commercial and noncommercial speech. In one footnote, the court gave this caution: "[We do not] mean to suggest that each of the characteristics present in this case must necessarily be present in order for speech to be commercial. For example, we express no opinion as to whether reference to any particular product or service is a necessary element of commercial speech."

In the other footnote, after observing that one of the pamphlets at issue discussed condoms in general without referring specifically to the corporation's own products, the court said: "That a product is referred to generically does not, however, remove it from the realm of commercial speech. For example, a company with sufficient control of the market for a product may be able to promote the product without reference to its own brand names. Or a trade association may make statements about a product without reference to specific brand names."

Thus, although the court in *Bolger, supra,* 463 U.S. 60, identified three factors—advertising format, product references, and commercial motivation—that in combination supported a characterization of commercial speech in that case, the court not only rejected the notion that any of these factors is *sufficient* by itself, but it also declined to hold that all of these factors in combination, or any one of them individually, is *necessary* to support a commercial speech characterization.

The high court also cautioned, as it had in past cases, that statements may properly be categorized as commercial "notwithstanding the fact that they contain discussions of important public issues," and that "advertising which 'links a product to a current public debate' is not thereby entitled to the constitutional protection afforded noncommercial speech," explaining further that "[a]dvertisers should not be permitted to immunize false or misleading product information from government regulation simply by including references to public issues."

Since its decision in *Bolger, supra,* 463 U.S. 60, the United States Supreme Court has acknowledged that "ambiguities may exist at the margins of the category of commercial speech." Justice Stevens in particular has remarked that "the borders of the commercial speech category are not nearly as clear as the Court has assumed," and he has suggested that the distinction cannot rest solely on the form or content of the statement, or the motive of the speaker, but instead must rest on the relationship between the speech at issue and the justification for distinguishing commercial from noncommercial speech. In his words, "any description of commercial speech that is intended to identify the category of speech entitled to less First Amendment protection should relate to the reasons for permitting broader regulation: namely, commercial speech's potential to mislead."

Analysis

The United States Constitution

The United States Supreme Court has not adopted an all-purpose test to distinguish commercial from noncommercial speech under the First Amendment, nor has this court adopted such a test under the state Constitution, nor do we propose to do so here. A close reading of the high court's commercial speech decisions suggests, however, that it is possible to formulate a limited-purpose test. We conclude, therefore, that *when a court must decide whether particular speech may be subjected to laws aimed at preventing false advertising or other forms of commercial deception,* categorizing a particular statement as commercial or noncommercial speech requires consideration of three elements: the speaker, the intended audience, and the content of the message.

In typical commercial speech cases, the *speaker* is likely to be someone engaged in commerce—that is, generally, the production, distribution, or sale of goods or services—or someone acting on behalf of a person so engaged, and the *intended audience* is likely to be actual or potential buyers or customers of the speaker's goods or services, or persons acting for actual or potential buyers or customers, or persons (such as reporters or reviewers) likely to repeat the message to or otherwise influence actual or potential buyers or customers. Considering the identity of both the speaker and the target audience is consistent with, and implicit in, the United States Supreme Court's commercial speech decisions, each of which concerned a speaker engaged in the sale or hire of products or services conveying a message to a person or persons likely to want, and be willing to pay for, that product or service. The high court has frequently spoken of commercial speech as speech proposing a commercial transaction, thus implying that commercial speech typically is communication between persons who engage in such transactions.

In *Bolger,* moreover, the court stated that in deciding whether speech is commercial two relevant considerations are advertising format and economic motivation. These considerations imply that commercial speech generally or typically is directed to an audience of persons who may be influenced by that speech to engage in a commercial transaction with the speaker or the person on whose behalf the speaker is acting. Speech in advertising format typically, although not invariably, is speech about a product or service by a person who is offering that product or service at a price, directed to persons who may want, and be willing to pay for, that product or service. Citing *New York Times* v. *Sullivan, supra,* 376 U.S. 254, which concerned a newspaper advertisement seeking contributions for civil rights causes, the court cautioned, however, that presentation in advertising format does not necessarily establish that a message is commercial in character. Economic motivation likewise implies that the speech is intended to lead to commercial transactions, which in turn assumes that the speaker and the target audience are persons who will engage in those transactions, or their agents or intermediaries.

Finally, the factual content of the message should be commercial in character. In the context of regulation of false or misleading advertising, this typically means that the speech consists of representations of fact about the business operations, products, or services of the speaker (or the individual or company that the speaker represents), made for the purpose of promoting sales of, or other commercial transactions in, the speaker's products or services. This is consistent with, and implicit in, the United States Supreme Court's commercial speech decisions, each of which has involved statements about a product or service, or about the operations or qualifications of the person offering the product or service.

This is also consistent with the third *Bolger* factor—product references. By "product references," we do not understand the United States Supreme Court to mean only statements about the price, qualities, or availability of individual items offered for sale. Rather, we understand "product references" to include also, for example, statements about the manner in which the products are manufactured, distributed, or sold, about repair or warranty services that the seller provides to purchasers of the product, or about the identity or qualifications of persons who manufacture, distribute, sell, service, or endorse the product. Similarly, references to services would include not only statements about the price, availability, and quality of the services themselves, but also, for example, statements about the education, experience, and qualifications of the persons providing or endorsing the services. This broad definition of "product references" is necessary, we think, to adequately categorize statements made in the context of a modern, sophisticated public relations campaign intended to increase sales and profits by enhancing the image of a product or of its manufacturer or seller.

Our understanding of the content element of commercial speech is also consistent with the reasons that the United States Supreme Court has given for denying First Amendment protection to false or misleading commercial speech. The high court has stated that false or misleading commercial speech may be prohibited because the truth of commercial speech is "more easily verifiable by its disseminator" and because commercial speech, being motivated by the desire for economic profit, is less likely than noncommercial speech to be chilled by proper regulation. This explanation assumes that commercial speech consists of factual statements and that those statements describe matters within the personal knowledge of the speaker or the person whom the speaker is representing and are made for the purpose of financial gain. Thus, this explanation implies that, at least in relation to regulations aimed at protecting consumers from false and misleading promotional practices, commercial speech must consist of factual representations about the business operations, products, or services of the speaker (or the individual or company on whose behalf the speaker is speaking), made for the purpose of promoting sales of, or other commercial transactions in, the speaker's products or services. The United States Supreme Court has never decided whether false statements about a product or service of a competitor of the speaker would properly be categorized as commercial speech. Because the issue is not presented here, we offer no view on how it should be resolved. . . .

Here, the first element—a commercial speaker—is satisfied because the speakers—Nike and its officers and directors—are engaged in commerce. Specifically, they manufacture, import, distribute, and sell consumer goods in the form of athletic shoes and apparel.

The second element—an intended commercial audience—is also satisfied. Nike's letters to university presidents and directors of athletic departments were addressed directly to actual and potential purchasers of Nike's products, because college and university athletic departments are major purchasers of athletic shoes and apparel. Plaintiff has alleged that Nike's press releases and letters to newspaper editors, although addressed to the public generally, were also intended to reach and influence actual and potential purchasers of Nike's products. Specifically, plaintiff has alleged that Nike made these statements about its labor policies and practices "to maintain and/or increase its sales and profits." To support this allegation, plaintiff has included as an exhibit a letter to a newspaper editor, written by Nike's director of communications, referring to Nike's labor policies practices and stating that "[c]onsumers are savvy and want to know they support companies with good products and practices" and that "[d]uring the shopping season, we encourage shoppers to remember that Nike is the industry's leader in improving factory conditions."

The third element—representations of fact of a commercial nature—is also present. In describing its own labor policies, and the practices and working conditions in factories where its products are made, Nike was making factual representations about its own business operations. In speaking to consumers about working conditions and labor practices in the factories where its products are made, Nike addressed matters within its own knowledge. The wages paid to the factories' employees, the hours they work, the way they are treated, and whether the environmental conditions under which they work violate local health and safety laws, are all matters likely to be within the personal knowledge of Nike executives, employees, or subcontractors. Thus, Nike was in a position to readily verify the truth of any factual assertions it made on these topics.

In speaking to consumers about working conditions in the factories where its products are made, Nike engaged in speech that is particularly hardy or durable. Because Nike's purpose in making these statements, at least as alleged in the first amended complaint, was to maintain its sales and profits, regulation aimed at preventing false and actually or inherently misleading speech is unlikely to deter Nike from speaking truthfully or at all about the conditions in its factories. To the extent that application of these laws may make Nike more cautious, and cause it to make greater efforts to verify the truth of its statements, these laws will serve the purpose of commercial speech protection by "insuring that the stream of commercial information flow[s] cleanly as well as freely."

Finally, government regulation of Nike's speech about working conditions in factories where Nike products are made is consistent with traditional government authority to regulate commercial transactions for the protection of consumers by preventing false and misleading commercial practices. Trade regulation laws have traditionally sought to suppress and prevent not only false or misleading statements about products or services in themselves but also false or misleading statements about where a product was made, or by whom.

Because in the statements at issue here Nike was acting as a commercial speaker, because its intended audience was primarily the buyers of its products, and because the statements consisted of factual representations about its own business operations, we conclude that the statements were commercial speech for purposes of applying state laws designed to prevent false advertising and other forms of commercial deception. Whether these statements could properly be categorized as commercial speech for some other purpose, and whether these statements could properly be categorized as commercial speech if one or more of these elements was not fully satisfied, are questions we need not decide here.

Nike argues that its allegedly false and misleading statements were not commercial speech because they were part of "an international media debate on issues of intense public interest." In a similar vein, our dissenting colleagues argue that the speech at issue here should not be categorized as commercial speech because, when Nike made the statements defending its labor practices, the nature and propriety of those practices had already become a matter of public interest and public debate. This argument falsely assumes that speech cannot properly be categorized as commercial speech if it relates to a matter of significant public interest or controversy. As the United States Supreme Court has explained, commercial speech commonly concerns matters of intense public and private interest. The individual consumer's interest in the price, availability, and characteristics of products and services "may be as keen, if not keener by far, than his interest in the day's most urgent political debate." And for the public as whole, information on commercial matters is "indispensable" not only "to the proper allocation of resources in a free enterprise system" but also "to the formation of intelligent opinions as to how that system ought to be regulated or altered."

In her dissent, Justice Brown states that our logic "erroneously assumes that false or misleading commercial speech . . . can never be speech about a public issue." On the contrary, we assume that commercial speech frequently and even normally addresses matters of public concern. The reason that it is "less necessary to tolerate inaccurate statements for fear of silencing the speaker" of commercial speech is not that such speech concerns matters of lesser public interest or value, but rather that commercial speech is both "more easily verifiable by its disseminator" and "less likely to be chilled by proper regulation."

In support of their argument that speech about issues of public importance or controversy must be considered noncommercial speech, our dissenting colleagues cite *Thomas* v. *Collins* (1945) and *Thornhill* v. *State of Alabama* (1940). The United States Supreme Court issued these decisions three decades before it developed the modern commercial speech doctrine in *Bigelow* v. *Virginia* and *Va. Pharmacy Bd.* v. *Va. Consumer Council.* Moreover, neither decision addressed the validity of a law prohibiting false or misleading speech. To the extent they hold that truthful and nonmisleading speech about commercial matters of public importance is entitled to constitutional protection, they are consistent with the modern commercial speech doctrine and with the decision we reach today. We find nothing in either decision suggesting that the state lacks the authority to prohibit false and misleading factual representations, made for purposes of maintaining and increasing sales and profits, about the speaker's own products, services, or business operations.

For purposes of categorizing Nike's speech as commercial or noncommercial, it does not matter that Nike was responding to charges publicly raised by others and was thereby participating in a public debate. The point is illustrated by a decision of a federal court of appeals about statements by a trade association denying there was scientific evidence that eating eggs increased the risk of heart and circulatory disease. The court held that these statement were commercial speech subject to regulation by the Federal Trade Commission (FTC) to the extent the statements were false or misleading, even though the trade association made the statements "to counteract what the FTC described as 'anticholesterol attacks on eggs which had resulted in steadily declining per capita egg consumption.'" Responding to the argument that the statements were noncommercial because they concerned a debate on a matter of great public interest, the federal court of appeals responded that "the right of government to restrain false advertising can hardly depend upon the view of an agency or court as to the relative importance of the issue to which the false advertising relates."

Here, Nike's speech is not removed from the category of commercial speech because it is intermingled with noncommercial speech. To the extent Nike's press releases and letters discuss policy questions such as the degree to which domestic companies should be responsible for working conditions in factories located in other countries, or what standards domestic companies ought to observe in such factories, or the merits and effects of economic "globalization" generally, Nike's statements are noncommercial speech. Any content-based regulation of these noncommercial messages would be subject to the strict scrutiny test for fully protected speech. But Nike may not "immunize false or misleading product information from government regulation simply by including references to public issues." Here, the alleged false and misleading statements all relate to the commercial portions of the speech in question—the description of actual conditions and practices in factories that produce Nike's products—and thus the proposed regulations reach only that commercial portion.

Asserting that the commercial and noncommercial elements in Nike's statement were "inextricably intertwined," our dissenting colleagues maintain that it must therefore be categorized as noncommercial speech, and they cite in support the United States Supreme Court's decision in *Riley* v. *National Federation of the Blind of North Carolina*. That decision concerned regulation of charitable solicitations, a category of speech that does not fit within our limited-purpose definition of commercial speech because it does not involve factual representations about a product or service that is offered for sale. More importantly, the high court has since explained that in *Riley* "the commercial speech (if it was that) was 'inextricably intertwined' because the state law required it to be included" and that commercial and noncommercial messages are not "inextricable" unless there is some legal or practical compulsion to combine them. No law required Nike to combine factual representations about its own labor practices with expressions of opinion about economic globalization, nor was it impossible for Nike to address those subjects separately.

We also reject Nike's argument that regulating its speech to suppress false and misleading statements is impermissible because it would restrict or disfavor expression of one point of view (Nike's) and not the other point of view (that of the critics of Nike's labor practices). The argument is misdirected because the regulations in question do not suppress points of view but instead suppress false and misleading statements of fact. As we have explained, to the extent Nike's speech represents expression of opinion or points of view on general policy questions such as the value of economic "globalization," it is noncommercial speech subject to full First Amendment protection. Nike's speech loses that full measure of protection only when it concerns facts material to commercial transactions—here, factual statements about how Nike makes its products.

Moreover, differential treatment of speech about products and services based on the identity of the speaker is inherent in the commercial speech doctrine as articulated by the United States Supreme Court. A noncommercial speaker's statements criticizing a product are generally noncommercial speech, for which damages may be awarded only upon proof of both falsehood and actual malice. A commercial speaker's statements in praise or support of the same product, by comparison, are commercial speech that may be prohibited entirely to the extent the statements are either false or actually or inherently misleading. To repeat, the justification for this different treatment, as the high court has explained, is that when a speaker promotes its own products, it is "less necessary to tolerate inaccurate statements for fear of silencing the speaker" because the described speech is both "more easily verifiable by its disseminator" and "less likely to be chilled by proper regulation."

Our dissenting colleagues are correct that the identity of the speaker is usually not a proper consideration in regulating speech that is entitled to First

Amendment protection, and that a valid regulation of protected speech may not handicap one side of a public debate. But to decide whether a law regulating speech violates the First Amendment, the very first question is whether the speech that the law regulates is entitled to First Amendment protection at all. As we have seen, commercial speech that is false or misleading receives no protection under the First Amendment, and therefore a law that prohibits only such unprotected speech cannot violate constitutional free speech provisions.

We conclude, accordingly, that here the trial court and the Court of Appeal erred in characterizing as noncommercial speech, under the First Amendment to the federal Constitution, Nike's allegedly false and misleading statements about labor practices and working conditions in factories where Nike products are made. . . .

As we have explained, the United States Supreme Court has indicated that economic motivation is relevant but not conclusive and perhaps not even necessary. The high court has never held that commercial speech must have as its *only* purpose the advancement of an economic transaction, and it has explained instead that commercial speech may be intermingled with noncommercial speech. An advertisement primarily intended to reach consumers and to influence them to buy the speaker's products is not exempt from the category of commercial speech because the speaker also has a secondary purpose to influence lenders, investors, or lawmakers.

Nor is speech exempt from the category of commercial speech because it relates to the speaker's labor practices rather than to the price, availability, or quality of the speaker's goods. An advertisement to the public that cherries were picked by union workers is commercial speech if the speaker has a financial or commercial interest in the sale of the cherries and if the information that the cherries had been picked by union workers is likely to influence consumers to buy the speaker's cherries. Speech is commercial in its content if it is likely to influence consumers in their commercial decisions. For a significant segment of the buying public, labor practices do matter in making consumer choices. . . .

Conclusion

As the United States Supreme Court has explained, false and misleading speech has no constitutional value in itself and is protected only in circumstances and to the extent necessary to give breathing room for the free debate of public issues. Commercial speech, because it is both more readily verifiable by its speaker and more hardy than noncommercial speech, can be effectively regulated to suppress false and actually or inherently misleading messages without undue risk of chilling public debate. With these basic principles in mind, we conclude that when a corporation, to maintain and increase its sales and profits, makes public statements defending labor practices and working conditions at factories where its products are made, those public statements are commercial speech that may be regulated to prevent consumer deception.

Sprinkled with references to a series of children's books about wizardry and sorcery, Justice Brown's dissent itself tries to find the magic formula or incantation that will transform a business enterprise's factual representations in defense of its own products and profits into noncommercial speech exempt from our state's consumer protection laws. As we have explained, however, such representations, when aimed at potential buyers for the purpose of maintaining sales and profits, may be regulated to eliminate false and misleading statements because they are readily verifiable by the speaker and because regulation is unlikely to deter truthful and nonmisleading speech.

In concluding, contrary to the Court of Appeal, that Nike's speech at issue here is commercial speech, we do not decide whether that speech was, as plaintiff has alleged, false or misleading, nor do we decide whether plaintiff's complaint is vulnerable to demurrer for reasons not considered here. Because the demurrers of Nike and the individual defendants were based on multiple grounds, further proceedings on the demurrers may be required in the Court of Appeal, the superior court, or both. Our decision on the narrow issue before us on review does not foreclose those proceedings.

The judgment of the Court of Appeal is reversed, and the matter is remanded to that court for further proceedings consistent with this opinion.

NO

Janice Brown

Dissenting Opinion
by Janice Brown

I respectfully dissent.

I

In 1942, the United States Supreme Court, like a wizard trained at Hogwarts, waved its wand and "plucked the commercial doctrine out of thin air." (Kozinski & Banner, *Who's Afraid of Commercial Speech* (1990) 76 Va. L.Rev. 627, 627.) Unfortunately, the court's doctrinal wizardry has created considerable confusion over the past 60 years as it has struggled to define the difference between commercial and noncommercial speech. The United States Supreme Court has, in recent years, acknowledged "the difficulty of drawing bright lines that will clearly cabin commercial speech in a distinct category." After tracing the various definitions of commercial speech used over the years, the court conceded that no "categorical definition of the difference between" commercial and noncommercial speech exists. Instead, the difference is a matter of "'common[]sense,'" and restrictions on speech "must be examined carefully to ensure that speech deserving of greater constitutional protection is not inadvertently suppressed." Consistent with these pronouncements, the United States Supreme Court has expressly refused to define the elements of commercial speech. Indeed, "the impossibility of specifying the parameters that define the category of commercial speech has haunted its jurisprudence and scholarship."

Despite this chaos, the majority, ostensibly guided by *Bolger*, has apparently divined a new and simpler test for commercial speech. Under this "limited-purpose test," "categorizing a particular statement as commercial or noncommercial speech requires consideration of three elements: the speaker, the intended audience, and the content of the message." Unfortunately, the majority has forgotten the teachings of H.L. Mencken: "every human problem" has a "solution" that is "neat, plausible, and wrong." Like the purported discovery of cold fusion over a decade ago, the majority's test for commercial speech promises much, but solves nothing. Instead of clarifying the commercial speech doctrine, the test violates fundamental principles of First Amendment jurisprudence by making the level of protection given speech dependent

California Supreme Court, May 2, 2002.

on the identity of the speaker—and not just the speech's content—and by stifling the ability of certain speakers to participate in the public debate. In doing so, the majority unconstitutionally favors some speakers over others and conflicts with the decisions of other courts.

Contrary to the majority's belief, our current First Amendment jurisprudence defies any simple solution. Under the commercial speech doctrine currently propounded by the United States Supreme Court, all speech is *either* commercial or noncommercial, and commercial speech receives less protection than noncommercial speech. The doctrine further assumes that all commercial speech is the *same* under the First Amendment. Thus, all commercial speech receives the *same* level of lesser protection. The state may therefore ban *all* commercial speech "that is fraudulent or deceptive without further justification."

This simple categorization presupposes that commercial speech is wholly distinct from noncommercial speech and that all commercial speech has the same value under the First Amendment. The reality, however, is quite different. With the growth of commercialism, the politicization of commercial interests, and the increasing sophistication of commercial advertising over the past century, the gap between commercial and noncommercial speech is rapidly shrinking. As several commentators have observed, examples of the intersection between commercial speech and various forms of noncommercial speech, including scientific, political and religious speech, abound.

Although the world has become increasingly commercial, the dichotomous nature of the commercial speech doctrine remains unchanged. The classification of speech as commercial or noncommercial determines the level of protection accorded to that speech under the First Amendment. Thus, the majority correctly characterizes the issue as "whether defendant corporation's false statements are commercial or noncommercial speech for purposes of constitutional free speech analysis under the state and federal Constitutions." If Nike's press releases, letters and other documents are commercial speech, then the application of Business and Professions Code sections 17204 and 17535—which establish strict liability for false and misleading ads—is constitutional. Otherwise, it is not.

Constrained by this rigid dichotomy, I dissent because Nike's statements are more like noncommercial speech than commercial speech. Nike's commercial statements about its labor practices cannot be separated from its noncommercial statements about a public issue, because its labor practices *are* the public issue. Indeed, under the circumstances presented in this case, Nike could hardly engage in a general discussion on overseas labor exploitation and economic globalization without discussing its own labor practices. Thus, the commercial elements of Nike's statements are "inextricably intertwined" with their noncommercial elements. This court should therefore "apply [the] test for fully protected expression," notwithstanding the majority's specious distinctions of the relevant case law. Under this test, a categorical ban on all false and misleading statements made by Nike about its labor practices violates the First Amendment.

Although this result follows from controlling United States Supreme Court precedent, I believe the commercial speech doctrine, in its current form, fails to account for the realities of the modern world—a world in which personal, political, and commercial arenas no longer have sharply defined boundaries. My sentiments are not unique; many judges and academics have echoed them. Even some justices on the high court have recently questioned the validity of the distinction between commercial and noncommercial speech. Nonetheless, the high court has apparently declined to abandon it. Given that the United States Supreme Court is not prepared to start over, we must try to make the commercial speech doctrine work—warts and all. To this end, I believe the high court needs to develop a more nuanced approach that maximizes the ability of businesses to participate in the public debate while minimizing consumer fraud.

II

According to the majority, all speech containing the following three elements is commercial speech: (1) "a commercial speaker"; (2) "an intended commercial audience"; and (3) "representations of fact of a commercial nature." The first element is satisfied whenever the speaker is engaged in "the production, distribution, or sale of goods or services" "or someone acting on behalf of a person so engaged." The second element is satisfied whenever the intended audience is "actual or potential buyers or customers of the speaker's goods or services, or persons acting for actual or potential buyers or customers, or persons (such as reporters or reviewers) likely to repeat the message to or otherwise influence actual or potential buyers or customers." The third element is satisfied whenever "the speech consists of representations of fact about the business operations, products, or services of the speaker (or the individual or company that the speaker represents), made for the purpose of promoting sales of, or other commercial transactions in, the speaker's products or services."

Although the majority constructed this limited-purpose test from its "close reading of the high court's commercial speech decisions," it conveniently dismisses those decisions that cast doubt on its formulation. As explained below, a closer review of the relevant case law reveals that the majority's test for commercial speech contravenes long-standing principles of First Amendment law.

First, the test flouts the very essence of the distinction between commercial and noncommercial speech identified by the United States Supreme Court. "If commercial speech is to be distinguished, it 'must be distinguished *by its content.*'" Despite this caveat, the majority distinguishes commercial from noncommercial speech using two criteria wholly unrelated to the speech's content: the identity of the speaker and the intended audience. In doing so, the majority strays from the guiding principles espoused by the United States Supreme Court.

Second, the test contravenes a fundamental tenet of First Amendment jurisprudence by making the identity of the speaker potentially dispositive. As the United States Supreme Court stated long ago, "[the] identity of the speaker is not decisive in determining whether speech is protected," and "speech does not lose its protection because of the corporate identity of the speaker." This is because corporations and other speakers engaged in commerce "contribute to the 'discussion, debate, and the dissemination of information and ideas' that the First Amendment seeks to foster." Thus, "[t]he inherent worth of the speech in terms of its capacity for informing the public does not depend upon *the identity of its source,* whether corporation, association, union, or individual." Despite these admonitions, the majority has made the identity of the speaker a significant, and potentially dispositive, factor in determining the scope of protection accorded to speech under the First Amendment. As a result, speech by "someone engaged in commerce" may receive less protection solely because of the speaker's identity. Indeed, the majority's limited-purpose test makes the identity of the speaker dispositive whenever the speech at issue relates to the speaker's business operations, products, or services, in contravention of United States Supreme Court precedent.

Third, the test violates the First Amendment by stifling the ability of speakers engaged in commerce, such as corporations, to participate in debates over public issues. The United States Supreme Court has broadly defined public issues as those issues "about which information is needed or appropriate to enable the members of society to cope with the exigencies of their period." "The general proposition that freedom of expression upon public questions is secured by the First Amendment has long been settled. . . ." "[S]peech on public issues occupies the 'highest rung of the hierarchy of First Amendment values,' and is entitled to special protection," because such speech "is more than self-expression; it is the essence of self-government." "The First and Fourteenth Amendments remove 'governmental restraints from the arena of public discussion, putting the decision as to what views shall be voiced largely into the hands of each of us, in the hope that use of such freedom will ultimately produce a more capable citizenry and more perfect polity. . . .'" Thus, the First Amendment "both fully protects and implicitly encourages" public debate on "'matters of public concern.'"

To ensure "uninhibited, robust, and wide-open" "debate on public issues," the United States Supreme Court has recognized that some false or misleading speech must be tolerated. Although "[u]ntruthful speech, commercial or otherwise, has never been protected for its own sake," "[t]he First Amendment requires that we protect some falsehood in order to protect speech that matters." The "erroneous statement is inevitable in free debate, and . . . it must be protected if the freedoms of expression are to have the 'breathing space' that they 'need to survive'. . . ." Because "a rule that would impose strict liability on a" speaker "for false factual assertions" in a matter of public concern "would have an undoubted 'chilling' effect" on speech "that does have constitutional value," "only those false statements made with the high degree of awareness of their probable falsity demanded by *New York Times* may be the subject of either civil or criminal sanctions."

The majority contends its limited-purpose test for commercial speech does not violate these principles because false or misleading commercial speech may be prohibited "entirely." This logic is, however, faulty, because it erroneously assumes that false or misleading commercial speech as defined by the majority can never be speech about a public issue. Under the majority's test, the content of commercial speech is limited only to representations regarding "business operations, products, or services." But business operations, products, or services may be public issues. For example, a corporation's business operations may be the subject of public debate in the media. These operations may even be a political issue as organizations, such as state, local, or student governments, propose and pass resolutions condemning certain business practices. Under these circumstances, the corporation's business operations undoubtedly become a matter of public concern, and speech about these operations merits the full protection of the First Amendment. Indeed, the United States Supreme Court has long recognized that speech on a public issue may be inseparable from speech promoting the speaker's business operations, products or services.

The majority, however, creates an overbroad test that, taken to its logical conclusion, renders all corporate speech commercial speech. As defined, the test makes any public representation of fact by a speaker engaged in commerce about that speaker's products made for the purpose of promoting that speaker's products commercial speech. A corporation's product, however, includes the corporation itself. Corporations are regularly bought and sold, and corporations market not only their products and services but also themselves. Indeed, business goodwill is an important asset of every corporation and contributes significantly to the sale value of the corporation. Because all corporate speech about a public issue reflects on the corporate image and therefore affects the corporation's business goodwill and sale value, the majority's test makes all such speech commercial notwithstanding the majority's assertions to the contrary.

In so doing, the majority violates a basic principle of First Amendment law. By subjecting all corporate speech about business operations, products and services to the strict liability provisions of sections 17204 and 17535, the majority's limited-purpose test unconstitutionally chills a corporation's ability to participate in the debate over matters of public concern. The chilling effect is exacerbated by the breadth of sections 17204 and 17535, which "prohibit 'not only advertising which is false, but also advertising which[,] although true, is either actually misleading or *which has a capacity, likelihood or tendency to deceive or confuse the public.'*" This broad definition of actionable speech puts a corporation "at the mercy of the varied understanding of [its] hearers and consequently of whatever inference may be drawn as to [its] intent and meaning." Because the corporation could never be sure whether its truthful statements may deceive or confuse the public and would likely incur significant burden and expense in litigating the issue, "[m]uch valuable information which a corporation might be able to provide would remain unpublished. . . ." As the United States Supreme Court has consistently held, such a result violates the First Amendment.

Finally, in singling out speakers engaged in commerce and restricting their ability to participate in the public debate, the majority unconstitutionally favors certain speakers over others. Corporations "have the right to be free from government restrictions that abridge [their] own rights in order to 'enhance the relative voice' of [their] opponents." The First Amendment does not permit favoritism toward certain speakers "based on the identity of the interests that [the speaker] may represent." Indeed, "self-government suffers when those in power suppress competing views on public issues 'from diverse and antagonistic sources.'" The majority, however, does just that. Under the majority's test, only speakers engaged in commerce are strictly liable for their false or misleading representations pursuant to sections 17204 and 17535. Meanwhile, other speakers who make the same representations may face no such liability, regardless of the context of their statements. Neither United States Supreme Court precedent nor our precedent countenances such favoritism in doling out First Amendment rights.

III

The majority's limited-purpose test is not only problematic in light of controlling high court precedent, the test appears to conflict with the analysis used by other courts in analogous contexts. These conflicts belie the majority's claim of doctrinal consistency and underscore the illusory nature of its so-called solution to the commercial speech quandary.

For example, the majority opinion conflicts with *Gordon & Breach Science Publishers v. AIP.* In *Gordon & Breach,* the defendant, a nonprofit publisher of scientific journals, published scientific articles touting its journals as "both less expensive and more scientifically important than those of for-profit publishers such as" the plaintiff. The defendant, as part of an advertising campaign designed to promote its journals, touted and defended the conclusions of these articles by, among other things, issuing press releases and writing letters to the editor responding to attacks on these articles. In light of these promotional activities, the plaintiff sued the defendant for false advertising under the Lanham Trademark Act and New York law.

In determining whether the defendant's advertising campaign constituted commercial speech, the district court identified the following dilemma: how to characterize "speech which, from one perspective, presents the aspect of protected, noncommercial speech addressing a significant public issue, but which, from another perspective, appears primarily to be speech 'proposing a commercial transaction.'" After analyzing the relevant United States Supreme Court precedent, the court concluded that the articles, press releases and letters to the editor constituted noncommercial speech fully protected by the First Amendment.[1] According to the court, this speech fell "too close to core First Amendment values to be considered 'commercial advertising or promotion' under the Lanham Act."

Application of the majority's test would, however, result in a different outcome. The defendant was engaged in commerce; it sold journals. The intended audience was undoubtedly potential customers. The articles, press releases and letters contained representations of fact about the defendant's products—its journals. Thus, they contain the three elements of commercial speech identified by the majority. The majority would therefore classify this speech as commercial speech even though it constitutes "fully protected commentary on an issue of public concern."

Similarly, the majority's test creates a conflict with *Oxycal Laboratories, Inc. v. Jeffers.* In *Oxycal,* the defendants published a book that denigrated the plaintiffs' products while promoting the defendants' products. The defendants allegedly promoted the book in an effort to boost the sales of their own products. The plaintiffs sued, alleging false advertising. Finding this case easy, the court concluded that the book was noncommercial speech because there were "sufficient noncommercial motivations" notwithstanding the commercial motivations. To the extent the book contained commercial elements promoting the defendants' products, these commercial elements were "intertwined" with and secondary to the noncommercial elements.

Once again, the majority's test would yield a contrary result. The defendants were engaged in commerce, and the intended audience for the book was potential consumers. The book contained representations of fact about the defendants' products, and the defendants undoubtedly made these representations for the purpose of promoting their products. Thus, under the majority's test, the book was commercial speech, and the defendants would have been strictly liable for any false or misleading statements about their products in the book.

Although we are not bound by these decisions, they are instructive and highlight the deficiencies in the majority's limited-purpose test for commercial speech. In divining a new test for commercial speech, the majority finds a deceptively simple answer to a complicated question. Unfortunately, the answer is flawed. By failing to recognize that a speaker's business operations, products, or services may be matters of public concern, the majority ignores controlling principles of First Amendment law. As a result, the majority erroneously draws a bright line when "a broader and more nuanced inquiry" is required.

IV

Of course, my rejection of the majority's limited-purpose test does not resolve the central issue in this case: What level of protection should be accorded to Nike's speech under the First Amendment? To answer this question, this court, as the majority correctly notes, must determine whether Nike's speech is commercial or noncommercial speech. Following the existing framework set up by the United States Supreme Court, I would conclude that Nike's speech is more like noncommercial speech than commercial speech because its commercial elements are inextricably intertwined with its noncommercial elements. Thus, I would give Nike's speech the full protection of the First Amendment.

When determining whether speech is commercial or noncommercial, courts must "ensure that speech deserving of greater constitutional protection is not inadvertently suppressed." In following this philosophy in cases involving hybrid speech containing both commercial and noncommercial elements, the United States Supreme Court has assessed the separability of these elements to determine the proper level of protection. If the commercial elements are separable from the noncommercial elements, then the speech is commercial and receives lesser protection. Thus, advertising that merely "links a product to a current public debate" is still commercial speech notwithstanding its noncommercial elements. Where the speaker may comment on a public issue without promoting its products or services, the speech is also commercial, even if the speaker combines a commercial message with a noncommercial message. Indeed, "[a]dvertisers should not be permitted to immunize false or misleading product information from government regulation simply by including references to public issues."

The United States Supreme Court has, however, recognized that commercial speech may be "inextricably intertwined" with noncommercial speech in certain contexts. Where regulation of the commercial component of certain speech would stifle otherwise protected speech, "we cannot parcel out the speech, applying one test to one phrase and another test to another phrase. Such an endeavor would be both artificial and impractical." In such cases, courts must apply the "test for fully protected expression" rather than the test for commercial speech.[2]

Although the United States Supreme Court has mostly found this intertwining of commercial and noncommercial speech in the charitable solicitation context, it has also done so in a factual context analogous to the one presented here. In *Thomas v. Collins*,[3] the United States Supreme Court held that a speech made by a union representative promoting the union's services and inviting workers to join constituted noncommercial speech fully protected by the First Amendment. Although the court acknowledged that the speech promoted the services of the union and sought to solicit new members, it found that these commercial elements were inextricably intertwined with the noncommercial elements addressing a public issue—unionism. "The feat would be incredible for a national leader, addressing such a meeting, lauding unions and their principles, urging adherence to union philosophy, not also and thereby to suggest attachment to the union by becoming a member." Indeed, "whether words intended and designed to fall short of invitation would miss that mark is a question both of intent and of effect. No speaker, in such circumstances, safely could assume that anything he might say upon the general subject would not be understood by some as an invitation."

Finding that the commercial elements of the union representative's speech should be accorded the full protection of the First Amendment, the court concluded that distinguishing between the speech's commercial and noncommercial elements "offers no security for free discussion." "In these conditions," making such a distinction "blankets with uncertainty whatever may be said. It compels the speaker to hedge and trim." "When legislation or its application can confine labor leaders on such occasions to innocuous and abstract discussion of the virtues of trade unions and so becloud even this with doubt, uncertainty and the risk of penalty, freedom of speech for them will be at an end. A restriction so destructive of the right of public discussion . . . is incompatible with the freedoms secured by the First Amendment."

This case presents a similar scenario because Nike's overseas labor practices have become a public issue. According to the complaint, Nike faced a sophisticated media campaign attacking its overseas labor practices. As a result, its labor practices were discussed on television news programs and in numerous newspapers and magazines. These discussions have even entered the political arena as various governments, government officials and organizations have proposed and passed resolutions condemning Nike's labor practices. Given these facts, Nike's overseas labor practices were undoubtedly a matter of public concern, and its speech on this issue was therefore "entitled to special protection." Because Nike could not comment on this public issue without discussing its overseas labor practices, the commercial elements of Nike's representations about its labor practices were inextricably intertwined with their noncommercial elements. As such, these representations must be fully protected as noncommercial speech in the factual context presented here.

The majority's assertion that Nike's representations about its overseas labor practices are distinct from its comments on "policy questions" is simply wrong. The majority contends Nike can still comment on the policy issues implicated by its press releases and letters because it can generally discuss "the degree to which domestic companies should be responsible for working conditions in factories located in other countries, or what standards domestic companies ought to observe in such factories, or the merits and effects of economic 'globalization' generally. . . ." The majority, however, conveniently forgets that Nike's overseas labor practices *are* the public issue. Thus, general statements about overseas labor exploitation and economic globalization do not provide Nike with a meaningful way to participate in the public debate over *its* overseas labor practices.

Even if the majority correctly characterizes the public issues implicated by Nike's press releases and letters, its assertion is still wrong. In light of the sophisticated media campaign directed at Nike's overseas labor practices and the close association between Nike's labor practices and the public debate over overseas labor exploitation and economic globalization, Nike could not comment on these public issues without discussing its own labor practices. Indeed, Nike could hardly condemn exploitation of overseas workers and discuss the virtues of economic globalization without implying that it helps overseas workers and does not exploit them. By limiting Nike to "innocuous and abstract discussion," the majority has effectively destroyed Nike's "right of public discussion." Under these circumstances, Nike no longer "has the full panoply of protections available to its direct comments on public issues. . . ." Accordingly, the factual representations in Nike's press releases and letters are fully protected under current First Amendment jurisprudence.

Such a conclusion is consistent with the commercial speech decisions of the United States Supreme Court. Most of these decisions involve core commercial speech that does "no more than propose a commercial transaction." Because speech that just proposes a commercial transaction, by definition, only promotes the sale of a product or service and does not address a public issue, these decisions are inapposite.

The United States Supreme Court decisions finding hybrid speech containing both commercial and noncommercial elements to be commercial are also distinguishable. In these cases, the court found that the commercial elements of the speech were separable from its noncommercial elements and were therefore unnecessary for conveying the noncommercial message. Because the commercial message was merely linked to—and not inextricably intertwined with—the noncommercial message, the court concluded that restrictions on the commercial message would not stifle the speaker's ability to engage in protected speech. As explained above, this case is different. Nike's overseas business operations have become the public issue, and Nike cannot comment on important public issues like overseas worker exploitation and economic globalization without implicating its own labor practices. Thus, the commercial elements of Nike's press releases, letters, and other documents were inextricably intertwined with their noncommercial elements, and they must be fully protected as noncommercial speech.

Finally, *Bolger*, the primary case relied on by the majority, is distinguishable. In *Bolger*, a contraceptive manufacturer wished to mail, among other things, informational pamphlets that discussed the problem of venereal disease and the benefits of condoms and referenced the manufacturer. The United States Postal Service banned the mailings, and the manufacturer challenged the constitutionality of the ban. In assessing the constitutionality of the ban, the United States Supreme Court concluded that the informational pamphlets constituted commercial speech "notwithstanding the fact that they contain discussions of important public issues." Unlike Nike's overseas business operations, however, the products at issue in *Bolger* had not become a public issue. Moreover, in the factual context of *Bolger*, the manufacturer could have commented on the issues of venereal disease and family planning through avenues other than promotional mailings and without referencing its own products. By contrast, Nike has *no* other avenue for defending its labor practices, given the breadth of sections 17204 and 17535, and Nike cannot comment on the issues of labor exploitation and economic globalization without referencing its own labor practices. Given these differences, *Bolger* does not compel the majority's conclusion.

Constrained by the United States Supreme Court's current formulation of the commercial speech doctrine, I would therefore conclude that Nike's press releases, letters, and other documents defending its overseas labor practices are noncommercial speech. Based on this conclusion, I would find the application of sections 17204 and 17535 to Nike's speech unconstitutional. Accordingly, I would affirm the judgment of the Court of Appeal. . . .

VI

In today's world, the difference between commercial and noncommercial speech is not black and white. Due to the growing politicization of commercial matters and the increased sophistication of advertising campaigns, the intersection between commercial and noncommercial speech has become larger and larger. As this gray area expands, continued adherence to the dichotomous, all-or-nothing approach developed by the United States Supreme Court will eventually lead us down one of two unappealing paths: either the voices of businesses in the public debate will be effectively silenced, or businesses will be able to dupe consumers with impunity.

Rather than continue down this path, I believe the high court must reassess the commercial speech doctrine and develop a more nuanced inquiry that accounts for the realities of today's commercial world. Without abandoning the categories of commercial and noncommercial speech, the court could develop an approach better suited to today's world by recognizing that not all speech containing commercial elements should be equal in the eyes of the First Amendment.

For example, the United States Supreme Court could develop an intermediate category of protected speech where commercial and noncommercial elements are closely intertwined. In light of the conflicting constitutional principles at play, this intermediate category could receive greater protection than commercial speech but less protection than noncommercial speech. Under such an approach, false or misleading speech that falls within the intermediate category could be actionable so long as states do not impose liability without fault.

Alternatively, the court could abandon its blanket rule permitting the proscription of all false or misleading commercial speech. Instead, the court could devise a test for determining whether governmental restrictions on false or misleading speech with commercial elements survive constitutional scrutiny. In doing so, the court could develop a more nuanced approach that maximizes the ability of businesses to participate in the public debate without allowing consumer fraud to run rampant.

Even if these suggestions are unworkable or problematic, the practical realities of today's commercial world require a new "'accommodation between [First Amendment] concern[s] and the limited state interest present in the context of'" strict liability actions targeting speech with inextricably intertwined commercial and noncommercial elements. Given the growing intersection between advertising and noncommercial speech, such as political, literary, scientific and artistic expression, this observation is equally cogent where the commercial speech is false or misleading.

I realize the task is not easy. Indeed, Justice Scalia has recently alluded to the intractability of the problem. Nonetheless, a new accommodation of the relevant constitutional concerns is possible, and the United States Supreme Court can and should devise a more nuanced approach that guarantees the ability of speakers engaged in commerce to participate in the public debate without giving these speakers free rein to lie and cheat.

For example, such an accommodation could permit states to bar *all* false or misleading representations about the characteristics of a product or service—i.e., the efficacy, quality, value, or safety of the product or service—without justification even if these characteristics have become a public issue. In such a situation, the governmental interest in protecting consumers from fraud is especially strong because these representations address the fundamental questions asked by every consumer when he or she makes a buying decision: does the product or service work well and reliably, is the product or service harmful and is the product or service worth the cost? Moreover, these representations are the traditional target of false advertising laws. Thus, the strong governmental interest in this context trumps any First Amendment concerns presented by a blanket prohibition on such false or misleading representations.

By contrast, the governmental interest in protecting against consumer fraud is less strong if the representations are unrelated to the characteristics of the product or service. In some situations involving these representations, the First Amendment concerns *may* trump this governmental interest. A blanket prohibition of false or misleading representations in such a situation would be unconstitutional because the prohibition may stifle the ability of businesses to comment on public issues. Indeed, this case offers a prime example. Making Nike strictly liable for any false or misleading representations about its labor practices stifles Nike's ability to participate in a public debate *initiated by others.* Accommodating the competing interests in this context precludes the blanket prohibition favored by the majority. Although strict liability is inappropriate, an actual malice standard may be too high because these representations undoubtedly influence some consumers in their buying decisions, and the government has a strong interest in minimizing consumer deception. Thus, a well-crafted test could give states the flexibility to define the standard of liability for false or misleading misrepresentations in this context so long as the standard is not strict liability.[4]

VII

The majority accuses me of searching for my own "magic formula or incantation" because I urge a reevaluation of the commercial speech doctrine. To this charge, I plead guilty. Unlike the majority who finds nothing unsettling about doctrinal incoherence, I readily acknowledge that some wizardry may be necessary if courts are to adapt the commercial speech doctrine to the realities of today's commercial world. Unfortunately, Merlin and Gandalf are busy, so the United States Supreme Court will have to fill the gap.

Although I make these magical references in jest, my point is serious: the commercial speech doctrine needs and deserves reconsideration and this is as good a place as any to begin. I urge the high court to do so here.

Notes

1. The court did find that the defendant's distribution of preprints of the articles to potential customers and its repeated dissemination of the conclusions of these articles to potential customers constituted commercial speech. (*Gordon & Breach, supra,* 859 F.Supp. at p. 1544.)

2. The majority's attempts to distinguish *Riley* are not persuasive. First, "charitable solicitations" *do* "involve factual representations about a product or service that is offered for sale," where, as in *Riley,* the charitable solicitations are made by professional fundraisers who solicit contributions for a fee. Second, *Fox* does not preclude the application of *Riley* in this case. It *is* "impossible for Nike to address" certain public issues without addressing its own labor practices, because these practices are the public issue and symbolize the current debate over overseas labor exploitation and economic globalization.

3. The majority contends *Thomas* and *Thornhill* are not relevant because "[t]he United States Supreme Court issued these decisions three decades before it developed the modern commercial speech doctrine in *Bigelow v. Virginia* [(1975)], and *Va. [Consumer Council].*" The majority, however, conveniently neglects to mention that both *Bigelow* and *Va. Consumer Council* cite *Thomas* and *Thornhill* with approval. Thus, the United States Supreme Court, in developing the commercial speech doctrine, did not intend to overrule or diminish the relevance of *Thomas* and *Thornhill.* In any event, the binding effect of a high court opinion does not diminish with age.

4. States may, however, adopt a strict liability standard for false and misleading representations unrelated to the characteristics of a product or service where the representations are not inextricably tied to a public issue.

POSTSCRIPT

Are Corporations Accused of Wrongdoing Protected by the First Amendment?

In September 2003, Nike announced that it was settling its dispute with social activist Marc Kasky. Nike had appealed the decision of the California Supreme Court to the U.S. Supreme Court. The Supreme Court Justices, after agreeing previously to hear the case, abruptly changed their minds and dismissed Nike's appeal. In light of this development, Nike decided not to continue the fight against Kasky and agreed to pay $1.5 million to the Fair Labor Association, a Washington-based special interest organization involved in promoting international labor causes (Oliva, 2003). It's interesting to note that the settlement does not contain an admission of guilt or wrongdoing from the Nike Corporation nor does it provide any legal precedent.

In the dissenting opinion, California Supreme Court Justice Brown raised two important points that supporters of the current separation between economic and social speech need to address. First, she argued that there is no historical or philosophical justification for the concept of "commercial" speech as distinct from other forms of speech. Thus, the responsibility lies with supporters of this idea to prove their case, something that, thus far, they have failed to do. Secondly, she argues that previous court decisions involving this issue have been so inconsistent and ambiguous as to render the distinction between commercial and non-commerical speech virtually meaningless.

Regardless of which side of this case you support, the decision of the U.S. Supreme Court not to hear Nike's appeal can only be described as disappointing. Numerous social critics have suggested the Supreme Court missed an excellent opportunity to help clarify and define the concept of "commercial" speech. As a result, our understanding of how far First Amendment protection extends to such corporate behavior has not been furthered, nor has the debate on whether there should be a legal distinction between commercial and non-commercial speech in the first place. Beyond the immediate impact on the two parties involved, a decision of some sort would have gone a long way toward the establishment of a coherent framework capable of guiding future court decisions involving corporate speech and First Amendment protections.

Suggested Readings

Soontae An, From a business pursuit to a means of expression: The Supreme Court's disputes over commercial speech from 1942 to 1976. 8 *Communication Law and Policy 201*, 2003.

Center for the Advancement of Capitalism, Supreme Court should end the distinction between political and economic speech. *Center for the Advancement of Capitalism,* 2003. `http://www.capmag.com/article.asp?id=2542`

Bruce Ledewitz, Corporate advertising's democracy. *12 Boston University Public Interest Law Journal 389,* 2003.

Earl M. Maltz, The strange career of commercial speech. *6 Chapman Law Review,* 161, 2003.

S.M. Oliva, "Nike" equals "Cowardice": Nike's pragmatic appeasement spells defeat for freedom of speech. *Capitalism Magazine,* September 13, 2003. `http://www.capmag.com/article.asp?id=3082`

ISSUE 5

Should Insider Trading Be Legalized?

YES: Robert B. Thompson, from "Insider Trading, Investor Harm, and Executive Compensation," *Case Western Reserve Law Review* (Winter 1999)

NO: Stephen Bainbridge, from "Why Regulate Insider Trading?" *Tech Central Station* (September 8, 2004)

ISSUE SUMMARY

YES: Legal scholar Robert B. Thompson presents Manne's argument on insider regulation. Thompson then provides us with an analysis of the status and relevance of Manne's position three decades after the publication of his seminal text.

NO: UCLA professor of law Stephen Bainbridge does not accept Manne's arguments. Bainbridge believes that insider trading ultimately causes inefficiency in the markets and, therefore, must be subject to regulation.

In October 2004, domestic diva and multimillionaire Martha Stewart began serving her prison sentence for obstructing justice during an investigation into alleged insider trading activities. Although Stewart was not convicted of insider trading, her trial, and the investigation that preceded it, placed the topic of insider trading on the front of business publications and newspapers across America. Interestingly, a number of observers—typically those defending Stewart—questioned whether insider trading should be considered a criminal activity in the first place. And, although the Stewart case drew much attention to the topic in the public domain, the regulation of insider trading has received considerable attention in the academic and legal professions in recent years. Indeed, since 1997, legal commentaries have seen print at the rate of about one per month.

The first systematic justification for regulating insider trading is typically attributed to the work of H. L. Wilgus in 1910. Wilgus, a legal scholar, argued from an appeal to fairness and morality perspective. In an article published in the *Michigan Law Review,* he concluded that insider trading was morally distasteful (Jonathan R. Macy, "Securities Trading: A Contractual Perspective," *Case*

Western Reserve Law Review, Winter 1999) Wilgus's writings first drew attention to the topic of insider trading; shortly thereafter, other legal scholars joined him in condemning the action in moral terms. (*Note:* Insider trading, as we know it today, was not illegal at this time.)

The move to regulate insider trading gained momentum in the aftermath of the stock market crash of 1929 and the depression that immediately followed. The public increasingly viewed governmental intervention as a necessary step in order to safeguard investors and restore public confidence in the securities markets. The views of Wilgus and others like-minded found fertile ground during the congressional hearings held in 1933 and 1934. These hearings ultimately led to the Securities Act of 1933 and the Securities Exchange Act of 1934, both of which contained provisions outlawing insider trading. These provisions were justified on two grounds, both of which were promulgated and defended by Wilgus and his supporters. The first defense is that insider trading is an abuse of information because the individual uses, for personal gain, information intended strictly for corporate ends. The second justification argues that it is inherently unfair for an individual to act on information he or she has access to but those with whom he or she is dealing does not (the general public, for example, when the insider is buying or selling stock).

The dominant view that insider trading is immoral and should, therefore, be subject to regulation went unchallenged until the publication of two seminal works by Henry Manne in 1966. Manne, now dean emeritus of the George Mason University School of Law, astounded the legal profession, the securities industry, and the federal government with the publication of his book, *Insider Trading and the Stock Market.* Drawing on work in economics and employing a property rights–based perspective, Manne's highly analytical approach argued for the abolition of insider trading laws. In so doing, he noted that, among other things, the congressional hearings of 1933 and 1934 "resulted in the practical adoption of many of the ideas of Wilgus and Bearle [an important legal scholar of the time] without any concrete explanation for their blanket acceptance" (Macey, 2004, p. 269). Manne's desire to examine the ideas of Wilgus played to a wider audience—solidified his position as the most important and serious critic of insider regulation—when he published *In Defense of Insider Trading* in the *Harvard Business Review* later that same year.

The following selections provide us with two different reponses to the question, should insider trading be legalized? The "yes" article is by legal scholar Robert B. Thompson, who distills Manne's argument into three main attacks on insider regulation. Thompson then provides us with an analysis of the status and relevance of Manne's position three decades after the publication of his seminal text. UCLA professor of law Stephen Bainbridge also addresses Manne's position. But while Thompson concludes that Manne's position is still very much valid today, Bainbridge cannot accept his arguments. Bainbridge, in direct contrast with Manne, believes that insider trading ultimately causes inefficiency in the markets and, thus, must be subject to regulation.

Robert B. Thompson

 **YES**

Insider Trading, Investor Harm, and Executive Compensation

T he core questions in most law school classes change little from year to year even as the contexts in which those questions are raised and the answers which are provided sometimes move dramatically to reflect cutting-edge adaptations and changing regulatory policy. Insider trading has been one of those core questions in corporate and securities law since the early 1960s when the Securities and Exchange Commission's decision in In re Cady, Roberts & Co.[1] propelled Rule 10b-5 into the center of the debate over the regulation of such conduct. With the publication of Henry Manne's book Insider Trading and the Stock Market five years later defending this practice,[2] the issue was joined in a way that still shapes how courts and writers frame the topic. This essay addresses insider trading at the turn of the century by looking at three key assertions from Manne's 1966 book: (1) there is no coherent theory explaining regulation of insider trading;[3] (2) there is no significant injury to corporate investors from insider trading;[4] and (3) insider trading constitutes the most appropriate device for compensating entrepreneurs in large corporations.[5] Each of the parts which follow this introduction identifies the underlying premise for each assertion, the flourish with which Dean Manne presented it, the extent to which it has shaped debate over the last thirty-three years, and its place in the current discussion.

I. The Absence of a Coherent Theory

Manne's book opens with chapters devoted to the assertion that "in the literature on insider trading almost no careful analysis of the subject exists."[6] In discussing the traditional legal approach and opinions from courts, commentators, and legislative hearings, Dean Manne's language was somewhat mild compared to the other topics addressed later in the book and he was ecumenical in suggesting that arguments on both sides were "disappointing"[7] and "conclusionary."[8] His underlying premise was that the existing doctrines based on morality or "it's just not right" provided no foundation for determining regulation of insider trading, but that economic analysis could.[9]

From *Case Western Reserve Law Review*, Vol. 50, No. 2, Winter 1999, pp. 291–304. Copyright © 1999 by Case Western Reserve Law Review. Reprinted by permission.

On this point Jon Macey's opening paragraph. "The same, of course, is true today"[10] is very apt. Commentators regularly assail the incoherence of the law of insider trading[11] terming it problematic,[12] if not "seriously flawed."[13] Since the Supreme Court's 1997 decision in United States v. O'Hagan,[14] legal commentaries have been appearing at an average of around one a month.[15] As summarized by former SEC commissioner Roberta Karmel, "despite the large number of articles discussing insider trading, a general consensus among commentators has not developed as to why insider trading is unlawful."[16]. . . .

It seems fair to say that after almost forty years of judicial and academic efforts to develop a coherent theory to explain federal insider trading regulation, the literature is no more coherent than it was in 1966.

II. Shareholders as a Whole Are Not Hurt by Insider Trading

The second assertion, the focus of the middle part of Manne's book, is that no significant injury to corporate investors results from insider trading.[17] The subtext here is one of efficiency of markets.[18] Insider trading makes the market more efficient by moving the price in the right direction. An event or information that alters the value of the company and its stock will create a gap between the stock's current value and what it will trade for once the market has incorporated the new information.

Time-function traders, whose trading decisions are based on reasons beyond a change in price, benefit by receiving a better price as compared to what they would have received absent the insider trading. The premise is that they would have traded anyway (and before the disclosure of the new information and the accompanying change in price), and therefore would have absorbed the entire gap related to the change in value. The time-function trader benefits by whatever amount toward the new price the insider trader causes the price to move.

In contrast, price-function traders, whose trading decisions are motivated by a change in price, can be disadvantaged as compared to where they would have been absent the insider trading. Absent the change in price caused by the insider trader entering the market, the price-function traders would not have traded and presumably still would have had their shares when the information was later announced and the price changed in response to that announcement. If this group is further segmented to focus on long-term investors rather than short-swing traders, and the lens is widened to focus on all such traders over time and not just those in a particular stock and a particular time, the magnitude of the loss defined this way gets considerably smaller. Indeed, Dean Manne does not hold back in how he describes this risk: "de minimis . . . almost infinitesimally small . . . [and] so small as to be unworthy of serious concern."[19]

On this point, the impact of Manne's work is substantial. The challenge to show investor harm has been difficult and complex.[20] Despite explicit congressional action authorizing a cause of action for those who trade contemporaneously with an insider,[21] private enforcement of insider trading is small and the heavy lifting has been left to the SEC and the Justice Department. Professor Donald Langevoort has concluded that the addition of section 20A to the

Securities Exchange Act of 1934 makes "private rights of action by marketplace traders something of relatively small practical importance in the world of insider trading enforcement."[22]

In the wake of the Private Securities Litigation Reform Act of 1995,[23] private actions for insider trading have taken on more importance as allegations of that conduct commonly are used as a way to meet the heightened pleading standards now required for securities class actions.[24] Insider trading is one of the two most common factors cited in securities class action complaints as evidence of particularized facts necessary for a pleading to survive the heightened standards required by the 1995 Act.[25] Yet, that statistic overstates the importance of private action for insider trading. Plaintiffs usually seek to use insider trading by individuals to reach not the traders, but the corporation that made false or incomplete disclosures. Based on data in the Stanford Securities Class Action Clearinghouse database, less than 10% of the cases alleging insider trading include a count seeking private relief under section 20A.[26] The thirty-seven complaints in the database as of June, 1999 that include a count based on section 20A reduce to only fifteen transactions because of multiple filings; there was no indication of recovery by that date for any of those lawsuits.[27]

There appears to be little, if any, overlap between those private cases and the insider cases brought by the government, which average around fifty per year.[28] Of the fifteen companies for which insider trading was alleged as part of a securities class action, all but one allege selling after inaccurate reports or that bad news was withheld or covered up.[29] For the government suits, the dominant setting is trading on the basis of good news, such as in advance of tender offers.[30] It may be that enforcement of insider trading might evolve into a division of responsibility with indirect private enforcement taking a stronger relative role where the insider's action is to cover up bad news. It is more likely that the relative unimportance of private enforcement in insider trading will continue.

Given the lack of observable direct insider trading harm to individual traders, the debate over insider trading has moved in a different direction. Professors Jon Macey and David Haddock adapted the S graphs from the middle portion of the Manne book to illustrate that direct costs of insider trading are borne first by market professionals and then passed along to market participants through higher spreads and trading costs.[31] They pursued this to a public choice explanation of regulation. Michael Dooley's work suggests similar conclusions,[32] as do Dean Manne's later writings about the SEC.[33]

The Supreme Court's current approach to insider trading regulation takes yet another approach to investor harm. In O'Hagan, there is no mention of individual harm in specific transactions. Rather, the focus is on harm from a decrease in public confidence in the market. This could be related to the harm to price function traders that was explicitly part of Manne's economic calculation. He discussed price function traders who might not otherwise have traded but who are induced to trade by the price effect from insider trading that moves the price off what the price function traders otherwise thought was the correct market price. The O'Hagan reasoning assumes traders will be pushed in the opposite direction—to put their money in a mattress or at least be less inclined to trade because of insider trading.[34] The focus, however, is not on the harm incurred from the foregone trade; such claims would not be easily susceptible to proof and would be difficult to calculate under the usual measures of damages. Instead of identifying individual loss in a specific transaction, the harm is the loss of market confidence and resulting loss of liquidity in the market generally.[35]

Dean Manne took on the investor confidence argument in his response to the critics of his book. He pointed to evidence in the 1920s and thereafter that "the public has never shown any signs of losing confidence in the stock market because of the existence of insider trading."[36] But it is difficult to separate and empirically test factors that would show such a connection. For example, similar national regimes under which one country banned insider trading and the other did not, or findings on liquidity before and after a change in the regulation of insider trading, cannot be easily isolated from other factors so as to observe the effect of insider trading. In the face of such challenges, with harm being so diffuse and difficult to measure, economics loses some of its relative advantage to politics as an explanatory tool for why we have government regulation.

In such a setting, understanding regulation may require not just the rational choice economics that is at the core of Manne's work, but also the learning of behavioral economics and cognitive psychology. Even if there is no loss or little individual effect as a result of insider trading, investors may still want the conduct regulated. There may be a parallel to preferences revealed in various experimental settings of the ultimatum game. In the ultimatum game, two parties are given a sum of money to divide. One of the parties is to propose the division; the other can then choose either to accept or reject. If accepted, the parties get to keep the proceeds as divided; if rejected, neither gets anything. Traditional rational choice economics and game theories based on similar assumptions of self-interested behavior would predict a small amount to be offered to the second party (so that the second party would be better off than if there were no transaction) but the disproportionate portion to the first party. Instead of such a split, many experiments find "offers typically average about 30–40 percent of the total, with a 50–50 split often the mode. Offers of less than 20 percent are frequently rejected."[37] Thus in some settings, players depart from the equilibrium predicted by rational self-interest and instead propose a division that is closer to equal sharing.[38] Similarly, shareholders may prefer to limit insider trading even if the harm is not immediately visible. Part of the attraction of the investor confidence argument for insider trading is likely a manifestation of the choices said to be evidenced by the outcome of the ultimatum game.

III. Insider Trading As Executive Compensation

The third assertion, and the one that provoked most of the uproar in the 1960s, was that insider trading constitutes the most appropriate device for compensating entrepreneurs in the large corporation. Again, Professor Macey has captured the underlying core of Manne's contribution and how it focused the debate on insider trading as a matter of intra-firm contract and private ordering; what

Macey terms "an applied executive compensation problem."[39] Manne's description was a bit more dramatic, asserting that insider trading "may be fundamental to the survival of our corporate system"[40] and that those pressing for a rule banning insider trading "may inadvertently be tampering with one of the wellsprings of American prosperity."[41]

On this assertion, Manne's analysis has not changed the legal result. Our corporate system has both survived and prospered in the last third of the twentieth century even as insider trading has become more regulated. The rest of the world has moved more in the direction of regulating insider trading rather than away from it.[42]

The executive compensation aspect has faltered in part because there has not been widespread acceptance of Manne's assertion that:

> Information is not a free good, and we should not assume, without more information than we now possess, that its distribution is generally capricious, arbitrary, random, or uncontrolled. Rational, self-serving individuals will not blithely and willingly allow information of tremendous value to pass freely to individuals who have no valid claim upon it. The safer assumption is that individuals with the power to control the flow of valuable information do so rationally and allocate it in a market-like system of exchange. . . .[43]

Yet except perhaps for Raymond Dirks, who was an entrepreneur of sorts and for whom the Supreme Court found no legal liability,[44] the defendants in the visible insider trading cases have not been entrepreneurs—the group for whom the compensation was seen as necessary. More illustrative is the lawyer, James O'Hagan, for whom takeover information provided a needed source of funds,[45] or Keith Loeb in the Chestman case,[46] two generations and one marriage removed from the entrepreneur. Despite Manne's recognition of leakage within the rational economic model,[47] and despite the possible distortions of the defendant pool because we no longer have a basis to test a control group in which insider trading is permitted,[48] the dominance of defendants like O'Hagan and Loeb continue to act as a drag on Manne's executive compensation argument.

More fundamentally, executive compensation has changed in a way that makes this prong of the insider trading argument less compelling. At the time of writing his book in 1966, Manne based part of his assertion for insider trading as executive compensation on his comparative analysis of the various alternatives for compensating entrepreneurs. Salary, bonus, profit-sharing plans, and stock options failed to meet the conditions for appropriately compensating entrepreneurs. Since 1966, changes in insider compensation have come closer to filling the need that Manne described. Not only has there been growth in executive compensation generally, but there is a richer array of forms that are regularly used.[49] The experience of venture capital financing has produced compensation agreements aimed directly at compensating start-up entrepreneurs and balancing their return with others who contribute to the enterprise. Options need not require that money already be invested, as concerned Manne in 1966, and there is a greater willingness to make differential awards that permit payment for entrepreneurial services.[50]

These various forms of compensation have some advantages over insider trading as entrepreneurial compensation. First, they seem less likely to reward the wrong people. Defining the target group is direct, although not perfect; information leakage is less likely. Second, this compensation is not secret, which makes it easier to monitor. The Securities and Exchange Commission requires extensive periodic disclosure of executive compensation for all public companies and also when companies are selling securities;[51] disclosure that was enhanced by extensive changes made in 1992.[52] In addition, these other forms of compensation typically require a corporate governance process prior to their initial availability, such as action by the directors or shareholders,[53] as opposed to insider trading, which is triggered by the insider's actions. Compensation is often a volatile issue and has been so for much of this century.[54] Currently, executive compensation is higher than in past periods,[55] and higher in the United States than in other countries.[56] In that setting, the disclosure and governance framework that governs non-insider trading compensation likely has a comparative advantage as compared to insider trading as compensation.

IV. Conclusion

The three central assumptions that Henry Manne used to present his defense of insider trading in 1966 remain as relevant signposts in the debate over regulation more than three decades later. There still is no coherent analytical approach to this topic, although we have been through several, sometimes-conflicting approaches during that period. Economics, particularly the property rights approach that flowed from Manne's work, has contributed to a richer understanding of insider trading and became especially influential in judicial doctrine at the beginning of this decade. To date, there has been no effective answer to the lack of investor harm as defined by Manne. Instead, the focus has shifted back to the larger and more amorphous harm to collective investors. Manne's two challenges to defects in the then-existing attacks on insider trading have fared better than the positive justification put forward for permitting insider trading. The argument that executive compensation in the form of insider trading is needed to facilitate entrepreneurial activity was a difficult argument to make in 1966 and has receded in its impact since then.

Notes

1. Securities Exchange Act of 1934 Release No. 8-3925, 40 S.E.C. 907 (Nov. 8, 1961). Federal regulation of insider trading existed prior to 1961 under section 16 of the Securities Exchange Act of 1934, 15 U.S.C. §78p, but the reach of that statute extended only to a limited set of insiders (officers, directors, or 10% shareholders) who engaged in two transactions, both buying and selling, within a six-month period for companies whose shares are traded in a national market. Under Rule 10b-5, the reach of regulation has been extended beyond these statutory insiders to include tippees, constructive insiders and misappropriators with only one transaction required for any security, not just those listed or traded on a national exchange.

2. HENRY G. MANNE, INSIDER TRADING AND THE STOCK MARKET (1966) [hereinafter INSIDER TRADING].

3. See id. chs. 1–3.

4. See id. chs. 4–7.

5. See id. chs. 8–10.

6. Id. at 15.

7. Id. at 5 (describing the position of Robert Walker in a 1923 article opposing regulation).

8. Id. at 5, 10 (describing arguments of Professor H.L., Wilgus in a 1910 article supporting regulation and in the House Report accompanying the Securities Exchange Act of 1934).

9. See id. at 15; see also id. at 46 ("There is in today's literature, however, very little analysis helpful to a court or a legislature asked to resolve the issues posed by the Texas Gulf Sulphur case.").

10. Jonathan R. Macey, Securities Trading: A Contractual Perspective, 50 CASE W. RES. L. REV. 269, 269 (1999).

11. See James D. Cox, Insider Trading and Contracting: A Critical Response to the "Chicago School," 1986 DUKE L.J. 628, 634 (asserting that aggressive enforcement of insider trading "without a coherent, let alone articulated, philosophy of regulation is one of the most unsettling aspects of the federal securities laws").

12. See Paula J. Dalley, From Horse Trading to Insider Trading: The Historical Antecedents of the Insider Trading Debate, 39 WM. & MARY L. REV. 1289, 1293–94 (1998).

13. See Jill E. Fisch, Start Making Sense: An Analysis and Proposal for Insider Trading Regulation, 26 GA. L. REV. 179, 184 (1991).

14. 521 U.S. 642 (1997).

15. See, e.g., Stephen M. Bainbridge, Insider Trading Regulation: The Path Dependent Choice Between Property Rights and Securities Fraud, 53 SMU L. REV. [Graphic Character Omitted] (1999); Victor Brudney, O'Hagan's Problems, 1997 SUP. CT. REV. 249; Dalley, supra note 12; Fisch, supra note 13; Donna Nagy, Reframing the Misappropriation Theory of Insider Trading Liability: A Post-O'hagan Suggestion, 59 OHIO ST. L.J. 1223 (1998); Richard W. Painter et al., Don't Ask, Just Tell: Insider Trading After United States v. O'Hagan, 84 VA. L. REV. 153 (1998); Alan Strudler & Eric W. Orts, Moral Principle in the Law of Insider Trading (1999) (unpublished manuscript, on file with author).

16. Roberta S. Karmel, Outsider Trading on Confidential Information—A Breach in Search of a Duty, 20 CARDOZO L. REV. 83, 83 (1998).

17. See INSIDER TRADING, supra note 2, at 182.

18. What is presented here as a subtext that insider trading promotes efficient market may be distinct from the injury to investors rationale if insider trading makes the market more efficient but shareholders are nonetheless injured. See STEPHEN BAINBRIDGE, SECURITIES LAW: INSIDER TRADING 128–36 (1999).

19. Id. at 110.

20. See William K.S. Wang, Trading on Material Nonpublic Information in Impersonal Stock Markets: Who is Harmed, and Who Can Sue Whom Under SEC Rule 10b-5?, 54 S. CAL. L. REV. 1217 (1981) (discussing the difficulty of identifying a victim of insider trading).

21. See 15 U.S.C. §78t-1 (1994). This section was originally enacted as the Insider Trading and Securities Fraud Enforcement Act of 1998.

22. Donald C. Langevoort, INSIDER TRADING: REGULATION, ENFORCEMENT AND PREVENTION, in 18 SEC. L. SER., 9–17 (1998).

23. See 15 U.S.C. § 78a (1995) (codifying, as amended, the Private Securities Litigation Reform Act of 1995, Pub. L. No. 104–67, 109 Stat. 737 (1995)).

24. Section 21D(b)(2) of the 1934 Act added by the 1995 Reform Act requires that plaintiff in any private action for money damages "state with particularly facts giving rise to a strong inference that the defendant acted with the required state of mind." 15 U.S.C. § 78u-4.

25. See Joseph A. Grundfest & Michael A. Perino, Securities Litigation Reform: The First Year's Experience (John M. Olin Program in Law & Economics, Working Paper No. 140) (reporting that more than half of securities class actions claims filed in the year after the 1995 Act included allegations of insider trading) (Feb. 1997) (on file with author).

26. See Federal Court Securities Class Actions (visited June 10, 1999) <http://securities.stanford.edu/complaints/complaints.html>. There were 761 cases in the database on that date, but only thirty-seven list section 20A. See id. Grundfest and Perino note that more than half of them mention insider trading. See Grundfest & Perino, supra note 47, at iii.

27. See Federal Court Securities Class Actions (visited June 10, 1999) <http://securities.stanford.edu/complaints/complaints.html>.

28. The Annual Reports of the SEC show the number of insider trading prosecutions around fifty per year during the 1990s.

29. That complaint was filed in Susser v. Florida Panthers Holdings, Inc., No. 97-6084 1997) (S.D. Fla. 1997), available in Stanford Securities Class Action Clearinghouse database, (visited June 10, 1999) <http://securities.stanford.edu/complaints/floridap/97cv06084/001.html> (alleging that defendants who were officers and directors covered up good news in order to buy shares at a bargain price).

30. See Lisa K. Meulbroek, An Empirical Analysis of Illegal Insider Trading, 47 J. FIN. 1661, 1678 (1992) (stating that 79% of all insider information is takeover related).

31. See David D. Haddock & Jonathon R. Macey. A Coasian Model of Insider Trading, 80 NW. U. L. REV. 1449, 1452–54, 1469 (1987).

32. See Michael P. Dooley, Enforcement of Insider Trading Restrictions, 66 VA. L. REV. 1 (1980) (measuring harm to investors and finding none).

33. See, e.g., Henry G. Manne, Insider Trading and the Law Professors, 23 VAND. L. REV. 547, 554 (1970); Henry G. Manne, Insider Trading and Property Rights in New Information, 4 CATO J. 933, 937–943 (1985).

34. See United States v. O'Hagan, 521 U.S. 642, 658 (1997) ("[I]nvestors likely would hesitate to venture their capital in a market where trading based on misappropriated nonpublic information is unchecked by law.").

35. See Victor Brudney, Insiders, Outsiders, and Informational Advantages Under the Federal Securities Laws, 93 HARV. L. REV. 322, 356 (1979) ("[S]ome investors will refrain from dealing altogether, and others will incur costs to avoid dealing with such transactors or corruptly to overcome their unerodable informational advantages.").

36. Henry G. Manne, Insider Trading and the Law Professors, 23 VAND. L. REV. 547, 577 (1970). For a current statement of that view, see BAINBRIDGE, supra note 40, at 155 ("The loss of confidence is further undercut by the stock market's performance since the insider trading scandals of the mid-1980s. . . . One can but conclude that insider trading does not seriously threaten the confidence of investors in the securities markets.").

37. Colin Camerer & Richard H. Thaler, Anomalies: Ultimatum, Dictators and Manners, J. ECON. PERSP., Spring 1995, at 209–10 (1995).

38. This behavior is sometimes discussed in the context of reciprocity norms. See, e.g., Jon D. Hanson & Douglas A. Kysar, Taking Behavioralism Seriously: The Problem of Market Manipulation, 74 N.Y.U.L. REV. 630, 680–81 (1999) ("Reciprocity norms manifest themselves in numerous ways, most of which seem

relevant to the market context. For example, individuals are often more willing to cooperate with those actors they feel are behaving cooperatively or fairly. On the other hand, individuals will often refuse to cooperate with others who are being uncooperative. Moreover, individuals are often willing to sacrifice to hurt others who are being unfair.") (citations omitted). See also Jennifer Arlen, Comment: The Future of Behavioral Economic Analysis of Law, 51 VAND. L. REV. 1765, 1776 (1998) ("[R]isk of perceived unfairness is greater that it might at first seem because people tend to have a self-serving assessment of what is fair.").

39. Jonathan R. Macey, Insider Trading, Henry Manne and Academic Life, 50 CASE W. RES. L. REV. 269, 281 (1999).

40. INSIDER TRADING, supra note 2, at 110.

41. Id.

42. In part, the preference may reflect an association with American prosperity of that period. More specifically it may reflect the efforts of American regulators. See also David D. Haddock, Academic Hostility and SEC Acquiescence: Henry Manne's Insider Trading, 50 CASE W. RES. L. REV. 313, 316–17 (1999) (discussing the status and evolution of government regulation of insider trading).

43. INSIDER TRADING, supra note 2, at 158.

44. See Dirks v. SEC, 463 U.S. 646, 665 (1983).

45. See United States v. O'Hagan, 521 U.S. 642, 648 (1997) (affirming O'Hagan's disbarrment and reversing his theft conviction resulting from an insider transaction).

46. See United States v. Chestman, 947 F.2d 551, 555 (2d Cir. 1991) (en banc), cert. denied, 503 U.S. 1004 (1992).

47. See INSIDER TRADING, supra note 2, at 169 (discussing possible information leakage but dismissing it as unimportant).

48. As Manne observed in discussing the economics of partial enforcement, "the absence of the more highminded participants from a segment of the securities field makes it that much more lucrative and attractive for those we least want to encourage." Henry G. Manne, Insider Trading and the Law Professors, 23 VAND. L. REV. 547, 555 (1970).

49. See generally John Balkcom & Roger Brossy. Executive Pay-Then, Now, and Ahead, 22 DIRS. & BDS., Fall 1997, 55, 58 (noting that "trends in executive pay have gone far to align the interests of the managers and the shareholder").

50. See INSIDER TRADING, supra note 2, at 140.

51. See 17 C.F.R. §§ 229.401–05 (1999) (republishing as administrative rules, SEC Regulation S-K).

52. See Securities Act of 1933 Release No. 33-6962, 52 SEC Docket 1961, 1963 (Oct. 16, 1992) (requiring new disclosure as to options and stock appreciation rights and requiring disclosure of the relationship between compensation and corporate performance designed to "furnish shareholders with a more understandable presentation of the nature and extent of executive compensation").

53. See generally Balkcom & Brossy, supra note 71, at 61.

54. See, e.g., Rogers v. Hill, 289 U.S. 582 (challenging the compensation program of the American Tobacco Company); Salary $12,000, Bonus $1,623,753, THE LITERARY DIGEST, Aug. 9, 1930, at 10 (publishing the annual compensation of the president of Bethlehem Steel).

55. See generally GRAEF S. CRYSTAL, IN SEARCH OF EXCESS: THE OVERCOMPENSATION OF AMERICAN EXECUTIVES 27 (1966) (explaining that executive pay was around thirty-five times the pay of the average manufacturing worker in 1974 and 120 times the average pay two decades later).

56. See, e.g., DEREK BOK, THE COST OF TALENT: HOW EXECUTIVES AND PRO-
FESSIONALS ARE PAID AND HOW IT AFFECTS AMERICA 95 (1993) (showing
that American levels of corporate compensation are not replicated in other
industrial nations); Deborah Orr, Damn Yankees, FORBES, May 17, 1999, at 206
(noting average U.S. chief executive's pay still far outpaces the rest of the world
because of long term-incentives like stock options, which while common here,
are rarer abroad).

Stephen Bainbridge  **NO**

Why Regulate Insider Trading?

T he Washington Post recently reported on the considerable attention the SEC and Justice Department are devoting to enforcement of the insider trading laws. Who can forget the recent high profile case against Martha Stewart, which is only the very tip of a large iceberg? Is this a useful expenditure of government resources?

Henry Manne's 1966 book *Insider Trading and the Stock Market* stunned the SEC and corporate law academy by daring to propose the deregulation of insider trading. Manne argued that insider trading benefits both society and the firm in whose stock the insider traded. First, he argued, insider trading causes the market price of the affected security to move toward the price that the security would command if the inside information were publicly available. If so, both society and the firm benefit through increased price accuracy. Second, he posited insider trading as an efficient way of compensating managers for having produced information. If so, the firm benefits directly (and society indirectly) because managers have a greater incentive to produce additional information of value to the firm.

Although I have tremendous respect for Manne's daring in proposing such provocative arguments, I'm afraid I don't buy either one. As to the first, Manne argued (correctly) that both firms and society benefit from accurate pricing of securities. The "correct" price of a security is that which would be set by the market if all information relating to the security had been publicly disclosed. But while U.S. securities laws purportedly encourage accurate pricing by requiring disclosure of corporate information, they in fact do not require the disclosure of all material information. Where disclosure would interfere with legitimate business transactions, disclosure by the corporation is usually not required unless the firm is dealing in its own securities at the time.

Manne argued insider trading is an effective compromise between the need for preserving incentives to produce information and the need for maintaining accurate securities prices. Suppose, for example, that a firm's stock currently sells at fifty dollars per share. The firm has discovered new information that, if publicly disclosed, would cause the stock to sell at sixty dollars. If insiders trade on this information, the price of the stock will gradually rise toward but will not reach the "correct" price. Absent insider trading or leaks, the stock's price will remain at fifty dollars until the information is publicly disclosed and then rapidly rise to the correct price of sixty dollars. Thus, insider trading acts as a replacement for public disclosure of the information, preserving market gains of correct pricing while permitting the corporation to retain the benefits of nondisclosure.

The problem with this argument is that insider trading affects stock market prices through what is known as "derivatively informed trading." First, those individuals possessing material nonpublic information begin trading. Their trading has only a small effect on price. Some uninformed traders become aware of the insider trading through leakage or tipping of information or through observation of insider trades. Other traders gain insight by following the price fluctuations of the securities. Finally, the market reacts to the insiders' trades and gradually moves toward the correct price. But while derivatively informed trading can affect price, it functions slowly and sporadically. Given the inefficiency of derivatively informed trading, the market efficiency justification for insider trading loses much of its force.

As for Manne's second argument, insider trading in fact appears to be a very inefficient scheme for compensating corporate managers. Even assuming a change in stock price that accurately measures the value of the innovation, the insider's "compensation" from insider trading is limited by the number of shares he can purchase. This, in turn, is limited by his wealth. As such, the insider's trading returns are based, not on the value of his contribution to the corporation, but on his wealth.

Another objection to the compensation argument is the difficulty of restricting trading to those who produced the information. Where information is concerned, production costs normally exceed distribution costs. As such, many firm agents may trade on the information without having contributed to its production.

A related objection is the difficulty of limiting trading to instances in which the insider actually produced valuable information. In particular, why should insiders be permitted to trade on bad news? Allowing managers to profit from inside trading reduces the penalties associated with a project's failure because trading managers can profit whether the project succeeds or fails. If the project fails, the manager can sell his shares before that information becomes public and thus avoid an otherwise certain loss. The manager can go beyond mere loss avoidance into actual profit making by short selling the firm's stock.

In sum, the arguments for deregulating insider trading are not very persuasive. But that doesn't answer the question, why do we regulate insider trading? Efficiency-based arguments for regulating insider trading (as opposed to those grounded on legislative intent, equity, or fairness) fall into three main categories: (1) insider trading harms investors and thus undermines investor confidence in the securities markets; (2) insider trading harms the issuer of the affected securities; and (3) insider trading amounts to theft of property belonging to the corporation and therefore should be prohibited even in the absence of harm to investors or the firm. Only the latter proves very persuasive.

There are essentially two ways of creating property rights in information: allow the owner to enter into transactions without disclosing the information or prohibit others from using the information. In effect, the federal insider trading prohibition vests a property right of the latter type in the party to whom the insider trader owes a fiduciary duty to refrain from self-dealing in confidential information. To be sure, at first blush, the insider trading prohibition admittedly does not look very much like most property rights. Enforcement of the insider trading prohibition admittedly differs rather dramatically from enforcement of, say, trespassing laws. The existence of property rights in a variety of intangibles, including information, however, is well-established. Trademarks, copyrights, and patents are but a few of the better known examples of this phenomenon. There are striking doctrinal parallels, moreover, between insider trading and these other types of property rights in information. Using another's trade secret, for example, is actionable only if taking the trade secret involved a breach of fiduciary duty, misrepresentation, or theft. Likewise, insider trading is only unlawful if the use of the information involves a breach of fiduciary duty by the insider.

The rationale for prohibiting insider trading is precisely the same as that for prohibiting patent infringement or theft of trade secrets: protecting the economic incentive to produce socially valuable information. As the theory goes, the readily appropriable nature of information makes it difficult for the developer of a new idea to recoup the sunk costs incurred to develop it. If an inventor develops a better mousetrap, for example, he cannot profit on that invention without selling mousetraps and thereby making the new design available to potential competitors. Assuming both the inventor and his competitors incur roughly equivalent marginal costs to produce and market the trap, the competitors will be able to set a market price at which the inventor likely will be unable to earn a return on his sunk costs. Ex post, the rational inventor should ignore his sunk costs and go on producing the improved mousetrap. Ex ante, however, the inventor will anticipate that he will be unable to generate positive returns on his up-front costs and therefore will be deterred from developing socially valuable information. Accordingly, society provides incentives for inventive activity by using the patent system to give inventors a property right in new ideas. By preventing competitors from appropriating the idea, the patent allows the inventor to charge monopolistic prices for the improved mousetrap, thereby recouping his sunk costs. Trademark, copyright, and trade secret law all are justified on similar grounds.

This argument does not provide as compelling a justification for the insider trading prohibition as it does for the patent system. A property right in information should be created when necessary to prevent conduct by which someone other than the developer of socially valuable information appropriates its value before the developer can recoup his sunk costs. Insider trading, however, often does not affect an idea's value to the corporation and probably never entirely eliminates its value. Legalizing insider trading thus would have a much smaller impact on the corporation's incentive to develop new information than would, say, legalizing patent infringement.

The property rights approach nevertheless has considerable justificatory power. Consider the prototypical insider trading transaction, in which an insider trades in his employer's stock on the basis of information learned solely because of his position with the firm. There is no avoiding the necessity of assigning the property right to either the corporation or the inside trader. A rule allowing insider trading assigns the property right to the insider, while a rule prohibiting insider trading assigns it to the corporation.

From the corporation's perspective, legalizing insider trading likely would have a relatively small effect on the firm's incentives to develop new information. In some cases, however, insider trading will harm the corporation's interests and thus adversely affect its incentives in this regard. This argues for assigning the property right to the corporation, rather than the insider.

Those who rely on a property rights-based justification for regulating insider trading also observe that creation of a property right with respect to a particular asset typically is not dependent upon there being a measurable loss of value resulting from the asset's use by someone else. Indeed, creation of a property right is appropriate even if any loss in value is entirely subjective, both because subjective valuations are difficult to measure for purposes of awarding damages and because the possible loss of subjective values presumably would affect the corporation's incentives to cause its agents to develop new information. As with other property rights, the law therefore should simply assume (although the assumption will sometimes be wrong) that assigning the property right to agent-produced information to the firm maximizes the social incentives for the production of valuable new information.

Because the relative rarity of cases in which harm occurs to the corporation weakens the argument for assigning it the property right, however, the critical issue may be whether one can justify assigning the property right to the insider. On close examination, the argument for assigning the property right to the insider is considerably weaker than the argument for assigning it to the corporation. As we have seen, Manne argued that legalized insider trading would be an appropriate compensation scheme. In other words, society might allow insiders to inside trade in order to give them greater incentives to develop new information. As we have also seen, however, this argument founders because insider trading in fact is an inefficient compensation scheme.

The economic theory of property rights in information thus cannot justify assigning the property right to insiders rather than to the corporation. Because there is no avoiding the necessity of assigning the property right to the information in question to one of the relevant parties, the argument for assigning it to the corporation therefore should prevail.

None of this is to say that the precise set of rules the SEC has adopted is ideal. To the contrary, as I detailed in my book on insider trading, there are serious problems with a number of features of the current enforcement regime. As to the basic question of whether we ought to regulate insider trading, however, economic efficiency commands an affirmative answer.

POSTSCRIPT

Should Insider Trading Be Legalized?

In addition to the Martha Stewart case, in virtually all of the major corporate scandals at the turn of the century—Enron, Global Crossing, Tyco Corporation, WorldCom—insider trading was identified as a major source of illegal activity. A natural outcome of this has been a revival of the debate over the moral and legal status of insider trading. Most observers have adopted the traditional viewpoint of insider trading as morally heinous behavior and deserving of criminal prosecution. But a growing chorus of dissenters have resurrected the work of Henry Manne and offered it as justification for legalizing insider trading. Although much of this dissention is rooted in academia, Manne's views are becoming known to a wider audience.

In a recent interview with syndicated talk radio show host and social commentator Larry Elder, Henry Manne reiterated his belief that insider trading should be legalized. In so doing, he highlighted an often neglected aspect of his earlier position. Manne contends that, independent of the economic, legal, or moral arguments against regulation, the reality is that insider trading is virtually impossible to detect and enforce: "That's, of course, why they didn't indict Martha Stewart for insider trading. The SEC does not win many of the cases they bring, and they don't bring many. It's really very interesting to wonder what kind of law is this that it is so difficult to prove that you've got a case" (Elder, "Legalize Insider Trading," *Capitalism Magazine*, September 24, 2004). He suggests that the SEC would be well advised to spend its time and money in other pursuits.

Regardless of whether enforcement is feasible or not, the fact is that most of the public, and virtually all of the political powers, are supportive of continued regulation of insider trading activities. In fact, a significant portion of the massive, landmark Sarbanes-Oxley Act of 2002 on corporate governance specifically addresses the issue of insider trading. Thus, whether you agree with Manne's viewpoint or not, there can be no debating that the current socio-political environment is characterized by the view that insider trading is harmful, immoral, illegal, and therefore, subject to governmental regulation.

Suggested Readings

Stephen M. Bainbridge, Insider trading: An overview. *Encyclopedia of Law and Economics*, 2000.

Andrew Bernstein, The injustice of insider trading laws. *The Ayn Rand Institute*, July 12, 2004. http://www.aynrand.org/site/News2?page=NewsArticle&id=9559

Larry Elder, Legalize insider trading. *Capitalism Magazine*, September 24, 2004. http://www.capmag.com/article.asp?ID=3933

Jonathan R. Macey, Securities trading: A contractual perspective. *Case Western Reserve Law Review*, vol. 50, no. 2, Winter 1999, p. 269.

On the Internet . . .

About.com: Affirmative Action

This site provides a myriad of links to help you understand the controversial topic of Affirmative Action as well as information on any current developments and reform initiatives.

```
http://racerelations.about.com/od/
          affirmativeaction/
```

Workplace Fairness

Workplace Fairness is a nonprofit organization that brings together employers, workers, policymakers, and others to ensure and promote fairness in the workplace and employment relationships.

```
http://www.nerinet.org/
```

Partnership for a Drug-Free America

This Web site has much information on drug use by young adults as well as links to related sites. Also features an updated news resource links.

```
http://www.drugfreeamerica.org/Home/
    default.asp?ws=PDFA&vol=1&grp=Home
```

Institute for Women's Policy Research

The Institute for Women's Policy Research (IWPR) is a public policy research organization dedicated to informing and stimulating the debate on public policy issues of critical importance to women and their families.

```
http://www.iwpr.org/
```

PART 2

Organizational Behavior and Human Resource Management

Affirmative action has been with us for several decades. There is no question that it has helped in obtaining more and better opportunities for minorities and females during this time. But, as some critics claim, has it become outdated? Do we still need it? Companies have the right to protect themselves from harm and to ensure a safe and drug-free workplace. But employees also have a right to privacy. So which right prevails when a company drug tests its employees? In the late 1950s, women made about 40 percent less than did males. In 2003, the male-female wage gap has only shrunk to 25 percent. Is discrimination still responsible for this difference? Part 2 explores these and other important questions for managers.

- Has Affirmative Action Outlived Its Usefulness in the Workplace?

- Is the Control of Drug Abuse in the Workplace More Important than Protecting Employee Privacy?

- Does Workplace Diversity Result in a More Productive Firm?

- Is Gender Discrimination the Main Reason Women Are Paid Less than Men?

- Is Blowing the Whistle an Act of Disloyalty?

ISSUE 6

Has Affirmative Action Outlived Its Usefulness in the Workplace?

YES: Walter E. Williams, from "Affirmative Action Can't Be Mended," *Cato Journal* (Spring/Summer 1997)

NO: Wilbert Jenkins, from "Why We Must Retain Affirmative Action," *USA Today Magazine* (September 1999)

ISSUE SUMMARY

YES: Cato Institute research fellow Dr. Walter Williams argues that affirmative action is no longer useful in the workplace. He likens affirmative action to a "zero-sum" game where one group benefits at the expense of all other groups.

NO: Dr. Wilbert Jenkins presents, and then rebuts, the major points critics of affirmative action typically raise. He also provides a discussion on the relationship between affirmative action and diversity in the workplace. He argues that since diversity is good business, and affirmative action encourages diversity, then affirmative action is good business.

One of the most important outcomes of the 1960s civil rights movement in America was the concept of affirmative action. In the workplace, affirmative action can be defined as the "process in which employers identify needs and take positive steps to create and enhance opportunities for protected class members [i.e., minorities and females]" (Robert L. Mathis and John H. Jackson, *Human Resource Management,* Thompson South-Western Publishers, 2003). For most private companies, implementing an affirmative action program is a voluntary decision. However, in addition to all state and federal government agencies, those businesses that contract government work are required by law to maintain affirmative action programs in their workplace. One of the effects of these requirements has been to increase the diversity of the workforce in corporate America. And while many people feel this is a positive result, there are many others who are, both in principle and in practice, vigorously opposed to the concept of affirmative action. Many of its detractors argue that it has accomplished its goals and is, at best, no longer needed and, at worst, damaging to the

American social fabric. Supporters contend that affirmative action has not yet met all its goals and is still very much needed in the workplace. The debate over the legitimacy and effectiveness of affirmative action is characterized by strong passions on both sides and represents one of the most important social issues of the early twenty-first century.

There are several compelling arguments on each side of the debate. Proponents of affirmative action believe that many of the current differences in racial and gender success in the workplace can be attributed to the effects of discrimination built up over many years. These effects cut both ways: Women and minorities suffer unfair employment treatment while males and non-minorities have received preferential treatment. Not surprisingly, supporters of affirmative action argue that it is needed to overcome the effects of past discrimination. A second argument rests on the observation that social ills like crime, drug abuse, and low educational attainment levels are most likely to occur among those at the lowest level of the socio-economic ladder, a rung that consists primarily of minorities. Since economic disparities will be reduced as a result of the increased employment and economic opportunities provided by affirmative action, social problems such as these could decline, thereby benefiting all members of our society.

The other side of the debate also has several strong points. An important consideration is the concept of reverse discrimination. Like it or not, the fact is that when we give preferential treatment to any group of individuals we necessarily discriminate against other groups. Critics of affirmative action argue that this occurs frequently, is reverse discrimination (usually against males and non-minorities), and requires adopting a "two wrongs make a right" viewpoint. Another line of reasoning against affirmative action involves the recognition that the overwhelming majority of non-protected class individuals have nothing to do with past discrimination—indeed, many were not even alive at the time—and yet it is exactly these people who are penalized by affirmative action programs. Opponents argue that it is patently unfair for these individuals to be penalized for discrimination that occurred in the past and in which they played no part.

In the two selections that follow, the question of whether affirmative action has outlived its usefulness in the workplace is addressed. The "yes" selection is presented by economist and Cato Institute Research Fellow Dr. Walter Williams. As you read his selection, pay close attention to the discussion concerning affirmative action as a "zero-sum" game. Do you find the logic behind this argument compelling? The "no" position is presented by Wilbert Jenkins, a professor of history at Temple University. During the course of this well-structured article, Dr. Jenkins presents, and then rebuts, the major points critics of affirmative action typically raise. In addition, he provides an interesting discussion on the relationship between affirmative action and diversity in the workplace arguing, in effect, that since diversity is good business, and affirmative action encourages diversity, then affirmative action is good business. Before turning to the articles themselves, one final point should be made: lest you think that the race of the authors themselves played a role in their views about affirmative action, consider that each is a male protected class member.

Affirmative Action Can't Be Mended

For the last several decades, affirmative action has been the basic component of the civil rights agenda. But affirmative action, in the form of racial preferences, has worn out its political welcome. In Gallup Polls, between 1987 and 1990, people were asked if they agreed with the statement: "We should make every effort to improve the position of blacks and other minorities even if it means giving them preferential treatment." More than 70 percent of the respondents opposed preferential treatment while only 24 percent supported it. Among blacks, 66 percent opposed preferential treatment and 32 percent supported it (Lipset 1992: 66–69).

The rejection of racial preferences by the broad public and increasingly by the Supreme Court has been partially recognized by even supporters of affirmative action. While they have not forsaken their goals, they have begun to distance themselves from some of the language of affirmative action. Thus, many business, government, and university affirmative action offices have been renamed "equity offices." Racial preferences are increasingly referred to as "diversity multiculturalism." What is it about affirmative action that gives rise to its contentiousness?

For the most part, post–World War II America has supported civil rights for blacks. Indeed, if we stick to the uncorrupted concept of civil rights, we can safely say that the civil rights struggle for blacks is over and won. Civil rights properly refer to rights, held simultaneously among individuals, to be treated equally in the eyes of the law, make contracts, sue and be sued, give evidence, associate and travel freely, and vote. There was a time when blacks did not fully enjoy those rights. With the yeoman-like work of civil rights organizations and decent Americans, both black and white, who fought lengthy court, legislative, and street battles, civil rights have been successfully secured for blacks. No small part of that success was due to a morally compelling appeal to America's civil libertarian tradition of private property, rule of law, and limited government.

Today's corrupted vision of civil rights attacks that civil libertarian tradition. Principles of private property rights, rule of law, freedom of association, and limited government are greeted with contempt. As such, the agenda of today's civil rights organizations conceptually differs little from yesteryear's restrictions that were the targets of the earlier civil rights struggle. Yesteryear civil rights organizations fought *against* the use of race in hiring, access to public schools, and university admissions. Today, civil rights organizations fight *for* the use of race in hiring, access to public schools, and university admissions. Yesteryear, civil rights organizations fought *against* restricted association in the forms of racially segregated schools, libraries, and private organizations. Today, they fight *for* restricted associations. They use state power, not unlike the racists they fought, to enforce racial associations they deem desirable. They protest that blacks should be a certain percentage of a company's workforce or clientele, a certain percentage of a student body, and even a certain percentage of an advertiser's models.

Civil rights organizations, in their successful struggle against state-sanctioned segregation, have lost sight of what it means to be truly committed to liberty, especially the freedom of association. The true test of that commitment does not come when we allow people to be free to associate in ways we deem appropriate. The true test is when we allow people to form those voluntary associations we deem offensive. It is the same principle we apply to our commitment to free speech. What tests our commitment to free speech is our willingness to permit people the freedom to say things we find offensive.

Zero-Sum Games

The tragedy of America's civil rights movement is that it has substituted today's government-backed racial favoritism in the allocation of resources for yesterday's legal and extra-legal racial favoritism. In doing so, civil rights leaders fail to realize that government allocation of resources produces the kind of conflict that does not arise with market allocation of resources. Part of the reason is that any government allocation of resources, including racial preferential treatment, is a zero-sum game.

A zero-sum game is defined as any transaction where one person's gain necessarily results in another person's loss. The simplest example of a zero-sum game is poker. A winner's gain is matched precisely by the losses of one or more persons. In this respect, the only essential difference between affirmative action and poker is that in poker participation is voluntary. Another difference is the loser is readily identifiable, a point to which I will return later.

The University of California, Berkeley's affirmative action program for blacks captures the essence of a zero-sum game. Blacks are admitted with considerably lower average SAT scores (952) than the typical white (1232) and Asian student (1254) (Sowell 1993: 144). Between UCLA and UC Berkeley, more than 2,000 white and Asian straight A students are turned away in order to provide spaces for black and Hispanic students (Lynch 1989: 163). The admissions gains by blacks are exactly matched by admissions losses by white and Asian students. Thus, any preferential treatment program results in a zero-sum game almost by definition.

More generally, government allocation of resources is a zero-sum game primarily because government has no resources of its very own. When government gives some citizens food stamps, crop subsidies, or disaster relief payments, the recipients of the largesse gain. Losers are identified by asking: where does government acquire the resources to confer the largesse? In order for government to give to some citizens, it must through intimidation, threats, and coercion take from other citizens. Those who lose the rights to their earnings, to finance government largesse, are the losers.

Government-mandated racial preferential treatment programs produce a similar result. When government creates a special advantage for one ethnic group, it necessarily comes at the expense of other ethnic groups for whom government simultaneously creates a special disadvantage in the form of reduced alternatives. If a college or employer has X amount of positions, and R of them have been set aside for blacks or some other group, that necessarily means there are $(X - R)$ fewer positions for which other ethnic groups might compete. At a time when there were restrictions against blacks, that operated in favor of whites, those restrictions translated into a reduced opportunity set for blacks. It is a zero-sum game independent of the race or ethnicity of the winners and losers.

Our courts have a blind-sided vision of the zero-sum game. They have upheld discriminatory racial preferences in hiring but have resisted discriminatory racial preferences in job layoffs. An example is the U.S. Supreme Court's ruling in *Wygant v. Jackson Board of Education* (1986), where a teacher union's collective-bargaining agreement protected black teachers from job layoffs in order to maintain racial balance. Subsequently, as a result of that agreement, the Jackson County School Board laid off white teachers having greater seniority while black teachers with less seniority were retained.

A lower court upheld the constitutionality of the collective bargaining agreement by finding that racial preferences in layoffs were a permissible means to remedy societal discrimination (*Wygant* 1982: 1195, 1201). White teachers petitioned the U.S. Supreme Court, claiming their constitutional rights under the Equal Protection clause were violated. The Court found in their favor. Justice Lewis F. Powell delivered the opinion saying, "While hiring goals impose a diffuse burden, only closing one of several opportunities, layoffs impose the entire burden of achieving racial equity on particular individuals, often resulting in serious disruption of their lives. The burden is too intrusive" (*Wygant* 1986: 283). . . .

There is no conceptual distinction in the outcome of the zero-sum game whether it is played on the layoff or the hiring side of the labor market. . . . The diffuseness to which Justice Powell refers is not diffuseness at all. It is simply that the victims of hiring preferences are less visible than victims of layoff preferences as in the case of *Wygant*. The petitioners in *Wygant* were identifiable people who could not be covered up as "society." That differs from the cases of hiring and college admissions racial preferences where those who face a reduced opportunity set tend to be unidentifiable to the courts, other people, and even to themselves. Since they are invisible victims, the Supreme Court and others can blithely say racial hiring goals (and admission goals) impose a diffuse burden.

Tentative Victim Identification

In California, voters passed the California Civil Rights Initiative of 1996 (CCRI) that says: "The state shall not discriminate against, or grant preferential treatment to, any individual or group on the basis of race, sex, color, ethnicity, or national origin in the operation of public employment, public education, or public contracting." Therefore, California public universities can no longer have preferential admission policies that include race as a factor in deciding whom to admit. As a result, the UCLA School of Law reported accepting only 21 black applicants for its fall 1997 class—a drop of 80 percent from the previous year, in which 108 black applicants were accepted. At the UC Berkeley Boalt Hall School of Law, only 14 of the 792 students accepted for the fall 1997 class are black, down from 76 the previous year. At the UCLA School of Law, white enrollment increased by 14 percent for the fall 1997 term and Asian enrollment rose by 7 percent. At UC Berkeley, enrollment of white law students increased by 12 percent and Asian law students increased by 18 percent (Weiss 1997). . . .

In the case of UC Berkeley's preferential admissions for blacks, those whites and Asians who have significantly higher SAT scores and grades than the admitted blacks are victims of reverse discrimination. However, in the eyes of the courts, others, and possibly themselves, they are invisible victims. In other words, no one can tell for sure who among those turned away would have gained entry to UC Berkeley were it not for the preferential treatment given to blacks. . . .

Affirmative Action and Supply

An important focus of affirmative action is statistical underrepresentation of different racial and ethnic groups on college and university campuses. If the percentages of blacks and Mexican-Americans, for example, are not at a level deemed appropriate by a court, administrative agency, or university administrator, racial preference programs are instituted. The inference made from the underrepresentation argument is that, in the absence of racial discrimination, groups would be represented on college campuses in proportion to their numbers in the relevant population. In making that argument, little attention is paid to the supply issue—that is, to the pool of students available that meet the standards or qualifications of the university in question.

In 1985, fewer than 1,032 blacks scored 600 and above on the verbal portion of the SAT and 1,907 scored 600 and above on the quantitative portion of the examination. There are roughly 58 elite colleges and universities with student body average composite SAT scores of 1200 and above (Sowell 1993: 142). If blacks scoring 600 or higher on the quantitative portion of the SAT (assuming their performance on the verbal portion of the examination gave them a composite SAT score of 1200 or higher) were recruited to elite colleges and universities, there would be less than 33 black students available per university. At none of those universities would blacks be represented according to their numbers in the population.

There is no evidence that suggests that university admissions offices practice racial discrimination by turning away blacks with SAT scores of 1200 or higher. In reality, there are not enough blacks to be admitted to leading colleges and universities on the same terms as other students, such that their numbers in the campus population bear any resemblance to their numbers in the general population.

Attempts by affirmative action programs to increase the percent of blacks admitted to top schools, regardless of whether blacks match the academic characteristics of the general student body, often produce disastrous results. In order to meet affirmative action guidelines, leading colleges and universities recruit and admit black students whose academic qualifications are well below the norm for other students. For example, of the 317 black students admitted to UC Berkeley in 1985, all were admitted under affirmative action criteria rather than academic qualifications. Those students had an average SAT score of 952 compared to the national average of 900 among all students. However, their SAT scores were well below UC Berkeley's average of nearly 1200. More than 70 percent of the black students failed to graduate from UC Berkeley (Sowell 1993: 144).

Not far from UC Berkeley is San Jose State University, not one of the top-tier colleges, but nonetheless respectable. More than 70 percent of its black students fail to graduate. The black students who might have been successful at San Jose State University have been recruited to UC Berkeley and elsewhere where they have been made artificial failures. This pattern is one of the consequences of trying to use racial preferences to make a student body reflect the relative importance of different ethnic groups in the general population. There is a mismatch between black student qualifications and those of other students when the wrong students are recruited to the wrong universities.

There is no question that preferential admissions is unjust to both white and Asian students who may be qualified but are turned away to make room for less-qualified students in the "right" ethnic group. However, viewed from a solely black self-interest point of view, the question should be asked whether such affirmative action programs serve the best interests of blacks. Is there such an abundance of black students who score above the national average on the SAT, such as those admitted to UC Berkeley, that blacks as a group can afford to have those students turned into artificial failures in the name of diversity, multiculturalism, or racial justice? The affirmative action debate needs to go beyond simply an issue of whether blacks are benefited at the expense of whites. Whites and Asians who are turned away to accommodate blacks are still better off than the blacks who were admitted. After all, graduating from the university of one's second choice is preferable to flunking out of the university of one's first choice.

To the extent racial preferences in admission produce an academic mismatch of students, the critics of California's Proposition 209 may be unnecessarily alarmed, assuming their concern is with black students actually graduating from college. If black students, who score 952 on the SAT, are not admitted to UC Berkeley, that does not mean that they cannot gain admittance to one of America's 3,000 other colleges. It means that they will gain admittance to some other college where their academic characteristics will be more similar to those of their peers. There will not be as much of an academic mismatch. To the extent this is true, we may see an *increase* in black graduation rates. Moreover, if black students find themselves more similar to their white peers in terms of college grades and graduation honors, they are less likely to feel academically isolated and harbor feelings of low self-esteem.

Affirmative Action and Justice

Aside from any other question, we might ask what case can be made for the morality or justice of turning away more highly credentialed white and Asian students so as to be able to admit more blacks? Clearly, blacks as a group have suffered past injustices, including discrimination in college and university admissions. However, that fact does not spontaneously yield sensible policy proposals for today. The fact is that a special privilege cannot be created for one person without creating a special disadvantage for another. In the case of preferential admissions at UCLA and UC Berkeley, a special privilege for black students translates into a special disadvantage for white and Asian students. Thus, we must ask what have those individual white and Asian students done to deserve punishment? Were they at all responsible for the injustices, either in the past or present, suffered by blacks? If, as so often is the case, the justification for preferential treatment is to redress past grievances, how just is it to have a policy where a black of today is helped by punishing a white of today for what a white of yesterday did to a black of yesterday? Such an idea becomes even more questionable in light of the fact that so many whites and Asians cannot trace the American part of their ancestry back as much as two or three generations.

Affirmative Action and Racial Resentment

In addition to the injustices that are a result of preferential treatment, such treatment has given rise to racial resentment where it otherwise might not exist. While few people support racial resentment and its manifestations, if one sees some of affirmative action's flagrant attacks on fairness and equality before the law, one can readily understand why resentment is on the rise.

In the summer of 1995, the Federal Aviation Administration (FAA) published a "diversity handbook" that said, "The merit promotion process is but one means of filling vacancies, which need not be utilized if it will not promote your diversity goals." In that spirit, one FAA job announcement said, "Applicants who meet the qualification requirements . . . cannot be considered for this position. . . . Only those applicants who do not meet the Office of Personnel Management requirements . . . will be eligible to compete" (Roberts and Stratton 1995: 141).

According to a General Accounting Office report that evaluated complaints of discrimination by Asian-Americans, prestigious universities such as UCLA, UC Berkeley, MIT, and the University of Wisconsin have engaged in systematic discrimination in the failure to admit highly qualified Asian students in order to admit relatively unqualified black and Hispanic students (U.S. GAO 1995).

In Memphis, Tennessee, a white police officer ranked 59th out of 209 applicants for 75 available positions as police sergeant, but he did not get promoted. Black officers, with lower overall test scores than he, were moved ahead of him and promoted to sergeant. Over a two-year period, 43 candidates with lower scores were moved ahead of him and made sergeant (Eastland 1996: 1–2).

There is little need to recite the litany of racial preference instances that are clear violations of commonly agreed upon standards of justice and fair play.

But the dangers of racial preferences go beyond matters of justice and fair play. They lead to increased group polarization ranging from political backlash to mob violence and civil war as seen in other countries. The difference between the United States and those countries is that racial preferences have not produced the same level of violence (Sowell 1990). However, they have produced polarization and resentment.

Affirmative action proponents cling to the notion that racial discrimination satisfactorily explains black/white socioeconomic differences. While every vestige of racial discrimination has not been eliminated in our society, current social discrimination cannot begin to explain all that affirmative action proponents purport it explains. Rather than focusing our attention on discrimination, a higher payoff can be realized by focusing on real factors such as fraudulent education, family disintegration, and hostile economic climates in black neighborhoods. Even if affirmative action was not a violation of justice and fair play, was not a zero-sum game, was not racially polarizing, it is a poor cover-up for the real work that needs to be done.

References

Eastland, T. (1996) *Ending Affirmative Action: The Case for Colorblind Justice.* New York: Basic Books.

Lipset, S. M. (1992) "Equal Chances Versus Equal Results." In H. Orlans and J. O'Neill (eds.) *Affirmative Action Revisited; Annals of the American Academy of Political and Social Science* 523 (September): 63–74.

Lynch, F. R. (1989) *Invisible Victims: White Males and the Crisis of Affirmative Action.* New York: Greenwood Press.

Roberts, P. C., and Stratton, L. M. (1995) *The Color Line: How Quotas and Privilege Destroy Democracy.* Washington, D.C.: Regnery.

Sowell, T. (1990) *Preferential Policies: An International Perspective.* New York: William Morrow.

Sowell, T. (1993) *Inside American Education: The Decline, The Deception, The Dogmas.* New York: The Free Press.

United States General Accounting Office (1995) *Efforts by the Office for Civil Rights to Resolve Asian-American Complaints.* Washington, D.C.: Government Printing Office. (December).

Weiss, K. R. (1997) "UC Law Schools' New Rules Cost Minorities Spots." *Los Angeles Times*, 15 May.

Wygant v. Jackson Board of Education (1982) 546 F. Supp. 1195.

Wygant v. Jackson Board of Education (1986) 476 U.S. 267.

NO

Wilbert Jenkins

Why We Must Retain Affirmative Action

The historical origins of affirmative action can be found in the 14th and 15th Amendments to the Constitution, the Enforcement Acts of 1870 and 1871, and the Civil Rights Acts of 1866 and 1875, which were passed by Republican-dominated Congresses during the Reconstruction period. This legislation set the precedent for many of the civil rights laws of the 1950s and 1960s—such as the Civil Rights Act of 1957, the Civil Rights Act of 1964, and the Voting Rights Act of 1965—and paved the way for what would become known as affirmative action.

In spite of the fact that laws designed to promote and protect the civil and political rights of African-Americans were enacted by Congress in the 1950s and 1960s, it was obvious that racism and discrimination against blacks in the area of education and, by extension, the workplace were huge obstacles that needed to be overcome if African-Americans were ever going to be able to carve an economic foundation. Thus, in the 1960s, affirmative action became a part of a larger design by Pres. Lyndon Johnson's War on Poverty program. In a historic 1965 speech at Howard University, the nation's top black school, Johnson illustrated the thinking that led to affirmative action: "You do not take a person who for years has been hobbled by chains and liberate him, bring him to the starting line and say you are free to compete with all the others." Civil rights leader Martin Luther King, Jr., also underscored this belief when he stated that "one cannot ask people who don't have boots to pull themselves up by their own bootstraps."

Policymakers fervently believed that more than three centuries of enslavement, oppression, and discrimination had so economically deprived African-Americans that some mechanism had to be put in place that would at least allow them a fighting chance. Blacks were locked out of the highest paid positions and made considerably fewer dollars than their white counterparts in the same jobs. Moreover, the number of African-Americans enrolling in the nation's undergraduate and graduate schools was extremely low. Affirmative action became a vehicle to correct this injustice. The original intent of affirmative action was not to provide jobs and other advantages to blacks solely because of the color of their skin, but to provide economic opportunities for those who are competent and qualified. Due to a history of discrimination, even those with outstanding credentials were often locked out. As the years wore on, it was deemed necessary to add other minorities—such as Native Americans, Hispanics, and Asian-Americans—as well as women to the list of those requiring affirmative action in order to achieve a measure of economic justice.

A number of conservatives—black and white—such as Armstrong Williams, Linda Chavez, Patrick Buchanan, Robert Novak, Ward Connerly, Clarence Thomas, Clint Bolick, Alan Keyes, and others argue that it is time to scrap affirmative action. This is necessary, they maintain, if the country is truly going to become a color-blind society like King envisioned. People would be judged by the content of their character, not by the color of their skin. Many among these conservatives also maintain that affirmative action is destructive to minorities because it is demeaning, saps drive, and leads to the development of a welfare dependency mentality. Minorities often come to believe that something is owed them.

Thus, conservatives argue against race-based admissions requirements to undergraduate and graduate schools, labeling them preferential treatment and an insult to anyone who is the beneficiary of this practice. In their opinion, it is psychologically, emotionally, and personally degrading for individuals to have to go through life realizing they were not admitted to school or given employment because of their credentials, but in order to fill some quota or to satisfy appearances. It is rather ironic, however, that they are so concerned about this apparent harm to black self-esteem, since there is little evidence that those who have been aided by affirmative action policies feel many doubts or misgivings. The vast majority of them believe they are entitled to whatever opportunities they have received—opportunities, in their estimation, which are long overdue because of racism and discrimination. Consequently, America is only providing them with a few economic crumbs which are rightfully theirs.

Although a number of affirmative action critics argue that lowering admissions standards for minorities creates a class of incompetent professionals—if they are somehow fortunate enough to graduate—the facts run counter to their arguments. For instance, a study conducted by Robert C. Davidson and Ernest L. Lewis of affirmative action students admitted to the University of California at Davis Medical School with low grades and test scores concluded that these students became doctors just as qualified as the higher-scoring applicants. The graduation rate of 94% for special-admissions students compared favorably to that of regular-admissions students (98%). Moreover, despite the fact that regular-admissions students were more likely to receive honors or A grades, there was no difference in the rates at which students failed core courses.

Many whites have been the recipients of some form of preferential treatment. For many years, so-called selective colleges have set less-demanding standards for admitting offspring of alumni or the children of the rich and famous. For example, though former Vice Pres. Dan Quayle's grade-point average was minuscule and his score on the LSAT very low, he was admitted to Indiana University's Law School. There is little evidence that Quayle or other recipients of this practice have developed low self-esteem or have felt any remorse for those whose credentials were better, but nonetheless were rejected because less-qualified others took their slots. The following example further underscores this practice. A number of opponents of affirmative action were embarrassed during 1996 in the midst of passage of Proposition 209, which eliminated affirmative action in California, when the *Los Angeles Times* broke a story documenting the fact that many of them and their children had received preferential treatment in acquiring certain jobs and gaining entry to some colleges.

Some opponents of affirmative action go so far as to suggest that it aggravates racial tensions and leads, in essence, to an increase in violence between whites and people of color. This simply does not mesh with historical reality. Discrimination against and violence toward the powerless always has increased during periods of economic downturns, as witnessed by the depressions of 1873 and 1893. There was nothing akin to affirmative action in this country for nearly two centuries of its existence, yet African-American women were physically and sexually assaulted by whites, and people of color were brutalized, murdered, and lynched on an unprecedented scale. Moreover, there were so many race riots in the summer of 1919 that the author of the black national anthem, James Weldon Johnson, referred to it as "the red summer." The 1920s witnessed the reemergence of a reinvigorated Ku Klux Klan. Many state politicians even went public with their memberships, and the governor of Indiana during this period was an avowed member of the Klan. The 1930s and 1940s did not bring much relief, as attested to by several race riots and Pres. Franklin D. Roosevelt's refusal to promote an anti-lynching bill.

Some of the African-American critics of affirmative action have actually been beneficiaries of such a program. It is unlikely that Clarence Thomas would have been able to attend Yale University Law School or become a justice on the U.S. Supreme Court without affirmative action. Yet, Thomas hates it with a passion, once saying he would be violating "God's law" if he ever signed his name to an opinion that approved the use of race—even for benign reasons—in hiring or admissions.

Opponents of affirmative action from various racial and ethnic backgrounds argue that it may lead to reverse discrimination, whereby qualified whites fail to acquire admission to school, secure employment, or are fired because of their race since prospective slots have to be preserved solely for minorities. It is difficult to say with any degree of certainty how many whites may have been bypassed or displaced because preferences have been given to blacks and other minorities. What can be said, though, with a large measure of accuracy is that whites have not lost ground in medicine and college teaching, despite considerable efforts to open up those fields. In addition, contrary to popular myth, there is little need for talented and successful advertising executives, lawyers, physicians, engineers, accountants, college professors, movie executives, chemists, physicists, airline pilots, architects, etc. to fear minority preference. Whites who lose out are more generally blue-collar workers or persons at lower administrative levels, whose skills are not greatly in demand.

Furthermore, some whites who are passed over for promotion under these circumstances may simply not be viewed as the best person available for the job. It is human nature that those not receiving promotions that go to minorities or not gaining admission to colleges and universities prefer to believe that they have been discriminated against. They refuse to consider the possibility that the minorities could be better qualified. Although some highly qualified white students may be rejected by the University of California at Berkeley, Duke, Yale, Harvard, Stanford, or Princeton, the same students often are offered slots at Brown, Dartmouth, Cornell, Columbia, Michigan, the University of Pennsylvania, and the University of North Carolina at Chapel Hill—all first-rate institutions of higher learning.

Although some white women have been the victims of affirmative action, females, for the most part, arguably have been the largest beneficiaries of it. Over the last quarter-century, their numbers have increased dramatically in such fields as law, medicine, accounting, engineering, broadcasting, architecture, higher education, etc. Nonetheless, many white women vehemently have attacked affirmative action. For example, according to an ABC News poll taken in November, 1996, 52% of white women in California voted to support Proposition 209, which sought to eliminate racial and gender preferences in hiring, college admissions, and Federal contracts. What explains this behavior?

White women believe affirmative action is denying their sons admission to some schools and taking jobs away from their sons and husbands. Many worry about the psychological and emotional toll this could have on their loved ones. In fact, a bipartisan Federal panel found in 1995 that white men hold 95% of the nation's top management jobs although they represent just 43% of the workforce. It thus is apparent that much ground still has to be covered in terms of providing adequate economic opportunities for minorities. Yet, when most critics of affirmative action who favor destroying it are asked the question of what they would replace it with, they are silent.

Tangible Benefits

Affirmative action has produced some tangible benefits for the nation as a whole. As a result of it, the number of minorities attending and receiving degrees from colleges and universities rose in the 1970s and 1980s. This led to an increase in the size of the African-American middle class. An attainment of higher levels of education, as well as affirmative action policies in hiring, helped blacks gain access to some professions that earlier had been virtually closed to them. For instance, it traditionally had been nearly impossible for African-Americans and other minorities to receive professorships at predominantly white schools. Some departments at these schools actively began to recruit and hire minority faculty as their campuses became more diverse.

As expected, African-American, Hispanic, Native American, and Asian-American students demanded that not only should more minority faculty be hired, but that the curriculum be expanded to include courses that deal with the cultural and historical experiences of their past. Some school administrators granted their demands, which has borne fruit in a number of ways. First, given the fact that the U.S. is steadily becoming even more multicultural, it is imperative that Americans learn about and develop an appreciation and respect for various cultures. This could enable those who plan to teach students from several different racial, cultural, and ethnic backgrounds in the public school system to approach their jobs with more sensitivity and understanding. Second, it is often crucial for minority faculty to act as role models, particularly on white campuses. Third, white students could profit by being taught by professors of color. Since a white skin provides everyday advantages, having to face people of color in positions of authority may awaken some whites to realities about themselves and their society they previously have failed to recognize. It also might become obvious to them that certain racial stereotypes fly out of the window in light of intellectual exchanges with professors and peers of color.

Since education is crucial to acquiring economic advancement, it is of paramount importance that as many educational opportunities as possible be extended to the nation's minorities, which many studies indicate will total 50% of the population by 2050. Although much more is needed than affirmative action in order for minorities to gain the necessary access to higher levels of education and hiring, it nevertheless is the best mechanism to ensure at least a small measure of success in this regard. However, it currently is under attack in the areas of higher education, hiring, and Federal contracts. Now is the perfect time to find ways of improving affirmative action, rather than developing strategies aimed at destroying it.

Although a large number of minorities were attending and graduating from colleges and universities in the 1970s and 1980s, this trend had subsided by the 1990s. Tougher admission requirements, rising college costs, cutbacks of scholarships and fellowships or their direct elimination, as well as a reduction of grants and loans to students are contributing factors. Budgetary cuts have had a devastating effect on faculty in general, and minority faculty in particular, since they are often the first to be released from jobs. At a time when tenure and promotion are difficult to attain for most academics, it is almost impossible for some minority faculty.

Indeed, the attack on affirmative action is real. In California, without a commitment to affirmative action, the number of black students has dipped sharply. Applications from "underrepresented" minorities in 1997 on the nine campuses of the University of California dropped five percent, while overall applications rose 2.6%. The losses were even more dramatic at Ues Boalt Hall Law School, where admissions of African-Americans dropped 81% and Hispanics 50%. What are the implications of this for the nation? Certainly there will not be as many choices or opportunities for students and employers who have learned the value of a diverse workforce. This onslaught is contributing to the creation of an atmosphere in which many whites feel comfortable making racially derogatory remarks they would not have dared make a few years ago. For example, a University of Texas law professor remarked that "Blacks and Mexican-Americans are not academically competitive with whites in selective institutions. It is the result primarily of cultural effects. They have a culture that seems not to encourage achievement. Failure is not looked upon with disgrace."

Impact

Three questions beg answering in this racially charged environment: What impact will the attack on affirmative action have on the recruitment of minority student-athletes? Will they eventually be subjected to the same rigorous admissions standards as other students? Even if they are not, will they continue to enroll in large numbers at predominantly white state-supported colleges and universities with steadily decreasing numbers of minority students and faculty? Since minority athletes bring millions of dollars to schools, which, in turn, are used to subsidize the education of whites, I seriously doubt that tougher admission standards will be applied to them so rigorously that they eventually will be driven away from these schools. Administrators could not afford to lose millions of dollars.

Let's for a second imagine what would happen to state colleges that tried to recruit minority athletes to their campuses if they were all white in terms of faculty and student body. Those schools would have a difficult time convincing them to come. Furthermore, private schools not subjected to the same admission requirements would be all too happy to offer minority athletes lucrative financial aid packages.

Many industries began downsizing in the late 1980s and the practice has continued in the 1990s, helping to reverse some of the earlier gains made by minorities. With American society steadily becoming even more multicultural, it makes good business sense to have a workforce that is reflective of this development. In order to make this a reality, affirmative action policies need to be kept in place, not abandoned. Why not use the expertise of African-Americans to target African-American audiences for business purposes or Asian-Americans to tap into potential Asian-American consumers? Businessmen who believe minorities will purchase products as readily from all-white companies as those which are perceived as diverse are seriously misguided.

A diverse workforce also can yield huge economic dividends in the international business sector, as became obvious in 1996 to Republicans who hoped to increase their majority in Congress and ride into the White House by attacking affirmative action policies in hiring. Rep. Dan Burton of Indiana, Speaker of the House Newt Gingrich, and presidential candidate Bob Dole, to name a few, applied pressure on businesses to end affirmative action policies in hiring. Executives informed them that this would be bad business and that the losses in revenue potentially would be staggering. In addition, it would be foolish public relations and substantially would reduce the pool of fine applicants. For the time being, the Republicans eased off.

A diverse workforce in a multicultural society makes practical and ethical sense. With all of the problems that need to be solved—such as disease, hunger, poverty, homelessness, lack of health care, racism, anti-Semitism, sexism, teenage pregnancy, crime, drugs, etc.—why should anyone's input be limited because of sex, race, color, class, or ethnic background? All Americans should be working together in this endeavor. It can best be accomplished by creating a truly diverse workforce through a continuation of affirmative action policies.

In spite of the fact that affirmative action has helped some African-Americans and other minorities achieve a middle-class status, not all have witnessed a significant improvement in their economic condition. For the most part, it has only helped the last generation of minorities. In order to make a significant impact, affirmative action policies need to be in place for several generations. Between 1970 and 1992, the median income for white families, computed in constant dollars, rose from $34,773 to $38,909, an increase of 11.9%. Black family income declined during this period, from $21,330 to $21,162. In relative terms, black incomes dropped from $613 to $544 for each $1,000 received by whites. Moreover, in 1992, black men with bachelor's degrees made $764 for each $1,000 received by white men with such degrees, and black males with master's degrees earned $870 for each $1,000 their white counterparts earned. Overall, black men received $721 for every $1,000 earned by white men.

Even more depressing for blacks is the fact that unemployment rates for them have remained at double-digit levels since 1975, averaging 14.9% for the 1980s, while the average was 6.3% for whites. The number of black children living below the poverty line reached 46.3% by 1992, compared to 12.3% of white children. At the same time, the overall poverty rate among Hispanics increased to 28.2%. Even in professions where blacks made breakthroughs by the early 1990s, they remained underrepresented. This was the case in engineering, law, medicine, dentistry, architecture, and higher education. Although blacks represented 10.2% of the workforce in 1992, they constituted just 3.7% of engineers, 2.7% of dentists, 3.1% of architects, and held 4.8% of university faculty positions.

Furthermore, while 27,713 doctoral degrees were awarded in 1992 to U.S. citizens and aliens who indicated their intention is to remain in America, 1,081, or 3.9%, of these doctorates went to blacks. Given the low percentage of African-Americans receiving doctoral degrees, most college departments in all likelihood will find it difficult to recruit black faculty. With the hatchet steadily chopping affirmative action programs, this may become virtually impossible in the near future. The same holds true for other professions.

The most feasible way to ensure that colleges, universities, and various occupations will not become lily-white again is by the continuation of affirmative action. It gives minority groups that traditionally have been locked out of the education system and the workforce the best opportunity to carve out a solid economic foundation in America. I agree with Pres. Clinton, who said, "Don't end it; mend it."

America has had over 200 years to deliver true justice, freedom, and equality to women and people of color. To believe that it now will make good the promise of equality without some kind of legislation to assist it is to engage in fantasy.

In advocating for affirmative action policies, people of color are not looking for government handouts. They merely are asking that some mechanism be kept in place to help provide the same social and economic opportunities most whites have had and continue to have access to.

POSTSCRIPT

Has Affirmative Action Outlived Its Usefulness in the Workplace?

In the 1960s, America was a society polarized across racial lines. Dr. Martin Luther King, in his famous "I have a dream" speech, presented his vision of an American society where skin color plays no role in securing economic and social opportunities. His hope was that harmony between the races would be possible if all were afforded the same opportunities to succeed. And, although he did not live long enough to see its emergence, there can be no doubt that King's civil rights activities helped pave the way for the development of affirmative action as an important vehicle for promoting a more diverse American workplace. But in a cruel twist of fate, it seems that affirmative action has given rise to the very scenario it was intended to alleviate. As Dr. Williams noted in his article, affirmative action can cause resentment and polarization between the races. Consider these comments from Dr. Onkar Ghate, a widely respected resident fellow at the influential Libertarian think tank, the Ayn Rand Institute: "The consequence of the spread of racial quotas [i.e., affirmative action] and multiculturalist ideas hasn't been harmony, but a precipitous rise in racial hatred throughout America, particularly in the classroom and the workplace."

Dr. Wilbert Jenkins disputes this viewpoint in his article. He points out that if affirmative action is applied in the manner and spirit in which it was originally intended, there need be no discrimination. He argues that employers have the right to demand that job applicants, for example, be at least minimally qualified before they are considered for the job. If no protected class members are qualified, then so be it; the employer can hire all the white males he wants and not be guilty of discrimination. However, under affirmative action, if there is a qualified protected class member in the applicant pool, the employer should select that individual for the position. In this instance, failing to do so constitutes discrimination whereas selecting the protected class member does not.

Suggested Readings

Affirmative Action and Diversity Project, The affirmative action and diversity project: A webpage for research, 2004. http://aad.english.ucsb.edu/

Dinesh D'Souza, The end of racism. *Free Press,* 1995.

Joe R. Feagin and Hernan Vera, White racism: The basics. *Routledge,* 1995.

Marie Gryphon, The affirmative action myth. *The Cato Institute,* July 10, 2004. http://www.cato.org/dailys/07-10-04.html

Edwin A. Locke, What we should remember on Martin Luther King day. *The Ayn Rand Institute,* January 14, 2002. http://www.aynrand.org/site/News2?page=NewsArticle&id=7903&news_iv_ctrl=1076

News press release, MLK Day: King's colorblind dream is being destroyed. *The Ayn Rand Institute,* January 10, 2001. http://www.aynrand.org/site/News2?page=NewsArticle&id=7637&news_iv_ctrl=1221

Philip F. Rubio, *A History of Affirmative Action.* University Press of Mississippi, 2001.

ISSUE 7

Is the Control of Drug Abuse in the Workplace More Important than Protecting Employee Privacy?

YES: Michael A. Verespej, from "Drug Users—Not Testing—Anger Workers," *Industry Week* (February 17, 1992)

NO: Jennifer Moore, from "Drug Testing and Corporate Responsibility: The 'Ought Implies Can' Argument," *Journal of Business Ethics* (vol. 8, 1989)

ISSUE SUMMARY

YES: Michael Verespej notes that for many employees, it is the drug users who are problematic, not the testing. He points out that both employees and managers are becoming increasingly intolerant of drugs in the workplace and, as a result, actually welcome drug testing.

NO: Scholar Jennifer Moore presents a philosophical discussion of why the individual rights of the employee trump the corporation's right to protect itself. In so doing, she reaches the conclusion that drug testing cannot be justified as a legitimate corporate policy.

Drug abuse in the United States is a major social problem and one that is not likely to be solved any time soon. In the workplace, substance abuse costs employers tens of millions of dollars every year as a result of the increased levels of absenteeism, work-related accidents, health care costs, and theft. The U.S. Department of Labor reports that 70 percent of illegal drug users are employed, a number exceeding 10 million workforce members (Robert L. Mathis and John H. Jackson, *Human Resource Management,* Thompson South-Western Publishers, 2003, p. 527). It's not surprising, then, that employers across the country have adopted various types of drug-testing policies as a way of fighting back. The federal government entered the battle with the passage of the Drug-free Workplace Act of 1988. This act requires all government agencies and firms with governmental contracts to take action toward eliminating drugs from the workplace.

Despite society's apparent acceptance of drug testing at work, firms need to be acutely aware of the threat it poses to employee privacy. Critics of workplace drug testing fear that it infringes on employee rights and, therefore, should not be allowed. On the other hand, corporations have a right to protect themselves.

Responses to this topic have generally fallen into one of three categories and can be thought of as comprising a continuum of viewpoints: At one end are those who are against drug testing in the workplace under any and all circumstances. They typically invoke a rights-based argument, contending that individual rights always trump organizational rights. America is a country founded on the belief in the supremacy of individual rights and, since drug testing violates an individual's right to privacy, organizations should not be allowed to implement them under any conditions.

At the opposite end of our continuum reside the pro-testing advocates. The view here is that organizations, often owners of private property and as much legal citizens as are individuals, have a right to protect themselves. Inasmuch as they can be held accountable for the moral and legal violations committed by their employees, they should be allowed to exercise reasonable control over the workplace. Given the tremendous damage drug abuse can cause an organization, drug testing is clearly a reasonable activity.

Perhaps the most commonly accepted view, representing the midpoint of our continuum, is that corporations should hold employee privacy as an important corporate principle. Testing can be done, but all effort should be made to protect employee privacy throughout the process, and it should be implemented only in cases with reasonable grounds for suspicion. Thus, determining employee drug use is fair game only when there is evidence that it results in undesirable behaviors such as lower productivity or increasing the likelihood of safety violations.

Before you read the following articles and develop your own opinion, some facts should be presented. It is important to know that the courts have consistently sided with the rights of corporations to test employees provided there was no evidence of discrimination in its implementation nor unwarranted targeting of individuals for testing. Courts have been particularly supportive of drug testing when the job in question is of a sensitive nature. The legality of workplace drug testing accounts in large measure for its widespread use by employers. Recent surveys of major American corporations indicate that nearly 90 percent of the firms use some form of drug testing in the workplace. Almost all firms surveyed use the tests as part of the applicant process and eliminate from consideration those individuals who failed (George Gray and Darrel Brown in Laura P. Hartman, ed., *Perspectives in Business Ethics,* 2nd ed., McGraw-Hill, 2002, p. 433.) Thus, workplace drug testing is both legal and widespread. But the question remains, does that make it right?

Michael Verespej, writing in *Industry Week* magazine, notes that for many employees it is the drug users who are problematic, not the testing. He points out that employees and managers are becoming fed up with drugs in the workplace and actually welcome drug testing. On the other side of the debate, business ethics scholar Jennifer Moore presents a philosophical discussion of why the individual rights of the employee trump the corporation's right to protect itself. And though she stops short of saying that there are no circumstances under which firms should be allowed to drug test, her conclusion is that drug testing cannot be justified as a legitimate corporate policy.

Michael A. Verespej  **YES**

Drug Users—Not Testing—
Anger Workers

Drug testing by companies still elicits an emotional response from employees. But it's a far different one from four years ago.

Back then, readers responding to an IW [*Industry Week*] survey angrily protested workplace drug testing as an invasion of privacy and argued that drug testing should be reserved for occasions in which there was suspicion of drug use or in an accident investigation.

Today's prevailing view, based on a recent IW survey covering essentially the same questions, stands as a stark contrast. Not only do fewer employees see drug testing as an invasion of privacy, but a significantly higher percentage think that companies should extend the scope of drug testing to improve safety and productivity in the workplace.

Why aren't employees as leery of workplace drug testing as they were four years ago?

First, both the numbers and the comments suggest that employees and managers are less worried that inaccurate drug tests will brand them as drug users. Just 19.3% of those surveyed say that they consider drug testing an invasion of privacy, compared with 30% in the earlier survey.

Second, the tight job market appears to have made non-drug-users resent the presence of drug users in the workplace. Third, in contrast to four years ago, employees and managers are more concerned about the potential safety problems that drug users cause them than whatever invasion of privacy might result from a drug test. The net result: Unlike four years ago, employee thinking is now in sync with the viewpoints held for some time by top corporate management. "Job safety and performance are more important than the slight invasion of privacy caused by drug testing," asserts Lee Taylor, plant manager at U.S. Gypsum Co.'s Siguard, Utah, facility. "Freedom and privacy end when others are likely to be injured," adds the president of a high-tech business in Fort Collins, Colo.

G. A. Holland, chief estimator for a Bloomfield, Conn., construction firm, agrees: "Drug testing may be an invasion of privacy, but, because drug use puts others in danger, [drug testing] is an acceptable practice. The safety of employees overrides the right to privacy of another." Adds D. S. McRoberts, manager of a

Green Giant food-processing plant in Buhl, Idaho: "The risks employees put themselves and their peers under when they use drugs justify testing."

Perhaps the most blunt response comes from Louis Krivanek, a consulting engineer with Omega Induction Services, Warren, Mich.: "I certainly wouldn't ride with a drinking alcoholic. Why should I work with a drug addict not under control?"

And the anti-drug-user attitude is not just a safety issue, either. "Drug users are also a financial risk to the employer," declares John Larkin, president of Overland Computer, Omaha, Nebr. "It's time to begin thinking about the health and welfare of the company," says William Pence, vice president and general manager of Kantronics Inc., Lawrence, Kans. "Drug testing is simply a preventive measure to ensure the future stability of a company."

The competitive factor also appears to be influencing workers' viewpoints. "A drug-free environment must exist if the quality of product and process is to be continuously improved," writes one employee.

"Productivity and company survival are too important to trust to an employee with a drug problem," says Jack VerMeulen, director of quality assurance at C-Line Products, Des Plaines, Ill. "Employees are a company's most valuable assets, and those assets must perform at the peak of their ability. Test them." One could argue that workers—and managers—have simply become conditioned to drug testing in the workplace because it is no longer the exception, but the rule. After all, 56% of the managers responding to the survey—twice as many as four years ago—say their companies have drug-testing programs in place.

But the real reason for the change in opinion appears to be that four years of day-in, day-out experience with workplace drug problems have made managers and employees less tolerant of users. The attitude appears to be: Drug users are criminals and shouldn't be protected by the absence of a drug-testing program.

"Users are, by definition, criminals," declares Nick Benson, senior automation engineer at Babcock & Wilcox, Lynchburg, Va. "Drug users are breaking the law," states Naomi Walter, a data-processing specialist at Gemini Marketing Associates, Carthage, Mo. "So why let them get an advantage?"

Layoffs and plant and store closings are also behind the new lack of tolerance for the drug user. "I believe that if a company is paying a person to work for them," says one IW reader, "that person should be drug-free. A job is a privilege, not a right."

⋯◉⋯

That lack of tolerance is reflected in significantly changed ideas of who in the workplace should be tested for drug use. A significantly higher percentage of respondents think that more workers should be tested at random or that *all* employees should be tested.

More than 45% of IW readers—compared with 29.6% four years ago—say that drug tests should be conducted at random. And 70.5% think all employees should be required to take drug tests. Only 60% felt that way in the last IW drug-testing survey. Not surprisingly, then, the percentage of readers who would take a drug test and who think that employers should be able to test employees for drug use is now 93%; it was 88% four years ago.

But several attitudes haven't changed. Workers and managers still think that when companies use drug testing, they should be required to offer rehabilitation through employee-assistance programs, that management should be tested as well as employees, and that alcohol problems are equally troublesome. "Employers should be prepared to help—not just fire someone if the drug or alcohol abuse is exposed," says H. A. Dellicker, programming manager at Siemens Nixdorf, Burlington, Mass. "You need a properly monitored rehabilitation program."

Readers are just as adamant that if the majority of employees is to be tested, then everyone should be included—all the way up to the CEO. "Drug testing should be conducted on all employees, from top management down to the lowest position," asserts Sharon Hyitt, a drafting technician at Varco Pruden Buildings, Van Wert, Ohio. And IW readers contend that any drug-testing program should test for alcohol abuse as well. "Drug testing stops short," argues a reader in Muncie, Ind. "Alcoholism is more widespread in our workplace and just as destructive."

A plant superintendent in Ohio agrees and laments, "Alcohol is the most abused drug in our workplace, but it is not covered under our testing program. While the 'heavy' drugs get the spotlight because of the violence associated with their distribution, alcohol does the most damage in the workplace."

A product-testing engineer agrees, "Alcohol should be included in the tests and then perhaps lunch-time drinking would decrease. Why is it O.K. for those who have three-martini lunches to come back to work and try to function?"

NO

Jennifer Moore

Drug Testing and Corporate Responsibility: The "Ought Implies Can" Argument

In the past few years, testing for drug use in the workplace has become an important and controversial trend. Approximately 30% of Fortune 500 companies now engage in some sort of drug testing or screening, as do many smaller firms. The Reagan administration has called for mandatory testing of all federal employees. Several states have already passed drug testing laws; others will probably consider them in the future. While the Supreme Court has announced its intention to rule on the testing of federal employees within the next few months, its decision will not settle the permissibility of testing private employees. Discussion of the issue is likely to remain lively and heated for some time.

Most of the debate about drug testing in the workplace has focused on the issue of privacy rights. Three key questions have been: Do employees have privacy rights? If so, how far do these extend? What kinds of considerations outweigh these rights? I believe there are good reasons for supposing that employees do have moral privacy rights,[1] and that drug testing usually (though not always) violates these, but privacy is not my main concern in this paper. I wish to examine a different kind of argument, the claim that because corporations are responsible for harms committed by employees while under the influence of drugs, they are entitled to test for drug use.

This argument is rarely stated formally in the literature, but it can be found informally quite often.[2] One of its chief advantages is that it seems, at least at first glance, to bypass the issue of privacy rights altogether. There seems to be no need to determine the extent or weight of employees' privacy rights to make the argument work. It turns on a different set of principles altogether, that is, on the meaning and conditions of responsibility. This is an important asset, since arguments about rights are notoriously difficult to settle. Rights claims frequently function in ethical discourse as conversation-stoppers or non-negotiable demands.[3] Although it is widely recognized that rights are not absolute, there is little consensus on how far they extend, what kinds of considerations should be allowed to override them, or even how to go about settling these questions. But it is precisely these thorny problems that proponents of drug testing must tackle

From *Journal of Business Ethics*, Vol. 8, 1989. Copyright © 1989R by Kluwer Academic Journals. Reprinted by permission.

if they wish to address the issue on privacy grounds. Faced with the claim that drug testing violates the moral right to privacy of employees, proponents of testing must either (1) argue that drug testing does not really violate the privacy rights of employees;[4] (2) acknowledge that drug testing violates privacy rights, but argue that there are considerations that override those rights, such as public safety; or (3) argue that employees have no moral right to privacy at all.[5] It is not surprising that an argument that seems to move the debate out of the arena of privacy rights entirely appears attractive.

In spite of its initial appeal, however, I will maintain that the argument does not succeed in circumventing the claims of privacy rights. Even responsibility for the actions of others, I will argue, does not entitle us to do absolutely anything to control their behavior. We must look to rights, among other things, to determine what sorts of controls are morally permissible. Once this is acknowledged, the argument loses much of its force. In addition, it requires unjustified assumptions about the connection between drug testing and the prevention of drug-related harm.

An "Ought Implies Can" Argument

Before we can assess the argument, it must be set out more fully. It seems to turn on the deep-rooted philosophical connection between responsibility and control. Generally, we believe that agents are not responsible[6] for acts or events that they could not have prevented. People are responsible for their actions only if, it is often said, they "could have done otherwise." Responsibility implies some measure of control, freedom, or autonomy. It is for this reason that we do not hold the insane responsible for their actions. Showing that a person lacked the capacity to do otherwise blocks the normal moves of praise or blame and absolves the agent of responsibility for a given act.

For similar reasons, we believe that persons cannot be obligated to do things that they are incapable of doing, and that if they fail to do such things, no blame attaches to them. Obligation is empty, even senseless, without capability. If a person is obligated to perform an action, it must be within his or her power. This principle is sometimes summed up by the phrase "ought implies can." Kant used it as part of a metaphysical argument for free will, claiming that if persons are to have obligations at all, they must be autonomous, capable of acting freely.[7] The argument we examine here is narrower in scope, but similar in principle. If corporations are responsible for harms caused by employees under the influence of drugs, they must have the ability to prevent these harms. They must, therefore, have the freedom to test for drug use.

But the argument is still quite vague. What exactly does it mean to say that corporations are "responsible" for harms caused by employees? There are several possible meanings of "responsible." Not all of these are attributable to corporations, and not all of them exemplify the principle that "ought implies can." The question of how or whether corporations are "responsible" is highly complex, and we cannot begin to answer it in this paper.[8] There are, however, four distinct senses of "responsible" that appear with some regularity in the argument. They can be characterized, roughly, as follows: (a) legally liable; (b) culpable or guilty;

(c) answerable or accountable; (d) bound by an obligation. The first is purely legal; the last three have a moral dimension.

Legal Liability

We do hold corporations legally liable for the negligent acts of employees under the doctrine of *respondeat superior* ("let the master respond"). If an employee harms a third party in the course of performing his or her duties for the firm, it is the corporation which must compensate the third party. *Respondeat superior* is an example of what is frequently called "vicarious liability." Since the employee was acting on behalf of the firm, and the firm was acting through the employee when the harmful act was committed, liability is said to "transfer" from the employee to the firm. But it is not clear that such liability on the part of the employer implies a capacity to have prevented the harm. Corporations are held liable for accidents caused by an employee's negligent driving, for example, even if they could not have foreseen or prevented the injury. While some employee accidents can be traced to corporate negligence,[9] there need be no fault on the part of the corporation for the doctrine of *respondeat superior* to apply. The doctrine of *respondeat superior* is grounded not in fault, but in concerns of public policy and utility. It is one of several applications of the notion of liability without fault in legal use today.

Because it does not imply fault, and its attendant ability to have done otherwise, legal liability or responsibility **a** cannot be used successfully as part of an "ought implies can" argument. Holding corporations legally liable for harms committed by intoxicated employees while at the same time forbidding drug-testing is not inconsistent. It could simply be viewed as yet another instance of liability without fault. Of course, one could argue that the notion of liability without fault is itself morally unacceptable, and that liability ought not to be detached from moral notions of punishment and blame. This is surely an extremely important claim, but it is beyond the scope of this paper. The main point to be made here is that we must be able to attribute more than legal liability to corporations if we are to invoke the principle of "ought implies can." Corporations must be responsible in sense **b**, **c**, or **d**—that is, *morally* responsible—if the argument is to work.

Moral Responsibility

Are corporations morally responsible for harms committed by intoxicated employees? Perhaps the most frequently used notion of moral responsibility is sense **b**, what I have called "guilt" or "culpability."[10] I have in mind here the strongest notion of moral responsibility, the sense that is prevalent in criminal law. An agent is responsible for an act in this sense if the act can be imputed to him or her. An essential condition of imputability is the presence in the agent of an intention to commit the act, or *mens rea*.[11] But does an employer whose workers use drugs satisfy the *mens rea* requirement? The requirement probably would be satisfied if it could be shown that the firm intended the resulting harms, ordered its employees to work under the influence of drugs, or even, perhaps (though this is less clear) turned a blind eye to blatant drug abuse in the workplace.[12] But these are all quite farfetched possibilities. It is reasonable to assume that most corporations do not intend the harms caused by their employees, and that they do not order employees to use drugs on the job. Drug use is quite likely to be prohibited by company policy. If corporations are morally responsible for drug-related harms committed [by] employees, then, it is not in sense **b**.

Corporations might, however, be morally responsible for harms committed by employees in another sense. An organization acts through its employees. It empowers its employees to act in ways in which they otherwise would not act by providing them with money, power, equipment, and authority. Through a series of agreements, the corporation delegates its employees to act on its behalf. For these reasons, one could argue that corporations are responsible, in the sense of "answerable" or "accountable" (responsibility **c**), for the harmful acts of their employees. Indeed, it could be argued that if corporations are not morally responsible for these acts, they are not morally responsible for any acts at all, since corporations can only act through their employees.[13] To say that corporations are responsible for the harms of their employees in sense **c** is to say more than just that a corporation must "pay up" if an employee causes harm. It is to assign fault to the corporation by virtue of the ways in which organizational policies and structures facilitate and direct employees' actions.[14]

Moreover, corporations presumably have the same obligations as other agents to avoid harm in the conduct of their business. Since they conduct their business through their employees, it could plausibly be argued that corporations have an obligation to anticipate and prevent harms that employees might cause in the course of their employment. If this reasoning is correct, corporations are morally responsible for the drug-related harms of employees in sense **d**—that is, they are under an obligation to prevent those harms. The "ought implies can" argument, then, may be formulated as follows:

1. If corporations have obligations, they must be capable of carrying them out, on the principle of "ought implies can."
2. Corporations have an obligation to prevent harm from occurring in the course of conducting their business.
3. Drug use by employees is likely to lead to harm.
4. Corporations must be able to take steps to eliminate (or at least reduce) drug use by employees.
5. Drug testing is an effective way to eliminate/reduce employee drug use.
6. Therefore corporations must be permitted to test for drugs.[15]

The Limits of Corporate Autonomy

This is surely an important argument, one that deserves to be taken seriously. The premise that corporations have an obligation to prevent harm from occurring in the conduct of their business seems unexceptional and consistent with the actual moral beliefs of society. There is not much question that drug use by employees, especially regular drug use or drug use on the job, leads to harms of various kinds. Some of these are less serious than others, but some are very serious indeed: physical injury to consumers, the public, and fellow employees—and sometimes even death.[16]

Moreover, our convictions about the connections between responsibility or obligation and capability seem unassailable. Like other agents, if corporations are to have obligations, they must have the ability to carry them out. The argument seems to tell us that corporations are only able to carry out their obligations to prevent harm if they can free themselves of drugs. To prevent corporations from drug testing, it implies, is to prevent them from discharging their obligations. It is to cripple corporate autonomy just as we would cripple the autonomy of an individual worker if we refused to allow him to "kick the habit" that prevented him from giving satisfactory job performance.

But this analogy between corporate and individual autonomy reveals the initial defect in the argument. Unlike human beings, corporations are never fully autonomous selves. On the contrary, their actions are always dependent upon individual selves who are autonomous. Human autonomy means self-determination, self-governance, self-control. Corporate autonomy, at least as it is understood here, means control over others. Corporate autonomy is essentially derivative. But this means that corporate acts are not the simple sorts of acts generated by individual persons. They are complex. Most importantly, the members of a corporation are frequently not the agents, but the objects, of "corporate" action. A good deal of corporate action, that is, necessitates doing something not only *through* corporate employees, but *to* those employees.[17] The act of eliminating drugs from the workplace is an act of this sort. A corporation's ridding itself of drugs is not like an individual person's "kicking the habit." Rather, it is one group of persons making another group of persons give up drug use.

This fact has important implications for the "ought implies can" argument. The argument is persuasive in situations in which carrying out one's obligations requires only *self*-control, and does not involve controlling the behavior of others. Presumably there are no restrictions on what one may do to oneself in order to carry out an obligation.[18] But a corporation is not a genuine "self," and there *are* moral limits on what one person may do to another. Because this is so, we cannot automatically assume that the obligation to prevent harm justifies employee drug testing. Of course this does not necessarily mean that drug testing is *unjustified*. But it does mean that before we can determine whether it is justified, we must ask what is permissible for one person or group of persons to do to another to prevent a harm for which they are responsible.

Are there any analogies available that might help to resolve this question? It is becoming increasingly common to hold a hostess responsible (both legally and morally) for harm caused by a drunken guest on the way home from her party. In part, this is because she contributes to the harm by serving her guest alcohol. It is also because she knows that drunk driving is risky, and has a general obligation to prevent harm. What must she be allowed to do to prevent harms of this kind? Persuade the guest to spend the night on the couch? Surely. Take her car keys away from her? Perhaps. Knock her out and lock her in the bathroom until morning? Surely not.

Universities are occasionally held legally and morally responsible for harms committed by members of fraternities—destruction of property, gang rapes, and injuries or death caused by hazing. What may they do to prevent such harms? They may certainly withdraw institutional recognition and support from the fraternity, refusing to let it operate on the campus. But may they expel students who live together off-campus in fraternity-like arrangements? Have university security guards police these houses, covertly or by force? These questions are more difficult to answer.

We sometimes hold landlords morally (though not legally) responsible for tenants who are slovenly, play loud music, or otherwise make nuisances of themselves. Landlords are surely permitted to cancel the leases of such tenants, and they are justified in asking for references from previous landlords to prevent future problems of this kind. But it is not clear that a landlord may delve into a tenant's private life, search his room, or tap his telephone in order to anticipate trouble before it begins.

Each of these situations is one in which one person or group of persons is responsible, to a greater or a lesser degree, for the prevention of harm by others, and needs some measure of control in order to carry out this responsibility.[19] In each case, there is a fairly wide range of actions which we would be willing to allow the first party, but there are some actions which we would rule out. Having an obligation to prevent the harms of others seems to permit us some forms of control, but not all. At least one important consideration in deciding what kinds of actions are permissible is the *rights* of the controlled parties.[20] If these claims are correct, we must examine the rights of employees in order to determine whether drug testing is justified. The relevant right in the case of drug testing is the right to privacy. The "ought implies can" argument, then, does not circumvent the claims of privacy rights as it originally seemed to do.

The Agency Argument

A proponent of drug testing might argue, however, that the relation between employers and employees is significantly different from the relation between hosts and guests, universities and members of fraternities, or landlords and tenants. Employees have a special relation with the firm that employs them. They are *agents*, hired and empowered to act on behalf of the employer. While they act on the business of the firm, it might be argued, they "are" the corporation. The restrictions that apply to what one independent agent may do to another thus do not apply here.

But surely this argument is incorrect, for a number of reasons. First, if it were correct, it would justify anything a corporation might do to control the behavior of an employee—not merely drug testing, but polygraph testing, tapping of telephones, deception, psychological manipulation, whips and chains, etc.[21] There are undoubtedly some people who would argue that some of these procedures are permissible, but few would argue that all of them are. The fact that even some of them appear not to be suggests that we believe there are limits to what corporations may do to control employees, and that one consideration in determining these limits is the employees' rights.

Secondly, the argument implies that employees give up their own autonomy completely when they sign on as agents, and become an organ or piece of the corporation. But this cannot be true. Agency is a moral and contractual relationship of the kind that can only obtain between two independent, autonomous parties. This relationship could not be sustained if the employee ceased to be autonomous upon signing the contract. Employees are not slaves, but autonomous agents capable of upholding a contract. Moreover, we expect a certain amount of discretion in employees in the course of their agency. Employees are not expected to follow illegal or immoral commands of their employers, and we find them morally and legally blameworthy when they do so. That we expect such independent judgment of them suggests that they do not lose their autonomy entirely.[22]

Finally, if the employment contract were one in which employees gave up all right to be treated as autonomous human beings, then it would not be a legitimate or morally valid contract. Some rights are considered "inalienable"—people are forbidden from negotiating them away even if it seems advantageous to them to do so. The law grants recognition to this fact through anti-discrimination statutes, minimum wage legislation, workplace health and safety standards, etc. Even if I would like to, I may not trade away, for example, my right not to be sexually harassed or my right to know about workplace hazards.

Again, these arguments do not show that drug testing is unjustified. They do show, however, that *if* drug testing is justified, it is not because the "ought implies can" argument bypasses the issue of employee rights, but because drug testing does not impermissibly violate those rights.[23] To think that obligation, or responsibility for the acts of others, can circumvent rights claims is to misunderstand the import of the "ought implies can" principle. The principle tells us that there is a close connection between obligation or responsibility and capability. But it does not license us to disregard the rights of others any more than it guarantees us the physical conditions that make carrying out our obligations possible. It may well prove that employees' right to privacy, assuming they have such a right, is secondary to some more weighty consideration. I take up this question briefly below. What has been shown here is that the issue of the permissibility of drug testing will not and cannot be settled *without* a close scrutiny of privacy rights. If we are to decide the issue, we must eventually determine whether employees have privacy rights, how far they extend, and what considerations outweigh them—precisely the difficult questions the "ought implies can" argument sought to avoid.

Is Drug Testing Necessary?

The "ought implies can" argument also has another serious flaw. The argument turns on the claim that forbidding drug testing prevents corporations from carrying out their obligation to prevent harm. But this is only true if drug testing is *necessary* for preventing drug-related harm. If it is merely one option among many, then forbidding drug testing still leaves a corporation free to prevent harm in other ways. For the argument to be sound, in other words, premise 5 would have to be altered to read, "drug testing is a necessary element in any plan to rid the workplace of drugs."

But it is not at all clear that drug testing *is* necessary to reduce drug use in the workplace. Its necessity has been challenged repeatedly. In a recent article in the *Harvard Business Review*, for example, James Wrich draws on his experience in dealing with alcoholism in the workplace and suggests the use of broadbrush educational and rehabilitative programs as alternatives to testing. Corporations using such programs to combat alcohol problems, Wrich reports, have achieved tremendous reductions in absenteeism, sick leave, and on-the-job accidents.[24] Others have argued that impaired performance likely to result in harm could be easily detected by various sorts of performance-oriented tests—mental and physical dexterity tests, alertness tests, flight simulation tests, and so on. These sorts of procedures have the advantage of not being controversial from a rights perspective.[25]

Indeed, many thinkers have argued that drug testing is not only unnecessary, but is not even an effective way to attack drug use in the workplace. The commonly used and affordable urinalysis tests are notoriously unreliable. They have a very high rate both of false negatives and of false positives. At best the tests reveal, not impaired performance or even the presence of a particular drug, but the presence of metabolites of various drugs that can remain in the system long after any effects of the drug have worn off.[26] Because they do not measure impairment, such tests do not seem well-tailored to the purpose of preventing harm—which, after all, is the ultimate goal. As Lewis Maltby, vice president of a small instrumentation company and an opponent of drug testing, puts it,

> . . . [T]he fundamental flaw with drug testing is that it tests for the wrong thing. A realistic program to detect workers whose condition put the company or other people at risk would test for the condition that actually creates the danger.[27]

If these claims are true, there is no real connection between the obligation to prevent harm and the practice of drug testing, and the "ought implies can" argument provides no justification for drug testing at all.[28]

Conclusion

I have made no attempt here to determine whether drug testing does indeed violate employees' privacy rights. The analysis . . . above suggests that we have reason to believe that employees have some rights. Once we accept the notion of employee rights in general, it seems likely that a right to privacy would be among them, since it is an important civil right and central for the protection of individual autonomy. There are also reasons, I believe, to think that most drug testing violates the right to privacy. These claims need much more defense than they can be given here, and even if they are true, this does not necessarily mean that drug testing is unjustified. It does, however, create a *prima facie* case against drug testing. If drug testing violates the privacy rights of employees, it will be justified only under very strict conditions, if it is justified at all. It is worth taking a moment to see why this is so.

It is generally accepted in both the ethical and legal spheres that rights are not absolute. But we allow basic rights to be overridden only in special cases in which some urgent and fundamental good is at stake. In legal discourse, such goods are called "compelling interests."[29] While there is room for some debate about what counts as a "compelling interest," it is almost always understood to be more than a merely private interest, however weighty. Public safety might well fall into this category, but private monetary loss probably would not. While more needs to be done to determine what kinds of interests justify drug testing, it seems clear that if testing does violate the basic rights of employees, it is only justified in extreme cases—far less often than it is presently used. Moreover, we believe that overriding a right is to be avoided wherever possible, and is only justified when doing so is *necessary* to serve the "compelling interest" in question. If it violates rights, then drug testing is only permissible if it is necessary for the protection of an interest such as public safety and if there is no other, morally preferable, way of accomplishing the same goal. As we have seen above, however, it is by no means clear that drug testing meets these conditions. There may be better, less controversial ways to prevent the harm caused by drug use; if so, these must be used in preference to drug testing, and testing is unjustified. And if the attacks on the effectiveness of drug testing are correct, testing is not only unnecessary for the protection of public safety, but does not serve any "compelling interest" at all.

What do these conclusions tell us about the responsibility of employers for preventing harms caused by employees? If it is decided that drug testing is morally impermissible, then there can be no duty to use it to anticipate and prevent harms. Corporations who fail to use it cannot be blamed for doing so. They cannot have a moral obligation to do something morally impermissible. Moreover, if it turns out that there is no other effective way to prevent the harms caused by drug use, then it seems to me we may not hold employers morally responsible for those harms. This seems to me unlikely to be the case—there probably are other effective measures to control drug abuse in the workplace. But corporations can be held responsible only to the extent that they are permitted to act. It would not be inconsistent, however, to hold corporations legally liable for the harms caused by intoxicated employees under the doctrine of *respondeat superior,* even if drug testing is forbidden, for this kind of liability does not imply an ability to have done otherwise.

Notes

1. Employees do not, of course, have legal privacy rights, although the courts seem to be moving slowly in this direction. Opponents of testing usually claim that employees have *moral* rights to privacy, even if these have not been given legal recognition. See, for example, Joseph Des Jardins and Ronald Duska, "Drug Testing in Employment," in *Business Ethics: Readings and Cases in Corporate Morality,* 2nd edition, ed. W. M. Hoffman and J. M. Moore (McGraw-Hill, forthcoming).

2. See, for example, "Work-Place Privacy Issues and Employer Screening Policies," Richard Lehr and David Middlebrooks, *Employee Relations Law Journal* 11, 407. Lehr and Middlebrooks cite the argument as one of the chief justifications for drug testing used by employers. I have also encountered the argument frequently in discussion with students, colleagues, and managers.

3. Ronald Dworkin has referred to rights as moral "trumps." This kind of language tends to suggest that rights overwhelm all other considerations, so that when they are flourished, all that opponents can do is subside in silence. Rights are frequently asserted this way in everyday discourse, and in this sense rights claims tend to close, rather than open, the door to fruitful ethical dialogue.

4. In his article "Privacy, Polygraphs, and Work," *Business and Professional Ethics Journal* 1, Fall, 1981, 19, George Brenkert has developed the idea that my privacy is violated when some one acquires information about me that they are not entitled, by virtue of their relationship to me, to have. My mortgage company, for example, is entitled to know my credit history; a prospective sexual partner is entitled to know if I have any sexually transmitted diseases. Thus their knowledge of this information does not violate my privacy. One could argue that employers are similarly entitled to the information obtained by drug tests, and that drug testing does not violate privacy for this reason. A somewhat different move would be to argue that testing does not violate privacy because employees give their "consent" to . . . drug testing as part of the employment contract. For a sustained attack on these and other Type 1 arguments, see Joseph Des Jardins and Ronald Duska, "Drug Testing in Employment."

5. One might defend this position on the ground that the employer "owns" the job and is therefore entitled to place any conditions he wishes on obtaining or keeping it. The problem with this argument is that it seems to rule out *all* employee rights, including such basic ones as the right to organize and bargain collectively, or the right not to be discriminated against, which have solid legal as well as ethical grounding. It also implies that ownership overrides all other considerations, and it is not at all clear that this is true. One might take the position that by accepting a job, an employee has agreed to give up all his rights save those actually specified in the employment contract. But this makes the employment contract look like an agreement in which employees sell themselves and accept the status of things without rights. And it overlooks the fact that we believe there are some things ("inalienable" rights) that persons ought not to be permitted to bargain away. Alex Michalos has discussed some of the limitations of the employment contract in "The Loyal Agent's Argument," in *Ethical Theory and Business,* 2nd edition, ed. Tom L. Beauchamp and Norman E. Bowie (Englewood Cliffs, NJ: Prentice-Hall, 1983), p. 247.

6. The term "responsibility" is deliberately left ambiguous here. Several different meanings of it are examined below.

7. See Immanuel Kant, *Critique of Practical Reason,* trans. Lewis White Beck (Indianapolis: Bobbs-Merril, 1956), p. 30.

8. In this paper I have tried to avoid getting embroiled in the question of whether or not corporations are themselves "moral agents," which has been the question to dominate the corporate responsibility debate. The argument I offer here does, I believe, have important implications for the problem of corporate agency, but does not require me to take a stand on it here. I am content to have those who reject the notion of corporations as moral agents read my references to corporate responsibility as shorthand for some complex form of individual or group responsibility.

9. One example would be negligent hiring, which is an increasingly frequent cause of action against an employer. Employers can also be held negligent if they give orders that lead to harms that they ought to have foreseen. Domino's Pizza is now under suit because it encouraged its drivers to deliver pizzas as fast as possible, a policy that accident victims claim should have been expected to cause accidents.

10. This understanding of moral responsibility often seems to overshadow other notions. In an article on corporate responsibility, for example, Manuel Velasquez concludes that because corporations are not responsible in this sense, they are "not responsible for anything they do." "Why Corporations Are Not Responsible For Anything They Do," *Business and Professional Ethics Journal* 2, Spring, 1983, 1.

11. There is also an *actus reus* requirement for this type of responsibility—that is, the act must be traceable to the voluntary bodily movements of the agent. Obviously, corporations do not have bodies, but the people who work for them do. The

question, then, has become when may we call an act by onemember of the corporation a "corporate act." If it is possible to do so at all, the decisive feature is probably the presence of some sort of corporate "intention." This is why I focus on intention here, and why intention has been central to the discussion of corporate responsibility.

12. There are some, like Velasquez, who hold that a corporation can never satisfy the *mens rea* requirement because this would require a collective mind. If this were true, the argument would collapse at the outset. Others believe that a *mens rea* can be attributed to corporations metaphorically, if it can be shown that company policy includes an "intention" to harm, and it is this model I follow here.

13. There are, of course, those who take precisely this position. See Velasquez, "Why Corporations Are Not Responsible For Anything They Do."

14. See, for example, Peter French, *Collective and Corporate Responsibility* (New York: Columbia University Press, 1984).

15. It is tempting to conclude from this argument that drug testing is not only permissible, but obligatory, but this is not the case. The reason why it is not provides a clue to one of the major weaknesses of the argument. Drug testing would be obligatory only if it were *necessary* for the prevention of harm due to drug use, but it is not clear that this is so. But [it] also means that it is not clear that corporations are deflected from their duty to prevent harm by a prohibition against drug testing. See below for a fuller discussion of this problem.

16. For example, it has been claimed that employees who use drugs cause four times as many work-related accidents as do other employees. The highly publicized Conrail crash in 1987 was determined to be drug-related. Of course there are harms to the company itself as well, in the form of higher absenteeism, lowered productivity, higher insurance costs, etc. But since these types of harm raise the question of what a company may do to preserve its self-interest, rather than what it may do to prevent harms to others for which they are responsible, I focus here on harm to employees, consumers, and the public.

17. In our eagerness to assign "corporate responsibility," this fact has frequently been overlooked. This in turn has led, I believe, to an oversimplified view of corporate action. I discuss this problem more fully in a paper in progress entitled "The Paradox of Corporate Autonomy."

18. It is an interesting question whether there are limitations on what individuals can do to themselves to control their own behavior. What about individuals who undergo hypnosis, or who have their jaws wired shut in order to lose weight? Are they violating their own rights? Undermining their own autonomy? It could be argued plausibly that these kinds of things are not permissible, on the Kantian ground that we have a duty not to treat ourselves as merely as means to an end. Of course, if there are such restrictions, it makes the "ought implies can" argument as applied to corporations even weaker.

19. None of these analogies is perfect. In the case of the hostess and guest, for example, the guest is clearly intoxicated. This is rarely true of employees who are tested for drugs; if the employee were visibly intoxicated, there would be no need to test. Moreover, in the hostess/guest case the hostess contributes directly to the intoxication. There are important parallels, however. In each case one party is held morally (and in two of the cases, legally) responsible for harms caused by others. Moreover, the first parties are responsible in close to the same way that employers are responsible for the acts of their employees: they in some sense "facilitate" the harmful acts, they have some capacity to prevent those acts, and they are thus viewed as having an obligation to prevent them. One main difference, of course, is that employees are "agents" of their employers. . . .

20. There are other, utility-related considerations, as well—for example, harm to employees who are unjustly dismissed, a demoralized workforce, the costs of testing, etc. I concentrate here on rights because they have been the primary focal point in the drug testing debate.

21. The assumption here is that persons are entitled to do whatever they wish to themselves. See Note 18.

22. See Michalos, "The Loyal Agent's Argument."

23. Some violations of right, of course, are permissible. . . .

24. James T. Wrich, "Beyond Testing: Coping with Drugs at Work," *Harvard Business Review* Jan.–Feb. 1988, 120.

25. See Des Jardins and Duska, "Drug Testing in Employment," and Lewis Maltby, "Why Drug Testing is a Bad Idea," *Inc.* June 1987. While other sorts of tests also have the potential to be abused, they are at least a direct measurement of something that an employer is entitled to know—performance capability. Des Jardins and Duska offer an extended defense of this sort of test.

26. See Edward J. Imwinkelreid, "False Positive," *The Sciences,* Sept.–Oct. 1987, 22. Also David Bearman, "The Medical Case Against Drug Testing," *Harvard Business Review* Jan.–Feb. 1988, 123.

27. Maltby, "Why Drug Testing is a Bad Idea," pp. 152–153.

28. It could still be argued that drug testing *deters* drug use, and thus has a connection with preventing harm, even though it doesn't directly provide any information that enables companies to prevent harm. This is an important point, but it is still subject to the restrictions discussed in the previous section. Not everything that has a deterrent value is permissible. It is possible that a penalty of capital punishment would provide a deterrent for rapists, or having one's hand removed deter shoplifting, but there are very few advocates for these penalties. Effectiveness is not the only issue here; rights and justice are also relevant.

29. The principle that fundamental rights may not be overridden by the state unless doing so is necessary to serve a "compelling state interest" is a principle of constitutional law, but it also reflects our moral intuitions about when it is appropriate to override rights. The legal principle would not apply to all cases of drug testing in the workplace because many of these involve private, rather than state, employees. But the principle does provide us with useful guidelines in the ethical sphere. Interestingly, Federal District Judge George Revercomb recently issued an injunction blocking the random drug testing of Justice Department employees on the ground that it did not serve a compelling state interest. Since there was no evidence of a drug problem among the Department's employees, the Judge concluded, there is no threat that would give rise to a compelling interest. See "Judge Blocks Drug Testing of Justice Department Employees," *New York Times* July 30, 1988, 7.

POSTSCRIPT

Is the Control of Drug Abuse in the Workplace More Important than Protecting Employee Privacy?

Beyond the right-to-privacy argument, offered here in Jennifer Moore's articles, critics have raised a host of concerns about workplace drug testing. Foremost among these is the accuracy of the tests themselves. Critics point out that the repercussions from inaccurate test scores can be devastating not only to the specific individuals involved, but also to the rest of the workforce. Employee confidence in management's neutrality as well as the appropriateness of testing can be severely eroded if innocent individuals are punished or guilty employees go undetected. Testing also seems to send a message of distrust from management to employees regardless of whether such a perception is accurate. A second concern is the expense of drug testing. There is, of course, a cost/accuracy trade-off: Cheap tests are notoriously undependable, and highly accurate tests are extremely expensive. Small firms may have no choice but to use inexpensive tests while large firms with thousands of employees might find the costs to be excessive. Finally, critics express concern about the information obtained from the tests and the manner in which management uses it. The most common type of test is urine analysis, and the amount and type of information it yields is far greater than merely determining the presence of illegal drugs. An individual's medical history can be ascertained from a urine sample as well as determining her susceptibility to many costly health threats. Critics are concerned that employers will use the information to target employees for dismissal on grounds that are completely unrelated to job performance (Gollot, Cohen, & Fillman, 1990).

In defense of drug testing, Michael Verespej argues that in most instances, both management and employees are for testing. He suggests that it is usually those individuals who have a reason to fear drug tests who are the most vocal against their use. An important research study on this topic provides support for Verespej's contention: Human resource scholars found that students who had never used drugs were much more likely to support workplace drug testing programs than were students who had used drugs in the past (Murphy, Thornton, & Reynolds, 1990).

Suggested Readings

Jane Easter Bahls, Drugs in the workplace. *HR Magazine,* February 1998.

Michael A. Gips, Industry comment shapes drug testing rule. *Security Management,* March 2001.

Thomas Gollot, Mark Cohen, and Eric Fillman, Is employee drug testing the answer? *State Government News,* November 1990. The Council of State Governments.

George R. Gray and Darrel R. Brown, Issues in drug testing for the private sector, in *Perspectives in Business Ethics,* 2nd ed., Laura P. Hartman, editor. McGraw-Hill Irwin, 2002.

Robert L. Mathis and John H. Jackson, *Human Resource Management,* 10th ed. Thompson South-Western, 2003.

A. McBay, Legal challenges to testing hair for drugs: A review. *The International Journal of Drug Testing,* no. 1, 2000.

Kevin Murphy, George Thornton, and Douglas Reynolds, College students' attitudes toward employee drug testing programs. *Personnel Psychology,* 1990.

150

ISSUE 8

Does Workplace Diversity Result in a More Productive Firm?

YES: Mary F. Salomon and Joan M. Schork, from "Turn Diversity to Your Advantage," *Research Technology Management* (July/August 2003)

NO: Thomas Kochan et al., from "The Effects of Diversity on Business Performance: Report of the Diversity Research Network," *Human Resource Management* (Spring 2003)

ISSUE SUMMARY

YES: Mary Salomon and Joan Schork answered "yes" and provided a detailed argument built on the idea that there is a business case for diversity. During the course of their article, the authors consider several commonly accepted arguments supportive of workplace diversity.

NO: Researcher Thomas Kochan and his colleagues reported findings from their complex, sophisticated research project. Despite their initial expectations, the researchers failed to find support for the effects of diversity on performance and, thus, provided this issue with its "no" response.

The composition of the U.S. workforce has changed dramatically over the last few decades. Prior to 1980, for example, the typical employee in corporate America was a married, white male with children and a wife at home who did not work. Consider that now, in the workplace of 2004, such an individual is actually in the minority! Indeed, as management scholar Stephen Robbins notes (*Organizational Behavior*, Prentice Hall, 2003, p. 15), 47 percent of the current U.S. labor force are females, many of whom are childless and/or single, while minorities, at about 25 percent, represent the fastest growing demographic segment of the workforce. This tremendous increase in workplace diversity—Robbins defines the concept as the recognition that organizations are becoming increasingly heterogeneous in terms of race, gender, ethnicity, and other diverse groups of employees—raises important questions for managers and their organizations as we move farther into the twenty-first century.

In the "yes" article that follows this introduction, Mary Salomon and Joan Schork present what is known as "the business case" for diversity. In this article, the authors consider several commonly accepted arguments supportive of workplace diversity; here, we briefly preview three. The first involves the recognition that talent shortages can be addressed by embracing a willingness to actively recruit, hire, and train minorities and females. Another argument in support of workplace diversity is based on the notion that the wide range of cultural and personal differences characteristic of diverse groups results in improved decision making and increases in creativity that, presumably, result in higher levels of productivity. And lastly, the fact is that in today's business environment, firms are practically required to diversify their workforce. Legal mandates (i.e., civil rights acts, anti-discrimination legislation) and strong social pressures virtually condemn to failure those organizations that fail to engage in at least some minimal level of diversity-based initiatives. Regardless of intent, firms that maintain a homogenous workforce risk not only legal action, but also being labeled as socially irresponsible. Salomon and Schork discuss these and several other points while making their case that diversity results in positive outcomes including increased productivity.

The view that workplace diversity *does not* result in consistent, predictable gains in productivity represents the thesis of the "no" article. Many scholars have granted that while diversity at work may indeed be a desirable organizational goal, the pursuit of such a goal should not be based on expectations of productivity gains. Indeed, according to Thomas Kochan et al., the extant research on this issue has provided virtually no support for the view that diversity leads to increases in productivity. There appear to be three major factors accounting for the lack of support for the expected relationship between diversity and organizational performance. The first concerns the ease and effectiveness of communications among diverse members. Research on group communications has consistently shown that homogenous groups communicate more effectively and more efficiently than do heterogeneous groups. The second factor involves decision-making processes. Although diverse groups provide both greater numbers and more creative solutions to decision situations, achieving group consensus is much more difficult than it is in homogenous groups. In fact, some research suggests that the additional costs—usually in terms of time and money expenditures—incurred by diverse groups trying to reach consensus outweigh the benefits provided by their membership diversity. The final factor involves the overall complexity of conducting research on the relationship between diversity and productivity. Kochan and his co-authors acknowledge that previous research has failed to account for the complexity inherent in the issue and, therefore, may have missed proving a relationship between diversity and productivity. Thus, they hoped that by recognizing the complexity in the relationship and structuring their research project to account for it, they would be able to show that there is indeed a relationship between diversity and organizational performance. In a sense, then, Kochan et al. were actually trying to provide research evidence in support of the "yes" side of this debate. Keep this in mind as you read their article and ask yourself if the conclusions they reach ultimately provide more support for the no side of the issue or for the yes side.

Mary F. Salomon
and Joan M. Schork

 **YES**

Turn Diversity to Your Advantage

. . . Today, nearly every U.S. corporation has a policy on diversity. Most define diversity in broad terms: "all the unique talents and capabilities possessed by individuals in the workforce" (Dow Corning) or "all of the differences that we bring" (Agilent). As indicated by the Air Products Diversity Iceberg, diversity is much more than the clearly visible parameters of race, age and gender. It includes religion, education, sexual orientation, personality type, and a variety of other factors that may or may not be obvious at a first meeting. SC Johnson and others choose to depict the dimensions of diversity as a wheel, with organizational dimensions in the outer circle and internal or personal dimensions in the inner circle. Ultimately, it is the diversity of perspective and thought that will benefit the corporation. This diversity is accessed from a workforce that is diverse in all dimensions.

Two recent Industrial Research Institute meetings have focused on the benefits of a diverse R&D staff. The May 2001 meeting included a report on a survey of published business cases and a panel discussion on corporate views on diversity. At the May 2002 meeting, women managers and directors spoke on the link between innovation and diversity. This article is based on the presentations and discussions at these two meetings and provides a collection of thoughts, viewpoints and practices from a number of IRI member companies and their representatives. Specifically, we address three diversity topics:

- Business Drivers For Diversity—What are the business drivers for recruiting and retaining a diverse workforce?
- Challenges—What are the challenges that keep the numbers of women and minorities so low in our research organizations?
- Best Practices—What are the best practices for creating and sustaining a diverse workforce?

Business Drivers for Diversity

Published studies indicate better financial performance for companies that have been recognized for their focus on diversity. For example, the 50 companies recognized by Fortune Magazine in 1998 as the best places for racial minorities to work had a total five-year return to shareholders of 201 percent versus 171 percent for the S&P 500. A 1998 American Management Association study based on demographic profiles of 1,000 senior managers provided evidence that diversity in senior management leads to favorable long-term financial performance, finding that organizations with women on the senior management team out-performed those organizations with an all-male team. For example, between 1996 and 1997, companies with women on the senior management team showed a 76 percent increase in sales vs. 69 percent for companies with an all-male senior management team.

There is considerable published information on the business case for diversity. There is remarkable consistency among these publications, as well as the IRI panelists, on the primary business drivers for diversity. Three key drivers are universally given:

- Enhanced access to a broader talent pool.
- Improved innovation.
- Stronger customer relationships.

Three additional business drivers are frequently cited:

- Improved productivity.
- Increased speed and agility.
- No choice: being demanded by key stakeholders.

Access to a Broader Talent Pool

The ability to attract, retain and motivate talent from all over is critical to business success. A research organization that aspires to recruit the best and brightest employees cannot afford to ignore any portion of the talent pool. Organizations that restrict themselves to only selected talent pools are forced to recruit deeper into the pool, to lower talent levels.

Women are a talent pool that cannot be ignored since they represent half of the world's intellectual resources. IRI member companies report positive benefits from the presence of women on the R&D staff. Women often have strengths as integrators and as experts on parallel processing and multi-tasking. Women tend to be more comfortable in ambiguous situations, which can be important for "the fuzzy front end" of research. Women also tend to have a more collaborative approach and are more effective team builders. One IRI member company surveyed project managers in the United Kingdom and found that the women performed significantly better than the men in the important area of project management. A possible reason cited for the better performance was more cohesive teams under female leadership.

Improved Innovation

Several reasons are given for the connection between innovation and diversity. First, the heart of innovation is being "new" and "different." A culture or organization that is open to diversity or "differences" will provide a more fertile ground for the growth of new ideas than a culture or organization that is comfortable only with "sameness." Second, problem solving is improved by having a team with a diverse set of perspectives, experiences and training. There are many examples of creative solutions coming from unexpected quarters or resulting from the merger of two very different ideas.

Similarly, a diverse workforce improves the rate and quality of innovation. Creativity is often looking at something familiar and seeing something new. The more "different" the idea-generators are from the original inventors, the more likely they are to provide new perspectives. Additionally, the more ideas put on the table, the more likely it will be that a "big winner" will be found. IBM, for example, feels so strongly about the importance of a globally diverse workforce that it establishes research labs around the world, thereby gaining access to ideas that arise from people who experience different economies and cultures.

Finally, some of the most creative periods in our civilization have occurred when people from very different backgrounds came together: "East met West" and the Renaissance resulted. The modern-day equivalent in the world of technology is the collaboration of people from different disciplines. The greatest innovations today are occurring at the interfaces between disciplines. The numerous examples include: the marriage of medicine and engineering to produce implantable microsensors and prosthetics, and the collaboration of physicists, materials scientists, and various branches of engineering in the development of nanotechnologies.

Stronger Customer Relationships

There are several customer-related benefits cited for moving toward more diverse research organizations. First, companies must be poised to market effectively to a broad global customer base. American women comprise 50 percent of the population and control around 80 percent of household spending, buying 81 percent of all products and services and writing 80 percent of all checks. A diverse workforce is needed to bring different perspectives on the development of products targeted to this important customer base.

Second, forging strong relationships with customers by developing relationships with individuals within the customer firms is crucial to business success. Customers insist on doing business with suppliers who understand and respect local conditions, both in geography and culture. They want suppliers to build, invest and become part of their community. When customers and business are global, investments in research, development and manufacturing must also be global for the business to have customer credibility.

Finally, diversity initiatives are becoming more prevalent within customer firms. As customers recognize the value of diversity in their workforces, they are demanding to see it in those of their suppliers. Customers want to hear about diversity programs, and they want to interface with teams that are diverse. One IRI panelist cited a case in which a key customer actually asked, "How can you explain your diversity program when you have six white males who turn up for a meeting with us?"

Productivity

An important part of maintaining a diverse workforce is sustaining an inclusive environment in which everyone feels valued as part of the team. Employees who feel this way are going to be more enthusiastic, more committed and more loyal; they will be more likely to "go the extra mile" or "chip in" for the good of the team. Obviously, this is the kind of environment desired for maximum productivity.

A tremendous amount of time and energy is wasted when the work environment is not inclusive. Senior women are often heard to say, "You just get tired," when commenting on the challenges of working in male-dominated organizations. It is exhausting to feel that you must continually work to be heard or accepted. In the worst case, productivity is hurt when there are conflicts, misunderstandings or any kind of disrespect.

Improved Speed and Agility

A diverse organization is adaptable by necessity, knowing how to deal internally with different types of people. These organizations also adapt more readily to changing markets. The open and direct communications needed in a diverse organization also result in enhanced speed and agility.

No Choice

Finally, it would appear that U.S. corporations have no choice but to embrace diversity. Boards of directors, executives, potential employees, and customers demand it. As stated by many corporate executives in various ways, there is no choice because diversity is a factor in being competitive. Any corporation that is going to be successful in the fast-paced, global business environment of today and tomorrow must strive for the fullest possible access to all talent and ideas.

Challenges to Integrating a Diverse Workforce

The potential value of diversity is very clear philosophically. However, the development and effective integration of a diverse workforce have proven amazingly difficult and typically taken far longer than anticipated. IRI companies have directed an enormous amount of effort toward increasing minority hiring, retention and advancement.

The need to establish a critical mass has been an impediment to effective diversity initiative implementation.

Critical mass is the point at which the minority group represents a large enough percentage of the population in question (e.g., candidate pool or work group) that its full participation can be sustained without extraordinary effort on the part of both management and the individual. Various authors have defined critical mass as being somewhere between 15 and 33 percent.

This range in definition is probably due to the fact that critical mass is important in a variety of ways. First, it affects the ability to recruit members of an underrepresented group. If a company has less than the critical mass of a certain group, bringing in new members of that group is difficult. Prospective employees observe the workplace and ask: "How can you convince me that this is not a hostile place for me? How can you convince me that this is going to be a place that's going to value my contribution?" Second, critical mass is important in employee inclusion and advancement. If the representation of a group is less than 15–20 percent, feelings of disaffection or not belonging tend to arise. Psychological studies indicate a critical mass of 25 percent must be reached in order for the abilities of the minority group members to be judged fairly.

Developing and integrating a diverse workforce is also a challenge because it represents change. Instituting this change means involving top management, combatting the inertia of the status quo, and meeting the concerns of the traditionally dominant, typically white male, workforce group.

What Companies Are Doing

The final section of this article explores "best practices" from IRI member companies seeking to address the challenges associated with recruiting, integrating and retaining diversity, as well as the challenges associated with leveraging the unique differences of a diverse workforce into competitive business advantage.

Changing the numbers of women and minorities in a workforce, especially in the higher-level positions, takes time and perseverance. Numerical goals are important as quantifiable indicators of progress. However, for a long-term change, an organization must concentrate on changing the environment. Concentrating on the numbers alone can lead to successful recruiting but poor retention.

Changing an environment includes changing the corporate culture—a truly daunting task that must have the support of those at the very top. Special attention must be paid to the pipeline, since it is recognized that it will take time to change the numbers "at the top."

Strategy Development and Implementation

IRI member companies have paid considerable attention to the development of corporate diversity strategies. Defining diversity is typically the first step, followed by developing a vision and then tying the vision to the business case. General Mills' vision is "Recognizing, understanding and respecting all the ways that we differ, and leveraging those differences for competitive business advantage." The Agilent vision involves achieving creativity, innovation and growth through diversity and inclusion.

Setting clear, specific goals is very important. These goals are often numerical, including representation at various levels over time. Because of the size and challenge of the initiative, many companies develop a multi-year plan with annual milestones for each specific business area. Some firms have a centralized head of diversity supported by champions with specific implementation responsibilities. Agilent has an interesting "diversity made real" initiative: it has a first year "launch" strategy, a second and third year "build" strategy to operationalize the strategy, and a fourth year and beyond "thrive" strategy to embed diversity in its culture.

During implementation, the strategy must be communicated loudly, widely and unapologetically. Regular surveys to measure progress help to keep the program on track. Public recognition of diversity contributions emphasizes the importance of, and corporate commitment to, the effort.

Management Involvement and Accountability

Commitment of executives is critical to the success of diversity initiatives and programs. A first step is often education of upper management, including having executives sit down with employee groups to hear their concerns. Executive committees such as Air Products' Executive Forum on Diversity may be formed to set strategy, create awareness and drive implementation. At IBM, each executive and senior manager is expected to take a personal leadership role in supporting the corporate view of the business case for diversity, personally exemplifying the values underlying the diversity vision, and communicating expectations down to the middle management and work teams across the company.

Effective diversity/inclusion initiatives require accountability throughout management ranks. Companies have used a variety of tools to promote accountability. Linking management's personal financial success with diversity progress has been effective in emphasizing the importance of diversity and making significant progress. Executive/management bonuses are often tied to both setting and achieving diversity goals. A 360-degree performance review survey that includes questions assessing behavior in the areas of respecting differences and diversity is another tool that has been used to increase awareness and individual accountability.

Training

Best practices include diversity training for the entire workforce and specific training for managers. Professionally developed programs are recommended. For many companies, this has meant working with a consultant to develop a program tailored to the company. Most workforce training programs take the form of 1-2-day workshops. Air Products devotes one week of its five-week Leadership Education program for managers to diversity.

The best training programs focus on inclusion. Everyone should understand diversity in its broadest terms. The J. Howard & Associates program was well received by the majority population at one IRI member firm. This program approaches diversity from the standpoint of workforce productivity, focusing on the impact of inclusion on workforce productivity improvement. Some programs include sessions in which people actually identify and work through real issues within the company. In addition to providing important "sensitivity" training, this can be an opportunity to facilitate real communication and begin tackling real issues.

Training can include more than formal classes, workshops or programs. Several IRI member firms have employee advisory groups to the CEO. These are used to increase executive awareness of diversity issues. Having small groups of employees share their experiences with a leader has been found to be an effective way of helping executives recognize and understand the barriers faced by others. Providing "eye-opening" experiences to help specific employees understand better the challenges faced by others has also been effective. An example is to assign an employee to a work situation in which he is the "outsider," e.g., a U.S. citizen in Japan.

Mentoring

Mentoring is important in gaining the full value from a diverse workforce, and programs are in place at many IRI companies. These programs need to be organization-specific, so the embodiments vary widely. Some mentoring programs are highly structured with formal training for mentees and mentors; other programs involve mentoring "circles" where a single mentor meets with a group of mentees. This approach has the advantages of reducing the time burden on mentors and providing opportunities for peer support. At IBM, inverse mentoring has also proven to be valuable. With inverse mentoring, an executive says, "I'm going to reach down in the organization and I'm going to ask someone who has a different set of life experiences and a different point of view to be my mentor."

Mentors serve many functions: they open doors, provide learning opportunities, help expand an individual's contributions to the organization, and provide a secure area in which to brainstorm ideas and solve problems. A mentor within the same workforce group, such as the same gender, is highly valued by some and can be particularly advantageous when the workforce group level is below critical mass.

Employee Networks and Conferences

Employee networks are formed to provide peer support, networking opportunities, forums for the discussion and advancement of common issues, and sponsorship of educational and awareness activities. One of the most common activities is the hosting of speakers. Most networks are grassroots organizations, but the most successful ones have the recognition and support of the company.

In 1999, Air Products held a global Women's Leadership Conference. The top 200 women were invited to participate in several days of activities that included leadership-training exercises, networking and discussion with Air Products executives. Feedback on the conference was positive: the participants felt that they had gained much from both the formal presentations and the networking opportunities. A highlight of the conference was a professionally produced Socratic dialogue in which a panel of Air Products male and female leaders were asked to respond spontaneously to hypothetical situations posed by the moderator. The result was entertaining and enlightening.

IBM held a similar conference in 1997. The company also holds an annual Women's Technical Conference. This meeting is an opportunity for IBM women from around the world to present their technical work to their female colleagues. About 500 women participate. As typical for any technical conference, papers are submitted and selected for presentation. Participation is by nomination. Similar conferences are held for gay and lesbian and multicultural employees.

External Pipeline Activities: Recruiting

The skills pipeline is receiving attention, particularly in areas where there is a general shortage of candidates or where the representation of a group in the educational pipeline is decreasing. Companies such as IBM conduct a lot of outreach work in pre-college education. Through National Engineers' Week and networks such as "Girl Geeks," IBM reaches out to high school and elementary school students to ensure that young people understand that opportunities are available for all people to join the high-tech industry.

Companies strive to strengthen ties to the universities where they recruit by encouraging employee networks to interact with similar student organizations. This can build synergies between universities and companies and develop valuable recruiting relationships. The use of diverse recruiters also clearly has benefits. When companies are below the 15 percent critical mass of a particular group, one approach is to attempt to recruit several members of the group simultaneously, explaining to the candidates that they have the opportunity to be an important part of significant change.

Internal Pipeline Activities: Retention and Advancement

It is human nature to be most comfortable with those who think and act like you. Thus, until an organization has achieved diversity throughout the ranks, special care must be taken to ensure that everyone is being given opportunity for advancement.

Many companies require that a diverse slate of candidates be developed, particularly when filling a senior position. A problem that often arises is the lack of qualified diverse candidates in the internal pipeline. One tactic to help fill the pipeline is to require that diverse candidates be included in succession plans; this must be coupled with a commitment to ensure that those listed receive the development that is required to be considered strong candidates when the opportunity arises. For example, IBM maintains and frequently reviews feeder lists for all key positions. It ensures that the feeder list contains the broadest possible coverage of diverse, talented candidates. People on these lists get development opportunities and assignments.

Succession planning addresses the pipeline at the top of the organization, but pipeline development efforts must extend down into the organization where diverse candidates are often lost. Mid-level managers and supervisors must be encouraged to identify and develop a diverse pool of candidates. Dow Corning addresses this issue by identifying "stepping stone" positions that traditionally have led to higher-level positions. Careful attention is given to how these stepping stone positions are filled so that a diverse pool of qualified candidates is developed for higher-level positions.

Work-Life

In order to attract and retain a highly motivated, productive workforce, firms today must have workplaces that respect employees' individual needs. Over the past decade, most large U.S. firms have established policies allowing some flexibility in work hours. Benefits included 50 percent less absenteeism among employees who used flexible work options and family leave policies compared to absenteeism for the workforce as a whole. There is concern, however, that some work-life policies are only "paper policies." Important meetings are scheduled outside of the core hours, making it difficult to practice flextime effectively, and employees feel that selecting a non-standard work schedule will be viewed negatively with regard to promotions and opportunities. Organizations leading the way in this area must ensure that work-life policies are not only in place but are truly accessible and working.

Implementation Remains a Challenge

The business drivers for recruiting and maintaining a diverse workforce are widely documented and consistently agreed upon. There is little question as to the importance of diversity to the corporate bottom line. The organizations that will flourish will be those that can take full advantage of the diversity in their workforces to enhance innovation, customer relations, productivity, and corporate speed and agility.

However, although the value of a diverse workforce is widely recognized, effective diversity implementation, particularly at higher levels in the company, remains a challenge. The daunting tasks of overcoming human prejudices and changing corporate culture must be undertaken. The agents for change must remain vigilant until self-sustaining critical mass populations are established. IRI member companies are engaged in a variety of diversity efforts reflected in the best practices discussed above, and R&D divisions are often in the forefront of implementation of these activities.

NO

Thomas Kochan et al.

The Effects of Diversity on Business Performance: Report of the Diversity Research Network

Introduction

Since 1996, a group of industry chief executives and human resource professionals have been working together under the auspices of a nonprofit organization called the Business Opportunities for Leadership Diversity (BOLD) Initiative to help American corporations learn how to leverage their cultural diversity for competitive advantage. These leaders espouse the now popular "business case" for diversity—the view that a more diverse workforce will increase organizational effectiveness. For them, providing more opportunities for women and minorities is a business imperative. Realizing, however, that they lacked clear evidence to support this view, either within their own organizations or more generally across American industry, these business leaders called for definitive research to assess the diversity-performance link. An initial study commissioned by BOLD found that no organizations were collecting the data needed to assess the effects of their diversity practices on firm performance. Therefore, in 1997, the BOLD Initiative asked a group of researchers from a cross section of universities to design a large-scale field research project to examine the relationships between gender and racial diversity and business performance.

This paper presents our conclusions from this five-year research effort. We believe this to be the largest field-based research project on this topic undertaken to date. We summarize our results here and their implications for managers and human resource practitioners and describe the challenges we encountered along the way in the hopes of advancing the study and practice of diversity in organizations in the future. . . .

Historical Context of the Business-Case Perspective

The recognition that diversity is a reality in the workforce has generated an enormous amount of activity over the years among leaders in business, government, and civil society alike. An outcome of the civil rights movement, Title VII

From *Human Resource Management*, Vol. 42, No. 1, Spring 2003, pp. 3–21. Copyright © 2003 by John Wiley & Sons. Reprinted by permission.

of the 1964 Civil Rights Act, made it illegal for organizations to engage in employment practices that discriminated against employees on the basis of race, color, religion, sex, and national origin (age and disability were legislated after 1964). Through these government actions, society made a statement: employers must provide equal employment opportunities to all people of similar qualifications and accomplishments. In addition, Executive Order 11246, issued in 1965, required government contractors to take affirmative actions to overcome past patterns of exclusion or discrimination. These societal mandates curtailed formal policies that discriminated against certain classes of workers and raised the costs to organizations that failed to implement fair employment practices. The laws remain a part of the legal responsibilities under which firms and other labor-market institutions, such as unions or job-matching organizations, operate today.

By the late 1970s and into the 1980s, there was growing recognition within the private sector that, while the legal mandates were necessary, they were not sufficient for ensuring the effective management of diversity within organizations. Although the workforces of many organizations became more diverse, entrenched organizational cultures, which remained inhospitable to traditionally underrepresented groups, were slow to change. To promote the development of more positive organizational cultures that would support the effective development of a more diverse workforce, many companies and consulting firms began to offer training programs aimed at "valuing diversity." These efforts focused on changing employees' attitudes and eliminating behaviors that reflected more subtle forms of discrimination and exclusion, which often inhibited effective interactions among people. The widespread adoption of such training programs expanded the concept of "diversity" as people began to realize that visible, legally recognized, demographic differences such as race and gender were not the only types of differences that affected work relationships among employees. Gradually, training initiatives proliferated, encouraging employees to value the wide range of physical, cultural, and interpersonal differences, which would presumably enhance decision making, problem solving, and creativity at work. Unfortunately, however, most studies show that such training rarely leads to the desired long-term changes in attitudes and behavior.

During the 1990s, diversity rhetoric shifted to emphasize the business case for supporting workforce diversity. Figure 1 reports how the former CEO of Hewlett Packard described the new rhetoric. Essentially, he was looking for a way to convince his fellow executives and managers that to manage diversity effectively is a business necessity not only because of the nature of labor and product markets today, but also because a more diverse work force—relative to a homogeneous one—produces better business results. He believed that providing evidence to support these claims would accelerate the rate of progress employers would make in hiring and developing a more diverse workforce and produce organizations that are more fully integrated across occupations and levels of hierarchy. Likewise, for diversity advocates, the new imperative was to find evidence to support the business-case argument.

In fact, as both the study commissioned by BOLD and our own reviews of the research literature have shown, there is little research conducted in actual

---

Figure 1

Lew Platt, former CEO of Hewlett Packard, comments to the Diversity Research Network, Stanford Business School, March 18, 1998.

The Business Case for Diversity

I see three main points to make the business case for diversity:

1. A talent shortage that requires us to seek out and use the full capabilities of all our employees.
2. The need to be like our customers, including the need to understand and communicate with them in terms that reflects their concerns.
3. Diverse teams produce better results.

This last point is not as easy to sell as the first two-especially to engineers who want the data. What I need is the data, evidence that diverse groups do better.

---

organizations that addresses the impact of diversity or diversity-management practices on financial success. While there are a large number of laboratory experiments that test specific diversity-performance hypotheses, there are few such studies in real organizations and fewer still that assess this hypothesis using objective performance measures. An exception is a study that compared companies with exemplary diversity-management practices to those that had paid legal damages to settle discrimination lawsuits. The results of this study showed that the exemplary firms also performed better as measured by their stock prices. Overall, however, the search for evidence that directly supports the business-case hypothesis has proved elusive.

Two reasons might explain this lack of evidence. First, diversity is extremely difficult to study in organizational settings because it raises sensitive issues that are difficult to discuss. In addition, organizations, including many we contacted during this project, are reluctant to share their experiences or data, given the legal climate and the potential for litigation. Another reason for the lack of evidence linking workforce diversity to business performance may be that the relationship between diversity and the bottom line is more complex than is implied by the popular rhetoric. Decades of research on the effects of diversity within teams and small groups indicate that diversity can have negative effects, as well as positive ones. The empirical literature does not support the simple notion that more diverse groups, teams, or business units necessarily perform better, feel more committed to their organizations, or experience higher levels of satisfaction. Instead, the evidence suggests that diversity may simultaneously produce more conflict and employee turnover as well as more creativity and innovation. For example, this pattern of mixed results was found in two studies that examined diversity within top management teams in the banking industry. In one study, diversity in top management teams was associated with greater innovation within bank branches. In another, diversity also associated with higher rates of turnover among top management team members. Thus, the research literature paints a more complex picture of the consequences of diversity than does the popular rhetoric.

The Diversity Research Network and Research Project

It was this mismatch between research results and diversity rhetoric that led us to agree to form a Diversity Research Network. Our purpose was to conduct a multi-firm study of the effects of racial and gender diversity on organizational performance. The Alfred P. Sloan Foundation, the Society of Human Resource Management (SHRM) Foundation, and the BOLD Initiative provided the funding for the Network's research. . . .

Specifically, the literature suggests that diversity, if unattended, is likely to have an adverse effect on group processes, such as communications, conflict, and cohesion. More specifically, diversity in a work group can produce lower cohesion and miscommunication among group members, which can lead to group conflict. Some of this conflict may be productive—if, for example, it avoids "groupthink" and brings additional points of view into the discussion— whereas other forms may worsen group performance.

. . . In fact, past research suggests that there may be no direct positive or negative relationship between diversity and performance outcomes. In some groups, diversity may improve performance, while in other groups, diversity may be detrimental to performance. If diversity has inconsistent effects across groups, then in studies that examine the relationship between diversity and performance across many groups, the positive and negative effects may cancel each other out so that no effect obtains. Therefore, our research model suggests that the relationship between diversity and performance may depend on the organizational context in which the work takes place. For example, the effects of diversity on organizational performance might be more favorable if group leaders and members build on team members' creativity and information. Diversity may also be more likely to improve performance when group members and leaders are trained to deal with group process issues, particularly those involved in communicating and problem solving in diverse teams. Presumably, HR practices for recruiting, selecting, training, motivating, and rewarding employees partially determine whether team members and leaders are skilled in communicating with and coordinating among members of diverse teams. When HR practices support the creation of a workforce that has the skills needed to turn diversity into an advantage, diversity is more likely to lead to positive performance outcomes. In other organizations, however, HR practices may inadvertently result in teams that are diverse but unskilled in diversity management. Such organizations are more likely to experience negative outcomes, such as disruptive conflict and increased turnover, which can harm performance. . . .

Data Collection

The BOLD Initiative first approached several of us in early 1997 with the idea of forming a collaborative industry-university research project to explore the business case for diversity. Researchers from a number of universities met twice to discuss whether such a project was feasible. We were well aware of the difficulties associated with field research on this topic. It raises politically and emotionally charged issues, as well as legal concerns. In addition, it would be difficult to develop and even more difficult to implement a research design that would enable us to draw valid, convincing conclusions about the causal effects of diversity on organizational outcomes. In an ideal world, such a design would entail longitudinal data collected from a large and representative sample of organizations, enabling us to track how changes in demography influence performance over time. We knew from past organizational research that the data needed to examine the impact of diversity on performance are quite extensive, seldom collected, or relatively inaccessible, and unlikely to be comparable across organizations. Yet we all shared the view that if we were to generate knowledge that would be useful to practitioners on the relationship between diversity and performance, we needed to move the research on this topic from the laboratory to the field. Moreover, we were intrigued by the potential benefits of forming a research network among those working on this topic, generating a common framework to guide research, and comparing results across multiple organizations. Some of us had had positive experiences in building and participating in a similar network to explore the relationship between human resource practices and firm performance, a topic that individual researchers had previously found equally difficult to study. Therefore, we decided to move ahead with the support of the Sloan Foundation, SHRM, and the BOLD Initiative.

The process of recruiting companies to provide the data and participate in the research proved to be even more difficult than we had expected. Over a two-year period (1998–2000), members of the research network and leaders of the BOLD Initiative initiated discussions with over 20 large and well-known Fortune 500 companies, all of which expressed considerable interest in the topic. However, after often considerable discussion of the data, confidentiality, and time commitments, all but four companies declined to participate. In some cases, the diversity advocates and professionals in the company lacked sufficient influence to convince line managers to spend the time required to collect the necessary data. In other cases, these professionals were reluctant to examine the effects of their organization's policies, with the view that they had sufficient top management support for their current initiatives and did not need to demonstrate a business case to maintain this support. In still other cases, we found that, even with the support of the CEO, objections raised by internal or external legal counsel and/or by other managers who would need to provide the data proved insurmountable. In the end, each of the firms that agreed to participate had a prior relationship with one or more members of the research team and/or leaders of BOLD Initiative and, therefore, had already established a high level of trust. Thus, the first lesson of this research was that not only had none of the organizations we contacted ever conducted a systematic examination of the effects of their diversity efforts on bottom-line performance measures, very few were interested in doing so. . . .

Summary and Implications

The studies reported here were conducted in large firms that have well-deserved reputations for their longstanding commitments to building a diverse workforce and managing diversity effectively. Each of these firms has taken steps to ensure that its formal policies support and reinforce its diversity objectives. While their specific practices vary, our investigation clearly documents the importance and value of firm-wide, diversity-sensitive managerial strategies, human resource policies, and organizational cultures. Despite the variability in industry contexts, specific practices, and the performance measures we examined, our quantitative results are strikingly similar.

We found that racial and gender diversity do not have the positive effect on performance proposed by those with a more optimistic view of the role diversity can play in organizations—at least not consistently or under all conditions—but neither does it necessarily have the negative effect on group processes warned by those with a more pessimistic view. Most analyses yielded no negative effects on team processes at all, but when racial diversity was shown to have a negative effect, it was mitigated by training and development-focused initiatives. Gender diversity had either no effects or positive effects on team processes. This is consistent with research that has shown that sex balanced groups have more positive interactions than either predominantly male or predominantly female groups.

There were few direct effects of diversity on performance—either positive or negative. Our findings suggest that, as we expected, this is likely because context is crucial in determining the nature of diversity's impact on performance. Conditions that exacerbated racial diversity's negative effects on performance included a highly competitive context among teams. Finally, there was some promising evidence to suggest that, under certain conditions, racial diversity may even enhance performance, namely when organizations foster an environment that promotes learning from diversity.

In general, we also found that gender diversity was less problematic than racial diversity. We expect that this may be, at least in part, because in the companies in these studies, women—typically White women—tended to be better represented than either men or women of color.

If these studies are representative of other leading companies with similarly strong commitments to diversity, our results may suggest that efforts to create and manage diverse workforces have generally paid off by eliminating many of the potentially negative effects of diversity on group processes and performance documented previously in the literature. Moreover, there appear to be some conditions under which diversity, if managed well, may even enhance performance.

An important goal of this research was to explore the feasibility of conducting research on diversity in organizational settings. Our experience demonstrated how difficult it is to conduct this type of field research and how little analytical attention practitioners pay to these issues in organizations today. Few companies are equipped to assess the impact of their diversity efforts on their performance. One clear implication of our work is that organizations need to do a better job of tracking and evaluating the impact of their strategies for managing a diverse workforce.

Managerial Implications

What implications do we draw from this work for managers? Given the limited nature of our sample and our findings, it would be inappropriate to propose broad or sweeping implications for managerial action. In the course of this project, however, we discussed the state of practice with managers from more than 20 large, well-known, and highly regarded firms as we sought their involvement in our research. Through these discussions we obtained what we believe is a valid picture of the state of practice in managing diversity in large organizations today. Moreover, while our empirical research is limited to four cases, to our knowledge, this research represents the first effort to test a model relating diversity to performance in multiple firms. Thus, with appropriate caution, we offer the following implications for practice.

Modify the business case.   The simplistic business case of the past is simply not supported in our research. Our experience and findings in these companies suggest that those who want to invoke a business case to advance the cause of diversity need to modify the way they frame the argument. They should start by recognizing that there is virtually no evidence to support the simple assertion that diversity is inevitably either good or bad for business. Based on our findings, we propose a more nuanced view, which focuses on the conditions that can leverage benefits from diversity or, at the very least, mitigate its negative effects. Our proposed reframing of the business case for diversity follows.

> Diversity is a reality in labor markets and customer markets today. To be successful in working with and gaining value from this diversity requires a sustained, systemic approach and long-term commitment. Success is facilitated by a perspective that considers diversity to be an opportunity for everyone in an organization to learn from each other how better to accomplish their work and an occasion that required a supportive and cooperative organizational culture as well as group leadership and process skills that can facilitate effective group functioning. Organizations that invest their resources in taking advantage of the opportunities that diversity offers should outperform those that fail to make such investments.

Look beyond the business case.   We believe this restatement of the business case accurately reflects both our results and the results from prior laboratory studies. However, our results may offer an even stronger implication. It may be that the business-case rhetoric has run its course. Diversity professionals, industry leaders, and researchers might do better to recognize that while there is no reason to believe diversity will naturally translate into better or worse results, diversity is both a labor-market imperative and societal expectation and value. Therefore managers might do better to focus on building an organizational culture, human resource practices, and the managerial and group process skills needed to translate diversity into positive organizational, group, and individual results. Our more specific recommendations for doing so follow.

Adopt a more analytical approach.   Despite the widespread availability and use of human resource information systems, we found that basic HR data about individuals or groups could not be readily linked to business-level performance data. Unable to link HR practices to business performance, HR practitioners will be limited in what they can learn about how to manage diversity effectively, and their claims for diversity as a strategic imperative warranting financial investments weakened accordingly. Human resource managers and other professionals in charge of diversity efforts should take a more analytical approach in performing their roles. Sophisticated data collection and analyses are needed to understand the consequences of diversity within organizations, and to monitor an organization's progress in managing diversity effectively. Currently, organizations typically assess their diversity efforts by simply comparing attitudes, performance, advancement, pay, and so on, among different groups of employees. These comparisons can be useful, but they are only a first step. Equally important but very different questions are: Under what conditions do work units that are diverse with respect to gender or race outperform or underperform work units that are more homogeneous? What conditions mitigate or exacerbate diversity's potential negative or positive effects?

Support experimentation and evaluation. More work is needed to design and evaluate specific interventions or experiments aimed at creating a positive link between diversity and performance. Of necessity, we relied on assessing this relationship by examining natural covariations in diversity and performance across groups, but there were many other factors that we could neither measure nor control, which may have influenced our findings and no doubt attenuated the size of true effects. Researchers who are better able to isolate effects by studying them in the controlled setting of the laboratory tend to find larger effects than we observed in the field research on which we reported here. Studies that can better replicate these experimental conditions in real organizational settings would increase control without the artificiality of the laboratory. To conduct such research, however, will require executives to commit to this type of experimentation and learning within their own organizations.

Train for group-process skills. Our results suggest that training programs must help managers to develop the leadership and group process skills needed to facilitate constructive conflict and effective communication. These are challenges that will inevitably arise for managers who attempt to make diversity a resource for learning, change, and renewal.

In summary, we believe that progress in both research and organizational practice will come through continuing collaborative efforts between researchers and managers as they design and evaluate new approaches to leveraging workforce diversity. Training programs that improve the skills of managers and team members may be particularly useful, but training alone is not likely to be sufficient. Organizations must also implement management and human resource policies and practices that inculcate cultures of mutual learning and cooperation.

This research was conducted in partnership with the BOLD Initiative. Support was provided by the Alfred P. Sloan Foundation and the Society for Human Resource Management Foundation. All views expressed here are solely those of the authors.

POSTSCRIPT

Does Workplace Diversity Result in a More Productive Firm?

Are firms that embrace workplace diversity more productive than firms that resist diversifying their mix of employees? That was the question addressed by the two articles comprising this issue. Authors Mary Salomon and Joan Schork answered "yes" and provided a detailed argument built on the idea that there is a business case for diversity. Researcher Thomas Kochan and his colleagues reported findings from their complex, sophisticated research project. As noted previously, their intent was to show that this relationship does exist and, in so doing, provide an authoritative voice to the rather weak body of research characterizing this topic. Surprisingly, despite their initial intentions, Kochan et al. failed to find support for the effects of diversity on performance and, thus, provided this issue with its "no" response.

Although the conclusions of one research study alone rarely represent the final word on a topic, the high degree of quality and sophistication of Kochan's investigation clearly place it at the pinnacle of research on workplace diversity and its effects (or lack thereof) on productivity. Consequently, the findings of this study need to be taken very seriously by anyone who argues that organizations should diversify primarily because of the expectations of productivity gains.

So, given the negative findings of this study, where do diversity advocates go from here? Are there legitimate reasons aside from expected productivity gains for organizations to embrace diversity in their workforce? Both sets of authors here provide a resounding "yes!" in response. Both point out that firms willing to embrace diversity open themselves up to a much larger pool of talent than those firms that resist diversifying their labor composition. Both papers note that there are important non-economic considerations arguing for the acceptance of workplace diversity. The current social, political, and cultural environment in America celebrates and encourages the acceptance of cultural, racial, and sexual differences and strongly discourages discriminatory mind-sets, philosophies, and practices. Thus, a diverse workforce is a business necessity in the sense that adopting such a policy reduces corporate exposure to legal action and allows the firm to align itself with socially desirable values and expectations.

It seems, then, that the case for adopting diversity in the workplace as a corporate philosophy and strategy is a strong one but, as explained in the conclusion of the Kochan et al. paper, part of that case is, apparently, not the assertion that diversity leads to productivity.

Suggested Readings

Building a competitive workforce: Diversity—The bottom line. *Forbes*, April 3, 2000, pp. 181–194.

Fay Hansen, Diversity's business case doesn't add up. *Workforce Management*, Crain Communications, Inc. April 1, 2003.

Demedre R. Heulett, BNA, Inc.: Effectively managing a diverse workforce. *The Metropolitian Corporate Counsel*, Northeast Edition, January 2004.

R. Koonce, Redefining diversity. *T+D*, December 2001, p. 25.

O.C. Richard and N.B. Johnson, Making the connection between formal human resource practices and organizational effectiveness: Beyond management fashion. *Performance Improvement Quarterly*, 12, pp. 77–96.

T.J. Rodgers, "Defense of non-diversity," in *Perspectives in Business Ethics* (2nd ed.). Edited by Laura P. Hartman. McGraw-Hill, 2002.

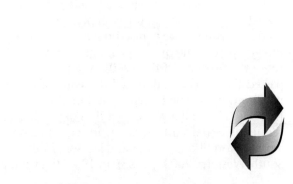

ISSUE 9

Is Gender Discrimination the Main Reason Women Are Paid Less Than Men?

YES: Stephen J. Rose and Heidi I. Hartmann, from "Still a Man's Labor Market: The Long-Term Earnings Gap," *Institute for Women's Policy Research* (2004)

NO: Naomi Lopez, from "Free Markets, Free Choices II: Smashing the Wage Gap and Glass Ceiling Myths," *Pacific Research Institute* (1999)

ISSUE SUMMARY

YES: Stephen J. Rose and Heidi I. Hartmann, scholars at the Institute for Women's Policy Research, argue in their 2004 study that discrimination is still the main reason for the persistence in the gender gap.

NO: Naomi Lopez, director of the Center for Enterprise and Opportunity at the Pacific Research Institute in San Francisco, provides evidence that the wage gap is a function of several different variables beyond gender discrimination. She concludes her analysis with the observation that we may never reduce the wage gap entirely and that such an outcome is not necessarily undesirable.

During the 1950s, female workers in the United States earned about 59 cents for every dollar males earned. Not surprisingly, the differential in pay between women and men—the "gender wage gap"—was assumed to be the result of sexual discrimination in the workplace. Critics and social reformers at this time made the issue of wage discrimination—gender, racial, or any other type—an integral part of the overall civil rights movement that was sweeping the country in the first part of the 1960s. As a result, two critically important laws were passed that directly addressed the issue of discrimination and the wage gaps produced by it. The Equal Pay Act of 1963 requires employers to pay equivalent rates for similar work regardless of gender. Similar pay must occur for jobs requiring equal skill, equal effort, equal responsibility, or jobs with similar working conditions (Mathis and Jackson, *Human Resource Management*, Thomson South-Western, 2003, p. 388). In 1964, the Civil Rights Act was passed, which, among other things, further solidified the basis of the Equal Pay Act as a discrimination barrier in the workplace. Over the next three decades, the gender wage gap slowly, but consistently, declined as women gained access to jobs and pay levels typically reserved for men. By the mid-1990s, women, on average, earned 70 cents on the male dollar, a fact generally interpreted as evidence that the legislative actions of the 1960s were having the desired effect on workplace gender discrimination.

Despite the apparent large gains women have made in this area over the last several decades, the question of gender discrimination in wage rates has seen renewed interest in the last few years. The main reason for this is data from the U.S. Census bureau indicating that the trend in female wage gains may be reversing. Women have seen their pay levels decline from 76.5 percent of male pay in 1999 to 75.5 percent in 2003 (U.S. Census Bureau, "Income, Poverty, and Health Insurance Coverage in the United States: 2003," U.S. Department of Commerce, Economics and Statistics Administration). This decline represents the largest move backward in women's wages since 1991 and has caused many social commentators to wonder if discrimination against women is on the upswing as we move into the twenty-first century. The comments of Dr. Barbara Gault, director of research at the Institute for Women's Policy Research (IWPR), are typical: "To address the continuing disparities between women and men, we need to raise the minimum wage, improve enforcement of Equal Employment Opportunity laws, help women succeed in higher-paying, traditionally male occupations, and create more flexible, family friendly workplace policies" (IWPR, "Women's Earning Fall: U.S. Census Bureau Finds Rising Gender Wage Gap," *IWPR News*, August 27, 2004).

Although there is no dispute about the existence of the gender wage gap, there is definitely a difference of opinion as to its cause. On one side are those who believe the answer is straightforward—the persistence of the wage gap is due to gender discrimination. The above comments of the IWPR director of research exemplify this position nicely. On the other side are those who argue that other factors play a more important role in the gender wage gap. According to Howard J. Wall, senior economist at the Federal Reserve Bank of St. Louis, "The weight of evidence suggests that little of the wage gap is related to wage discrimination at all. Instead, wage discrimination accounts for, at most, about one-fourth of the gap, with the remainder due to differences between men and women in important determinants of earnings such as the number of hours worked, experience, training and occupation. Moreover, even this one-fourth of the gap may have less to do with wage discrimination than with the accumulated effects of shorter hours and interrupted careers on women's earnings and promotion prospects" (Wall, "The Gender Wage Gap and Wage Discrimination: Illusion or Reality," *The Regional Economist,* October 2000).

In the following selections, Stephen J. Rose and Heidi I. Hartmann, scholars at the IWPR, argue that discrimination is still the main reason for the persistence in the gender gap. Naomi Lopez, director of the Center for Enterprise and Opportunity at the Pacific Research Institute in San Francisco, provides evidence that the wage gap is a function of several different variables beyond gender discrimination.

Stephen J. Rose and
Heidi I. Hartmann

Still a Man's Labor Market: The Long-Term Earnings Gap

Many argue that women's prospects in the labor market have steadily incre-ased and that any small remaining gap in earnings between women and men is not significant. They see the remaining differences as resulting from women's own choices. Others believe that with women now graduating from college at a higher rate than men and with the economy continuing its shift toward ser-vices, work and earnings differences between women and men may disappear entirely.

Although the wage gap, measured by conventional methods, *has* narrowed in the last several decades, with women who work full-time full-year now earn-ing 77 percent of what men earn (compared with 59 cents on the male dollar 40 years ago), its sweeping effects are largely unacknowledged because its measure-ment is limited to a single year and restricted to only a portion of the workforce. *When accumulated over many years for all men and women workers, the losses to women and their families due to the wage gap are large and can be devastating.*

For many families, the quality of children's care and education suffers from women's low earnings throughout their child rearing years. Even with increased time in the labor market after their children are grown, women cannot make up the loss in lifetime earnings. Moreover, most women enter retirement without pensions, either from their own or their husband's employment, and thus lack security in old age.

A New Measure Highlights Wage Gap Understatement

The conventional way of measuring the differences in earnings and labor force experience between women and men is misleading because it fails to capture the difference in men's and women's total lifetime earnings. The more com-monly cited wage ratio is based on comparing the annual earnings of women and men who work full-time, full-year in a given year. Using a more inclusive 15-year time frame (1983–1998), and taking into account women's lower work hours and their years with zero earnings due to family care, this study finds that women workers, in their prime earning years, make only 38 percent of what men earn. *Across the 15 years of the study, the average prime age working woman earned only $273,592 while the average working man earned $722,693 (in 1999 dollars).* This gap of 62 percent is more than twice as large as the 23 percent gap commonly reported.

This new measure of the long-term earnings gap is based on comparing the average annual earnings, across 15 years, of prime-age workers between the ages of 26 and 59 years, regardless of how many hours they worked or how many years they had earnings. The data used are from the Panel Study of Income Dynamics, a longitudinal data set that tracks the same groups of women and men over many years. *Compared with men, women are more likely to work part-time, less likely to work year-round, and more likely to have entire years out of the labor force.* Thus, the conventional 77 cent comparison underplays all of these factors by focusing only on the earnings of the approximately half of women and the 85 percent of men who work full-time for at least 50 weeks in a given year. To measure the access women and men have to economic resources through working, earnings for all prime-age women and men is a more relevant statistic.

Across 15 years, the majority (52 percent) of women but just 16 percent of men have at least one complete calendar year without any earnings. A career interruption like this has a large effect on the earnings of both men and women independent of their education and previous experience, and such interruptions partially account for women's lower life-time earnings. But even among men and women who have earnings in all 15 years, men's average annual earnings are $49,068 while women's are $29,507, or 57 cents on the dollar. Again, this figure is considerably below the commonly cited 77-cent comparison.

Women Are More Likely to Be Long-Term Low Earners

Women's lower average earnings mean that women are much more likely than men to be low earners overall. Even among those who have earnings every year in the 15-year study, 17 percent of women but only 1 percent of men average less than $15,000 per year in earnings—just above the poverty line for a family of three. Women are less likely than men to move up and out of low-wage work. In fact, more than 90 percent of long-term low earners among prime-age adults are women. Furthermore, in the new economy, one's educational background plays more of a role than ever before. Yet, women with a bachelor's degree earn less than men with only a high school diploma or less (even when the comparison is restricted to those with earnings in all 15 study years).

Again when only committed workers, those with earnings in all 15 years, are considered, the earnings range of $25,000–$49,999 annually is the most common earnings range for both men and women with nearly half of both sexes earning in that range. But for men, that range is effectively the bottom, since 42 percent of men earn more than $50,000 annually, while for women it is effectively the top, since only 9 percent of women average above that amount.

Gender Segregation in the Labor Market Results in Lower Pay for Women

One major reason for the gender gap in earnings is that women work in 'women's jobs'—jobs that are predominantly done by women, while men work in 'men's jobs'—those predominantly done by men. This phenomenon is known as the gender segregation of the labor market.

In this report, we develop a three-tier schema of elite, good, and less-skilled jobs; within each tier, there is a set of occupations that are predominantly male and a set that are predominantly female. In the elite tier, women are concentrated in teaching and nursing while men are business executives, scientists, doctors, and lawyers; in middle tier jobs, women are secretaries while men are skilled blue collar workers, police, and fire fighters; and in the lowest tier, women are sales clerks and personal service workers while men work in factory jobs. Among prime-age workers who are continuously employed (have earnings every year in the 15-year study period), nearly 60 percent are employed consistently at least 12 of 15 years in one of these six occupational clusters.

Within each of the six gender-tier categories, at least 75 percent of the workers are of one gender. In each tier, women's jobs pay significantly less than those of their male counterparts even though both sets of occupations tend to require the same level of educational preparation.

Perhaps largely because of the generally low pay scales in the female career occupations, only 8 percent of men work in them. In contrast, 15 percent of continuously employed women, apparently more eager to seek higher-paying male jobs, work consistently in male occupations. These women, however, earn one-third less than their male counterparts in male elite and less-skilled jobs. Among the few women who make it into the middle tier of good male jobs (the skilled, blue collar jobs), the more formal wage structures (due to unions and civil service regulations) mean that their pay lags men's by only one-fifth. Increasing women's entry into this tier of male good jobs would thus increase their earnings substantially.

For the preponderance of women who remain in the female sector of each tier, earnings are strikingly low. In general, even restricting the comparison to women who work full-time, women in women's jobs earn less than men in men's jobs one tier below: women in female elite jobs earn less than men in male good jobs, and women in female good jobs earn less than men in male less-skilled jobs.

Time Spent in Family Care Limits Women's Own Earnings

Women's working experience is conditioned on their experience in families, where they often do most of the child and elder care and family and household maintenance. Because the United States lags behind many other countries in providing subsidized childcare and paid family leave, families are left to their own resources to meet the challenges of combining family care and paid work.

Most women spend the majority of their prime-age years married. As a result, women's average standard of living (as measured by average household income over 15 years, assuming that all family members share equally in this income) lags men's by only 10 percent (despite women's much lower earnings). For married women, it is still their connection to men that insulates them at least partially from their own low earnings. For women with few years of marriage, however, their family income lags men's with similar marital histories by more than 25 percent.

Women's lack of own earning power limits their options (in the worst case, they may feel forced to stay in an abusive relationship) and exposes them to great risk of poverty and near poverty when they divorce or if they never marry (especially if there are children present). Women who never experienced a year as a single parent during the 15-year study period had an average annual income of $70,200, compared with women who experienced single parenthood in at least 5 of 15 years, who had an average annual income of less than $35,800. Moreover, after the prime earnings years observed in this study, approximately half of women enter the retirement years alone, no longer married even if they once were. Women's low earnings come home to roost in old age, when widowed, divorced, and never married women all share high poverty rates of approximately 20 percent.

The Gendered Division of Labor Is Self-Reinforcing But Increasingly Unstable

Another major reason for the gender gap in cumulative earnings is the self-reinforcing gendered division of labor in the family and its implications for women's labor market time. First, families need childcare and other activities to be performed. Second, since the husband usually earns more than his wife, less income is lost if the lower earner cuts back on her labor force participation. Third, employers, fearing that women will leave their jobs for family responsibilities, are reluctant to train or promote them and may take advantage of women's limited opportunities by paying them less than they would comparable men. Fourth, a set of jobs evolves with little wage growth or promotion opportunities but part-time hours and these jobs are mainly held by women. Fifth, an ideology develops that proclaims this the natural order, resulting in many more men in men's jobs with higher pay and long work hours and many more women working in women's jobs with lower pay and spending considerable time on family care. Women without men particularly suffer from this ideology since they often support themselves and their families on jobs that pay women's wages.

This self-reinforcing arrangement, while long lasting, is also increasingly unstable. Women are demanding more independence and greater economic security throughout the life cycle, whether single or married. Many women and men believe that women's talents are being underutilized and undercompensated.

In the United States, the flipside of women typically being the caregivers and men typically the breadwinners has led to very high working hours, especially for men. Compared with other advanced countries, the United States has developed a set of institutions that leads to significantly longer labor market hours and considerably less leisure.

Policy Changes Can Bring Improvement

Several policy recommendations are offered to help move U.S. institutions toward supporting greater equity between women and men. Among them are: strengthening enforcement of existing equal opportunity laws, increasing access to education and training in high paying fields in which women are currently underrepresented, developing new legal remedies for the comparable worth problem (the tendency of 'women's jobs' to pay less at least partly because women do them), making work places more 'family friendly' through more flexible hours, providing more job-guaranteed and paid leaves of absence for sickness and family care, encouraging men to use family leave more, increasing subsidies for childcare and early education, encouraging the development of more part-time jobs that pay well and also have good benefits, and improving outcomes for mothers and children after divorce. Certainly, the United States should be able to develop a better way to share responsibility for family care and work, resulting in increased gender equity in earnings, family work, and leisure and greater long-term economic security for both women and men.

Policy Implications

While experts disagree about the significance that should be attributed to the remaining differences found in women's and men's work experiences in and out of the labor market, we argue in this report that they are significant for many reasons.

- First, the gender gap in earnings has a major influence on families' life choices and poverty rates, on older women's retirement security, and on single mothers' ability to provide for their children's care and education. More and more women, both single mothers and married women, are contributing to their family's income through their paid work. Nearly all families with women earners or would-be earners would have a higher standard of living if women's wages and lifetime earnings were higher.
- Second, there is ample evidence that women's low earnings are not primarily the result of their preferences for low-wage work. Rather women face discrimination in the labor market and in pre-labor market preparation as well. The degree of sex segregation in the labor market is striking and women's jobs at all educational levels pay less than men's jobs at the same level. Women's access to the better paying jobs and occupations is still constrained. Women deserve equal opportunity in the labor market.
- Third, while many women spend more time on family care than many men, the choices women and men make in allocating their time between work and family are heavily constrained. The lack of societal provisions for family care such as subsidized child and elder care means that most families have to fend for themselves. Women's lower earnings, of course, make it more practical for the family to sacrifice the woman's rather than the man's earnings and, given the loss of the woman's earnings, the man often works even more hours.

- Thus, a kind of perverse internal logic perpetuates a system with a rigid division of labor both in the workplace and in the home. Employers may feel justified in discriminating against women workers if they think they will be less devoted to their jobs because of family responsibilities. They may structure jobs as part-time and dead-end for this reason and many women may accept them because they cannot find better-paying jobs. Labor market discrimination means lower earnings for women; women's low earnings mean women spend more time in family care; women's commitments to family care contribute to discrimination against them. Single mothers especially suffer as they must attempt to support their families on women's lower wage levels.
- Finally, such a system surely fails to use human talent productively. How much total output is lost to society because the skills of women are not developed and put to work in the most productive way? To what extent are economic resources misallocated because of the constraints noted above? To what extent are both men and women denied the opportunity to allocate their time between home and work as they would most prefer? . . .

As this study demonstrates, the pay gap remains quite large and is bigger than many people think. Women still retain primary responsibility for family care in many families, making it difficult for women workers to compete equally with their male counterparts. Ideological attacks on women's equality also seem to be growing (or in any case not abating). Every few years, the media reassert that working moms may be hurting their children and wearing themselves out under the strain of the double burden.[1] In late 2002, Allison Pearson's *I Don't Know How She Does It: The Life of Kate Reddy, Working Mother* (Anchor Books) provided an example of this trend. And in late 2003 Lisa Belkin in "The Opt-Out Revolution" (*New York Times Magazine,* October 26) argued that highly educated and high earning women (with high earning husbands) are increasingly stepping off the fast track voluntarily, without presenting much evidence to support an actual increase. Her article also seemed to down play the evidence she had collected in her interviews of this small, select group, showing that several of the women dropped out only because their employers would not offer more family friendly work schedules. The cultural war over the demands of childrearing and work represents a real dilemma that society must face. The critics of working mothers and the champions of at-home mothers, however, tacitly assume that it is primarily the responsibility of women alone to solve the problem.

The genie is out of the bottle. Women, even those with young children, are working for significant portions of their lives. And, despite the economic slowdown and the continuing critique of women's increased employment, women continue to devote more and more hours to work and fewer to family care. They don't appear to be changing their minds and going back home.[2] While many married women are partially insulated from the effects of their own lower earnings by living with higher earning men, overall women are acting to reduce their economic dependence on husbands and to protect themselves from the vulnerabilities of divorce. Women are choosing the path to greater independence, arranging childcare, balancing their work and care giving tasks as best they can, and trying to get their partners to put in their fair share of housework and care giving.[3] Women are spending less of their adult lives in marriage, marrying later, and having fewer children. One third of prime age working women have at least one year as a single parent. Women's needs for equal earnings are increasing as they spend less time living with men.

The current system also places a burden on American men, who have the longest work hours in the advanced industrialized world, and the least leisure. The relative lack of infrastructure to support working parents in the United States (subsidized childcare, paid family leave) means that families are left to cope on their own. Most do so by increasing male work hours, enabling women to work less and spend more time on family care in the short run, but increasing women's economic vulnerability in the long run.

And to the extent that women's unequal pay contributes to poverty, it places a strain on our social safety net. The cumulative effect of years of lower earnings for women raises the cost to our welfare system, and reduces tax revenues.

Can the system change to become more conducive to women's equality? Certainly nothing is fixed in the long run, but many barriers remain in the United States. If Women in the United States hope to improve their economic standing and achieve greater economic parity with male workers, there must be a systematic change in both practices and policies with regard to work and family life. Among the policy strategies that are needed are the following:

- Strengthening equal employment opportunity (EEO) enforcement, by increasing federal support for government oversight agencies, both the Equal Employment Opportunity Commission (EEOC) and the Office for Federal Contract Compliance Programs (OFCCP). Complaints could be resolved more quickly with more resources, and, if more cases were resolved in the plaintiffs' favor, due to stronger and more timely enforcement efforts, employers would have larger incentives to improve their employment practices. The OFCCP could target federal contractors in egregious industries (e.g. construction) to encourage them to adhere to their affirmative action plans, much like mining and banking were targeted in the 1970s. One promising approach might be to audit many large employers regularly for discrimination, much the way large federal contractors have their financial transactions continually monitored by on-site auditors. Women's greater entry into predominately male jobs in the middle tier—in fire fighting, police work, or skilled trades—would be especially important in raising women's wages since women's jobs in this tier are particularly underpaid relative to men's jobs.
- Opening up educational and job training opportunities. Unfortunately there are still too many women who have been discouraged from pursuing higher education and/or job training for occupations that are not traditionally held by women. Jobs in the skilled trades and in the computer industry, for example, frequently require pre-job preparation that women are less likely to have access to. Programs that help women get to the starting gate with equal skills will benefit women tremendously.
- Developing new EEO remedies to address unequal pay for jobs of comparable worth (the tendency for jobs done disproportionately by women to pay less than jobs that require similar skill, effort, and responsibility but are traditionally held by men). Employers could be required to show that comparable jobs are paid fairly, using tools such as job evaluation systems that measure job content on many dimensions. Both men and women

in jobs that are underpaid because they are done predominantly by women would stand to gain from comparable worth implementation.

- Improving workers' bargaining power in the workplace, such as through encouraging increased unionization in unorganized sectors and raising the minimum wage, especially since women are over-represented among the non-unionized and low-wage work force. Living wage campaigns and efforts to tie the federal or state minimum wages to cost of living increases all raise public awareness about the importance of setting a reasonable wage floor. A reasonable wage floor disproportionately benefits women workers and the children they support.

- Creating more good part-time jobs that provide decent pay, benefits, and promotion opportunities. A less than optimal equilibrium may have formed in the labor market where many good jobs require more than 40 hours of work per week. This prevents workers from entering such jobs if they want to work fewer hours, and employers miss the opportunity to learn whether part-time workers in these jobs can contribute equally (on a per hour basis). Career part-time jobs could be fostered by public sector employers and, if successful, private sector employers could be encouraged to follow suit. Single parents would also be especially helped by the greater availability of part-time jobs with good hourly pay and benefits since their family care responsibilities generally limit their hours to less than full-time.

- Making work places 'family friendly'—including flexible hours, parental and other family care leave (including paid leave), and paid sick leave. Too often it is the lowest-paid workers who have the least access to these benefits since they are not legally required of most employers. Yet if such leaves were made more available and if they were used equally by both sexes, new workplace norms would be developed that recognize that all workers, male or female, have responsibilities to others that sometimes take them away from their jobs. Such paid leave programs could be provided through social insurance schemes, such as the recent expansion of the Temporary Disability Insurance system in California to include paid leave for family care. More wide spread use of leaves should, over time, reduce the earnings penalties observed for time out of the labor market.

- Providing more high quality, affordable childcare, through subsidized childcare centers at workplaces and in the community, and more public subsidies for higher education as well. Since well-reared and well-educated children are an asset to the whole society it makes no economic sense that most parents shoulder the financial responsibility for children's care and education alone. This arrangement disadvantages single mothers particularly since they have only one wage, and a lower one at that, with which to provide for their children.

- Encouraging men to be full participants in family care. Such sharing can be encouraged by government requirements for both parents to share available parental leave (as is done in the Nordic countries) and by utilizing the bully pulpit to educate employers and the public about the positive benefits of encouraging men to exercise options for flexible work arrangements when available and spend more time with children and less time working. A full-scale public education campaign against the double-standard in parenting, in which mothers seem to be expected to meet a higher standard of care than fathers, is needed.

- Reducing income tax rates on secondary earners, most often women, and reducing the 'marriage penalty' for dual earner couples. Higher tax rates for married couples are found up and down the income scale and they generally depress the work effort of the lower earning member of the couple.
- Improving access to non-custodial fathers' incomes or otherwise raising incomes in single mother families. Since single mothers and their children suffer disproportunately from poverty and near-poverty, even when the mother works (as the mothers in this study do), additional measures are needed to improve their income and support their work effort. In addition to paid leave and other family-friendly benefits, benefits such as subsidized housing or child care should be extended further up the income scale. Child support should be increased and income and property settlements at divorce should be more generous to the custodial parent. A strong safety net and work supports are necessary for low-income parents to maintain their employment and enable them to gain from long-term, steady employment.
- Democratizing the 'old boy' network. Since many positions in the economy depend on strong social interactions, these seemingly non-work relationships have economic consequences. The refusal of the Augusta National Golf Club to admit women in the spring of 2003 is one example of a principal location where the 'old boy' network remains intact. More surprising, perhaps, is the failure of male corporate leaders to resign from the club quickly once its exclusive membership policies became generally known. Federal EEO regulations and tax laws could be strengthened to clarify that employer support of such networks is discriminatory and not allowable as a business related tax deduction.
- Reducing working time norms. As long work hours increasingly become the standard, women can be more easily excluded because they are less likely to be able to meet this requirement. Most European countries manage to both provide more public support for parenting and have lower working hours on average. Reducing work hour norms, perhaps through eliminating or setting a cap on mandatory overtime, increasing the required premium paid for overtime work, or reducing the standard work week to 35 hours could spread the work and jobs more equitably across all members of society, increase gender equality in family care time, and increase the time available for leisure and civic engagement.

Achieving equality in the work place will likely require several more decades. The important thing is to keep the momentum going and prevent backsliding toward the reestablishment of the feminine mystique or 1950s family values. Instead, we must continue the progress our society has been making toward equal opportunity and fair compensation for women in the labor market and the more equitable sharing of family care between women and men.

Notes

1. Interestingly, research shows that mothers today, despite spending much more time working for pay, spend about as much time directly interacting with their children as mothers a generation ago (Bianchi 2000).

2. While data show a small drop from 1998–2002 in the labor force participation of mothers with infants (children less than one year of age), at approximately the same time the economic recession and slow recovery reduced labor force participation generally. The long-run trend in the labor force participation of mothers has been one of considerable increase. For mothers of infants, for example, the proportion in the labor force increased from 31 percent in 1976 to 55 percent in 1995, roughly the same as the 2002 figure of 54.6 percent (U.S. Census Bureau 2003b: Figure 2).

3. In an overview of changes in women's well-being, Blau (1998) shows that housework time decreased for almost everyone between 1978 and 1988. Married men were the only group to increase their housework time, indicating that married women were having some success in getting household tasks reallocated.

Naomi Lopez

 **NO**

Free Markets, Free Choices II: Smashing the Wage Gap and Glass Ceiling Myths

Executive Summary

Despite women's rapid gains in the working world, gender preference advocates and the media often portray working women as victims of rampant discrimination. This discrimination, such advocates argue, results in a wage gap and renders women powerless in the face of an impenetrable glass ceiling. While discrimination does exist in the workplace, levels of education attainment, field of education, and time spent in the workforce play a far greater role in determining women's pay and promotion.

Today, the average American woman earns about 74 cents for every dollar the average man earns. Women compose about 11 percent of corporate officers in the Fortune 500 companies. While such statistics are routinely used as evidence of gender discrimination, they ignore the many variables that affect position and earnings. More important, these claims serve to devalue women's choices—such as family, volunteer work, and self-employment—when they are not geared towards the corporate boardroom.

The reality is that, when considering men and women with similar fields of study, educational attainment, and continuous time spent in the workforce, the wage gap disappears. This is true for some women in high-paying "male" fields such as engineering, chemistry, and computer science.

Women make up 60 million of the nation's 138 million workers and have more than doubled their salaries, in real terms, over the past 50 years. These trends are only expected to continue as more women pursue higher education and seek professional career tracks.

Today, many women's groups have abandoned equal opportunity and are now calling for government action to create gender preferences that aim to guarantee women equal outcomes in earnings and representation in management. These advocates presume that unequal outcomes are due to discrimination, ignoring individual differences, preferences, and decisions.

When gender discrimination does occur, a formal, legal process exists to compensate alleged victims and protect them from retaliation from employers. The process also punishes alleged perpetrators and protects them from false claims.

Women's most dramatic employment gains occurred well before equal-pay legislation, civil-rights legislation, and affirmative-action programs. Furthermore, women's greatest gains in earnings occurred during the early 1980s—without hiring quotas and comparable-worth pay.

Women's continued success in the workplace will be secured by promotion of the original intent of the Civil Right's Act—equal opportunity, not special preferences. Enforcement of anti-discrimination laws also has a role to play, along with free-market economic policies, such as reducing the tax and regulatory burdens for small business. In these ways, the United States can create and maintain equal opportunity for women and all Americans.

Introduction

Women's dramatic gains in academia, the workplace, and the political world are well documented and cause for celebration. But as feminist leaders continue to use the wage gap and glass ceiling as rallying cries for further government action, some have come to believe that, absent gender preferences, women would not have achieved dramatic gains in these areas. There is no doubt that technological advances, attitudinal changes towards women's roles, and the women's movement profoundly contributed to these gains. The role of government in attempting to eliminate gender discrimination, however, deserves careful attention.

Women's labor force participation has dramatically increased since the turn of the century. Economist and Nobel laureate Gary Becker points out that market forces play a powerful role in determining women's labor force participation and earnings. Becker notes that:

> . . . the growth in employment and earnings of women over time is explained mostly by market forces rather than by civil rights legislation, affirmative-action programs, or the women's movement. Such programs can hardly explain the steady growth in the employment of women prior to 1950, or its accelerated growth during the 1950s and 1960s, since neither civil rights programs nor women's movements were yet widespread. Nor can equal-pay-for-equal-work legislation alone explain the narrowing earnings gap between men and women in the past 15 years. For one thing, the gap also narrowed in countries, such as Italy and Japan, that did not introduce such legislation.

By failing to examine historic trends in women's labor force participation—including participation in white collar jobs, such as managers—and educational attainment, one can mistakenly over-credit civil rights and equal-pay legislation for many of the opportunities women now enjoy. That is not to say that women have not benefited from equal protection under the law, but it is important to realize there is a significant distinction between opportunity and preference. Opportunity, however unequal, is responsible for many of the gains and successes that women now enjoy.

Whether at the turn of the century or today, the single necessary condition of women's success is affirmative action in its original sense—equality of opportunity. This should be the guiding principle of today's women's movement. According women anything beyond the same rights and opportunities as men, without special preferences, assumes that women will not continue to succeed.

The Wage Gap

The wage gap is the alleged difference between female and male earnings. In 1959, women earned about 59 cents for every dollar a man earned. Today, the wage gap has narrowed to about 74 cents for every dollar a man earns. When we compare educational attainment, we still find a significant gap even as education rises. Based on these disturbing numbers, it is easy to see why there is so much interest in this issue. But this is only part of the story.

Women do earn less than men, even at the highest educational levels. Upon further examination, however, we find that field of study has a major role in determining earnings. A 1970 U.S. Census Bureau study revealed that, among men with four-year degrees or higher who had earnings in 1966, fields of study accounted for wide disparities in subsequent earnings. Men specializing in law, health professions, and engineering garnered the highest earnings, while men specializing in religion, the humanities, education, and the biological sciences earned lower. While we know that women made significant strides in educational attainment earlier in the century; we do not have detailed information on their field of study until the mid-1960s.

A 1976 Census Bureau study examined field of study for two- and four-year college students between 1966 and 1974. While this study did not provide information on matriculation, level of degree earned, or highest degree earned, it indicated the rapid entrance of women into higher education; the dramatic increases of women in most non-humanities fields of study; and, with the notable exception of the health profession, a concentration of women in lower-yield fields of study.

Decades later, whether between men and men or men and women, field of study is still an important factor in subsequent earnings. In fact, many of the high-yield fields in the mid-1960s continue to be among the most lucrative today. Women are continuing their pursuit of these fields as evidenced by a continuous gravitation towards these high-yield fields and attainment of graduate degrees in these fields.

What is particularly striking is that, for women between the ages of 25 and 34 with bachelor's degrees, there does not appear to be a wage gap with their male counterparts in some of the same fields of study that require "men's" quantitative and scientific aptitudes. Architecture and environmental design are male-dominated fields but women's earnings in this area are a full 95 percent of men's. Engineering, another male-dominated field, yielded women 99 percent of men's earnings. Women earned 97 percent of men's earnings in chemistry and 94 percent in computer and information sciences.

Women between the ages of 35 and 44 with bachelor's degrees leaped ahead of men in architecture and environmental design, at a rate of 109 percent.

Economics, another male-dominated field, saw women break even at 100 percent of men's earnings. One must question how these women managed to fare this well in some of the most competitive, highest-paying, and male-dominated fields in the face of rampant gender discrimination, which some claim begins in the earliest years of one's education.

Love and Marriage

The remaining piece of the wage gap puzzle lies in continuous time spent in the workforce. This factor is critical because it is not readily apparent at first glance. For example, knowing that six out of every ten women were in the workforce in 1997 does not reveal whether they were the same six still in the workforce in 1999.

According to U.S. Bureau of the Census and Bureau of Labor Statistics data, men consistently log more work activity than women, regardless of educational level. In the aggregate, however, women are actually earning more per hour than men. In these ways, time spent away from the workforce adversely affects earnings and seniority.

As women's roles have changed from homemaker to breadwinner, women still assume a disproportionate share of housework. Economists Joni Hersch and Leslie S. Stratton found that wives' domestic responsibilities adversely affect income and that time spent on housework is responsible for eight or more percent of the wage gap. While this may not come as a surprise to mature wives, there are indications that Generation X couples are likely to more equally divide domestic responsibilities which should mitigate this housework/income trade-off for wives.

Since the early 1970s, never-married women in their thirties with continuous labor force participation earn slightly higher incomes than their male counterparts with the same background. Furthermore, women without children have earnings approaching 98 percent of men's.

In addition to changing the composition of the American workforce, married women are also "bringing home the bacon." Today, about one out of five married women is earning more than her husband. This trend will likely continue in the future, especially as men assume more domestic responsibilities and as women have fewer children and bear them later in life. Some households are now relocating to new cities to accommodate the wife's job, a trend almost unheard of in the 1960s.

Personal decision making—choices such as level of education attainment, field of study, time spent in the workforce, and, yes, time spent in the kitchen—plays a far greater role in determining women's pay and promotion than gender discrimination.

The Glass Ceiling

Good For Business: Making Full Use of the Nation's Human Capital, the report of the 1995 Federal Glass Ceiling Commission, claimed that only five percent of senior managers at Fortune 1000 companies are women. This finding has since become a rallying cry for advocates of gender-based preference policies. The "glass ceiling" refers to the idea that discrimination against women in the workplace remains a formidable barrier to their upward mobility in the corporate world.

While disturbing, this figure both fails to reveal the dramatic gains women have made in management over the past few decades and the future trend of women in these positions. This figure overlooks the fact that, of the qualified labor pool, women are accurately reflected in these senior management positions. Furthermore, this five percent figure is a minuscule portion of managers in a small, select group of companies, not reflecting the wide array of management positions in the broader workforce.

U.S. Department of Labor statistics reveal that, though they represent only 46 percent of the U.S. labor force, women hold about half of all management jobs, and in the aggregate, hold fewer bachelor's and higher degrees than their male counterparts. Since the Glass Ceiling Commission report was released, the number of women in Fortune 500 senior management positions has tripled.

What about the future prospects of women in the Fortune 500? The typical qualifications for senior corporate management positions are a MBA and 25 years in the labor force. Looking back 25 years, fewer than 7 percent of MBA graduates were women. Assuming that no women left the workforce over the 25-year period between 1974 and 1999, one would only expect to find around 7 percent of women holding these jobs—far less than the current 11 percent. And with women representing more than one third of MBA graduates, women are now in the "pipeline" for these positions.

Rather than choosing to climb the ladder in corporate America, many women are instead seeking success in their own firms and are fulfilling their desire for more flexibility and independence.

Today, women-owned businesses account for one third of all firms in the United States. According to the National Foundation of Women Business Owners (NFWBO), there were almost 8 million women-owned businesses in the United States in 1996. Estimates also reveal that the number of women-owned firms grew by 78 percent between 1987 and 1996 and that employment in those firms grew by 183 percent.

Women are also engaging in job-sharing arrangements and telecommuting in greater numbers, reflecting both the individual's desire for a more flexible lifestyle and employers' desire to allow greater freedom.

The End of Discrimination? Not Likely

There is no doubt that women face gender discrimination in the workplace, but a statistical disparity or the mere appearance of discrimination does not make it so. For example, the parents of a child that receives several injuries over the course of a year—far more than the average child—are not automatically guilty of child abuse or neglect. Accompanied by additional evidence, however, such a case might be proven true. Attempting to use statistical disparities, which are often the rule rather than the exception in America, as the sole arbitrator of discriminatory practices sets a dangerous precedent.

According to the U.S. Equal Employment Opportunity Commission (EEOC), fewer than one in five sexual harassment charges results in a meritorious outcome and fewer than one in twenty is found to have reasonable cause. Of sex-based charges, about one in eight charges result in a meritorious outcome. Only one in 25 is found to have reasonable cause. A formal, legal process, based on evidence not conjecture, exists to compensate alleged victims and protect them from retaliation. The process also punishes alleged perpetrators and protects them from false claims. Equating seeming disparities in pay to discrimination, without carefully scrutinizing the facts, undermines the important legal protections and processes that have been carefully established.

Many women's groups are abandoning these legal protections that ensure equal opportunity in pursuit of government action to create gender preferences that aim to guarantee women equal outcomes in earnings and representation in management. These advocates presume that unequal outcomes are due to discrimination, ignoring individual choices, preferences, and personal decisions. This, in turn, undermines opportunity, however unequal, which has been the cornerstone of women's achievements throughout this century.

Conclusion

Women may never achieve parity with men in the workplace, but that is not bad news for women. Some will choose not to work, while others will set their sights to lead the top corporations in America. The majority of women will fall somewhere in between.

Women's dramatic gains in academia, the workplace, and the political world are cause for celebration. The record confirms that these dramatic gains were achieved without government gender preferences. Whether at the turn of the century or today, the single necessary condition of women's success in affirmative action in its original sense—equality of opportunity. This should be the guiding principle of today's women's movement. According women anything beyond the same rights and opportunities as men, without special preferences, assumes that women will not continue to succeed.

The record shows otherwise, and refutes the notion that women need special preferences and government programs. No rehashing of shopworn grievances can change the facts. Given equal opportunity, women achieve at the highest levels and their record of achievement will continue to grow.

POSTSCRIPT

Is Gender Discrimination the Main Reason Women Are Paid Less Than Men?

Another way of viewing the wage gap debate is understanding it as an "equality of outcome" versus "equality of opportunity" issue. The goal of the former approach is equality in the sense that people are economically, socially, and legally equal. Regardless of where they start, this view holds that equity exists only when everyone enjoys the same results. Persistent differences in outcomes are indicative of discriminatory forces and can only be remedied through social initiatives designed to provide redress to victims. At the workplace, this approach argues that, within reason, all groups should be equally represented at each level of the organization. There should also be no persistent differences in pay between males and females. To the extent that there is, gender discrimination is presumed to be the cause. And, as researchers Stephen J. Rose and Heidi I. Hartmann note in their article here, women's access to high-paying career paths is constricted, thus indicating that "women face discrimination in the labor market and in the pre-labor market preparation as well."

Those who believe our societal obligations extend no further than providing everyone with a level playing field argue from a perspective of equal opportunity. Advocates of this view recognize that what accounts for the differences in women and men's pay and other indicators of corporate success has little to do with discrimination and much more to do with factors such as motivation levels, skill differences, and willingness to work hard. In the article you just read, Naomi Lopez has strong words for those who disagree with her viewpoint: "These advocates [equality of outcome supporters] presume that unequal outcomes are due to discrimination, ignoring individual choices, preferences, and personal decisions. This, in turn, undermines opportunity, however unequal, which has been the cornerstone of women's achievements throughout this century."

Suggested Readings

Samuel Cohn, Why are women paid less than men? *Race and Gender Discrimination at Work*. Westview Press, 2000.

Government Accountabililty Office (GAO), Women's Earnings: Work Patterns Partially Explain Difference between Men's and Woman's Earnings. *Reports and Testimony, GAO-04-35*, October 31, 2003.

Sally J. Haymann, The widening gap: Why America's working families are in jeopardy and what can be done about it. Basic Books, 2000.

Wendy McElroy, Wage gap reflects women's priorities. Foxnews.com, September 22, 2004. http://www.foxnews.com/story/0,2933, 133088,00.html

Staffs of Representatives John D. Dingell and Carolyn B. Maloney, A new look through the glass ceiling: Where are the women? *U.S. General Accounting Office,* January 2002.

Howard J. Wall, The gender wage gap and wage discrimination: Illusion or reality. *The Regional Economist,* October 2000. http://stlouisfed .org/publications/re/2000/d/pages/economic-backgnd.html

ISSUE 10

Is Blowing the Whistle
an Act of Disloyalty?

YES: Sissela Bok, from "Whistleblowing and Professional Responsibility," *New York University Education Quarterly* (Summer 1980)

NO: Robert A. Larmer, from "Whistleblowing and Employee Loyalty," *Journal of Business Ethics* (vol. 11, 1992)

ISSUE SUMMARY

YES: In presenting her view that whistle-blowing is usually a form of disloyalty, business ethics scholar Sissela Bok examines the nature of the whistle-blowing act itself as well as the motives of the individual exposing the wrongdoing.

NO: In contrast with Bok, University of New Brunswick philosophy professor Robert Larmer argues that it is not a breach of trust and, therefore, not an act of disloyalty.

On December 2, 2001, energy giant Enron Corporation filed for bankruptcy protection, the largest such action in the history of the United States. This action represented the final step in an amazingly fast downward spiral that started just a few months before in August 2001 when Enron VP Sherron Watkins wrote a memo to CEO Kenneth Lay outlining her discovery of and concern about illegal accounting practices involving various limited partnership investments held by Enron. Not satisfied by Lay's response to her concerns, she shared her knowledge with Enron's accounting firm Arthur Anderson, an act that ultimately led to the disclosure that Enron was worth over $1 billion less than it claimed, due mostly to losses from the partnerships they had created in the 1990s. This disclosure and the resulting massive devaluation of their stock forced the company to declare bankruptcy. Print and television media around the country portrayed Watkins as a heroic whistle-blower, a courageous individual who decided to expose corporate greed and immoral behavior committed by her superiors and co-workers.

Generally speaking, whistle-blowing occurs when an employee tells the public of illegal or immoral behavior on the part of his or her employer or co-workers. Since going public almost always results in harm to the organization, the decision to blow the whistle is usually an act of last resort. Further, it is important to realize that whistle-blowing carries considerable risk for the individual: The literature on this topic is rife with cases of employer retaliation against employees who publicly exposed their improper business behaviors. It is not uncommon for a whistle-blower to lose his or her job and have to relocate, often having to settle for a lower paying position. This isn't particularly surprising considering that a reputation for being a whistle-blower does not make things easier in the job market. And although they are extreme cases, there have been instances where the individual's personal safety was at risk. Indeed, two hugely popular Hollywood movies—*Silkwood* and *The Insider*—portrayed the harrowing, real-life stories of two courageous whistle-blowers who went public with damaging information about their firms' illegal practices and found themselves and their families in danger.

In a fascinating study of 55 whistle-blower cases (*The Whistle-Blowers: Exposing Corruption in Government and Industry*, Basic Books, 1989), business scholars Myron and Penina Glazer identified a strong belief in personal responsibility as the most common trait shared by the individuals who exposed wrongdoing. And, consistent with other research, they reported the majority felt their actions were morally correct and would blow the whistle again under similar circumstances. This comment is typical: "A corrupt system can happen only if the individuals who make up that system are corrupt. You are either going to be part of the corruption or part of the forces working against it. . . . Someone, someday, has to take a stand; if you don't, maybe no one will. And that is wrong." (Quote taken from Newton & Ford, *Taking Sides: Clashing Views on Controversial Issues in Business Ethics and Society*, 8th ed., McGraw-Hill Dushkin, 2004, p. 173.)

Although most whistle-blowers regard their behavior as morally correct, many business ethics scholars (not to mention organizational executives!) consider it an act of disloyalty to the firm. They argue that the motivation of the individual exposing the wrong-doing needs to be taken into account—many disgruntled employees have gone public specifically to cause harm to the company and without any real concern about whether their actions were in the best interest of the employees, the firm, or the general public. As scholar Daryl Koehn notes, "if and when a whistleblower's motives are mixed, we have some reason to wonder, on the one, hand, whether is trustworthy and, on the other hand, to perhaps be more sympathetic to a company who charges that the whistleblower has betrayed it and the public as well." (Quote from Hartman, *Perspectives in Business Ethics,* 2nd ed., McGraw-Hill, 2002, p. 459.)

The following two selections address the question, is blowing the whistle an act of disloyalty? Business ethics scholar Sissela Bok believes that it is and presents her argument here first. University of New Brunswick philosophy professor Robert Larmer argues that it is not a breach of trust and, therefore, not an act of disloyalty. As you read through these sections, ask yourself what you would do if you were faced with a potential whistle-blowing situation. Would concern for you, your family, or your career affect your ultimate decision? Do you consider whistle-blowing to be an act of disloyalty?

Sissela Bok  **YES**

Whistleblowing and Professional Responsibility

Whistleblowing" is a new label generated by our increased awareness of the ethical conflicts encountered at work. Whistleblowers sound an alarm from within the very organization in which they work, aiming to spotlight neglect or abuses that threaten the public interest.

The stakes in whistleblowing are high. Take the nurse who alleges that physicians enrich themselves in her hospital through unnecessary surgery; the engineer who discloses safety defects in the braking systems of a fleet of new rapid-transit vehicles; the Defense Department official who alerts Congress to military graft and overspending: all know that they pose a threat to those whom they denounce and that their own careers may be at risk.

Moral Conflicts

Moral conflicts on several levels confront anyone who is wondering whether to speak out about abuses or risks or serious neglect. In the first place, he must try to decide whether, other things being equal, speaking out is in fact in the public interest. This choice is often made more complicated by factual uncertainties: Who is responsible for the abuse or neglect? How great is the threat? And how likely is it that speaking out will precipitate changes for the better?

In the second place, a would-be whistleblower must weigh his responsibility to serve the public interest against the responsibility he owes to his colleagues and the institution in which he works. While the professional ethic requires collegial loyalty, the codes of ethics often stress responsibility to the public over and above duties to colleagues and clients. Thus the United States Code of Ethics for Government Servants asks them to "expose corruption wherever uncovered" and to "put loyalty to the highest moral principles and to country above loyalty to persons, party, or government."[1] Similarly, the largest professional engineering association requires members to speak out against abuses threatening the safety, health, and welfare of the public.[2]

A third conflict for would-be whistleblowers is personal in nature and cuts across the first two: even in cases where they have concluded that the facts

From *New York University Education Quarterly*, Vol. 11, Summer 1980, pp. 2–7. Copyright © 1980 by Sissela Bok. Reprinted by permission of the author.

warrant speaking out, and that their duty to do so overrides loyalties to colleagues and institutions, they often have reason to fear the results of carrying out such a duty. However strong this duty may seem in theory, they know that, in practice, retaliation is likely. As a result, their careers and their ability to support themselves and their families may be unjustly impaired.[3] A government handbook issued during the Nixon era recommends reassigning "undesirables" to places so remote that they would prefer to resign. Whistleblowers may also be downgraded or given work without responsibility or work for which they are not qualified; or else they may be given many more tasks than they can possibly perform. Another risk is that an outspoken civil servant may be ordered to undergo a psychiatric fitness-for-duty examination,[4] declared unfit for service, and "separated" as well as discredited from the point of view of any allegations he may be making. Outright firing, finally, is the most direct institutional response to whistleblowers.

Add to the conflicts confronting individual whistleblowers the claim to self-policing that many professions make, and professional responsibility is at issue in still another way. For an appeal to the public goes against everything that "self-policing" stands for. The question for the different professions, then, is how to resolve, insofar as it is possible, the conflict between professional loyalty and professional responsibility toward the outside world. The same conflicts arise to some extent in all groups, but professional groups often have special cohesion and claim special dignity and privileges.

The plight of whistleblowers has come to be documented by the press and described in a number of books. Evidence of the hardships imposed on those who chose to act in the public interest has combined with a heightened awareness of professional malfeasance and corruption to produce a shift toward greater public support of whistleblowers. Public service law firms and consumer groups have taken up their cause; institutional reforms and legislation have been proposed to combat illegitimate reprisals.[5]

Given the indispensable services performed by so many whistleblowers, strong public support is often merited. But the new climate of acceptance makes it easy to overlook the dangers of whistleblowing: of uses in error or in malice; of work and reputations unjustly lost for those falsely accused; of privacy invaded and trust undermined. There comes a level of internal prying and mutual suspicion at which no institution can function. And it is a fact that the disappointed, the incompetent, the malicious, and the paranoid all too often leap to accusations in public. Worst of all, ideological persecution throughout the world traditionally relies on insiders willing to inform on their colleagues or even on their family members, often through staged public denunciations or press campaigns.

No society can count itself immune from such dangers. But neither can it risk silencing those with a legitimate reason to blow the whistle. How then can we distinguish between different instances of whistleblowing? A society that fails to protect the right to speak out even on the part of those whose warnings turn out to be spurious obviously opens the door to political repression. But from the moral point of view there are important differences between the aims, messages, and methods of dissenters from within.

Nature of Whistleblowing

Three elements, each jarring, and triply jarring when conjoined, lend acts of whistleblowing special urgency and bitterness: dissent, breach of loyalty, and accusation.

Like all dissent, whistleblowing makes public a disagreement with an authority or a majority view. But whereas dissent can concern all forms of disagreement with, for instance, religious dogma or government policy or court decisions, whistleblowing has the narrower aim of shedding light on negligence or abuse, or alerting to a risk, and of assigning responsibility for this risk.

Would-be whistleblowers confront the conflict inherent in all dissent: between conforming and sticking their necks out. The more repressive the authority they challenge, the greater the personal risk they take in speaking out. At exceptional times, as in times of war, even ordinarily tolerant authorities may come to regard dissent as unacceptable and even disloyal.[6]

Furthermore, the whistleblower hopes to stop the game; but since he is neither referee nor coach, and since he blows the whistle on his own team, his act is seen as a violation of loyalty. In holding his position, he has assumed certain obligations to his colleagues and clients. He may even have subscribed to a loyalty oath or a promise of confidentiality. Loyalty to colleagues and to clients comes to be pitted against loyalty to the public interest, to those who may be injured unless the revelation is made.

Not only is loyalty violated in whistleblowing, hierarchy as well is often opposed, since the whistleblower is not only a colleague but a subordinate. Though aware of the risks inherent in such disobedience, he often hopes to keep his job.[7] At times, however, he plans his alarm to coincide with leaving the institution. If he is highly placed, or joined by others, resigning in protest may effectively direct public attention to the wrongdoing at issue.[8] Still another alternative, often chosen by those who wish to be safe from retaliation, is to leave the institution quietly, to secure another post, and then to blow the whistle. In this way, it is possible to speak with the authority and knowledge of an insider without having the vulnerability of that position.

It is the element of accusation, of calling a "foul," that arouses the strongest reactions on the part of the hierarchy. The accusation may be of neglect, of willfully concealed dangers, or of outright abuse on the part of colleagues or superiors. It singles out specific persons or groups as responsible for threats to the public interest. If no one could be held responsible—as in the case of an impending avalanche—the warning would not constitute whistleblowing.

The accusation of the whistleblower, moreover, concerns a present or an imminent threat. Past errors or misdeeds occasion such an alarm only if they still affect current practices. And risks far in the future lack the immediacy needed to make the alarm a compelling one, as well as the close connection to particular individuals that would justify actual accusations. Thus an alarm can be sounded about safety defects in a rapid-transit system that threaten or will shortly threaten passengers, but the revelation of safety defects in a system no longer in use, while of historical interest, would not constitute whistleblowing. Nor would the revelation of potential problems in a system not yet fully designed and far from implemented.[9]

Not only immediacy, but also specificity, is needed for there to be an alarm capable of pinpointing responsibility. A concrete risk must be at issue rather than a vague foreboding or a somber prediction. The act of whistleblowing differs in this respect from the lamentation or the dire prophecy. An immediate and specific threat would normally be acted upon by those at risk. The whistleblower assumes that his message will alert listeners to something they do not know, or whose significance they have not grasped because it has been kept secret.

The desire for openness inheres in the temptation to reveal any secret, sometimes joined to an urge for self-aggrandizement and publicity and the hope for revenge for past slights or injustices. There can be pleasure, too—righteous or malicious—in laying bare the secrets of co-workers and in setting the record straight at last. Colleagues of the whistleblower often suspect his motives: they may regard him as a crank, as publicity-hungry, wrong about the facts, eager for scandal and discord, and driven to indiscretion by his personal biases and shortcomings.

For whistleblowing to be effective, it must arouse its audience. Inarticulate whistleblowers are likely to fail from the outset. When they are greeted by apathy, their message dissipates. When they are greeted by disbelief, they elicit no response at all. And when the audience is not free to receive or to act on the information—when censorship or fear of retribution stifles response—then the message rebounds to injure the whistleblower. Whistleblowing also requires the possibility of concerted public response: the idea of whistleblowing in an anarchy is therefore merely quixotic.

Such characteristics of whistleblowing and strategic considerations for achieving an impact are common to the noblest warnings, the most vicious personal attacks, and the delusions of the paranoid. How can one distinguish the many acts of sounding an alarm that are genuinely in the public interest from all the petty, biased, or lurid revelations that pervade our querulous and gossip-ridden society? Can we draw distinctions between different whistleblowers, different messages, different methods?

We clearly can, in a number of cases. Whistleblowing may be starkly inappropriate when in malice or error, or when it lays bare legitimately private matters having to do, for instance, with political belief or sexual life. It can, just as clearly, be the only way to shed light on an ongoing unjust practice such as drugging political prisoners or subjecting them to electroshock treatment. It can be the last resort for alerting the public to an impending disaster. Taking such clear-cut cases as benchmarks, and reflecting on what it is about them that weighs so heavily for or against speaking out, we can work our way toward the admittedly more complex cases in which whistleblowing is not so clearly the right or wrong choice, or where different points of view exist regarding its legitimacy—cases where there are moral reasons both for concealment and for disclosure and where judgments conflict. . . .

Individual Moral Choice

What questions might those who consider sounding an alarm in public ask themselves? How might they articulate the problem they see and weigh its injustice before deciding whether or not to reveal it? How can they best try to make sure their choice is the right one? In thinking about these questions it helps to keep in mind the three elements mentioned earlier: dissent, breach of loyalty, and accusation. They impose certain requirements—of accuracy and judgment in dissent; of exploring alternative ways to cope with improprieties that minimize the breach of loyalty; and of fairness in accusation. For each, careful articulation and testing of arguments are needed to limit error and bias.

Dissent by whistleblowers, first of all, is expressly claimed to be intended to benefit the public. It carries with it, as a result, an obligation to consider the nature of this benefit and to consider also the possible harm that may come from speaking out: harm to persons or institutions and, ultimately, to the public interest itself. Whistleblowers must, therefore, begin by making every effort to consider the effects of speaking out versus those of remaining silent. They must assure themselves of the accuracy of their reports, checking and rechecking the facts before speaking out; specify the degree to which there is genuine impropriety; consider how imminent is the threat they see, how serious, and how closely linked to those accused of neglect and abuse.

If the facts warrant whistleblowing, how can the second element—breach of loyalty—be minimized? The most important question here is whether the existing avenues for change within the organization have been explored. It is a waste of time for the public as well as harmful to the institution to sound the loudest alarm first. Whistleblowing has to remain a last alternative because of its destructive side effects: it must be chosen only when other alternatives have been considered and rejected. They may be rejected if they simply do not apply to the problem at hand, or when there is not time to go through routine channels or when the institution is so corrupt or coercive that steps will be taken to silence the whistleblower should he try the regular channels first.

What weight should an oath or a promise of silence have in the conflict of loyalties? One sworn to silence is doubtless under a stronger obligation because of the oath he has taken. He has bound himself, assumed specific obligations beyond those assumed in merely taking a new position. But even such promises can be overridden when the public interest at issue is strong enough. They can be overridden if they were obtained under duress or through deceit. They can be overridden, too, if they promise something that is in itself wrong or unlawful. The fact that one has promised silence is no excuse for complicity in covering up a crime or a violation of the public's trust.

The third element in whistleblowing—accusation—raises equally serious ethical concerns. They are concerns of fairness to the persons accused of impropriety. Is the message one to which the public is entitled in the first place? Or does it infringe on personal and private matters that one has no right to invade? Here, the very notion of what is in the public's best "interest" is at issue: "accusations" regarding an official's unusual sexual or religious experiences may well appeal to the public's interest without being information relevant to "the public interest."

Great conflicts arise here. We have witnessed excessive claims to executive privilege and to secrecy by government officials during the Watergate scandal in order to cover up for abuses the public had every right to discover. Conversely, those hoping to profit from prying into private matters have become adept at invoking "the public's right to know." Some even regard such private matters as threats to the public: they voice their own religious and political prejudices in the language of accusation. Such a danger is never stronger than when the accusation is delivered surreptitiously. The anonymous accusations made during the McCarthy period regarding political beliefs and associations often injured persons who did not even know their accusers or the exact nature of the accusations.

From the public's point of view, accusations that are openly made by identifiable individuals are more likely to be taken seriously. And in fairness to those criticized, openly accepted responsibility for blowing the whistle should be preferred to the denunciation or the leaked rumor. What is openly stated can more easily be checked, its source's motives challenged, and the underlying information examined. Those under attack may otherwise be hard put to defend themselves against nameless adversaries. Often they do not even know that they are threatened until it is too late to respond. The anonymous denunciation, moreover, common to so many regimes, places the burden of investigation on government agencies that may thereby gain the power of a secret police.

From the point of view of the whistleblower, on the other hand, the anonymous message is safer in situations where retaliation is likely. But it is also often less likely to be taken seriously. Unless the message is accompanied by indications of how the evidence can be checked, its anonymity, however safe for the source, speaks against it.

During the process of weighing the legitimacy of speaking out, the method used, and the degree of fairness needed, whistleblowers must try to compensate for the strong possibility of bias on their part. They should be scrupulously aware of any motive that might skew their message: a desire for self-defense in a difficult bureaucratic situation, perhaps, or the urge to seek revenge, or inflated expectations regarding the effect their message will have on the situation. (Needless to say, bias affects the silent as well as the outspoken. The motive for holding back important information about abuses and injustice ought to give similar cause for soul-searching.)

Likewise, the possibility of personal gain from sounding the alarm ought to give pause. Once again there is then greater risk of a biased message. Even if the whistleblower regards himself as incorruptible, his profiting from revelations of neglect or abuse will lead others to question his motives and to put less credence in his charges. If, for example, a government employee stands to make large profits from a book exposing the inequities in his agency, there is danger that he will, perhaps even unconsciously, slant his report in order to cause more of a sensation.

A special problem arises when there is a high risk that the civil servant who speaks out will have to go through costly litigation. Might he not justifiably try to make enough money on his public revelations—say, through books or public speaking—to offset his losses? In so doing he will not strictly speaking have *profited* from his revelations: he merely avoids being financially crushed by their sequels. He will nevertheless still be suspected at the time of revelation, and his message will therefore seem more questionable.

Reducing bias and error in moral choice often requires consultation, even open debate[10]: methods that force articulation of the moral arguments at stake and challenge privately held assumptions. But acts of whistleblowing present special problems when it comes to open consultation. On the one hand, once the whistleblower sounds his alarm publicly, his arguments will be subjected to open scrutiny; he will have to articulate his reasons for speaking out and substantiate his charges. On the other hand, it will then be too late to retract the alarm or to combat its harmful effects, should his choice to speak out have been ill-advised.

For this reason, the whistleblower owes it to all involved to make sure of two things: that he has sought as much and as objective advice regarding his choice as he can *before* going public; and that he is aware of the arguments for and against the practice of whistleblowing in general, so that he can see his own choice against as richly detailed and coherently structured a background as possible. Satisfying these two requirements once again has special problems because of the very nature of whistleblowing: the more corrupt the circumstances, the more dangerous it may be to seek consultation before speaking out. And yet, since the whistleblower himself may have a biased view of the state of affairs, he may choose not to consult others when in fact it would be not only safe but advantageous to do so; he may see corruption and conspiracy where none exists.

Notes

1. Code of Ethics for Government Service passed by the U.S. House of Representatives in the 85th Congress (1958) and applying to all government employees and office holders.

2. Code of Ethics of the Institute of Electrical and Electronics Engineers, Article IV.

3. For case histories and descriptions of what befalls whistleblowers, see Rosemary Chalk and Frank von Hippel, "Due Process for Dissenting Whistle-Blowers," *Technology Review* 81 (June–July 1979); 48–55; Alan S. Westin and Stephen Salisbury, eds., *Individual Rights in the Corporation* (New York: Pantheon, 1980); Helen Dudar, "The Price of Blowing the Whistle," *New York Times Magazine*, 30 October 1979, pp. 41–54; John Edsall, *Scientific Freedom and Responsibility* (Washington, D.C.: American Association for the Advancement of Science, 1975), p. 5; David Ewing, *Freedom Inside the Organization* (New York: Dutton, 1977); Ralph Nader, Peter Petkas, and Kate Blackwell, *Whistle Blowing* (New York: Grossman, 1972); Charles Peter and Taylor Branch, *Blowing the Whistle* (New York: Praeger, 1972).

4. Congressional hearings uncovered a growing resort to mandatory psychiatric examinations.

5. For an account of strategies and proposals to support government whistleblowers, see Government Accountability Project, *A Whistleblower's Guide to the Federal Bureaucracy* (Washington, D.C.: Institute for Policy Studies, 1977).

6. See, e.g., Samuel Eliot Morison, Frederick Merk, and Frank Friedel, *Dissent in Three American Wars* (Cambridge: Harvard University Press, 1970).

7. In the scheme worked out by Albert Hirschman in *Exit, Voice and Loyalty* (Cambridge: Harvard University Press, 1970), whistleblowing represents "voice" accompanied by a preference not to "exit," though forced "exit" is clearly a possibility and "voice" after or during "exit" may be chosen for strategic reasons.

8. Edward Weisband and Thomas N. Franck, *Resignation in Protest* (New York: Grossman, 1975).

9. Future developments can, however, be the cause for whistleblowing if they are seen as resulting from steps being taken or about to be taken that render them inevitable.

10. I discuss these questions of consultation and publicity with respect to moral choice in chapter 7 of Sissela Bok, *Lying* (New York: Pantheon, 1978); and in *Secrets* (New York: Pantheon Books, 1982), Ch. IX and XV.

NO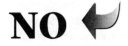

Robert A. Larmer

Whistleblowing and Employee Loyalty

Whistleblowing by an employee is the act of complaining, either within the corporation or publicly, about a corporation's unethical practices. Such an act raises important questions concerning the loyalties and duties of employees. Traditionally, the employee has been viewed as an agent who acts on behalf of a principal, i.e., the employer, and as possessing duties of loyalty and confidentiality. Whistleblowing, at least at first blush, seems a violation of these duties and it is scarcely surprising that in many instances employers and fellow employees argue that it is an act of disloyalty and hence morally wrong.[1]

It is this issue of the relation between whistleblowing and employee loyalty that I want to address. What I will call the standard view is that employees possess *prima facie* duties of loyalty and confidentiality to their employers and that whistleblowing cannot be justified except on the basis of a higher duty to the public good. Against this standard view, Ronald Duska has recently argued that employees do not have even a *prima facie* duty of loyalty to their employers and that whistleblowing needs, therefore, no moral justification.[2] I am going to criticize both views. My suggestion is that both misunderstand the relation between loyalty and whistleblowing. In their place I will propose a third more adequate view.

Duska's view is more radical in that it suggests that there can be no issue of whistleblowing and employee loyalty, since the employee has no duty to be loyal to his employer. His reason for suggesting that the employee owes the employer, at least the corporate employer, no loyalty is that companies are not the kinds of things which are proper objects of loyalty. His argument in support of this rests upon two key claims. The first is that loyalty, properly understood, implies a reciprocal relationship and is only appropriate in the context of a mutual surrendering of self-interest. He writes,

> It is important to recognize that in any relationship which demands loyalty the relationship works both ways and involves mutual enrichment. Loyalty is incompatible with self-interest, because it is something that necessarily requires we go beyond self-interest. My loyalty to my friend, for example, requires I put aside my interests some of the time. . . . Loyalty depends on ties that demand self-sacrifice with no expectation of reward, e.g., the ties of loyalty that bind a family together.[3]

From *Journal of Business Ethics*, Vol. 11, 1992, pp. 125–128. Copyright © 1992 by Kluwer Academic Journals. Reprinted by permission.

The second is that the relation between a company and an employee does not involve any surrender of self-interest on the part of the company, since its primary goal is to maximize profit. Indeed, although it is convenient, it is misleading to talk of a company having interests. As Duska comments,

> A company is not a person. A company is an instrument, and an instrument with a specific purpose, the making of profit. To treat an instrument as an end in itself, like a person, may not be as bad as treating an end as an instrument, but it does give the instrument a moral status it does not deserve . . .[4]

Since, then, the relation between a company and an employee does not fulfill the minimal requirement of being a relation between two individuals, much less two reciprocally self-sacrificing individuals, Duska feels it is a mistake to suggest the employee has any duties of loyalty to the company.

This view does not seem adequate, however. First, it is not true that loyalty must be quite so reciprocal as Duska demands. Ideally, of course, one expects that if one is loyal to another person that person will reciprocate in kind. There are, however, many cases where loyalty is not entirely reciprocated, but where we do not feel that it is misplaced. A parent, for example, may remain loyal to an erring teenager, even though the teenager demonstrates no loyalty to the parent. Indeed, part of being a proper parent is to demonstrate loyalty to your children whether or not that loyalty is reciprocated. This is not to suggest any kind of analogy between parents and employees, but rather that it is not nonsense to suppose that loyalty may be appropriate even though it is not reciprocated. Inasmuch as he ignores this possibility, Duska's account of loyalty is flawed.

Second, even if Duska is correct in holding that loyalty is only appropriate between moral agents and that a company is not genuinely a moral agent, the question may still be raised whether an employee owes loyalty to fellow employees or the shareholders of the company. Granted that reference to a company as an individual involves reification and should not be taken too literally, it may nevertheless constitute a legitimate shorthand way of describing relations between genuine moral agents.

Third, it seems wrong to suggest that simply because the primary motive of the employer is economic, considerations of loyalty are irrelevant. An employee's primary motive in working for an employer is generally economic, but no one on that account would argue that it is impossible for her to demonstrate loyalty to the employer, even if it turns out to be misplaced. All that is required is that her primary economic motive be in some degree qualified by considerations of the employer's welfare. Similarly, the fact that an employer's primary motive is economic does not imply that it is not qualified by considerations of the employee's welfare. Given the possibility of mutual qualification of admittedly primary economic motives, it is fallacious to argue that employee loyalty is never appropriate.

In contrast to Duska, the standard view is that loyalty to one's employer is appropriate. According to it, one has an obligation to be loyal to one's employer and, consequently, a *prima facie* duty to protect the employer's interests. Whistleblowing constitutes, therefore, a violation of duty to one's employer and needs strong justification if it is to be appropriate. Sissela Bok summarizes this view very well when she writes

> The whistleblower hopes to stop the game; but since he is neither referee nor coach, and since he blows the whistle on his own team, his act is seen as a violation of loyalty. In holding his position, he has assumed certain obligations to his colleagues and clients. He may even have subscribed to a loyalty oath or a promise of confidentiality. Loyalty to colleagues and to clients comes to be pitted against loyalty to the public interest, to those who may be injured unless the revelation is made.[5]

The strength of this view is that it recognizes that loyalty is due one's employer. Its weakness is that it tends to conceive of whistleblowing as involving a tragic moral choice, since blowing the whistle is seen not so much as a positive action, but rather the lesser of two evils. Bok again puts the essence of this view very clearly when she writes that "a would-be whistleblower must weigh his responsibility to serve the public interest *against* the responsibility he owes to his colleagues and the institution in which he works" and "that [when] their duty [to whistleblow] . . . *so overrides loyalties to colleagues and institutions,* they [whistleblowers] often have reason to fear the results of carrying out such a duty."[6] The employee, according to this understanding of whistleblowing, must choose between two acts of betrayal, either her employer or the public interest, each in itself reprehensible.

Behind this view lies the assumption that to be loyal to someone is to act in a way that accords with what that person believes to be in her best interests. To be loyal to an employer, therefore, is to act in a way which the employer deems to be in his or her best interests. Since employers very rarely approve of whistleblowing and generally feel that it is not in their best interests, it follows that whistleblowing is an act of betrayal on the part of the employee, albeit a betrayal made in the interests of the public good.

Plausible though it initially seems, I think this view of whistleblowing is mistaken and that it embodies a mistaken conception of what constitutes employee loyalty. It ignores the fact that

> The great majority of corporate whistleblowers . . . [consider] themselves to be very loyal employees who . . . [try] to use 'direct voice' (internal whistleblowing), . . . [are] rebuffed and punished for this, and then . . . [use] 'indirect voice' (external whistleblowing). They . . . [believe] initially that they . . . [are] behaving in a loyal manner, helping their employers by calling top management's attention to practices that could eventually get the firm in trouble.[7]

By ignoring the possibility that blowing the whistle may demonstrate greater loyalty than not blowing the whistle, it fails to do justice to the many instances where loyalty to someone constrains us to act in defiance of what that person believes to be in her best interests. I am not, for example, being disloyal to a friend if I refuse to loan her money for an investment I am sure will bring her financial ruin; even if she bitterly reproaches me for denying her what is so obviously a golden opportunity to make a fortune.

A more adequate definition of being loyal to someone is that loyalty involves acting in accordance with what one has good reason to believe to be in that person's best interests. A key question, of course, is what constitutes a good reason to think that something is in a person's best interests. Very often, but by no means invariably, we accept that a person thinking that something is in her best interests is a sufficiently good reason to think that it actually is. Other times, especially when we feel that she is being rash, foolish, or misinformed we are prepared, precisely by virtue of being loyal, to act contrary to the person's wishes. It is beyond the scope of this paper to investigate such cases in detail, but three general points can be made.

First, to the degree that an action is genuinely immoral, it is impossible that it is in the agent's best interests. We would not, for example, say that someone who sells child pornography was acting in his own best interests, even if he vigorously protested that there was nothing wrong with such activity. Loyalty does not imply that we have a duty to refrain from reporting the immoral actions of those to whom we are loyal. An employer who is acting immorally is not acting in her own best interests and an employee is not acting disloyally in blowing the whistle.[8] Indeed, the argument can be made that the employee who blows the whistle may be demonstrating greater loyalty than the employee who simply ignores the immoral conduct, inasmuch as she is attempting to prevent her employer from engaging in self-destructive behaviour.

Second, loyalty requires that, whenever possible, in trying to resolve a problem we deal directly with the person to whom we are loyal. If, for example, I am loyal to a friend I do not immediately involve a third party when I try to dissuade my friend from involvement in immoral actions. Rather, I approach my friend directly, listen to his perspective on the events in question, and provide an opportunity for him to address the problem in a morally satisfactory way. This implies that, whenever possible, a loyal employee blows the whistle internally. This provides the employer with the opportunity to either demonstrate to the employee that, contrary to first appearances, no genuine wrongdoing had occurred, or, if there is a genuine moral problem, the opportunity to resolve it.

This principle of dealing directly with the person to whom loyalty is due needs to be qualified, however. Loyalty to a person requires that one acts in that person's best interests. Generally, this cannot be done without directly involving the person to whom one is loyal in the decision-making process, but there may arise cases where acting in a person's best interests requires that one act independently and perhaps even against the wishes of the person to whom one is loyal. Such cases will be especially apt to arise when the person to whom one is loyal is either immoral or ignoring the moral consequences of his actions. Thus, for example, loyalty to a friend who deals in hard narcotics would not imply that I speak first to my friend about my decision to inform the police of his activities, if the only effect of my doing so would be to make him more careful in his criminal dealings. Similarly, a loyal employee is under no obligation to speak first to an employer about the employer's immoral actions, if the only response of the employer will be to take care to cover up wrongdoing.

Neither is a loyal employee under obligation to speak first to an employer if it is clear that by doing so she placed herself in jeopardy from an employer who will retaliate if given the opportunity. Loyalty amounts to acting in another's best interests and that may mean qualifying what seems to be in one's own interests, but it cannot imply that one take no steps to protect oneself from the immorality of those to whom one is loyal. The reason it cannot is that, as has already been argued, acting immorally can never really be in a person's best interests. It follows, therefore, that one is not acting in a person's best interests if one allows oneself to be treated immorally by that person. Thus, for example, a father might be loyal to a child even though the child is guilty of stealing from him, but this would not mean that the father should let the child continue to steal. Similarly, an employee may be loyal to an employer even though she takes steps to protect herself against unfair retaliation by the employer, e.g., by blowing the whistle externally.

Third, loyalty requires that one is concerned with more than considerations of justice. I have been arguing that loyalty cannot require one to ignore immoral or unjust behaviour on the part of those to whom one is loyal, since loyalty amounts to acting in a person's best interests and it can never be in a person's best interests to be allowed to act immorally. Loyalty, however, goes beyond considerations of justice in that, while it is possible to be disinterested and just, it is not possible to be disinterested and loyal. Loyalty implies a desire that the person to whom one is loyal take no moral stumbles, but that if moral stumbles have occurred that the person be restored and not simply punished. A loyal friend is not only someone who sticks by you in times of trouble, but someone who tries to help you avoid trouble. This suggests that a loyal employee will have a desire to point out problems and potential problems long before the drastic measures associated with whistleblowing become necessary, but that if whistleblowing does become necessary there remains a desire to help the employer.

In conclusion, although much more could be said on the subject of loyalty, our brief discussion has enabled us to clarify considerably the relation between whistleblowing and employee loyalty. It permits us to steer a course between the Scylla of Duska's view that, since the primary link between employer and employee is economic, the ideal of employee loyalty is an oxymoron, and the Charybdis of the standard view that, since it forces an employee to weigh conflicting duties, whistleblowing inevitably involves some degree of moral tragedy. The solution lies in realizing that to whistleblow for reasons of morality is to act in one's employer's best interests and involves, therefore, no disloyalty.

Notes

1. The definition I have proposed applies most directly to the relation between privately owned companies aiming to realize a profit and their employees. Obviously, issues of whistleblowing arise in other contexts, e.g., governmental organizations or charitable agencies, and deserve careful thought. I do not propose, in this paper, to discuss whistleblowing in these other contexts, but I think my development of the concept of whistleblowing as positive demonstration of loyalty can easily be applied and will prove useful.

2. Duska, R.: 1985, 'Whistleblowing and Employee Loyalty,' in J. R. Desjardins and J. J. McCall, eds., *Contemporary Issues in Business Ethics* (Wadsworth, Belmont, California), pp. 295–300.

3. Duska, p. 297.

4. Duska, p. 298.

5. Bok, S.: 1983, 'Whistleblowing and Professional Responsibility,' in T. L. Beauchamp and N. E. Bowie, eds., *Ethical Theory and Business*, 2nd ed. (Prentice-Hall Inc., Englewood Cliffs, New Jersey), pp. 261–269, p. 263.

6. Bok, pp. 261–2, emphasis added.

7. Near, J. P. and P. Miceli: 1985, 'Organizational Dissidence: The Case of Whistle-Blowing,' *Journal of Business Ethics* 4, pp. 1–16, p. 10.

8. As Near and Miceli note 'The whistle-blower may provide valuable information helpful in improving organizational effectiveness . . . the prevalence of illegal activity in organizations is associated with declining organizational performance' (p. 1).

    The general point is that the structure of the world is such that it is not in a company's long-term interests to act immorally. Sooner or later a company which flouts morality and legality will suffer.

POSTSCRIPT

Is Blowing the Whistle
an Act of Disloyalty?

The concept of "whistle-blower" was first defined in the Federal False Claims Act of 1863. At the time, the intention of this act was to combat fraud perpetrated against the federal government by military suppliers. This act sat dormant until 1986 when Congress updated it as a means of protecting and rewarding anyone who publicly reported knowledge of illegal business activities directed at defrauding the federal government. Under the new version of the act, "whistle-blowers can receive a percentage of the money recovered or damages won by the government in fraud cases they expose. The act also protects whistle-blowers from wrongful dismissal, allowing for reinstatement with seniority, double back pay, interest on back pay, compensation for discriminatory treatment, and reasonable legal fees" (*Information Please:* http://www.infoplease.com/ce6/society/A0852064.html). This act, in conjunction with legislation passed in the 1970s making retaliation against whistle-blowers illegal, has spawned a dramatic increase in the number of whistle-blowing cases.

For our purposes here, it's reasonable to wonder how many of these individuals are acting out of concern for the public's interest or out of concern for the potential monetary damages they can receive. Sissela Bok would argue that many are acting out of self-interest and, thus, are engaging in behavior disloyal to their organization. What do you think?

Philosophical questions such as those posed by this topic are always difficult to resolve. Perhaps the best we can do is to heed the advise of philosopher Norm Bowie who says that whistle-blowing is not justified unless the following conditions are met:

1. It is done based on a proper moral motive.
2. The individual has exhausted all internal channels for dissent.
3. The individual's belief regarding the inappropriate conduct is based on evidence that would persuade a reasonable person.
4. The individual has carefully analyzed the situation to determine the serious nature of the violation, the immediacy of the violation, and the specificity of the violation.
5. The individual's action is commensurate with responsibility for avoiding and/or exposing moral violations.
6. The individual's action has some chance of success, exposing and/or avoiding the moral violation (Norm Bowie, in Hartman, *Perspectives in Business Ethics,* 2nd ed., McGraw-Hill, 2002, p. 458).

Suggested Readings

Myron Peretz Glazer and Penina Migdal Glazer, *The Whistle-Blowers: Exposing Corruption in Government and Industry*. Basic Books, 1989.

L. Gomes, A whistleblower finds jackpot at the end of his quest, *The Wall Street Journal*, April 27, 1998.

Daryl Koehn, Whistleblowing and trust: Some lessons from the ADM scandal. In *Perspectives in Business Ethics*, 2nd ed., Laura Hartman, ed. McGraw-Hill, 2002, pp. 457–63.

Paula M. Miceli and Janet P. Near, *Blowing the Whistle*. Lexington, 1992.

The Cato Institute

The Cato Institute is a non-profit public policy think tank based on the traditional American "principles of limited government, individual liberty, free markets and peace." Cato has published policy commentary on a wide array of important business topics including outsourcing.

http://www.cato.org/

The Sarbanes-Oxley Act Community Forum

This site is an interactive portal designed to assist organizations that are attempting to comply with the massive requirements and regulations of Sarbanes-Oxley. Additional tips, resources, and links are also provided.

http://www.sarbanes-oxley-forum.com/

The International Corporate Governance Network (ICGN)

ICGN is a leading international authority on corporate governance. The organization provides research and policy recommendations to governments and organizations across the globe in order to elevate the quality of corporate governance.

http://www.icgn.org/

Institute for Women's Policy Research

The Institute for Women's Policy Research (IWPR) is a public policy research organization dedicated to informing and stimulating the debate on public policy issues of critical importance to women and their families.

http://www.iwpr.org/

PART 3

Strategic Management

*D*uring *the course of his 2004 Democratic presidential campaign, John Kerry accused President George W. Bush of betraying American workers by refusing to condemn corporations that transferred American jobs to offshore countries. Kerry's complaint was not that outsourcing is not an effective cost-reduction strategy; his antagonism was based on his belief that it is unpatriotic. On the surface, this sounds very plausible; however, many economists and social critics argue that not only is outsourcing not unpatriotic but, in some instances, failing to do so is unpatriotic! This emotionally charged question is one of three that comprise Part 3 of this book.*

- Is the Corporate Strategy of Outsourcing Unpatriotic?

- Are U.S. CEOs Overpaid?

- Corporate Governance Reform: Is Sarbanes-Oxley the Answer?

ISSUE 11

Is the Corporate Strategy of Outsourcing Unpatriotic?

YES: Sarah Anderson and John Cavanagh, from "Outsourcing: A Policy Agenda," *Foreign Policy in Focus* (April 2004)

NO: Daniel W. Drezner, from "The Outsourcing Bogeyman," *Foreign Affairs* (May/June 2004)

ISSUE SUMMARY

YES: Sarah Anderson and John Cavanagh argue that outsourcing is a real threat to the economic health of the United States and provide several suggestions as to the types of governmental actions necessary to keep American jobs from moving overseas. Included in their discussion is an analysis of the views of the two 2004 presidential candidates, John Kerry and George W. Bush.

NO: Dr. Daniel Drezner argues that the controversy surrounding outsourcing is not new and that its current form is more hype than substance. He shows how outsourcing is actually economically beneficial to America, despite the warnings of critics. Dr. Drezner also asserts that the concept of outsourcing is consistent with a solid understanding of free-market capitalism and an appreciation of traditional American principles and values.

As his Democratic party foes constantly pointed out during the 2004 election year, President George W. Bush's early years in the White House were characterized by, among other things, a steady increase in the number of jobs lost as a result of the recession, which started almost immediately upon his taking office in 2001. An interesting residual effect of this situation was the increased attention both economists and politicians gave to outsourcing. Indeed, if one were to believe the media, offshore outsourcing—the transferring of work previously done by Americans to foreign countries as a strategic response to pressures to keep costs low—occurred at epic rates and was partly responsible for the economic downturn of the early part of the decade. Democratic presidential nominee John Kerry campaigned on a platform built, in part, on the promise that he would keep American jobs in America. The implication, of course, is that outsourcing is unpatriotic. On the surface, such corporate behavior would indeed appear to be unpatriotic—after all, what could be more anti-American than moving American jobs to foreign countries? But is this indeed the case?

Those who argue that outsourcing is bad business and anti-American maintain this is so simply because it moves jobs out of America. Sarah Anderson and John Cavanagh note that this is no small trend: Millions of jobs have left American shores in recent years, and many millions more are vulnerable. Critics also point to the alarming growth of outsourcing in the service sector. The historical justification for outsourcing was built on the belief that jobs lost in manufacturing would be replaced by jobs in the service sector as the United States shifted from an industrial to a service-based economy. Since the current outsourcing wave is primarily service-based, the concern is that outsourcing will accelerate further as we move toward a service-oriented society. Finally, many charge that outsourcing is nothing more than American firms exploiting cheaper labor in other countries in order to increase profits (see Issue 17 regarding sweatshops for further insight into this contentious topic). Do you agree with this point and, if so, how patriotic is this type of corporate behavior?

Proponents of outsourcing have strong points on their side of the issue as well. The call to end outsourcing is, in their view, merely protectionism in disguise, a concept entirely at odds with traditional American political and economic principles. American capitalism and prosperity were built on free trade; forcing American firms to forego cheap overseas labor in the name of patriotism will ultimately cause U.S. firms, and society, to suffer. In terms of the exploitation of foreign labor argument, supporters respond that it is not exploitation at all. Consider these comments by Edwin Locke, Dean's Professor of Leadership and Motivation at the University of Maryland, and Ayn Rand, Institute contributing author:

> ... the claim that multinational companies [e.g., American firms] exploit workers in poor countries by paying lower wages than they would pay in their home countries. Well, what is the alternative? It is: no wages! The comparative advantage of poorer countries is precisely that their wages are low, thus reducing the costs of production. If multinational corporations had to pay the same wages as in their home countries, they would not bother to invest in poorer countries at all and millions of people would lose their livelihoods.

In the following selections, you will be exposed to both sides of this controversial topic. Sarah Anderson and John Cavanagh defend an anti-outsourcing perspective. During the course of their discussion, the authors present an analysis of the viewpoints on outsourcing held by Democratic nominee John Kerry and Republican President George W. Bush just prior to the 2004 presidential election. Daniel Drezner, professor of political science at the University of Chicago, provides a pro-outsourcing perspective in his article. Among other things, Professor Drezner invites his readers to consider the following question: In today's increasingly competitive global marketplace, wouldn't domestic political actions designed to curb outsourcing ultimately make American firms less competitive?

Sarah Anderson and
John Cavanagh

 **YES**

Outsourcing: A Policy Agenda

D on't worry; they'll get better jobs in the service sector." During the last three decades of the 20th century, this was the mantra of most government and business leaders when corporations transferred auto or apparel jobs to Mexico or China. That line doesn't work anymore, since U.S. companies have started shifting a wide range of service jobs as well—from high-skill computer programming to entry-level call center jobs—to India and other lower-wage nations. This breaching of the final frontier of American jobs has caused understandable anxiety and has become a hot-button issue in the presidential election campaign.

The trend toward foreign "outsourcing" of service jobs is an extension of a longstanding practice of cutting costs by subcontracting parts of business operations to nonunion shops within the United States. The practice has gone global, in part because of technological changes. Massive amounts of information can now be transmitted across the world at low cost, making geographic distances less important. International financial institutions and trade agreements have also facilitated the trend by promoting investment liberalization and privatization of public services, creating new opportunities for U.S. corporations in overseas markets.

Forrester Research estimates that about 40 percent of Fortune 1,000 firms have already outsourced some work and that at least another 3 million service jobs will leave the United States by 2015, led by information technology work. A study by the University of California, Berkeley estimates that 14 million U.S. jobs (11 percent of the total work force) are vulnerable to being outsourced.

Although the number of jobs lost so far is small relative to the total work force, these layoffs have a huge impact on the affected communities, and the potential for white-collar jobs to be offshored is deeply unsettling for many American workers. In addition to job cuts, service workers must now also contend with the enhanced power of highly mobile, increasingly unregulated global corporations to bargain down U.S. wages and working conditions by threatening to move jobs elsewhere.

According to McKinsey and Company, a consulting firm that helps businesses develop offshore operations, U.S. companies make up about 70 percent of the global outsourcing market. Their top destination in the developing world is currently India, where domestic subcontractors perform a range of services for

From *Foreign Policy In Focus Brief*, Volume 9, No. 2, April 2004, pp. 1–3. Copyright © 2004 by Foreign Policy In Focus. Reprinted by permission.

the U.S. market. At the low-skill end, Indian workers earn $1 or less per hour to handle customer service calls for firms like Earthlink and Travelocity. Among the higher-skill workers are Indian computer programmers, who earn about one-tenth the pay of their U.S. counterparts to write code for multinational corporations like Citigroup. Given a lack of other economic opportunities, Indian workers are often eager to secure new jobs catering to the U.S. market. However, there is also a nagging fear that these jobs may evaporate as soon as companies can find lower costs elsewhere.

China, of course, looms on the horizon. It is already the second-biggest developing-country draw for service work, offering rock-bottom wages and an official ban on basic union rights. Though it lacks India's English-speaking advantage, this may not be the case forever, as Beijing is heavily promoting English-language education. Mexico's experience in competing with China over manufacturing jobs could foreshadow events to come. Although employment in Mexico's border export zone more than doubled after the implementation of the North American Free Trade Agreement (NAFTA) in 1994, the country has in recent years lost several hundred thousand of these jobs, partly in economic flight to lower-wage China. India has even lost some foreign manufacturing jobs to China.

Public pressure has galvanized U.S. state and federal legislators to introduce a flurry of bills to curb outsourcing, primarily by requiring that government contract work not be performed overseas. However, there is stiff resistance from the corporate lobby, such as the new Coalition for Economic Growth and American Jobs, which represents some 200 trade groups, including the U.S. Chamber of Commerce and the Information Technology Association of America. These and other pro-outsourcing groups argue that the practice is good for U.S. workers, because it lowers the cost of services for U.S. consumers and enhances the overall competitiveness of U.S. companies. Another common claim is that recent job losses are due to productivity gains, not outsourcing. However, because workers are facing a "jobless" recovery and see few personal benefits from enhanced productivity, these arguments convince very few.

One reflection of public opinion is that concerns about U.S. trade policy have spread up the income ladder. Lower- and middle-class workers have been consistently skeptical of U.S. trade policies, but a February 2004 University of Maryland poll showed that even among Americans earning over $100,000 a year, support for actively promoting more "free trade" has dropped from 57 percent in 1999 to 28 percent in 2004.

Problems with Current U.S. Policy

As they vie for votes in layoff-ridden swing states, both presidential candidates are offering solutions to the prevailing American angst about trade and outsourcing. Railing against "Benedict Arnold" companies, Sen. John Kerry has vowed to eliminate government incentives for outsourcing. For example, he would place conditions on most government contracts to require that the work be performed in the United States. He would also eliminate a tax break that currently allows U.S. businesses to defer tax payments on income earned abroad, and he proposes to use the resulting revenue to lower the overall corporate tax rate from 35 to 33.25 percent. Similarly, Kerry would offer incentives to encourage transnational corporations to repatriate earnings and would then channel these revenues into an employer tax credit for new hires. Regarding trade, Kerry has vowed to include stronger labor and environmental protections in future trade pacts and to review all existing agreements.

The Bush administration has delivered mixed messages regarding outsourcing. Two prominent officials have publicly endorsed the practice—Treasury Secretary John Snow and Gregory Mankiw, chairman of the Council of Economic Advisers. Both have argued that foreign outsourcing of service jobs is good for the American economy, because it helps companies become more efficient. Meanwhile, President Bush has sought to distance himself from such statements and instead to focus public attention on his administration's new "21st Century" jobs plan. Bush argues that the real driving forces behind outsourcing are "frivolous" lawsuits, excessive regulation, and high taxes. He also claims that NAFTA and other trade agreements have been good for U.S. workers, and he promises that by breaking down even more trade barriers his policies will boost export-related jobs. "The best product on any shelf anywhere in the world says, 'Made in the USA,'" Bush told an audience of women entrepreneurs in Cleveland.

But the Bush administration's jobs plan ignores the historical record and thus misdiagnoses the problem. Government figures show that U.S. employment for American multinational corporations grew only 25 percent between 1982 and 2001, while employment at their overseas affiliates increased 47 percent. (These figures likely underestimate foreign expansion, because they do not include information on employment through subcontractors, data the U.S. government does not require businesses to report). This period of rapid overseas expansion has coincided with increased trade and investment liberalization and a declining corporate tax burden. U.S. employers are leaders in outsourcing, even though their share of the national tax bill is considerably lower than the average for employers in other industrial nations.

Bush's claim that companies are fleeing "Big Government" is also dubious. McKinsey and Company claims that U.S. corporations have led the outsourcing trend not to escape burdensome regulations, but because the relatively unregulated U.S. labor market facilitates sending jobs abroad. McKinsey, a pro-outsourcing consulting firm, points out that compared to most European counterparts, the United States has "liberal employment and labor laws that allow companies greater flexibility in reassigning tasks and eliminating jobs."

Kerry's early jobs plan is encouraging, but it addresses only one side of the issue. His proposal to end taxpayer subsidies for outsourcing, whether through government contracting or tax breaks, is long overdue. Citizens should not have to pay higher taxes to subsidize the evaporation of their jobs. To ensure effectiveness, any reforms must be carefully crafted to prevent potential loopholes. More effort will also be needed to address the threat posed by existing international agreements to domestic legislation that requires public contract work to be performed in the United States. For example, under World Trade Organization rules, the Government Procurement Agreement bans governments from favoring domestic firms in procurement contracts. Although only 25 countries have signed the agreement thus far, plans are under way to expand its scope and incorporate similar rules in other trade pacts.

Kerry's primary focus on domestic measures will have only a modest impact on the jobs issue, because these policies cannot make up for the extreme gap in labor costs, which is the primary driving force behind outsourcing. McKinsey estimates that global pay gaps result in a net cost savings for outsourcers of at least 45–55 percent (after accounting for higher infrastructure and other costs). If this is true, figures in a 2003 University of California, Berkeley study suggest that companies could save around $300 billion a year if they outsourced all of the estimated 14 million U.S. service jobs considered feasible to transfer overseas.

Kerry's promises to change U.S. trade policy are also a step in the right direction. If there were effective international mechanisms to strengthen labor rights enforcement, developing-country workers would have a better chance of obtaining fair wages. Research commissioned by the AFL-CIO indicates that labor rights violations in China artificially depress wages by 47–86 percent and that if the country were to respect basic internationally recognized labor rights, wages would likely increase 90 to 95 percent. However, the goal of strengthening labor rights protections should be pursued as part of a broader strategy to uplift conditions generally in poorer countries. Without overall economic improvements, developing-country governments will continue to face strong pressure to attract foreign investment by offering lax labor rights enforcement, thereby undermining efforts to maintain high standards in the richer countries.

Toward a New Foreign Policy

The overall goal of U.S. policy on outsourcing should be to attack the factors that make workers—in the U.S. as well as around the world—vulnerable to exploitation by increasingly mobile and unregulated global corporations. The approach needs to recognize that raising standards overseas is vital to retaining stable and substantial jobs at home. This requires a multifaceted response encompassing changes in domestic tax, procurement and labor laws as well as in multilateral trade, finance and aid policies.

On the domestic side, a first step should be to reform tax and procurement policies at all levels of government to ensure that they support good jobs in the United States. Additional subsidies that enhance the incentives for corporations to shift jobs overseas should also be eliminated. These include risk insurance and loan guarantees provided by the Overseas Private Investment Corporation as well as technical assistance and other supports offered by the U.S. Trade and Development Agency. Moreover, the U.S. government should ensure that U.S. authorities, as well as their counterparts around the world, have the right to use tax and procurement policies as instruments to support social goals without being undermined by international trade agreements.

The domestic policy response should also involve labor law reforms that reduce current obstacles to union organizing and that beef up rules related to laying off workers. Most European countries require that corporations guarantee higher severance pay based on years of service, which substantially raises the cost of moving jobs. Many European countries also oblige companies that are planning to close an operation to consult with unions and sometimes to negotiate over the decision. By contrast, under U.S. law, unions may only bargain over the effects of a closure. Thus, although European countries also experience outsourcing-related job loss, the practice is not as advanced as in the United States.

However, domestic measures, while significant, do not address the biggest incentive for outsourcing—extreme wage gaps. Tackling this problem will require a long-term commitment to supporting sustainable economic activity in poor countries and should focus on the factors that make workers around the world vulnerable to exploitation by global companies.

One of these factors is lax enforcement of internationally recognized labor rights, which artificially depresses wages. U.S. policymakers must learn from the failure of NAFTA's weak labor rights mechanism and should develop a better model. The Hemispheric Social Alliance has proposed involving the International Labor Organization in monitoring compliance and investigating complaints related to rights violations. If necessary, assistance would be provided to help countries achieve compliance. Only if this approach was unsuccessful would sanctions be applied, and if the perpetrator was a specific company, the punishments would be targeted at the company rather than at the host government.

Any labor rights initiative, however, should be integrated within a broader strategy toward poorer nations. Other factors that make workers vulnerable are high unemployment and poverty. Although national governments are not without responsibility for these problems, international financial institutions and trade agreements have played an exacerbating role. For example, the World Bank, the International Monetary Fund and the World Trade Organization all threaten the livelihoods of tens of millions of farmers by pressuring poor-country governments to eliminate tariffs and agricultural subsidies. Likewise, privatization supported by these international financial institutions has often resulted in mass layoffs and weakened social services. These multilateral agencies should instead join governments in promoting "global green deal" policies that stimulate stable and substantial employment while protecting the environment.

Regarding trade, Washington should withdraw its support for rules—such as in Chapter 11 of NAFTA—that grant excessive protection to U.S. investors against public interest laws and other host government actions that diminish profits. Such trade rules undermine democracy and encourage U.S. firms to shift jobs overseas.

To enhance this new and broader strategy toward poorer nations, the U.S. government should advocate for stronger international mechanisms to transfer resources from richer to poorer countries. Where appropriate, this would include debt reduction or cancellation. Washington could also promote the adoption of international taxes on both foreign exchange transactions and arms sales to generate revenues for development purposes. The U.S. must also revamp its development aid policies to emphasize anti-poverty measures, healthy communities and a clean environment rather than handouts to U.S. corporations like Halliburton and Bechtel.

In short, a comprehensive response to corporate outsourcing requires a sea change in the outlook of both the U.S. public and its politicians toward

America's role in the world. Just as Americans are less secure when much of the world is plagued by extreme poverty, inequality and instability, worker exploitation overseas translates into exploited workers and less secure jobs at home. The electoral debate over outsourcing offers an opportunity to create a new policy approach that combines solidarity with self-interest in a whole-scale effort to benefit the entire world.

Sources for More Information

Organizations

Economic Policy Institute
1660 L St. N.W., Suite 1200
Washington, DC 20036
Voice: (202) 775-8810
Fax: (202) 775-0819
Email: epi@epinet.org
Web site: http://www.epinet.org/

WashTech
2900 Eastlake Avenue East, Suite 200
Seattle, WA 98102
Voice: (206) 726-8580
Fax: (206) 323-6966
Email: contact@washtech.org
Web site: http://www.washtech.org/

Publications

Ashok Deo Bardhan and Cynthia A. Kroll, "The New Wave of Outsourcing," Fisher Center for Real Estate and Urban Economics, University of California, Berkeley, available at: <http://www.haas.berkeley.edu/news/Research_Report_Fall_2003.pdf>.

Hemispheric Social Alliance, "Alternatives for the Americas," available at <http://www.art-us.org/docs/alternatives%20dec%202002.pdf>.

McKinsey Global Institute, "Offshoring: Is It a Win-Win Game?" available at: <http://www.mckinsey.com/knowledge/mgi/offshore/>.

North American Alliance for Fair Employment, "Outsource This? American Workers, the Jobs Deficit and the Fair Globalization Solutions," available at: <http://www.fairjobs.org/docs/OutsourceThis!.pdf>.

Web sites

Communications Workers of America
http://www.cwa-union.org/outsourcing/

India Resource Center
http://www.corpwatchindia.org/

Daniel W. Drezner  **NO**

The Outsourcing Bogeyman

The Truth Is Offshore

When a presidential election year coincides with an uncertain economy, campaigning politicians invariably invoke an international economic issue as a dire threat to the well-being of Americans. Speechwriters denounce the chosen scapegoat, the media provides blanket coverage of the alleged threat, and legislators scurry to introduce supposed remedies.

The cause of this year's commotion is offshore outsourcing—the alleged migration of American jobs overseas. The depth of alarm was strikingly illustrated by the firestorm of reaction to recent testimony by N. Gregory Mankiw, the head of President George W. Bush's Council of Economic Advisers. No economist really disputed Mankiw's observation that "outsourcing is just a new way of doing international trade," which makes it "a good thing." But in the political arena, Mankiw's comments sparked a furor on both sides of the aisle. Democratic presidential candidate John Kerry accused the Bush administration of wanting "to export more of our jobs overseas," and Senate Minority Leader Tom Daschle quipped, "If this is the administration's position, I think they owe an apology to every worker in America." Speaker of the House Dennis Hastert, meanwhile, warned that "outsourcing can be a problem for American workers and the American economy."

Critics charge that the information revolution (especially the Internet) has accelerated the decimation of U.S. manufacturing and facilitated the outsourcing of service-sector jobs once considered safe, from backroom call centers to high-level software programming. (This concern feeds into the suspicion that U.S. corporations are exploiting globalization to fatten profits at the expense of workers.) They are right that offshore outsourcing deserves attention and that some measures to assist affected workers are called for. But if their exaggerated alarmism succeeds in provoking protectionist responses from lawmakers, it will do far more harm than good, to the U.S. economy and to American workers.

Should Americans be concerned about the economic effects of outsourcing? Not particularly. Most of the numbers thrown around are vague, overhyped estimates. What hard data exist suggest that gross job losses due to offshore outsourcing have been minimal when compared to the size of the entire U.S. economy.

From *Foreign Affairs*, May/June 2004. Copyright © 2004 by Foreign Affairs. Reprinted by permission.

The outsourcing phenomenon has shown that globalization can affect white-collar professions, heretofore immune to foreign competition, in the same way that it has affected manufacturing jobs for years. But Mankiw's statements on outsourcing are absolutely correct; the law of comparative advantage does not stop working just because 401(k) plans are involved. The creation of new jobs overseas will eventually lead to more jobs and higher incomes in the United States. Because the economy—and especially job growth—is sluggish at the moment, commentators are attempting to draw a connection between offshore outsourcing and high unemployment. But believing that offshore outsourcing causes unemployment is the economic equivalent of believing that the sun revolves around the earth: intuitively compelling but clearly wrong.

Should Americans be concerned about the political backlash to outsourcing? Absolutely. Anecdotes of workers affected by outsourcing are politically powerful, and demands for government protection always increase during economic slowdowns. The short-term political appeal of protectionism is undeniable. Scapegoating foreigners for domestic business cycles is smart politics, and protecting domestic markets gives leaders the appearance of taking direct, decisive action on the economy.

Protectionism would not solve the U.S. economy's employment problems, although it would succeed in providing massive subsidies to well-organized interest groups. In open markets, greater competition spurs the reallocation of labor and capital to more profitable sectors of the economy. The benefits of such free trade—to both consumers and producers—are significant. Cushioning this process for displaced workers makes sense. Resorting to protectionism to halt the process, however, is a recipe for decline. An open economy leads to concentrated costs (and diffuse benefits) in the short term and significant benefits in the long term. Protectionism generates pain in both the short term and the long term.

The Sky Is Falling

Outsourcing occurs when a firm subcontracts a business function to an outside supplier. This practice has been common within the U.S. economy for some time. (Witness the rise of large call centers in the rural Midwest.) The reduction of communication costs and the standardization of software packages have now made it possible to outsource business functions such as customer service, telemarketing, and document management. Other affected professions include medical transcription, tax preparation, and financial services.

The numbers that are bandied about on offshore outsourcing sound ominous. The McKinsey Global Institute estimates that the volume of offshore outsourcing will increase by 30 to 40 percent a year for the next five years. Forrester Research estimates that 3.3 million white-collar jobs will move overseas by 2015. According to projections, the hardest hit sectors will be financial services and information technology (IT). In one May 2003 survey of chief information officers, 68 percent of IT executives said that their offshore contracts would grow in the subsequent year. The Gartner research firm has estimated that by the end of this year, 1 out of every 10 IT jobs will be outsourced overseas. Deloitte Research predicts the outsourcing of 2 million financial-sector jobs by 2009.

At first glance, current macroeconomic indicators seem to support the suspicion that outsourcing is destroying jobs in the United States. The past two years have witnessed moderate growth and astonishing productivity gains, but overall job growth has been anemic. The total number of manufacturing jobs has declined for 43 consecutive months. Surely, many observers insist, this must be because the jobs created by the U.S. recovery are going to other countries. Morgan Stanley analyst Stephen Roach, for example, has pointed out that "this is the first business cycle since the advent of the Internet—the enabler of a new real-time connectivity to low-cost offshore labor pools." He adds, "I don't think it's a coincidence that this jobless recovery has occurred in such an environment." Those who agree draw on anecdotal evidence to support this assertion. CNN's Lou Dobbs routinely harangues U.S. companies engaged in offshore outsourcing in his "Exporting America" series.

Many IT executives have themselves contributed to this perception. When IBM announced plans to outsource 3,000 jobs overseas this year, one of its executives said, "[Globalization] means shifting a lot of jobs, opening a lot of locations in places we had never dreamt of before, going where there's low-cost labor, low-cost competition, shifting jobs offshore." Nandan Nilekani, the chief executive of the India-based Infosys Technologies, said at this year's World Economic Forum, "Everything you can send down a wire is up for grabs." In January testimony before Congress, Hewlett-Packard chief Carly Fiorina warned that "there is no job that is America's God-given right anymore."

That last statement chills the blood of most Americans. Few support the cause of free trade for its own sake, out of pure principle. The logic underlying an open economy is that if the economy sheds jobs in uncompetitive sectors, employment in competitive sectors will grow. If hi-tech industries are no longer competitive, where will new jobs be created?

Inside the Numbers

Before answering that question, Americans need to separate fact from fiction. The predictions of job losses in the millions are driving the current outsourcing hysteria. But it is crucial to note that these predictions are of gross, not net, losses. During the 1990s, offshore outsourcing was not uncommon. (American Express, for one, set up back-office operations in India more than a decade ago.) But no one much cared because the number of jobs leaving U.S. shores was far lower than the number of jobs created in the U.S. economy.

Similarly, most current predictions are not as ominous as they first sound once the numbers are unpacked. Most jobs will remain unaffected altogether: close to 90 percent of jobs in the United States require geographic proximity. Such jobs include everything from retail and restaurants to marketing and personal care—services that have to be produced and consumed locally, so outsourcing them overseas is not an option. There is also no evidence that jobs in the high-value-added sector are migrating overseas. One thing that has made offshore outsourcing possible is the standardization of such business tasks as data entry, accounting, and IT support. The parts of production that are more complex, interactive, or innovative—including, but not limited to, marketing, research, and development—are much more difficult to shift abroad. As an International Data Corporation analysis on trends in IT services concluded, "the activities that will migrate offshore are predominantly those that can be viewed as requiring low skill since process and repeatability are key underpinnings of the work. Innovation and deep business expertise will continue to be delivered predominantly onshore." Not coincidentally, these are also the tasks that generate high wages and large profits and drive the U.S. economy.

As for the jobs that can be sent offshore, even if the most dire-sounding forecasts come true, the impact on the economy will be negligible. The Forrester prediction of 3.3 million lost jobs, for example, is spread across 15 years. That would mean 220,000 jobs displaced per year by offshore outsourcing—a number that sounds impressive until one considers that total employment in the United States is roughly 130 million, and that about 22 million new jobs are expected to be added between now and 2010. Annually, outsourcing would affect less than .2 percent of employed Americans.

There is also reason to believe that the unemployment caused by outsourcing will be lower than expected. Gartner assumed that more than 60 percent of financial-sector employees directly affected by outsourcing would be let go by their employers. But Boston University Professor Nitin Joglekar has examined the effect of outsourcing on large financial firms and found that less than 20 percent of workers affected by outsourcing lose their jobs; the rest are repositioned within the firm. Even if the most negative projections prove to be correct, then, gross job loss would be relatively small.

Moreover, it is debatable whether actual levels of outsourcing will ever match current predictions. Despite claims that the pace of onshore and offshore outsourcing would quicken over time, there was no increase in 2003. In fact, TPI Inc., an outsourcing advisory firm, even reports that the total value of business process outsourcing deals in the United States fell by 32 percent in 2003.

There is no denying that the number of manufacturing jobs has fallen dramatically in recent years, but this has very little do with outsourcing and almost everything to do with technological innovation. As with agriculture a century ago, productivity gains have outstripped demand, so fewer and fewer workers are needed for manufacturing. If outsourcing were in fact the chief cause of manufacturing losses, one would expect corresponding increases in manufacturing employment in developing countries. An Alliance Capital Management study of global manufacturing trends from 1995 to 2002, however, shows that this was not the case: the United States saw an 11 percent decrease in manufacturing employment over the course of those seven years; meanwhile, China saw a 15 percent decrease and Brazil a 20 percent decrease. Globally, the figure for manufacturing jobs lost was identical to the U.S. figure—11 percent. The fact that global manufacturing output increased by 30 percent in that same period confirms that technology, not trade, is the primary cause for the decrease in factory jobs. A recent analysis of employment data from U.S. multinational corporations by the U.S. Department of Commerce reached the same conclusion.

What about the service sector? Again, the data contradict the popular belief that U.S. jobs are being lost to foreign countries without anything to replace them. In the case of many low-level technology jobs, the phenomenon has been somewhat exaggerated. For example, a Datamonitor study found that global call-center operations are being outsourced at a slower rate than previously thought—only five percent are expected to be located offshore by 2007. Dell and Lehman Brothers recently moved some of their call centers back to the United States from India because of customer complaints. And done properly, the offshore outsourcing of call centers creates new jobs at home. Delta Airlines outsourced 1,000 call-center jobs to India in 2003, but the $25 million in savings allowed the firm to add 1,200 reservation and sales positions in the United States.

Offshore outsourcing is similarly counterbalanced by job creation in the high-end service sector. An Institute for International Economics analysis of Bureau of Labor Statistics employment data revealed that the number of jobs in service sectors where outsourcing is likely actually increased, even though total employment decreased by 1.7 percent. According to the Bureau of Labor Statistics "Occupation Outlook Handbook," the number of IT-related jobs is expected to grow 43 percent by 2010. The case of IBM reinforces this lesson: although critics highlight the offshore outsourcing of 3,000 IT jobs, they fail to mention the company's plans to add 4,500 positions to its U.S. payroll. Large software companies such as Microsoft and Oracle have simultaneously increased outsourcing and domestic payrolls.

How can these figures fit with the widespread perception that IT jobs have left the United States? Too often, comparisons are made to 2000, an unusual year for the technology sector because Y2K fears and the height of the dot-com bubble had pushed employment figures to an artificially high level. When 1999 is used as the starting point, it becomes clear that offshore outsourcing has not caused a collapse in IT hiring. Between 1999 and 2003, the number of jobs in business and financial operations increased by 14 percent. Employment in computer and mathematical positions increased by 6 percent.

It is also worth remembering that many predictions come from management consultants who are eager to push the latest business fad. Many of these consulting firms are themselves reaping commissions from outsourcing contracts. Much of the perceived boom in outsourcing stems from companies' eagerness to latch onto the latest management trends; like Dell and Lehman, many will partially reverse course once the hidden costs of offshore outsourcing become apparent.

If offshore outsourcing is not the cause of sluggish job growth, what is? A study by the Federal Reserve Bank of New York suggests that the economy is undergoing a structural transformation: jobs are disappearing from old sectors (such as manufacturing) and being created in new ones (such as mortgage brokering). In all such transformations, the creation of new jobs lags behind the destruction of old ones. In other words, the recent recession and current recovery are a more extreme version of the downturn and "jobless recovery" of the early 1990s—which eventually produced the longest economic expansion of the post-World War II era. Once the structural adjustments of the current period are complete, job growth is expected to be robust. (And indeed, current indicators are encouraging: there has been a net increase in payroll jobs and in small business employment since 2003 and a spike in IT entrepreneurial activity.)

Offshore outsourcing is undoubtedly taking place, and it will likely increase over the next decade. However, it is not the tsunami that many claim.

Its effect on the U.S. economy has been exaggerated, and its effect on the U.S. employment situation has been grossly exaggerated.

The Upside of Outsourcing

To date, the media's coverage of outsourcing has focused on its perceived costs. This leaves out more than half of the story. The benefits of offshore outsourcing should not be dismissed.

The standard case for free trade holds that countries are best off when they focus on sectors in which they have a comparative advantage—that is, sectors that have the lowest opportunity costs of production. Allowing countries to specialize accordingly increases productivity across all countries. This specialization translates into cheaper goods, and a greater variety of them, for all consumers.

The current trend of outsourcing business processes overseas is comparative advantage at work. The main driver of productivity gains over the past decade has been the spread of information technology across the economy. The commodification of simple business services allows those benefits to spread further, making growth even greater.

The data affirm this benefit. Catherine Mann of the Institute for International Economics conservatively estimates that the globalization of IT production has boosted U.S. GDP by $230 billion over the past seven years; the globalization of IT services should lead to a similar increase. As the price of IT services declines, sectors that have yet to exploit them to their fullest—such as construction and health care—will begin to do so, thus lowering their cost of production and improving the quality of their output. (For example, cheaper IT could one day save lives by reducing the number of "adverse drug events." Mann estimates that adding bar codes to prescription drugs and instituting an electronic medical record system could reduce the annual number of such events by more than 80,000 in the United States alone.)

McKinsey Global Institute has estimated that for every dollar spent on outsourcing to India, the United States reaps between $1.12 and $1.14 in benefits. Thanks to outsourcing, U.S. firms save money and become more profitable, benefiting shareholders and increasing returns on investment. Foreign facilities boost demand for U.S. products, such as computers and telecommunications equipment, necessary for their outsourced function. And U.S. labor can be reallocated to more competitive, better-paying jobs; for example, although 70,000 computer programmers lost their jobs between 1999 and 2003, more than 115,000 computer software engineers found higher-paying jobs during that same period. Outsourcing thus enhances the competitiveness of the U.S. service sector (which accounts for 30 percent of the total value of U.S. exports). Contrary to the belief that the United States is importing massive amounts of services from low-wage countries, in 2002 it ran a $64.8 billion surplus in services.

Outsourcing also has considerable noneconomic benefits. It is clearly in the interest of the United States to reward other countries for reducing their barriers to trade and investment. Some of the countries where U.S. firms have set up outsourcing operations—including India, Poland, and the Philippines—are vital allies in the war on terrorism. Just as the North American Free Trade Agreement

(NAFTA) helped Mexico deepen its democratic transition and strengthen its rule of law, the United States gains considerably from the political reorientation spurred by economic growth and interdependence.

Finally, the benefits of "insourcing" should not be overlooked. Just as U.S. firms outsource positions to developing countries, firms in other countries outsource positions to the United States. According to the Bureau of Labor Statistics, the number of outsourced jobs increased from 6.5 million in 1983 to 10 million in 2000. The number of insourced jobs increased even more in the same period, from 2.5 million to 6.5 million.

Political Economy

When it comes to trade policy, there are two iron laws of politics. The first is that the benefits of trade diffuse across the economy, but the costs of trade are concentrated. Thus, those made worse off by open borders will form the more motivated interest group. The second is that public hostility toward trade increases during economic downturns. When forced to choose between statistical evidence showing that trade is good for the economy and anecdotal evidence of job losses due to import competition, Americans go with the anecdotes.

Offshore outsourcing adds two additional political pressures. The first stems from the fact that technological innovation has converted what were thought to be nontradeable sectors into tradeable ones. Manufacturing workers have long been subject to the rigors of global competition. White-collar service-sector workers are being introduced to these pressures for the first time—and they are not happy about it. As Raghuram Rajan and Luigi Zingales point out in "Saving Capitalism From the Capitalists," globalization and technological innovation affect professions such as law and medicine that have not changed all that much for centuries. Their political reaction to the threat of foreign competition will be fierce.

The second pressure is that the Internet has greatly facilitated political organization, making it much easier for those who blame outsourcing for their troubles to rally together. In recent years, countless organizations—with names such as Rescue American Jobs, Save U.S. Jobs, and the Coalition for National Sovereignty and Economic Patriotism—have sprouted up. Such groups have disproportionately focused on white-collar tech workers, even though the manufacturing sector has been much harder hit by the recent economic slowdown.

It should come as no surprise, then, that politicians are scrambling to get ahead of the curve. During the Democratic primary in South Carolina—a state hit hard by the loss of textile jobs—billboards asked voters, "Lost your job to free trade or offshore outsourcing yet?" Last Labor Day, President Bush pledged to appoint a manufacturing czar to get to the bottom of the outflow of manufacturing positions. In his stump speech, John Kerry bashes "Benedict Arnold CEOs [who] send American jobs overseas."

Where presidential candidates lead, legislators are sure to follow. Senator Charles Schumer (D-N.Y.) claimed in a January "New York Times" op-ed authored with Paul Craig Roberts that because of increased capital mobility, the law of comparative advantage is now null and void. Senator Tom Daschle (D-S.D.) has observed, "George Bush says the economy is creating jobs. But let me tell you, China is one long commute. And let me tell you, I'm tired of watching jobs shift overseas." Senator Christopher Dodd (D-Conn.) and Representative Nancy Johnson (R-Conn.) are sponsoring the USA Jobs Protection Act to prevent U.S. companies from hiring foreign workers for positions when American workers are available. In February, Senate Democrats announced their intentions to introduce the Jobs for America Act, requiring companies to give public notice three months in advance of any plan to outsource 15 or more jobs. In March, the Senate overwhelmingly approved a measure banning firms from federal contracts if they outsource any of the work overseas. In the past two years, more than 20 state legislatures have introduced bills designed to make various forms of offshore outsourcing illegal.

Splendid Isolation?

There are clear examples of jobs being sent across U.S. borders because of U.S. trade policy—but not for the reasons that critics of outsourcing believe. Consider the example of candy-cane manufacturers: despite the fact that 90 percent of the world's candy canes are consumed in the United States, manufacturers have sent much of their production south of the border in the past five years. The attraction of moving abroad, however, has little to do with low wages and much to do with protectionism. U.S. quotas on sugar imports have, in recent years, caused the domestic price of sugar to become 350 percent higher than world market prices. As candy makers have relocated production to countries where sugar is cheaper, between 7,500 and 10,000 workers in the Midwest have lost their jobs—victims not of outsourcing but of the kind of protectionism called for by outsourcing's critics.

A similar story can be told of the steel tariffs that the Bush administration foolishly imposed from March 2002 until December 2003 (when a ruling by the World Trade Organization prompted their cancellation). The tariffs were allegedly meant to protect steelworkers. But in the United States, steel users employ roughly 40 times more people than do steel producers. Thus, according to estimates by the Institute for International Economics, between 45,000 and 75,000 jobs were lost because higher steel prices made U.S. steel-using industries less competitive.

These examples illustrate the problem with relying on anecdotes when debating the effects of offshore outsourcing. Anecdotes are incomplete narratives that fail to capture opportunity costs. In the cases of steel and sugar, the opportunity cost of using protectionism to save jobs was the much larger number of jobs lost in sectors rendered less productive by higher input prices. Trade protectionism amounts to an inefficient subsidy for uncompetitive sectors of the economy, which leads to higher prices for consumers and a lower rate of return for investors. It preserves jobs in less competitive sectors while destroying current and future jobs in sectors that have a comparative advantage. Thus, if barriers are erected to prevent offshore outsourcing, the overall effect will not be to create jobs but to destroy them.

So if protectionism is not the answer, what is the correct response? The best piece of advice is also the most difficult for elected officials to follow: do no harm.

Politicians never get credit for inaction, even when inaction is the best policy. President George H.W. Bush, for example, was pilloried for refusing to follow Japan's lead by protecting domestic markets—even though his refusal helped pave the way for the 1990s boom by letting market forces allocate resources to industries at the technological frontier. Restraint is anathema to the political class, but it is still the most important response to the furor over offshore outsourcing. As Robert McTeer, president of the Federal Reserve Bank of Dallas, said when asked about policy responses to outsourcing, "If we are lucky, we can get through the year without doing something really, really stupid."

The problem of offshore outsourcing is less one of economics than of psychology—people feel that their jobs are threatened. The best way to help those actually affected, and to calm the nerves of those who fear that they will be, is to expand the criteria under which the Trade Adjustment Assistance (TAA) program applies to displaced workers. Currently, workers cannot apply for TAA unless overall sales or production in their sector declines. In the case of offshore outsourcing, however, productivity increases allow for increased production and sales—making TAA out of reach for those affected by it. It makes sense to rework TAA rules to take into account workers displaced by offshore outsourcing even when their former industries or firms maintain robust levels of production.

Another option would be to help firms purchase targeted insurance policies to offset the transition costs to workers directly affected by offshore outsourcing. Because the perception of possible unemployment is considerably greater than the actual likelihood of losing a job, insurance programs would impose a very small cost on firms while relieving a great deal of employee anxiety. McKinsey Global Institute estimates that such a scheme could be created for as little as four or five cents per dollar saved from offshore outsourcing. IBM recently announced the creation of a two-year, $25 million retraining fund for its employees who fear job losses from outsourcing. Having the private sector handle the problem without extensive government intervention would be an added bonus.

The Best Defense

Until robust job growth returns, the debate over outsourcing will not go away— the political temptation to scapegoat foreigners is simply too great.

The refrain of "this time, it's different" is not new in the debate over free trade. In the 1980s, the Japanese variety of capitalism—with its omniscient industrial policy and high nontariff barriers—was supposed to supplant the U.S. system. Fifteen years later, that prediction sounds absurd. During the 1990s, the passage of NAFTA and the Uruguay Round of trade talks were supposed to create a "giant sucking sound" as jobs left the United States. Contrary to such fears, tens of millions of new jobs were created. Once the economy improves, the political hysteria over outsourcing will also disappear.

It is easy to praise economic globalization during boom times; the challenge, however, is to defend it during the lean years of a business cycle. Offshore outsourcing is not the bogeyman that critics say it is. Their arguments, however, must be persistently refuted. Otherwise, the results will be disastrous: less growth, lower incomes—and fewer jobs for American workers.

POSTSCRIPT

Is the Corporate Strategy of Outsourcing Unpatriotic?

The controversy surrounding foreign outsourcing not only incites strong passions, but cuts across party lines. Consider the following comments from Democrats John Kerry, "Unlike the Bush Administration, I want to repeal every tax break and loophole that rewards any Benedict Arnold CEO or corporation for shipping American jobs overseas" and Hillary Rodham Clinton, "I don't think losing American jobs is a good thing. The folks at the other end of Pennsylvania Avenue apparently do." Republican House Speaker Dennis Hastert said of a Bush economist's support for outsourcing, "[His] theory fails a basic test of real economics. An economy suffers when jobs disappear." (Quotes taken from Daniel T. Griswold, 2004.)

The war on American outsourcing has moved beyond the talking stage: In March 2004, the Senate passed an amendment that denies certain federal contracts from being awarded to organizations that outsource work overseas. This action has been echoed at the state level as well. Indiana, for example, cancelled a contract with an Indiana-based firm to upgrade the state's computer systems when it was discovered that the company employed workers in India. Instead, they spent $8 million more of taxpayer's money and awarded the contract to another firm. Clearly, the alarmist tone of the above quotes is manifesting itself in the concrete actions of federal and state legislation designed to penalize firms that choose to send work overseas. Is this a wise response to the current wave of corporate outsourcing? Is outsourcing unpatriotic and bad for American business? Where do you stand on this important management topic?

Both of the articles presented here raised important points and presented strong evidence in support of their views. Sarah Anderson and John Cavanagh argue that outsourcing is a real threat to the economic health of the United States and provide several suggestions as to the types of government actions necessary to keep American jobs from moving overseas. Dr. Daniel Drezner argues that the controversy surrounding outsourcing is more hype than substance, is actually economically beneficial to America, and is consistent with American principles and values.

Suggested Readings

For anti-outsourcing articles, see the last page of the Anderson and Cavanagh article.

Radley Balko, Outsourcing debate tainted by myths, misconceptions. Foxnews.com, April 22, 2004.

Daniel T. Griswold Outsource, outsource, and outsource some more. *Center for Trade Policy Studies,* The Cato Institute, May 3, 2004. http://www.freetrade.org/pubs/articles/dg-05-03-04.html

Edwin A. Locke, On May Day celebrate capitalism. *The Ayn Rand Institute.* April 24, 2003. http://www.aynrand.org/site/News2?page=NewsArticle&id=7449

McKinsey Global Institute, "Offshoring: Is It a Win-Win Game?" San Francisco, CA, August 2003.

ISSUE 12

Are U.S. CEOs Overpaid?

YES: Lisa H. Newton, from "The Care and Feeding of the Truly Greedy: CEO Salaries in World Perspective," *Taking Sides: Business Ethics and Society* (McGraw-Hill Dushkin, 2000)

NO: Ira T. Kay and Steven E. Rushbrook, from "The U.S. Executive Pay Model: Smart Business or Senseless Greed?" *WorldatWork Journal* (First Quarter, 2001)

ISSUE SUMMARY

YES: Lisa Newton believes that the typical U.S. CEO should not receive ten or more times the annual pay of CEOs in other industrial countries. She also points out, in no uncertain terms, that CEOs are only partly responsible for the ultimate success of their organization and the accompanying increase in shareholder wealth.

NO: Ira Kay and Steven Rushbrook believe that U.S. CEOs are entitled to whatever levels of pay they receive. They argue from a free-market perspective where labor, like every other business input, is subject to free-market forces. They also provide a discussion on the incredible amount of wealth U.S. CEOs have created for their shareholders.

O ver the last 15 years or so, it has become a spring ritual as nearly anticipated in some circles as the first pitch of the new baseball season. Business magazines and newspapers across the country, in blazing titles written to arouse reader antipathy, report on the incredible pay received by chief executive officers (CEOs) in the previous year at some of the nation's largest corporations. Often, the articles include photos with a prominently displayed figure—the number of employees laid off the previous year by these apparently shameless and greedy CEOs! The intent of such prejudicial headlines is, obviously, to sell copy by painting CEOs as gluttonous fat cats and thereby appealing to the consumer's sense of fairness. But beyond the legitimate economic objective of generating revenues, articles of this sort raise an important question for corporate America: On the whole, are U.S. CEOs overpaid? For many individuals whose sole exposure to this topic comes through popular media publications and news outlets, the answer is obviously "yes." But, like most things in life, there are two sides to this story. In academic circles and corporate boardrooms across the country, there is much passionate debate on CEO pay with plenty of advocates on both sides. So, by way of introduction, let us consider a few points on each side of the question.

Those who argue that U.S. CEOs are overpaid raise several interesting points in support of their position. One of their most powerful arguments appeals to the apparent unfairness of paying a CEO tens of millions of dollars while the corporation is simultaneously laying off hundreds or even thousands of employees. Why should a CEO be rewarded for cutting the workforce? Related to this is the fact that some boards of directors have shown a willingness to award large bonuses not just to high-performing CEOs but also to CEOs whose organizations were clear underperformers the previous year. Such actions suggest that a CEO's pay may not be tied to how well he or she performs, a situation that most would agree is not fair. Perhaps the strongest argument put forth by those who think U.S. CEOs are overpaid is based on a comparison of the CEO pay–to–worker pay ratio in America to that of other industrialized countries. Critics frequently point out that U.S. executives typically make several hundred times more in annual income than the lowest paid employees in their firms. In other countries, however, the ratio is considerably smaller. In Japan, for example, the typical CEO makes only about 15 times the lowest worker, and many member countries of the European Union restrict top executive pay to around 20 times the lowest worker's pay.

On the other side of the debate, defenders of current U.S. CEO pay point out that CEO pay is, like most jobs in America, subject to labor market influences. Currently, the market for quality CEOs is very tight, and wage-increasing bidding wars are the norm. Thus, CEO pay is clearly subject to labor market conditions. In response to the layoff issue, proponents of existing CEO pay levels argue that CEOs are paid to make and execute difficult decisions. They point out that often the alternative to downsizing and staying in business is laying off no one and going out of business entirely. Another reason that U.S. CEOs deserve their pay is because of the incredible amount of wealth created by their organizations over the last two decades. When compared to how much wealth CEOs have made for their shareholders, their pay levels look very reasonable.

The two articles that follow address the issue of whether or not U.S. CEOs, as a group, are overpaid. Lisa H. Newton argues that they are overpaid. In so doing, she raises and addresses several of the points made above. As you read her article, ask yourself whether you find her position convincing, particularly the last section where she argues that high CEO pay is against the public interest. The "no" article was written by Ira T. Kay and Steven E. Rushbrook. Their article covers all the points typically espoused by CEO pay advocates and throws in a few more for good measure. Particularly noteworthy is their discussion on the amount of wealth created by American CEOs over the last 20 years. Do you find this point to be particularly influential in the debate?

Lisa H. Newton  **YES**

The Care and Feeding of the Truly Greedy: CEO Salaries in World Perspective

In 1996, Jack Welch, CEO of General Electric, received $21.4 million in salary and performance bonuses (and about $18 million in stock options); Lawrence Coss of the Green Tree Financial Corporation received $102.4 million in salary and bonus (plus stock options worth at least $38 million). Michael Eisner of Disney added $196 million in stock to his previous holding, somewhere around a third of a billion. The list goes on: Intel's Andrew Grove took home $97.6 million, Traveler's Group Sanford Weill made $94.2 million, and Citicorp's John Reed got $43.6 million. (These figures from John Cassidy's piece, aptly titled "Gimme," in *The New Yorker* of April 21, 1997; See also "The Top Ten List" in *The Nation*, December 8, 1997.) According to a preliminary study of 60 companies by Pearl Meyer & Partners, the CEO of a multibillion-dollar company received an average of $4.37 million in compensation in 1995. That was a 23% increase from 1994. (That number from an anonymous squib, "Checking in on the CEO's Pay," in *HR Focus*, May 1996, p. 15.) As Cassidy points out, we're not supposed to think those figures excessive:

> But, according to *Business Week*, when you add together salary, bonuses, and options packages the typical C.E.O. at a large company saw his pay envelope grow by just fifty-four per cent—barely eighteen times the increase necessary to keep pace with the cost of living. (All told, his pay-check was only two hundred and nine times as big as the average factory employee's.)

Meanwhile, World Resource Institute figures from a few years earlier show that average annual compensation for a citizen (or Gross Domestic Product per capita, which is as close to the same thing as we can get in largely non-cash economies), in U.S. dollars, was less than $100 in Mozambique and Tanzania, less than $200 in seven other African countries (Burundi, Chad, Malawi, Rwanda, Sierra Leone, Somalia, Uganda), plus Nepal and Vietnam, under $300 in another 15 countries worldwide. (That list from *World Resources 1996–1997*, published by the World Resources Institute, p. 166.) We are not living in a rich world. But some CEO's are rich, very rich.

How, the untaught observer might ask, is this kind of disparity justified? How can it be that one of the world's inhabitants has a yearly compensation equal to the combined resources of 43,700 other of the world's inhabitants? We can understand that some people are lucky (born with perfect pitch) and others are not (born without arms). But the agreement to compensate an executive to the tune of tens of millions is not a matter of luck. It's a human decision if ever there was one. What on earth could make it the right human decision?

Justifications abound. Justifications are products, and like all products, are for sale for a fair market price. They are not always necessary or desirable, but become so very quickly if something not quite right—something that just doesn't *smell* very good—is happening. Having an annual compensation 209 times that of your employees, and 43,700 times that of fellow humans across the world, is one of those conditions that assaults the nostrils, so CEO's need justifications; and with that much money to spend, there's bound to be some left after the mortgage and the groceries to splurge on a justification or two. It's a perfect free market situation: a willing buyer (the CEO and his loyal staff) meets a willing seller (a well-educated and articulate wordsmith who really needs money), and a justification changes hands. A rudimentary knowledge of human psychology tells you that the wordsmith will instantly convince himself (or herself: this is an equal opportunity sellout) that CEO's really are worth the enormous amount of money they're getting, and that the CEO will instantly convince himself (never herself: equal opportunity has not yet reached this level) that the justification is sound. But it isn't. As we might expect of products turned out at such speed in such an uncritical market, the quality isn't the best. It might be worthwhile to count some of the errors.

It won't do, for instance, to claim that the CEO contributes 43,700 times as much value to the world as the shepherd in Tanzania or the farmer in Chad. Even if the movies, or software, or candy bars produced by the CEO's company are really worth that many times the wool or corn produced by the Africans, they are not made by the CEO, who never goes near the production floor, but by the minions of the company, making 1/209 their CEO's annual pay. Whatever value the company produces, in short, could equally well be produced with a CEO making half that annual compensation, or, most likely, no CEO at all. (That suggestion might be worth examining.)

Nor will it do to claim that a company simply *has* to pay that much for such rare talent, that you really *can't* get a good CEO these days for under that price, given all the competition. The reason why that rings somehow false is that these decisions are made by the Board of Directors of the company, being a very small club of similarly compensated executives (on whose Boards of Directors the CEO will also sit), and the whole decision stays within that little overpaid group. One wonders if, given another Search Committee, someone could not have been found to do the job for, say, $2,000,000 per annum. Or maybe $650,000, which will pay most of the bills that a CEO might run up in the course of a year.

Comparisons with other high-paid talent also ring false. Entertainers, to be sure, make big bucks, singing or acting or shooting baskets. But here we have direct value for money, paid by those who are entertained. The entertainers make a lot of money: but their careers come to an end as soon as *our* tastes change or attention wanders, and for the time being, they are at least fun to watch. Careers can also end in a minute with a car accident or even a badly twisted knee. But the CEO is not at all fun to watch, and he seems to be immune to the changing of consumer tastes or accidental assaults on the body; he can write his memos from a wheelchair.

Now we come to the crux of the value! He writes memos. What is he *writing,* in those memos, that makes him so valuable? For an answer to that question, a review of the incentive structures of the publicly held corporation is needed:

The Corporation From Cradle to Grave

How does the corporation get started? An investor, or a group of investors, decide that there is a good market for a good or service (i.e. a high demand coupled with the money to buy that which will fill the demand), and that the revenue from sales will exceed the cost of making the good or service available by a healthy margin (i.e. they're going to make a lot of money), so they buy the machinery and supplies and office space and talent required for the production of this good or service, and the production and marketing and advertising begin. In a magic metaphysical moment the articles of incorporation are signed, and a bouncing baby company is launched. Pretty soon the money's rolling in and the investors are very happy.

Now, it's always possible for one of these investors to decide he wants his money back, possibly to invest in some other enterprise; he can try to sell out his share in the enterprise, to one of the other investors or to a stranger. He may have problems doing that if the enterprise is not doing well or if he owns a very large share. To make a long story very short, that problem and myriads of others were solved by a common Stock Market where all such shares can be bought and sold. In the present day, if an investor decides he no longer wants to be a shareholder, an investor, in Acme Corporation, he can sell his shares on the open market and invest instead in Beter Corporation. His choice.

Why would a shareholder want to sell out? The reason he bought in was to make money, and the company he set up is doing fine. If he wants continuing income, he'll do better to hang on to the stock and continue collecting dividends. But suppose he just wants lots of cash right now: fine, he sells his shares, "liquidates" his share of the assets of the company, and he gets the cash. Now of course, if all the original investors early in the company's history decided to do that at once, the whole company would be liquidated. But that's not likely to happen. (In the contemporary stock market, it's almost impossible, just because of the huge volume of stock traded; some mutual funds turn over their entire portfolio in the course of the year, and stray stocks are likely to be picked up.)

Why is it not likely to happen, at least in the original model of shareholdership? Because a funny thing happens when you put your money into a company as an investor. You begin to think of the company as "yours," which is appropriate, because it is, in part. You become anxious for its fortunes, not only for the monetary value of your initial investment, but for its own sake, as you would be anxious for the fortunes of a nephew. You watch its coverage in the press, cheering when it is favorable, grousing when it is not. You get attached to the company. You don't call your broker and have him sell it if it goes down a few points. For one thing, by the time you got hold of your broker and he got the stock offered for sale, the whole situation would have changed; for another, his fee would wipe out any gains; but for a third, your sense of ownership has become tinged with loyalty: you don't "sell out" until something really big, college or retirement or a new house, comes along. Besides, the individual shareholder is important in the company. If you are the owner of the company, even a part owner, you are the "principal," and all the company's employees are your "agents"—they act for you and for your interests. The CEO has to please you or (in theory: it almost never happened) you can wage a proxy fight at the annual meeting, bring about the election of your own Board of Directors, and have them hire a new CEO who will represent your interests more perfectly. So the CEO wants to keep you happy. But what does the CEO of your company have to do to please you? Not much: keep the company on an even keel, no scandals, distribute profits regularly, but remember to keep some of those profits to reinvest for the long term, because the long term is what you're in for.

That was the American shareholder up into the 1960's. There were mutual funds, of course, that owned stock, effectively pooling the investment funds of small shareholders to give them a diversified portfolio. Mutual funds did not operate like individual shareholders, for their managers, under the same fiduciary obligation to *their* shareholders, were not permitted to get attached to the companies they held—their job was to increase the total amount of stock value in the fund, and they didn't care what companies they had to hold shares in, in order to do that. But the funds were not really big players at the time.

They could become big players if they were joined by the vast money salted away in huge trust funds—pension funds and the like, and the endowments of not-for-profit institutions of all kinds. But these funds always invested in bonds, for the sake of safety; they didn't buy stocks. Until the 1960's, that is. Then these huge funds decided that 1929 was a long time ago, that stocks were quite as safe as bonds, and that it was time to trade in creditorship for ownership. Slowly they moved into the market, and took it over.

Again: what a fund manager wants from the investments he makes is rapid growth, the swift increase in the total amount of money in the fund. If it is a pension fund, that money is what the workers are going to retire on, and he (or she) works for the workers. If the fund is an investment pool, the manager works for the investors; if it is the endowment fund of a University, the manager works for the University. He will keep his huge funds invested in a company for the long term only if it is pouring money into his fund at a rate unmatched anywhere else in the market, or if he really has no choice. For a long time, the customs of the market and the available technology kept the funds' money moving slowly through the market, as well-weighted decisions moved the cash from blue chip to blue chip. But in the 1980's, the established ways of the market broke down, the white-shod country clubbers were shoved aside by the new breed of traders and arbitragers, and computer technology advanced to the point of allowing program trading (programming your computer to make trades automatically, in a split second, in response to certain changes in the market) and otherwise very rapid shifts of money from one stock to another.

Then it all came together. The new breed of trader talked the managers of the huge slowmoving funds into becoming players in a new rapid-fire market, and their money funded the leveraged buyouts, the mergers and acquisitions, and the infamous hostile takeovers for which the 1980's became famous. In the process a new breed of fund manager was born, one who is acutely aware, first, that his fund (for instance, my favorite pension fund), CREF, owns very large chucks of (say) Acme Company, second, that the Acme Board of Directors had therefore better take CREF's interests seriously or he'll have them replaced (he may even demand, and get, his own Director on the Board), third, that his obligation is to increase the amount of money in CREF as rapidly as possible, fourth, that therefore the Acme Board of Directors must instruct the Acme CEO to run the company in such a way that CREF's stock position appreciates, and fifth, that if the CEO is unresponsive to that instruction, the Board must fire him and get a more responsive one. This is what we call an "active" investor: no longer does the fund manager simply sell Acme and buy Beter when Acme is not running the way he wants it to run. He gets in there and makes it do what he wants. (Oh, but doesn't CREF offer a "social responsibility" track, in which only stocks in socially responsible corporations are purchased, for conscientious investors? Yes indeed; and CREF's fund manager manages those funds just as aggressively as all the others.)

Once a CEO is on board who promises to extract money from the company's workings and move it into shareholder hands faster than ever, the Board kind of makes *sure* he doesn't forget what to do by structuring incentives to help his memory: the more the dividends flow and the price per share of the stock goes up, the greater his bonus.

That, of course, is the link between the new way of doing business and the CEO's compensation.

Now, what was on that memo? How does the CEO suddenly put lots more money into shareholder hands? We know that the size profit to be divided among the shareholders is based in part on the ratio of corporate revenue to corporate costs—best understood as a fraction with revenue as a numerator and costs as the denominator—so the CEO has to increase the numerator, the revenue stream, or cut costs, the denominator, or, preferably, both. Let me count the ways he might do that: (1) He can discover that the company's operations were rife with waste, inefficiency, theft, whatever; tighten it up, get things working the way they should, and the company saves oodles of money, squeezing down the denominator, without changing operations at all. He'll always say that's what he's doing, but it's unlikely that much savings will be got that way. (2) He can try to raise the numerator, the revenue, by raising price. In some markets he can get away with that for awhile, but in a highly competitive market that's just likely to reduce sales, theoretically to zero. (3) He can try to raise revenue by developing new products, new markets, or both. That's a good idea, but it requires more investment, therefore lower distributions of profits right now. CREF is not interested in waiting. It wants money now. (4) There aren't any other ways to raise revenue, so he has to cut costs. He can cut the paper clip budget and pick up cheaper raw materials for his manufacturing, and he'll do that, but it's not enough. The big item in any company is payroll, not only for the meager salaries and wages the workers make, but also for those infinitely expensive medical and other insurance plans the company signed on for and now can't back out of. Fire a worker, and you save all that money. Fire (lay off) lots of workers, and you save lots of money. The denominator goes way down, raising profits, and the stock price goes way up. And that was the object of the expedition.

So that's what the memo was about. The CEO was setting the ball in motion to lay off thousands of workers. CREF will see the stock price go way up, and will be happy when the Board of Directors presents the CEO with a wonderful year-end bonus. That's why CEO compensation is so high, millions of dollars for successfully pink-slipping the company.

What does CREF do next? Sells the stock, obviously. After all, the prospects for the company are not good. They've cut way back on the quality of their materials, refused to reinvest in better plant or equipment, and laid off the folks who were doing the work, all to cut costs and send the price of the stock way up. In effect, they sold off some fraction of the value of the company, "liquidated" it, for quick cash, and distributed the cash. Now the company is worth a lot less, and CREF has no intention of holding on to worthless goods. Seeing the stock go up, investors who do not know why it went up will buy into Acme now on the expectation that it will go higher. CREF will take their cash and invest in the stock of (say) Beter, and promptly insist that Beter go through the same round of liquidation—cost-cutting, laying off, and neglecting reinvestment. Then Beter's stock will go up, CREF will sell it, and repeat the process. And all other funds are doing the same thing. In theory, the process could lead to the liquidation of the entirety of American industry. The grave of the productive corporation is already prepared; we await the death rattle. However long it takes, the CEO's will be well paid throughout.

In the Public Interest

What's wrong with very high CEO compensation? Two things: First, it is bad stewardship for people to take more than they can use, and unjust that some people should be making 43,700 times what other people make, especially when at least some of those other people are starving. John Locke, high priest of private property, put the case for the morality of private property very simply: each man may take from the commons (the world resources available to all) only as much as he can use, and only as long as enough and as good is left for others. The CEO fails on both counts.

Second, this compensation system is destroying American industry. It is commonplace by now that our cost-saving schemes have cost us the economy: our products made obsolete by foreign companies that invested in R & D [research and development] when we did not, and invested in new plants when we did not, our industrial jobs lost as our obsolete plants have to be shuttered, as pink slips flutter from the corner offices in the most recent "downsizings" and "rightsizings," as the actual work is assigned to East Asian and Mexican factories and American workers are handed over to unemployment. We are moving, we are told, from an era of manufacturing to an era of information-driven service industries. These are precisely the industries for which the vast majority of the population is not prepared and from which they cannot profit. We are condemning a majority of working-age adults to temporary, underpaid, service jobs, while the tiny minority feeds off the global wealth generated by the exploitation of the rest of the world. The entire system is unjust, and cries out to heaven, and to an informed citizenry, for remedy. The compensation of the truly greedy might be a good place to start.

**Ira T. Kay and
Steven E. Rushbrook**

The U.S. Executive Pay Model

Ceo pay has been under media scrutiny for more than 20 years, but the nature of that scrutiny has shifted recently. During the mid- to late-1980s, critics argued that compensation for CEOs and other executives was largely unrelated to the financial or stock market performance of their companies. These critics included the media, government, government agencies (e.g., Securities and Exchange Commission, Internal Revenue Service, Financial Accounting Standards Board), and institutional investors, including public employee pension funds.

During the mid-1990s, while some criticism was exaggerated, there was a marked move to strengthen the relationship between CEO pay and the stock price of their companies, primarily through increases in stock option grants and executive stock ownership. This pay/stock price linkage, combined with improved proxy disclosure and better governance by compensation committees, has played a role in motivating the increase in the value of the U.S. stock market.

Today the criticism continues, but the focus has again shifted. Executive pay has continued to rise dramatically along with the stock market. E-commerce, the Internet and technology sectors have created enormous wealth among founders and key employees. This new wealth has put significant pressure on boards to increase pay for their own CEOs, including those in the traditional economy. Critics contend that:

- CEOs are not worth their pay.
- CEO pay is too high in general.
- CEO pay is unrelated to performance.
- CEO pay went up because the stock market went up; the U.S. stock market would have performed just as well without stock options.
- CEO pay will not go down if the stock market goes down.
- CEO pay is part of a "winner-take-all" society.

This article will examine:

- Some of the reasons for record CEO pay levels
- The reasons that CEO performance is so vital to our economy

From *WorldatWork Journal*, First Quarter 2001, pp. 8–18. Copyright © 2001R by WorldatWork.
Reprinted by permission.

- The arguments for and against CEO worth
- When to measure CEO performance against pay
- The academic and author research relevant to this analysis
- A prognosis for the future.

Why CEO Pay Is So High

There is little doubt that executive pay has risen faster (10 to 15 percent annually) than average employee earnings (3 to 4 percent annually) and the rate of inflation (less than 3 percent annually).

However, increases in CEO compensation packages should be kept in perspective. Arguably, three primary factors account for the rapid escalation of CEO pay packages:

1. **A scarcity of CEO talent creates "bidding wars."** Despite occasional performance failures, boards are willing to pay breathtaking sums to CEOs who can generate record financial performance. Clearly, the escalation of CEO packages is due in large part to the scarcity of proven CEO talent. Boards now are turning to outside candidates more frequently in search of talent to help them compete in an increasingly competitive global business community. The notion of promoting from within is being balanced by boards that need to globalize their operations and find proven talent quickly. Research has shown that the percentage of CEOs hired from the outside has risen dramatically in the past 10 years (nearly one in five). The high technology sector has exploded in the last two years, and the executive talent drain is apparent. Even with the NASDAQ market correction starting in early 2000, old-line companies continue to compete with high tech companies in search of scarce CEO talent. Subsequently, the equity packages offered by the high tech firms are escalating CEO packages at all companies even further.

2. **The "winner take all" mentality is pervasive.** The CEO and the senior executive team work under significant pressure and public scrutiny, and the most successful CEO candidates are often those who are able to assume extraordinarily high levels of risk and still win. In contrast to Japan and Germany, where senior executives function more often as a risk-sharing team, the typical U.S. model requires the CEO to assume the greatest risk and responsibility. It is certainly true that this model has worked successfully in the United States for at least the past 10 years. CEO pay packages often provide the counterbalance to the risk inherent in these positions, and boards are willing to pay such packages to a limited pool of candidates.

3. **CEOs are compensated for making unpopular decisions.** As CEOs become celebrities, unpopular decisions such as downsizing, mergers and divestitures rest squarely on their shoulders. Increased media attention on the business community exacerbates this effect. In addition, large institutional shareholders often are quite vocal about CEO pay packages and company performance, and their actions exert significant control over a company's stock price. As a result, high CEO packages, in part, compensate for the stigma associated with the position.

Is CEO Performance Important?

The obvious answer is yes. High-performing CEOs are essential to the success of most companies. But the real answer is less obvious and has far-reaching social consequences beyond the executive suite.

Stronger Job Security and Better Career Opportunities for All Employees

CEOs who perform well are more likely to create and sustain successful companies and, in turn, employees are more likely to enjoy greater job security and better career opportunities. In the late 1980s and early 1990s, when downsizing was prevalent, employees who survived these waves of change were better positioned for the long term.

Today, while downsizing is less common, the pace of mergers and acquisitions has increased, and the U.S. economy has created a record number of jobs in the past decade. Successful CEOs, driven in large part by stock-based incentives, have created larger, more international companies serving a global customer base.

Stronger Retirement Security for Employees and Their Dependents

One aspect of higher CEO performance is an increase in the value of pension plan assets, thereby increasing the security of all pension plans. It is a great irony that public employee pension funds sometimes breed the most vocal opponents of pay-for-performance CEO plans because they, as well as state and local government employees, benefit so directly from the superior stock performance of Corporate America.

Over-funded pension plans, the result of higher stock values, allow companies to increase earnings per share (EPS). Increases in stock prices also contribute to portable retirement plans, such as the 401(k), allowing individual investment alternatives and mobility.

Are CEOs Worth It?

Spectacular headline CEO pay packages, especially in the e-commerce sector, have caused a flurry of media coverage. Obviously, that influences the general labor market for CEOs and executives, but it is not limited to them.

A study completed in the April 2000 issue of Forbes found 12 CEOs recruited within the prior 12 months from the traditional sector to the dot-com sector with packages valued at more than $100 million. Examples include Richard Braddock of Priceline and Margaret Whitman of eBay at more than $1 billion each. Are they worth it? Is this labor market "efficient"?

Because CEOs have alternatives, the labor market appears efficient. They could become consultants or venture capitalists or entrepreneurs, or go to another dot-com. Thus, the real question becomes, 'What do you have to pay them to buy them out of their risk to go?'

For example, a well-known executive changes companies from one telecommunications company to another and he gets reimbursed first class airfare for his mother. Another high technology executive is given a $40 million jet with a tax gross-up to cover the jet's value.

On the other hand, the Wilshire 5000, one of the broadest market indices available, recorded total market capitalization at $15.8 trillion dollars for 2000, up 24 percent from 1999, and a 300-plus percent increase from 1995. In addition, according to the Crystal Report, aggregate total CEO pay went up 43 percent from 1995 to 1999, but the figure represented only a fraction of a percent (.3 percent) of the market capitalization for those companies. While the stock market has corrected in the last half of 2000, the crucial point remains: While CEOs are well paid, they have created enormous economic value.

During 1999, the Standard & Poor's (S&P) 500 Index yielded a 21 percent return, and the bull market span has extended nearly 20 years. Annually, the S&P 500 Index has earned 19.9 percent (or 20 times) the original investment since August 1982. In addition, the Internet boom has pushed U.S. economic growth to record levels. Internet market capitalization represented well above 10 percent of the entire U.S. equity market at its peak. Internet companies also were responsible for more than 50 percent of stock market gains in 1999, as a result of 140 percent return and significant market weighting. In 1999, 257 Internet companies went public with a combined market capitalization of $242 billion. Even factoring in the correction of 2000, the returns remain quite remarkable.

Depending on how it is analyzed, the average large company CEO pay package is currently valued between $10 million and $20 million. The average increase was between 10 and 40 percent. But in sum, it still adds up to just 30 basis points—again, .3 percent of market capitalization for those companies.

Is mankind in the midst of a modern industrial revolution with all of the productivity and benefits to humanity? Or is it a decade of greed with people being paid what they're really not worth? There is a sense of paradox. The question is, can theory or hypothesis explain it? In short, yes.

In economic terms, the fundamental question is "Are the best resources being allocated to their optimal use?" In effect, the labor market is saying that Margaret Whitman will add more to eBay, and to society, under Adam Smith's invisible hand, than she would at her former employer. Are the resources (executives, in this case) being put to optimal use?

The theory behind executive pay rests on the principle that CEOs are the agents of shareholders; they are separate from owners. Occasionally, this agent/owner gap creates a conflict of interest. Executive pay programs, especially stock ownership and stock options, are explicitly designed to close the gap and create alignment between CEOs and shareholders. This "agency theory" clearly states that CEO pay opportunity could help create an increase in performance.

When Do You Measure CEO Performance?

The most fundamental question is whether pay causes performance. To examine whether causation exists, an appropriate methodology and performance period should be chosen. Frequently, an inappropriate time period is chosen and hence, an erroneous conclusion is drawn.

The following two perspectives yield the most valid results:

- **Pay Opportunity vs. Subsequent Performance.** Current pay opportunity should be correlated with future performance. A high pay opportunity today (e.g., annual cash bonus opportunity or stock option grants) should cause a CEO to create future high performance for the organization. For example, examine the cash bonus opportunity three years ago and then consider performance in subsequent years.
- **Actual Pay vs. Prior Performance.** Current actual pay, such as cash bonuses or stock option profits, should be correlated with prior performance in the past several years. Often, in journal articles and media clips, attempts to correlate past pay-outs with subsequent performance, or current pay opportunities (e.g., stock option grants) with past performance (e.g., three-year total returns to shareholders) result in wholly inappropriate perspectives that mislead the audience.

To measure and assess pay for performance, two criteria should be considered: pay and stock ownership. Consider today's pay, plus "in-the-money" options, compared to total shareholder return (TSR) in the past five years. As for stock ownership, take the opposite perspective and consider past stock ownership with performance in the subsequent five years.

For example, consider Company A and Company B, each of which granted 1 million options to their CEOs at $20 each in 1998.

- Company A had a $15 stock price in 1996, a $20 stock price in 1998 and a $20 stock price in 2000. Its Black-Scholes present value was approximately 50 percent, or $10 million in 1998, and there were no other stock option grants.
- Company B had a stock price that went from $25 to $20 to $40. The Black-Scholes value also is $10 million. But in-the-money value is $20 million in 2000.

One method would be to consider the 1998 Black-Scholes value compared with the 1996 to 1998 TSR, which includes the increase in stock price plus dividends.

- Company A had $10 million in pay, and 33 percent TSR from 1996 to 1998; the stock price increased from $15 to $20.
- Company B had $10 million in Black-Scholes value, but the stock price fell $5 from $25 to $20, down 20 percent.

At first glance, it is assumed that no pay for performance exists because both companies had CEO pay of $10 million under this methodology, one with TSR of positive 33 percent and the other with a negative 20 percent TSR.

The alternative methodology is more appropriate because it considers the correct time period—actual pay in the year 2000 vs. TSR for the prior three years. For Company A, there is zero pay and zero TSR. For Company B, there is $20 million pay and 100 percent TSR. With this alternative, the conclusion is that there is pay for performance.

The answer depends completely on the methodology. A case could be made that the large option grant motivated Company B's CEO to succeed, and while Company A did not succeed, there was no pay for that low performance.

Academic Research

The following six points categorize questions that most researchers seek to answer in relation to CEO pay:

1. Is there pay for performance? Is a CEO's pay sensitive to company performance? Is there a correlation?
2. Does stock ownership matter? In other words, can companies ignore CEO stock ownership and grant stock options? If stock ownership is important, do stock ownership guidelines work? Do stock ownership guidelines create CEO ownership, which improves company performance?
3. Are there motivational differences between stock ownership and stock options? Are executives afraid to buy stock if the price is volatile? Do large stock option grants motivate expensive company stock repurchase programs?
4. Do stock options create ownership?
5. Are poor performing CEOs terminated?
6. Is the U.S. model being exported?

According to Research Findings

Is There Pay for Performance?

CEO pay, including stock, is highly sensitive to company performance. CEO compensation in Year 1 is positively correlated with corporate performance in Year 2, the appropriate measurement period.

This demonstration of the pay/performance link is particularly important in light of the criticism that CEOs receive high pay for superior performance, and receive high severance packages when poor performance leads to termination.

Does CEO Stock Ownership Matter?

CEO stock ownership has increased dramatically, and company performance is positively correlated with the percentage of stock held by managers. In addition, executive stock ownership guidelines improve company performance.

Are There Motivational Differences Between Stock Ownership and Stock Options?

Large stock option grants are correlated with increased stock price volatility, suggesting that CEOs who receive large stock option grants may subsequently cause stock price volatility. Companies with volatile stock prices have executives with less stock ownership, confirming that executives are reluctant to purchase highly volatile stock. Stock option grants, without stock ownership guidelines, may increase stock price volatility and reduce executive stock ownership levels. In addition, stock options are correlated with lower stock dividends and increased stock repurchase levels.

Stock Dividends

Because the current stock price is inversely related to the expected future stream of dividends, lower dividend payments to shareholders will likely result in higher future stock prices and therefore greater potential stock option gains.

Company Stock Repurchases

Companies are repurchasing shares at an unprecedented rate to fuel their stock option programs. To fund these repurchases, companies are either using cash or borrowing funds, increasing both their debt/equity ratios and their risk significantly, and reducing the risk adjusted value of their stock.

Do Stock Options Create Ownership?

Stock options do not create stock ownership but tend to serve as an imperfect proxy for stock ownership. Stock options can help, but they must be combined with executive stock ownership guidelines and vehicles to assist executives achieve the required ownership levels. Stock option gains, even those for e-billionaires, can evaporate quickly during an economic downturn.

One way to promote stock ownership is a management stock purchase plan, which allows executives to purchase discounted company stock with a portion of their cash bonus and/or salary. This plan has significant tax, accounting and financial planning advantages.

Are Poor Performing CEOs Terminated?

Several sources of academic literature indicate that poor performing CEOs are, in fact, terminated.

Is the U.S. CEO Pay Model Being Exported?

Yes, the U.S. CEO pay model is being exported, but with significantly less performance sensitivity than the U.S. models. For example, Germany, Japan, France and other nations are incorporating pay-for-performance plans, but on a more limited basis.

Comparisons of U.S. and overseas CEO pay packages are difficult given the vastly different size of the countries and companies. Because CEO pay tracks with company size, given the complexity and risk involved, the U.S. CEO pay packages are likely to be larger than those found overseas. In addition, international studies often do not account for differences in culture, local welfare benefits and tax rates.

CEO Pay Study 2000–2001

U.S. executive pay, especially CEO pay, continues to generate controversy, with some in the media believing that it has gone beyond appropriate limits. Others, including most institutional investors, believe that the way U.S. CEOs are paid is a source of significant competitive advantage.

Can America's Economic Success Be Attributed to CEO Pay-for-Performance?

While there are outliers—such as high paying companies with low performance, and low paying companies with high performance—on the average, there is a strong correlation between CEO pay and company performance. Having shown this correlation, causation is difficult to prove. Still, the greater the CEO's financial stake in a company, the more likely he/she is to act in the best interests of shareholders.

Is CEO Cash Compensation Sensitive to Market Performance?

Yes, in terms of total shareholder return (TSR), a CEO's total cash compensation is sensitive to a company's stock market performance. In a Watson Wyatt survey sample, CEOs with above-median change in total cash compensation (TCC, or base salary plus cash bonus) correlated with an 18.8-percent five-year annualized TSR, vs. 9.8 percent annualized TSR for CEOs with below-median change in TCC....

Does CEO Stock Ownership Correlate With Market Value?

An effective way to examine this issue is to first calculate Tobin's Q, the ratio of stock market valuation plus long-term debt divided by the replacement cost of the company's assets. This measure, developed by James Tobin of Yale University, also is known as intellectual capital, or the premium that the market is willing to pay for how well the company manages its assets (including human capital). Values above 1.0 imply that the market views the company as more valuable than the sum of its assets. Then, after examining CEO stock and the ratio of CEO ownership to CEO base salary, the Tobin's Q of companies with high CEO stock ownership proved to be 40 percent greater than that of companies with low CEO stock ownership.

Evidently, the market is willing to pay a premium for companies with leaders who have aligned their interests with the shareholders'.

The New Millennium

Given the dramatic change in the past decade, predicting even the near future seems a daunting task. Based on client work and continuing research, the following should hold true in the next 10 years:

- Pay-for-performance plans will continue at the CEO and executive levels, and will spread deeper into organizations. Companies with broad-based stock plans will continue to significantly outperform those with narrow stock plan coverage.

- CEO total pay increases will level off as salary increases have done in the recent past. Many incentive plans may have already reached optimal leverage levels. Continued outcry by the media and public are likely to check pay excesses for the executive team in most cases.
- Individual investors and large institutional shareholders will resist further stock option overhang and the expensive share repurchase programs that have fueled record stock option grant levels.
- Stock option overhang will level off in the 10 to 15 percent range for most industries, and at 20 to 25 percent for the high technology sector, including e-commerce. Push-back from investors, combined with sufficient incentive pay plan opportunities, has already started to level off overhang levels.
- Stock ownership levels, particularly for the CEO and the senior executive team, will continue to rise.
- European and Pacific Rim companies will emulate the U.S. executive pay model, including pay-for-performance and stock ownership. While overseas compensation professionals may view this as executive greed, most companies probably will tailor plans to suit their own cultures.
- Actual year-to-year CEO pay levels will fluctuate with stock market and economic performance indicators. While compensation opportunities, including stock options, will grow modestly, actual payouts are likely to decline if the stock market corrects further. Any future stock market correction will be smaller because of significant CEO stock ownership levels, which have provided the U.S. economy with a "cushion" of high performance.
- Pay programs at traditional companies and new economy companies will converge, with proven best practices being adopted by the majority.
- And finally, CEO pay will, of course, remain controversial.

Undoubtedly, U.S. companies are on the right track given the record financial performance of the past decade. Performance-based pay for CEOs, combined with programs that encourage stock ownership, should fuel steady job creation and financial success in the future.

The answer to the question of whether U.S. CEOs are overpaid depends on who answers. Clearly shareholders, including private investors and large institutional shareholders, would respond with a resounding "no." The record performance-based CEO pay packages are a small price to pay for unprecedented productivity and growth.

On the contrary, some would argue that the average worker should share in the success to a greater extent. As research indicates, including all employees in pay-for-performance and stock-based incentives should result in even higher levels of performance.

POSTSCRIPT

Are U.S. CEOs Overpaid?

So, how high are U.S. CEO salaries? In 2001, the *average* U.S. CEO annual income was $13 million (*Business Week*, April 16, 2001, pp. 77–108). While this figure may seem large, consider that it includes the extremely few—though highly publicized—cases of exorbitant CEO pay such as the $293 million, $164 million, and $157 million recently paid to the heads of Citigroup, AOL/Time Warner, and Cisco Systems, respectively. A few extreme cases such as these can easily skew the numbers, suggesting that there are many CEOs in America making considerably less than the $13 million average. Nevertheless, figures such as these beg the question: Are American CEOs overpaid?

You have just read two different answers to this question. Lisa Newton believes that the typical U.S. CEO should not receive ten or more times the annual pay of CEOs in other industrial countries. She also points out, in no uncertain terms, that CEOs are only partly responsible for the ultimate success of their organization and the concomitant increase in shareholder wealth. Further, she argues, no matter how much responsibility a CEO actually does carry, it isn't enough to justify the levels of compensation currently being paid to top executives in America. She concludes her argument with an appeal to the reader's emotions by declaring that it is immoral, in effect, for a CEO to "take" more than he/she can use, particularly "when people in the world are starving." Despite its emotional appeal, one must be careful to embrace this last line of attack without considerable thought: After all, it has more than a little in common with the basic tenets and principles of communism.

Ira Kay and Steven Rushbrook believe that U.S. CEOs typically earn every nickel they make and are, therefore, entitled to whatever levels of pay they receive. Theirs is a free-market view—that labor, like every other business input, is subject to free-market forces. For the typical CEO, annual compensation accurately reflects his or her worth in the market. According to these authors, in this sense, U.S. CEO pay is both fair and equitable.

Suggested Readings

Louis Aguilar, Exec-worker pay gap widens to gulf. *The Denver Post,* July 8, 2001, p. 16a.

Kerry A. Dolan, The age of the $100 million CEO. *Forbes,* April 3, 2000, vol. 165, issue 8.

Jack Dolmat, Executive pay for performance. *WorldatWork Journal,* First Quarter 2001, pp. 19–27.

Elan Journo, Why are CEOs paid so much? *The Ayn Rand Institute,* April 12, 2004. `http://www.aynrand.org/site/News2?page=NewsArticle&id=8404`

Louis Lavelle, Executive pay. *Business Week,* April 16, 2001, pp. 77–108.

Louis Lavelle, CEO pay: The more things change. . . . *Business Week,* October 6, 2000, pp. 106–108.

Kevin J. Murphy, Top executives are worth every nickel they get. *Harvard Business Review,* March/April 1986.

Alan Reynolds, CEO pay parade. *The Cato Institute,* April 18, 2004. `http://www.cato.org/dailys/04-18-04.html`

ISSUE 13

Corporate Governance Reform: Is Sarbanes-Oxley the Answer?

YES: Federal News Service, from "Conference Report on Corporate Responsibility Legislation," Capital Hill Hearing, *Federal News Service* (July 24, 2002)

NO: Alan Reynolds, from "Sarbanes-Oxley in Retrospect," *The State of Corporate Governance: A Retrospective on Sarbanes-Oxley* (Hill Briefing, December 12, 2003)

ISSUE SUMMARY

YES: Actual testimony taken from a congressional hearing just prior to the vote on the act itself is presented in this article. Included are comments from the authors of the act, Paul Sarbanes (D-MD) and Michael Oxley (R-OH).

NO: Cato Institute senior fellow Alan Reynolds provides his audience with a scathing indictment of the mind-set and philosophy beyond the creation of the act in his argument that Sarbanes-Oxley was not a positive reaction to the call for corporate governance change.

On July 30, 2002, President George W. Bush signed into law the Sarbanes-Oxley Act, an enormous piece of legislation spawned in the wake of the massive World-Com and Enron scandals that rocked Wall Street and corporate America just a few years beforehand. This act is routinely considered to be the most comprehensive and significant legislative action directed at corporate governance activities since the Securities Act of 1933 and the Securities Exchange Act of 1934 (Mondaq Business Briefing, Mondaq Ltd., August 9, 2004). Interestingly, at the time of these scandals, there were numerous pieces of independent corporate governance legislation that, for various reasons, were floundering in Congress and had not been enacted. The Enron and WorldCom scandals enraged the public to the point that political action was considered necessary, the result of which is the Sarbanes-Oxley Act of 2002.

Sarbanes-Oxley was designed to address the numerous violations of corporate governance rules and procedures executives committed during the wave of scandals that affected corporate America over the last five years. Sarbanes-Oxley expert Jorge E. Guerra provides the following list of the most common transgressions (Guerra, "The Sarbanes-Oxley Act and Evolution of Corporate Governance," *The CPA Journal*, March 2004, p. 14): (1) executive compensation grossly disproportionate to corporate results, (2) misuse of corporate funds, (3) trading on insider information, particularly managers exercising stock options that have rewarded short-term thinking, (4) misrepresentation of true earnings and financial condition by too many companies, and (5) obstruction of justice by concealing activities or destroying evidence.

The net result of these wrongdoings is a crisis of investor confidence in corporations, their executives, and corporate governance policies and procedures. So, who is to blame? Guerra again provides us with a list: (1) passive, nonindependent, and rubber-stamping boards of directors, (2) nonaccountable CEOs and senior management involved in serious conflicts of interest, (3) transaction-driven investment bankers and market-makers, and biased and nonindependent investment analysts, (4) nonindependent public accounting firms, and (5) regulators paying more attention to the manifestations of the problem than to the systemic conflicts of interest at the core of poor governance practices (Guerra, 2004).

The Sarbanes-Oxley Act was the government's reaction to the public's growing skepticism about the ability of existing corporate governance laws and regulations to control and discourage immoral and illegal business activities. Guerra notes that "Corporate governance reengineering should begin with a clear definition of the authority, duties, and accountability of the board of directors and management. Special emphasis must be placed on the accountability (duty to account) of the board of directors to the shareholders, and on its independence from management" (Guerra, 2004). The Sarbanes-Oxley Act has numerous provisions and requirements addressing virtually all aspects of corporate governance. Some of the principal areas of emphasis of the act include: (1) increased regulation and oversight of the accounting profession, (2) more stringent auditor and audit committee independence requirements, (3) greater corporate responsibility and accountability, (4) increased issuer disclosure, (5) increased regulation of securities analysts, (6) increased criminal penalties, and (7) new professional responsibility standards for attorneys (Mondaq Business Briefing, Mondaq Ltd., August 9, 2004).

Given the tremendous increase in governmental oversight of corporate behavior that this act entails, it is not at all surprising that there are many who are vehemently against it. In the two articles that follow, you will be exposed to both sides of the question of whether or not this act is good for American business. The first article is actual testimony taken from a congressional hearing just prior to the vote on the act itself. Included are comments from the authors of the act, Paul Sarbanes (D-MD) and Michael Oxley (R-OH), as well as other members of the senate. Not surprisingly, their comments about the legislation are extremely positive in nature. The second article is a speech given by Cato Institute Senior Fellow Alan Reynolds at a Hill Briefing on the act. Reynolds provides his audience with a scathing indictment of the mind-set and philosophy beyond the creation of the act and condemns it as "more rules and regulations piled on top of others rules and regulations that had clearly failed."

Conference Report on Corporate Responsibility Legislation

July 24, 2002 Wednesday
Capitol Hill Hearing
Rayburn House Office Building,
Washington, D.C.

REP. OXLEY: (Strikes gavel.) The committee will come to order.

The committee is meeting today to consider the conference report on H.R. 3763, the only business in order at this meeting. All members will given three minutes to make opening remarks. The chair now recognizes himself for a briefing opening statement.

This has been a difficult period for those who love and cherish the free enterprise system. Our capital markets, the most respected in the world, have suffered a series of blows, mostly self-inflicted, which have led to the loss of literally trillions of investor dollars. "Investor confidence" is almost an oxymoron these days. Good, honest companies have been caught in this indiscriminate crossfire and thoroughly punished by angry and disillusioned investors.

It is important to remember that the market decline is not the result of any fundamental change in the ability of American companies to compete and excel. The fundamentals are strong. Rather, the market drop is tied to a series of high-profile scandals involving corporate officials misleading investors in order to line their own pockets and some accountants looking the other way.

The free market system relies primarily on trust and full and accurate disclosures. These tenets have been violated. It is not a systemic problem, but sadly, it is more than just a few bad apples.

Today offers a great deal of encouraging news. In addition to this bipartisan agreement, the Dow has increased nearly 500 points in just one day—perhaps the beginning of a restoration of confidence in the markets, although we're never sure. Additionally, the U.S. attorney and the Securities and Exchange Commission are to be commended for the strong action they have taken against the shocking fraud at Adelphia Communications. And that was just today.

In April, the House acted first in response to this crisis of confidence. Legislation was passed by the House on a bipartisan basis which would require the creation of a regulatory body for auditors, an unprecedented regulatory body with real teeth, possessing the power to sanction accountants for violating standards of ethics, competence and independence. The bill also increased disclosure to Investors and required greater corporate responsibility.

Earlier this month, Senator Sarbanes built on these ideas to produce legislation aimed towards the same goals. Today we meet to consider a conference committee report that will implement the reforms we all agree are needed to make market participants more accountable to America's 85 million investors.

When we began this process last Friday, I announced it was the House's intention to build on both bodies' efforts by incorporating four key ideas into the final product. These were the adoption of Richard Baker's FAIR proposal to ensure investors receive the proceeds of sanctions levied on malfeasant corporate executives, the adoption of real-time disclosure provisions as passed by the House, the adoption of tougher criminal penalties also as adopted by the House, and increased SEC oversight of the Auditor Oversight Board.

I'm happy to report that the agreement we consider today includes all these ideas as well as other improvements which will make this legislation stronger and more responsive to the needs of investors. I am pleased, and I know Senator Sarbanes shares this view, that we now have a bill that is superior to legislation passed by either body. The language we consider today will make the capital markets more accountable to investors, increase the transparency that serves as a foundation of our markets, and make corporate executives who break the law and abuse the public trust pay severely.

Jail time for corporate executives who commit crimes is clearly in order.

Having said all that, all of us know, however, that there is no law that can make all corporate officials act responsibly. After all, we have laws against bank robberies, and they occur every day. The fact that the vast majority of American businessmen and women are enterprising, honest and hard-working is what has made American in its brief 200-plus years the most prosperous civilization the world has ever known.

There is no law Congress can pass which would match the entrepreneurial talents of the American people. Indeed, it is quite often the case that we can run the risk of restraining those talents when we rush to legislate in times of crisis. In this area Congress must proceed with extreme caution, because there is a direct correlation between the amount of freedom in a society and its ultimate success of failure.

I want to take this time to commend the senior senator from Maryland, Senator Sarbanes, for the wisdom, professionalism and bipartisanship that he has brought to this process. As I stated on Friday, it was our intention to work in good faith, and we expected the other body to do the same. Senator Sarbanes has returned our good faith, and then some. His willingness to move constructively has allowed us within a very short period of time to produce a document which reflects the best intentions of all of us.

Senator Sarbanes, thank you for your good work. I know that American investors will benefit from your efforts.

I now recognize the senator from Maryland for an opening statement. . . .

❧❦❧

SEN. SARBANES: . . . This week, we will send to the president legislation to ensure accounting and auditor integrity, to set high standards for corporate governance, higher penalties for failure of corporate governance, address stock analyst conflict of interest and provide adequate funding resources for the Securities and Exchange Commission. This legislation reflects our determination to see that the confidence of investors in our capital markets is restored. For when trust is lost, the markets falter, with serious consequences for our economy. Indeed, with serious consequences for the world economy.

It has been our great and urgent challenge to come to agreement on the reform measures that will accomplish our objective. This has obviously not been an easy task. The problems we confront are both numerous and complex, and they are not amenable to easy solutions. From time to time, we obviously have disagreed amongst ourselves about the most effective means to resolve them, but I think we've been steady in our approach. We've worked through each problem in a careful and determined way, seeking out the best advice from experts in the field and consulting across party lines.

Traditionally, our markets have been the fairest, the most efficient and the most transparent in the world. We intend to see that they merit that reputation.

It's obviously time to act decisively, and I'm pleased that we will shortly send to the president a strong bill and that we now can look forward to this legislation becoming law. I think it's important for the Congress to set in place a statutory framework to address the challenges with which we are confronted, within which framework the regulatory agencies and the private sector can then go to work to do the many things that they have to do in order to address this situation. I have said repeatedly that unless we can bring this situation under control, I'm concerned that the economy, in the end, will suffer in a major way, with all of the implications of such a development. . . .

We hope that the SEC and other responsible agencies will be able to move swiftly to implement the provisions of this legislation, lay a strong and credible foundation for the restoration of investor confidence in our marketplace, which is critical to our economic well-being. . . .

⋅⊰❦⊱⋅

REP. JOHN LAFALCE (D-NY): Thank you very much, Mr. Chairman.

The agreement that we will reach today on corporate accountability legislation is an enormous victory. It's a victory for workers, it's a victory for investors. By moving quickly in conference on a strong bipartisan basis to essentially embrace the Sarbanes bill, which in so many key respects parallels legislation that we had introduced much earlier this year when this process began, we are prescribing exactly the strong medicine necessary to restore market integrity and confidence and help move our economy forward.

This conference report will include many major reforms which will fundamentally reshape the way our financial markets operate, which will toughen regulatory oversight and offer new protections to investors. Our conference report will end accounting industry self-regulation, which has proved to be a considerable failure, through the establishment of a strong, independent, legislatively created public accounting oversight board with legislatively defined powers.

The board will have full investigatory, disciplinary and standard-setting powers and full authority to enforce the securities laws that apply to the public accounting firms that the board will regulate.

The bill will also set high standards for auditor independence. Our conference report retains the strong auditor independence standards that are necessary to prohibit the conflicts that auditors currently face. Auditors will essentially be prohibited from providing consulting services that create conflicts. Audit committees will be given full authority over the hiring, the firing, the compensation of auditors and will be required to pre-approve any services provided by auditors.

The conference report retains the Senate provisions that give the new board full authority to implement the statutory standards of independence and auditor conduct through regulations. Foreign accounting firms will not be exempted from the act, and the SEC will not have authority to create exemptions.

Our conference report will ensure punishment of corporate wrongdoers. The final bill takes the increased penalties provided in Mr. Sensenbrenner's bill, but it retains the stronger provisions of Senator Leahy's amendment to the Senate legislation, including providing a private right of action for whistle-blowers, restoring the statute of limitations on private rights of actions under the securities laws, and stronger document-shredding prohibitions.

The final conference report will maintain reliable and independent funding for the new board and for FASB. The final conference report will reject the proposal to give the SEC complete control over the setting of fees that are to fund the new board and FASB, and permits issuers to join the two boards as auxiliary members.

The final bill will also maintain the provision that permits the new board and FASB to play a central role in the setting of fees that support them.

The final conference report will also hold corporate executives legally accountable for the accuracy of their companies' financial statements. It includes my proposal, which requires CEO's to conduct a detailed inquiry into the preparation of the company's financial statements so that they cannot claim ignorance of deceptive and misleading practices, requires CEO's to certify to the accuracy of those statements and imposes substantial penalties for the filing of false statements. . . .

✦

SEN. PHIL GRAMM (R-TX): I want to thank you. I want to congratulate you and Senator Sarbanes.

I believe that you have put together a bill that will do more good than harm, but I do not believe that the bill does as much good as it could do. I think it does more harm than it should do because it doesn't address the practical problems of making this new law work, not just for the Dow Jones industrial average companies, not just for the S&P 500, but for the 16,254 companies that will be governed by this law. I am afraid that we have written a one-size-fits all prescription when that one size clearly does not fit all.

We have the ability of the board to grant waivers on an individual basis, but the way the law is structured, it is almost destined to mean that thousands of small incorporated businesses that have their stocks traded publicly will be forced to hire lawyers and to hire lobbyists and to come to Washington and to ask for individual waivers. And yet once the board has granted 2,000 waivers under exactly the same conditions, it can't grant a blanket waiver to everybody else who would potentially benefit from that waiver. I am concerned that companies that have resources will hire—be able to hire the people to get the waiver; those that are often in need will not be able to do that. I am very concerned about the avenues of new litigation that will occur under this bill. I am concerned about what I see as an unnecessary change in a law passed earlier that was aimed at preventing strike lawsuits.

So I'm not saying that this bill is not an improvement over the status quo, I'm expressing disappointment that in conference, when you normally try to deal with practical problems and you try to address how is this law going to work, and can we make it practical in applying to all the circumstances in all of the companies it will apply to, in the environment that we're in today, that has been impossible. And so, I hope that this does the maximum amount of good it can do. I hope the harm it does is minimal. But I am concerned about it. I am convinced that we will be back here next year or the year after, correcting problems in the bill I think that could have been avoided, and I am disappointed by that. . . .

And so, while I'm not happy with the final product today, while I think it could have easily been much better, as tough as you want it to be, but reasonable and practical—and I think people have gotten confused between the two—it certainly could have been worse. If I were investing billions of dollars on Wall Street, I would look at this bill and conclude what I've concluded; that is, A, it's going to be very unworkable, it's going to create endless paperwork, there are going to be too may lawsuits. But in the end, we'll come back after the fact and fix it, and the American economy can continue to prosper under this bill.

I'm not going to vote for this bill because it could have and should have been better. These things should have been dealt with. But I'm not here saying the world's coming to and end because of its adoption. . . .

⸙

SEN. CHRISTOPHER DODD (D-CT): . . . This is an historic piece of legislation. It's not one size fits all. I appreciate the comments of my friend from Texas, but we went out of our way, as a result of the efforts of Senator Enzi and others to make sure that we did not reach too far to create the cascading effects that you could produce if we did not try to limit this to public companies, where the public is invested, where the public makes judgments based on the claims or assertions by the accounting industry and others that the condition of public companies are such that you have enough confidence in them to invest hard-earned dollars.

And certainly, there are larger and smaller public companies, but it's not too much to ask to see to it that when the certified public accountants make assertions about companies, that that information ought to be basically correct. And too often, it has not been so. And as a result, it was needed to pass this legislation.

In fact, this legislation was needed before the events of last October, but it took the events of last October and subsequent events to provoke this institution to begin to respond to them. So, I am pleased that we have put this bill together. . . .

The purpose of the original securities laws, passed more than 70 years ago, was to increase the public trust in America's public companies and financial markets, and the reliability of disclosed corporate information, financial information. These laws, which are part of the economic foundation of our country, were designed to promote market efficiency and inspire investor confidence. The resulting market confidence and the statements of financial health of publicly owned companies has paved the way for America's economic expansion over these decades. . . .

⋆⟨⊙⟩⋆

SEN. PATRICK LEAHY (D-VT): Thank you. . . . The criminal-law parts that I was involved with are nearly identical to the Corporate and Criminal Fraud Accountability Act, which we introduced in February and the Senate Judiciary Committee voted in April. We've—today's report will have a tough new crime and securities fraud (sic). It will cover any scheme or artifice to defraud investors—worked (sic) with the House counterparts. This provision is ample, with a 25-year maximum term.

Now there are three central provisions in here from the Senate bill that I think are extremely important: We extend the statute of limitations in security-fraud cases—something that would've helped so many people who were defrauded by Enron and others. We include meaningful protections for corporate whistle-blowers. We learned from Sharon Watkins of Enron that Enron lawyers said that Texas law would allow them to just ignore her and would not have her protected. We've taken care of that. And we include new anti-shredding crimes. We want to make sure that key documents don't get shredded in the first place. It only takes a few minutes to shred something; it might take years to put together a case. This makes sure the cases will be there.

Lastly, I would say that while we can't stop greed, we can stop greed from succeeding. And nothing is going to focus someone's moral compass more than knowing that if they don't do what is right and moral, they're going to be a guest of the state behind iron bars for a long, long time. . . .

⋆⟨⊙⟩⋆

SEN. ROBERT BENNETT (R-UT): Thank you, Mr. Chairman, . . . I will once again part company with my leader on the committee, Senator Gramm, in that I will vote for the conference report and I will vote—I will sign the conference report and I will vote for the bill.

I do find it easy, however, to restrain my overwhelming enthusiasm for everything in the bill, and that makes me something of a dissenting voice here for the chorus that I'm hearing.

I believe that adjustments will be made in the accounting profession to the new reality of this bill. And accountants, be they the CFOs or the auditing firms, once they get acquainted with the new rules and the new circumstances, will go forward with their business in as professional a fashion as they have in the past. I think we will probably see a net improvement, but the net improvement will come from their desire to see to it that they attract investors to the stock and that they attract customers to their accounting firms every bit as much as it will be that they will try to comply with the law.

I think while adjustments will be made and the accounting profession will survive just fine under this law, costs will go up as they make those adjustments, and those costs will be passed on to the consumer as they always are.

And unfortunately, stupidity will not disappear. The folks at Enron believed that their schemes would pay off. They didn't go into those partnerships expecting disaster, they went into those partnerships expecting glorious profits. And they were in an area they didn't understand. They were being stupid, and they got caught by the realities of the marketplace, and they have paid the price the marketplace always demands when somebody makes a stupid business decision.

The market is the fastest, quickest punisher of stupidity. And that's what happened.

Now, maybe as a result of this law we will know a little sooner than we would have known before that the stupidity had taken place. But we cannot tell ourselves that by virtue of passing this law stupidity will disappear. I'm reminded that Alan Greenspan warned against irrational exuberance in terms of where the stock market was, and it was approaching the stratospheric level of 6,000 on the Dow, which is more than 2,000 below where we are now. A large part of the problem that we have had is not because we didn't pass the proper laws, it was because there was a culture that existed in the mid- to late '90s that everything you touched turned to gold, every decision you made would have a multiple attached to it of 10, 20, 50, a hundred times, and markets have always told us those kinds of multiples don't exist over time and we have to come back to earth.

So I think this bill is a positive step forward. I think the Congress had to act to demonstrate that we were aware of the problem. But I think all of us should take a somewhat sobering dose of humility and recognize that the markets don't pay as much attention to us as we pay to ourselves. . . .

e<§>o

REP. CHRISTOPHER COX (R-CA): Thank you very much, Mr. Chairman. . . . Fraud and unfair dealing are the enemies of the free enterprise system.

And as we can see from the turmoil in our markets, our country is paying a very high price because those in power have broken faith with their employees and their investors.

We have tough laws on the books to deal with all manner of crime, including corporate crime. But just as bacteria mutate to defeat antibiotics, those who cook the books practice a devious art and constantly change their recipes, and we must keep our laws and our remedies up to date.

The legislation we're adopting today is carefully tailored to the abuses that were uncovered in House and Senate hearings and investigations. Enron and Global Crossing and WorldCom and other cases in which investors have been defrauded, all have centered around accounting. Abuses of accounting rules were central to each of these scandals. And so, using the regulatory thicket of detailed accounting rules as cover, the malefactors in these cases intentionally structured sham transactions in order to hide their true financial position. That is why the central reform in both the House-passed legislation and the Senate-passed legislation that we are reconciling here today has been the creation of an Accounting Oversight Board that will delve deeply into the ways that accounting and accountants have become accomplices to deceit. Its mission is to see to it that accounting standards once again make financial reports truthful, honest and clear.

Using existing laws, our government will, undoubtedly, soon put those most culpable into prison, I have no doubt. But today we are enacting good, tough, strong, new rules.

I should add, in conclusion, that no amount of new rules, no amount of government enforcement can eliminate the importance of honesty and character and ethics in our capital markets and in our places of work. (Brief audio break)—problems of ethics. And in this, the leadership of President Bush has been essential.

He has asked every American to meet a higher standard. And as we raise the legal standard here today, we should bear in mind our obligation to do still more to ensure that the best and the brightest will still want to join the accounting profession, to make sure that our most experienced citizens, possessed of good judgment and good reputation, will be willing to perform the crucial oversight functions of the board of directors, and that entrepreneurs will still take the risks and dream boldly, without fear of being second-guessed if the race is not won. . . .

Alan Reynolds  **NO**

Sarbanes-Oxley in Retrospect

Sarbanes-Oxley was based on a dubious analysis of the nature of the problem to be solved, and of the goals to be achieved. The problem was thought to be merely a matter of accounting, as though better bookkeeping could have somehow kept Enron and WorldCom solvent. And the stated objective was "to restore investor confidence" in the short term rather than preventing future Enron-like crises by making lasting improvements in institutional constraints and incentives.

The key congressional assumption appeared to be that any problems in business or accounting must be the fault of businessmen and accountants, not the fault of any governmental institutions (such as the IRS, SEC or FASB), or any laws (such as the 1968 Williams Act to protect spendthrift managers against hostile takeovers). So the solution, as usual, was more rules and regulations piled on top of other rules and regulations that had clearly failed.

I believe Sarbanes Oxley was unnecessary, harmful and inadequate.

It was *unnecessary* because the SEC had ample authority to oversee, investigate and enforce honest accounting and auditing. It is already proving to be *harmful* in ways I'll explain later, mainly because it greatly increases the costs and risks of doing business as a publicly traded U.S. corporation and increases the risks of serving as a director or officer. Finally, it is *inadequate* because it failed to encourage the development of institutions and incentives (including an excessive incentive to retain earnings before the individual tax on dividends was reduced) to improve corporate governance over the long haul.

I am first going to highlight a few prominent showpieces of the law, and then cite a few studies and news reports suggesting things are not working out as expected—that the law is already creating many "unintended consequences" but no apparent benefits (except to a growing industry of corporate governance consultants).

Perhaps the most visible symbolic change is that Sarbanes-Oxley required the CEO and CFO to certify that their financial statements "fairly" represent "financial conditions and results," and face prison sentences if they are wrong. The SEC always had the power to require such a certification ceremony, and in fact did so before Sarbanes-Oxley was enacted. But Section 302(a) is more extreme.

It threatens prison sentences of up to 20 years for executives who *"willfully"* certify incorrectly that reports have *"fairly"* presented "financial conditions and results," or 10 years for doing so "knowingly." Executives can be banned from serving as an officer or director because of undefined "misconduct." They can be required to forfeit one year of back pay if earnings have to be restated due to "material noncompliance." Nobody can know in advance what "willfully" or "fairly" or "misconduct" or "material noncompliance" means, so all these potentially capricious punitive measures fail to live up to the rule of law. Certification puts the CEO in the position of a nervous auditor—a job few CEOs are qualified to do—rather than a general manager who properly delegates such specialized chores to experts.

Another significant changes it that Sarbanes-Oxley required that each Board's audit committee be comprised entirely of independent directors with no company experience, plus one financial expert who claims to understand all 4500 pages of generally accepted accounting principles. The pretentious effort to redesign corporate boards in Washington D.C. certainly did not follow from any analysis of what went wrong at Enron. The Enron board was 86 percent independent, with a dozen non-employee outsiders including five CEOs and four academics. It was chaired by an accounting professor from the Stanford business school.

In 2000, *Chief Executive* magazine rated Enron's board among the five best. By contrast, the check-the-box formulas being peddled by corporate governance consultants invariably give Berkshire Hathaway a terrible rating because Warren Buffet has too many people on the Board who know him and his business very well. Yet Berkshire Hathaway's stock beat the S&P 500 for all but four years since 1965. Stockholders know more than legislators about who should be directors and officers of the companies they invest in.

A particularly grandiose gesture in Sarbanes-Oxley was the creation of a new Public Company Accounting Oversight Board, financed by what is essentially a tax on stockholders. That taxing authority—as well as the power to put some accounting firms out of business and favor others—raises serious questions about the Constitutionality of the new Board. The Board evades the rules governing federal agencies, such as the rules for appointments and salaries ($452,000), by pretending to be a private nonprofit—a dot-org, not a dot-gov. But no genuinely private organization can force us to both pay and obey.

Sarbanes-Oxley requires that non-accountants be a majority of the Board overseeing accounting, which is like having non-physicians oversee the practice of medicine. They will obviously need to rely on accountants, and Board is expected to hire about a hundred of them to do what the SEC and FASB were supposed to do. Having held a job with the Board will look terrific on any accountant's resume, of course, so the Board came up with a code of ethics in the hope of throwing a little sand in the revolving door. That is it's only accomplishment to date.

Let's outline a few of Sarbanes-Oxley's most obvious problems—those that [have] even been noticed by the press:

First, Sarbanes-Oxley makes it harder to attract and retain qualified directors, particularly the required financial expert. "Many companies are having trouble filling this slot," reports *The Wall Street Journal* (July 29, 2002), "because candidates fear they will be held responsible for auditing problems." Compensation of outside directors has increased to compensate for increased responsibilities and risks. A study of the Fortune 1000 firms, by Axentis LLC found that compensation of outside directors rose from $40,000 to $100,000.

Second, Sarbanes-Oxley reduces the availability of liability insurance for directors and officers, and greatly increases the cost of such insurance for those who can get it. The Axentis study found the premiums for D&O insurance quadrupled. "Directors' Insurance Fees Get Fatter" was the headline of a *Wall Street Journal* report (July 12, 2002) that found premiums up by as much as 100–300 percent despite reductions in coverage. This is partly due to Sarbanes-Oxley mandates, such as extending the statue of limitations for securities litigation to five years, and to the risk that the law will dramatically expand the potential liability of directors and officers.

A survey of 32 mid-sized companies by the law firm Foley & Lardner found the average price of being a public firm nearly doubled after Sarbanes-Oxley, from $1.3 million to almost $2.5 million. The cost of D&O insurance rose from $329,000 to $639,000. Directors' fees doubled, as did accounting, audit and legal fees.

Third, Sarbanes-Oxley makes it harder (particularly for smaller firms) to attract and retain qualified CEOs and CFOs. A new survey by Burson-Marsteller found that 73 percent of chief executive officers said they have thought about quitting, a record high. And 35 percent of other senior executives said they'd turn down the job of CEO if it were offered, up from 27 percent in 2001. When the talent pool shrinks, either the pay of American CEO's will rise (which was certainly an unintended consequence) or the quality of American CEOs will fall. The best executive talent may be lured to private or foreign firms.

Fourth, the punitive approach of Sarbanes-Oxley appears likely to make executives overly timid, afraid to take make bold investments in risky new technologies or products. Jeffrey Garten, Dean of Yale's School of Management, predicts, "CEOs are going to become more risk-averse and big investments on risky projects are going to be held back." This makes sense, and it is consistent with the unusually slow recovery of business investment since the 2001 recession. *Washington Post* columnist David Ignatius, in his column "Risk-Takers, Look Out" (June 26, 2002), also worried that, "The new rules and regulations will apply Washington's 'zero-defect culture"—its tendency to criminalize failure— to corporate America. . . . In a zero defect culture, the engine of economic growth begins to freeze up. For this is a barren landscape where only lawyers can survive for long."

Fifth, Sarbanes-Oxley is a "Boon for Slew of Consultants," to quote a recent headline from *The Wall Street Journal* story (August 19, 2003). The article went on to describe "a corporate governance gold rush." The reason is the Sarbanes-Oxley contains so many ambiguities and contradictions that companies faced with draconian punishments for vaguely defined offenses have no choice but to hire expensive consulting services. What is income to the consultants, however, is just like another tax on corporate stockholders—like the fees used to finance the well-paid Accounting Oversight Board.

Sixth, Sarbanes-Oxley makes it much less attractive to be a publicly traded U.S. firm. An article on "Why Companies Harbor Doubts on Doing IPOs" in *The Wall Street Journal* (March 24, 2003) noted that "it costs 60% to 100% more for an audit" because of the increased risk to auditing firms, and "insurance coverage for directors and officers' liability has risen drastically as well." The number of companies going public, though initial public offerings, dropped from 352 in 2000 to 27 in the first nine months of 2003. Fewer public companies means fewer investment opportunities for smaller investors and less public information about U.S. business (because private firms can keep their information private).

In "The Case for going private" (January 25, 2003) *The Economist* notes that an unusually large number of publicly traded U.S. firms have been taken private since Sarbanes-Oxley became law (26 percent more by one calculation). *The Economist* adds that taking public firms private "will seem even more tempting as the latest round of corporate governance reforms take effect in public firms." Foreign companies such as Porsche have also said they will not list on the New York stock exchange because doing so would subject them to Sarbanes-Oxley rules, some of which are offensive or illegal in their home countries. The EU complains of this effort to impose U.S. regulations beyond our borders. Concessions to foreign firms are inevitable, but such concessions will then leave foreign firms with the advantage of lower regulatory costs and litigation risks.

Seventh, Sarbanes-Oxley is drastically shrinking the number of accounting firms willing and able to do audits. A *Washington Post* report, "Small Accounting Firms Exit Auditing" (August 27, 2003) noted that many small accounting firms are planning to abandoning auditing of public companies, partly because of difficulty and expense of insuring themselves if something goes wrong. The GAO recently noted with some alarm that the Big Four accounting firms, down from the Big Eight in 1980, now audit 78 percent of the publicly traded companies in the U.S. Small companies report difficulty finding anyone willing to do their auditing, even at the inflated fees prevalent since this law was passed.

In short, the most concrete consequences of Sarbanes-Oxley are reduced profitability and competitiveness of U.S. public corporations due to higher costs of regulatory compliance, greater exposure to the legal expenses of class action suits, and greater expenses for insurance and directors' compensation to compensate for added personal risks of civil and criminal penalties.

What was *done* in Sarbanes-Oxley clearly created many more costs than benefits (if there are any benefits). Yet what was left *undone* may well be more important. Sarbanes-Oxley suffers from delusions of adequacy.

POSTSCRIPT

Corporate Governance Reform: Is Sarbanes-Oxley the Answer?

One of the major goals of the Sarbanes-Oxley Act of 2002 was to restore investor and public faith in the ability of corporations to govern themselves in an ethical, forthright manner. Two years after the act was signed into law, public opinion appears to be supportive, although not to levels that might be expected: A Harris poll taken in early 2004 found that 59 percent feel the act will help protect their stock investments, while 57 percent indicate that they would be very unlikely to invest in a company that did not comply with the provisions of the act.

But what of businesses? How do they feel about the law two years into its existence? *The Wall Street Journal (WSJ)* set out to get answers to this question and reported its findings in a June 2004 article by Judith Burns entitled, "Corporate Governance: Is Sarbanes-Oxley Working?" (June 21, 2004, pg. R8). Below are some typical responses from the experts queried by *WSJ*:

Janet Dolan, president and CEO of Tennant Co., a Minneapolis maker of industrial cleaning products "complains that the law is especially burdensome for smaller-cap firms such as Tennant. . . . 'We're all having to do about the same thing, but it's less of a burden for General Electric than for us. . . .' Ms. Dolan says that outside audit fees may double over 2003 as a result of complying with all the Sarbanes-Oxley requirements.

Logan Robinson, vice president and general counsel, Delphi Corp., an auto-parts supplier in Troy, Michigan "believes there's a 'lot more right than wrong' with Sarbanes-Oxley. The law 'was an appropriate response to a real crisis . . . the core of the law is a good law that has defended our capital markets.' But 'reporting out is more of a problem . . . if you turn all the lawyers in the world into enforcement agents who are compelled to run to the SEC, there's going to be a huge problem in getting people to tell their lawyers anything.

Nell Minow, editor of the Corporate Library, a Portland, Maine, research firm specializing in corporate governance: "Ms. Minow says she wouldn't make any 'substantive changes' to Sarbanes-Oxley, although she does believe it can use some 'fine-tuning' . . . she says, mandating that the role of chairman being separate from the chief executive is 'meaningless.' She says a better approach might be to let shareholders vote on who should chair the company's board.

Suggested Readings

Yaron Brook and Alex Epstein, The cost of the 'ethical' assault on honest-businessmen. Media release, *The Ayn Rand Institute*, July 8, 2003. `http://www.aynrand.org/site/News2?page=NewsArticle&id=7307`

Del Jones, Sarbanes-Oxley: Dragon or White Knight? *The USA Today*, October 20, 2003, p. 1B.

Floyd Norris, Too much regulation? Corporate bosses sing the Sarbanes-Oxley blues. *The New York Times*, January 23, 2004, p. C1.

Paul Volcker and Arthur Levitt, Jr., In defense of Sarbanes-Oxley. *The Wall Street Journal*, June 14, 2004, p. A16.

About GlobalWarming.org

The purpose of this organization is to dispel the myths of global warming by exposing flawed economic, scientific, and risk analysis. Coalition members will also follow the progress of the international Global Climate Change Treaty negotiations.

http://www.globalwarming.org/about.htm

Environmental Justice

The U.S. Environmental Protection Agency is charged with enforcing the laws and regulations passed by the law-making bodies in America. The goal is to reduce threats to the environment by increasing compliance through incentives and criminal prosecution.

http://www.epa.gov/compliance/

The Ayn Rand Institute (ARI)

The ARI is a non-profit educational organization whose goals are to spread the concepts and ideas contained in its revolutionary philosophy of Objectivism. Their members appear frequently in the national media and have widespread influence in colleges and universities across America. In staunchly defending capitalism and limited government, ARI provides unique insight into numerous topics of interest to business, including globalization.

www.aynrand.org

Globalization Guide.org

This site is the product of the Australian Apec Study Center and is designed to introduce students to the pros, cons, myths, and facts of globalization. Additional resources and access to other globalization links are also provided.

http://www.globalisationguide.org/

PART 4

Environmental and International Management

Images of young children working long hours in inhumane conditions for less than substance wages were a common sight on television news programs and covers of popular magazines during the 1990s. Major American firms like Nike and The Gap had been accused of running sweatshops in Third World countries as a means of keeping their production costs down. But beyond these terrible images lies a sophisticated defense of sweatshops, one that gets a hearing in the debate on sweatshops presented here. The question of sweatshops is related to another topic we debate: whether or not economic globalization is good for humankind. These two issues, along with two others, form the fourth and final section of this text.

- Is the Condition of the Environment Really as Bad as Environmentalists Claim?

- Can Economic Incentives Induce Top Management to Voluntarily Regulate Their Firm's Environmentally Harmful Behaviors?

- Is Economic Globalization Good for Humankind?

- Are Global Sweatshops Exploitative?

ISSUE 14

Is the Condition of the Environment Really as Bad as Environmentalists Claim?

YES: David Pimentel, from "Skeptical of the Skeptical Environmentalist," *Skeptic* (vol. 9, no. 2, 2002)

NO: Denis Dutton, from "Greener Than You Think," *Washington Post On-line Edition* (October 21, 2001)

ISSUE SUMMARY

YES: In his review of *The Skeptical Environmentalist*, David Pimentel disagrees with Lomborg's optimistic assessment. He also accuses Lomborg of selectively presenting advantageous data while simultaneously ignoring evidence that is damaging to his position.

NO: Denis Dutton, professor of philosophy at the University of Canterbury in New Zealand, agrees with Lomborg that the environment is much better off than the environmentalists would have us believe.

It is standard fare nowadays for introductory-level management textbooks to include a chapter exploring the environmental context in which business management takes place. Among the myriad of topics covered is, inevitably, a discussion on the impact business activities have on the natural environment. In varying degrees, this discussion usually blames business for much of the damage done to the environment and offers guidelines as to what corporations need to do to become more socially responsible. The following quote from a highly respected management text is typical: "[M]uch remains to be done. Companies need to develop economically feasible ways to avoid contributing to acid rain and global warming; to avoid depleting the ozone layer; and to develop alternative methods of handling sewage, hazardous wastes, and ordinary garbage. . . . Companies also need to develop safety policies that cut down on accidents with potentially disastrous environmental results" (Rickey W. Griffin, *Management*, 7th ed., Houghton Mifflin Company, 2002). Some texts argue that management needs to adopt policies of "sustainable development," an approach that emphasizes restricting economic growth to levels that won't outstrip the replenishment rate of our natural resources (Post, Lawrence, and Weber, *Business and Society*, 9th ed., Irwin McGraw-Hill, 1999).

The vast majority of discussions about the state of our natural environment share at least three important assumptions: (1) the earth's environment is in bad shape, (2) it is getting worse all the time, and (3) the primary source of the problem is global business activity. These assumptions are so commonly accepted as true that to question them is to leave oneself open for severe ridicule and criticism. Nevertheless, over the past 20 years or so, a growing number of social commentators, academicians, and environmental movement observers have wondered out loud whether things are really as bad as the environmentalists portray them to be.

The first prominent contrarian voice belonged to University of Maryland professor of economics, Julian Simon (1932–1998). Simon, who argued that human ingenuity was the "ultimate resource," set out to assess the true state of the earth's health in his 1981 tome, *The Ultimate Resource* (Princeton University Press). Using statistics readily available to the public, Simon's startling conclusion was that "Every measure of material and environmental welfare in the United States and in the world has improved rather than deteriorated. All long-run trends point in exactly the opposite direction from the direction of the doomsayers" (quote from Frank Miele, "Living without Limits: An Interview with Julian Simon," *Skeptic,* vol. 5, no. 1, 1997, p. 54). Science correspondent and Society of Environmental Journalists member Ronald Bailey edited a collection of articles by noted environmental scholars addressing various ecological issues. Although not as aggressively optimistic as Simon's work, the consensus of *Earth Report 2000* (McGraw-Hill, 2000) was, nevertheless, a resoundingly positive assessment of the health of our planet. Of all the voices that followed Simon's seminal work, however, that of former Greenpeace-activist-turned-environmental-optimist Bjorn Lomborg has unquestionably been the most controversial.

Lomborg, associate professor of statistics at the University of Aarhus in Denmark, set out to debunk Simon's findings in the late 1990s. Much to his surprise, the data strongly supported Simon's conclusions. Lomborg published his findings in a series of four newspaper articles in 1997 and 1998, thus triggering an intense debate in the Danish media. Ultimately, this debate led to the publication of his highly controversial, *The Skeptical Environmentalist: Measuring the Real State of the Earth* (Cambridge University Press, 2001).

Lomborg contends that the purpose of his book is not so much to attack or provoke the environmental doomsayers but, rather, to provide "a careful democratic check on the environmental debate, by knowing the real state of the world—having knowledge of the most important facts and connections in the essential areas of our world" (p. xx). The crucial point, according to Lomborg, is that we can only make wise and beneficial decisions if we have accurate information and a willingness to act on it.

Denis Dutton, professor of philosophy at the University of Canterbury in New Zealand, agrees with Lomborg that the environment is much better off than the environmentalists would have us believe. In the first selection, Cornell University professor David Pimentel disagrees with Lomborg's optimistic assessment. He also accuses Lomborg of selectively presenting advantageous data while simultaneously ignoring evidence that is damaging to his position.

David Pimentel  **YES**

Skeptical of the Skeptical Environmentalist

Bjorn Lomborg discusses a wide range of topics in his book and implies, through his title, that he will inform readers exactly what the real state of world is. In this effort, he criticizes countless world economists, agriculturists, water specialists, and environmentalists, and furthermore, accuses them of misquoting and/or organizing published data to mislead the public concerning the status of world population, food supplies, malnutrition, disease, and pollution. Lomborg bases his optimistic opinion on his selective use of data. Some of Lomborg's assertions will be examined in this review, and where differing information is presented, extensive documentation will be provided.

Lomborg reports that "we now have more food per person than we used to." In contrast, the Food and Agricultural Organization (FAO) of the United Nations reports that food per capita has been declining since 1984, based on available cereal grains (Figure 1). Cereal grains make up about 80% of the world's food. Although grain yields per hectare (abbreviated ha) in both developed and developing countries are still increasing, these increases are slowing while the world population continues to escalate. Specifically from 1950 to 1980, U.S. grains yields increased at about 3% per year, but after 1980 the rate of increase for corn and other grains has declined to only about 1% (Figure 2).

Obviously fertile cropland is an essential resource for the production of foods but Lomborg has chosen not to address this subject directly. Currently, the U.S. has available nearly 0.5 ha of prime cropland per capita, but it will not have this much land if the population continues to grow at its current rapid rate. Worldwide the average cropland available for food production is only 0.25 ha per person. Each person added to the U.S. population requires nearly 0.4 ha (1 acre) of land for urbanization and transportation. One example of the impact of population growth and development is occurring in California where an average of 156,000 ha of agricultural land is being lost each year. At this rate it will not be long before California ceases to be the number one state in U.S. agricultural production.

In addition to the quantity of agricultural land, soil quality and fertility is vital for food production. The productivity of the soil is reduced when it is eroded by rainfall and wind. Soil erosion is not a problem, according to

From *Skeptic* by David Pimentel, vol. 9 no. 2, 2002, pp. 90–93. Copyright © 2002 by David Pimentel. Reprinted by permission of the author.

Figure 1

Cereal Grain Production Per Capita in the World From 1961 to 1999

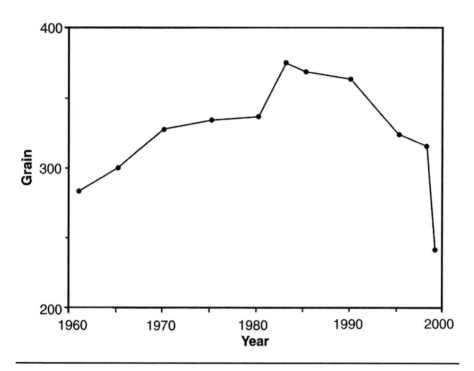

FAO, 1961–1999

Lomborg, especially in the U.S. where soil erosion has declined during the past decade. Yes, as Lomborg states, instead of losing an average of 17 metric tons per hectare per year on cropland, the U.S. cropland is now losing an average of 13 t/ha/yr. However, this average loss is 13 times the sustainability rate of soil replacement. Exceptions occur, as during the 1995–96 winter in Kansas, when it was relatively dry and windy, and some agricultural lands lost as much as 65 t/ha of productive soil. This loss is 65 times the natural soil replacement in agriculture.

Worldwide soil erosion is more damaging than in the United States. For instance, the India soil is being lost at 30 to 40 times its sustainability. Rate of soil loss in Africa is increasing not only because of livestock overgrazing but also because of the burning of crop residues due to the shortages of wood fuel. During the summer of 2000, NASA published a satellite image of a cloud of soil from Africa being blown across the Atlantic Ocean, further attesting to the massive soil erosion problem in Africa. Worldwide evidence concerning soil loss is substantiated and it is difficult to ignore its effect on sustainable agricultural production.

Contrary to Lomborg's belief, crop yields cannot continue to increase in response to the increased applications of more fertilizers and pesticides. In fact,

Figure 2

Corn Grain Yields From 1910 to 1999

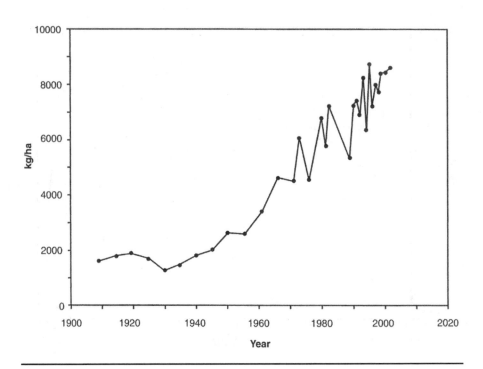

USDA, 1910–2000

field tests have demonstrated that applying excessive amounts of nitrogen fertilizer stresses the crop plants, resulting in declining yields. The optimum amount of nitrogen for corn, one of the crops that require heavy use of nitrogen, is approximately 120 kg/ha.

Although U.S. farmers frequently apply significantly more nitrogen fertilizer than 120 kg/ha, the extra is a waste and pollutant. The corn crop can only utilize about one-third of the nitrogen applied, while the remainder leaches either into the ground or surface waters. This pollution of aquatic ecosystems in agricultural areas results in the high levels of nitrogen and pesticides occurring in many U.S. water bodies. For example, nitrogen fertilizer has found its way into 97% of the well-water supplies in some regions, like North Carolina. The concentrations of nitrate are above the U.S. Environmental Protection Agency drinking-water standard of 10 milligrams per liter (nitrogen) and are a toxic threat to young children and young livestock. In the last 30 years, the nitrate content has tripled in the Gulf of Mexico, where it is reducing the Gulf fishery.

In an undocumented statement Lomborg reports that pesticides cause very little cancer. Further, he provides no explanation as to why human and other nontarget species are not exposed to pesticides when crops are treated. There is abundant medical and scientific evidence that confirms that pesticides cause significant numbers of cancers in the U.S. and throughout the world. Lomborg also neglects to report that some herbicides stimulate the production of toxic chemicals in some plants, and that these toxicants can cause cancer.

In keeping with Lomborg's view that agriculture and the food supply are improving, he states that "fewer people are starving." Lomborg criticizes the validity of the two World Health Organization [WHO] reports that confirm more than 3 billion people are malnourished. This is the largest number and proportion of malnourished people ever in history! Apparently Lomborg rejects the WHO data because they do not support his basic thesis. Instead, Lomborg argues that only people who suffer from calorie shortages are malnourished, and ignores the fact that humans die from deficiencies of protein, iron, iodine, and vitamin A, B, C, and D.

Further confirming a decline in food supply, the FAO reports that there has been a three-fold decline in the consumption of fish in the human diet during the past seven years. This decline in fish per capita is caused by overfishing, pollution, and the impact of a rapidly growing world population that must share the diminishing fish supply.

In discussing the status of water supply and sanitation services, Lomborg is correct in stating that these services were improved in the developed world during the 19th century, but he ignores the available scientific data when he suggests that these trends have been "replicated in the developing world" during the 20th century. Countless reports confirm that developing countries discharge most of their untreated urban sewage directly into surface waters. For example, of India's 3,119 towns and cities, only eight have full waste water treatment facilities. Furthermore, 114 Indian cities dump untreated sewage and partially cremated bodies directly into the sacred Ganges River. Downstream the untreated water is used for drinking, bathing, and washing. In view of the poor sanitation, it is no wonder that water borne infectious diseases account for 80% of all infections worldwide and 90% of all infections in developing countries.

Contrary to Lomborg's view, most infectious diseases are increasing worldwide. The increase is due not only to population growth but also because of increasing environmental pollution. Food-borne infections are increasing rapidly worldwide and in the United States. For example, during 2000 in the U.S. there were 76 million human food-borne infections with 5,000 associated deaths. Many of these infections are associated with the increasing contamination of food and water by livestock wastes in the United States.

In addition, a large number of malnourished people are highly susceptible to infectious diseases, like tuberculosis (TB), malaria, schistosomiasis, and AIDS. For example, the number of people infected with tuberculosis in the U.S. and the world is escalating, in part because medicine has not kept up with the new forms of TB. Currently, according to the World Health Organization, more than 2 billion people in the world are infected with TB, with nearly 2 million people dying each year from it.

Consistent with Lomborg's thesis that world natural resources are abundant, he reports that the U.S. Energy Information Agency for the period 2000 to 2020 projects an almost steady oil price over the next two decades at about

$22 per barrel. This optimistic projection was crossed late in 2000 when oil rose to $30 or more per barrel in the United States and the world. The best estimates today project that world oil reserves will last approximately 50 years, based on current production rates.

Lomborg takes the World Wildlife Fund (WWF) to task for their estimates on the loss of world forests during the past decade and their emphasis on resulting ecological impacts and loss of biodiversity. Whether the loss of forests is slow, as Lomborg suggests, or rapid as WWF reports, there is no question that forests are disappearing worldwide (Figure 3). Forests not only provide valuable products but they harbor a vast diversity of species of plants, animals and microbes. Progress in medicine, agriculture, genetic engineering, and environmental quality depend on maintaining the species diversity in the world.

This reviewer takes issue with Lomborg's underlying thesis that the size and growth of the human population is not a major problem. The difference between Lomborg's figure that 76 million humans were added to the world population in 2000, or the 80 million reported by the Population Reference Bureau, is not the issue, thought the magnitude of both projections is of serious concern. Lomborg neglects to explain that the major problem with world population growth is the young age structure that now exists. Even if the

Figure 3

Number of Hectares in Forests Worldwide (x 1 million ha) From 1961 to 1994

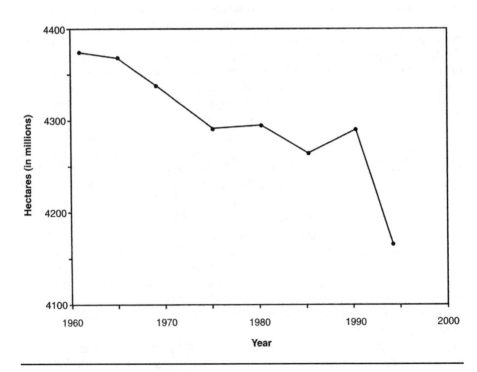

FAOSTAT Database, consulted September 3, 2001

world adopted a policy of only two children per couple tomorrow, the world population would continue to increase for more than 70 years before stabilizing at more than 12 billion people. As an agricultural scientist and ecologist, I wish I could share Lomborg's optimistic views, but my investigations and those of countless scientists lead me to a more conservative outlook. The supply of basic resources, like fertile cropland, water, energy, and an unpolluted atmosphere that support human life is declining rapidly, as nearly a quarter million people are daily added to the Earth. We all desire a high standard of living for each person on Earth, but with every person added, the supply of resources must be divided and shared. Current losses and degradation of natural resources suggest concern and a need for planning for future generations of humans. Based on our current understanding of the real state of the world and environment, there is need for conservation and protection of vital world resources.

Denis Dutton

Greener Than You Think:
The Skeptical Environmentalist: Measuring the Real State of the World by Bjorn Lomborg

That the human race faces environmental problems is unquestionable. That environmental experts have regularly tried to scare us out of our wits with doomsday chants is also beyond dispute. In the 1960s overpopulation was going to cause massive worldwide famine around 1980. A decade later we were being told the world would be out of oil by the 1990s. This was an especially chilly prospect, since, as Newsweek reported in 1975, we were in a climatic cooling trend that was going to reduce agricultural outputs for the rest of the century, leading possibly to a new Ice Age.

Bjorn Lomborg, a young statistics professor and political scientist at the University of Aarhus in Denmark, knows all about the enduring appeal—for journalists, politicians and the public—of environmental doomsday tales, having swallowed more than a few himself. In 1997, Lomborg—a self-described left-winger and former Greenpeace member—came across an article in Wired magazine about Julian Simon, a University of Maryland economist. Simon claimed that the "litany" of the Green movement—its fears about overpopulation, animal species dying by the hour, deforestation—was hysterical nonsense, and that the quality of life on the planet was radically improving. Lomborg was shocked by this, and he returned to Denmark to set about doing the research that would refute Simon.

He and his team of academicians discovered something sobering and cheering: In every one of his claims, Simon was correct. Moreover, Lomborg found on close analysis that the factual foundation on which the environmental doomsayers stood was deeply flawed: exaggeration, prevarications, white lies and even convenient typographical errors had been absorbed unchallenged into the folklore of environmental disaster scenarios.

Lomborg still feels at one with the basic sentiments that underlie the Green movement: that we should strive toward a cleaner, healthier world for everyone, including animals (he's a vegetarian with ethical objections to eating

From *Washington Post Online*, October 21, 2001. Copyright © 2001 by Washington Post Writers Group. Reprinted by permission.

flesh). But his aim in this new catalogue of environmental issues is to counter the gloom with a clear, scientifically based picture of the true state of the Earth and to take a rational view of what we can expect in the next century.

In a massive, meticulously presented argument that extends over 500 pages, supported by nearly 3,000 footnotes and 182 tables and diagrams, Lomborg revisits a number of heartening breakthroughs in the recent life of the planet. Chief among these is the decline of poverty and starvation across the world. Starvation still exists, but there is less of it than ever, as our capacity to produce abundant quantities of food continues to improve. Likewise with other dire scenarios of resource depletion: We are emphatically not running out of energy and mineral resources, the population bomb is fizzling, and, far from killing us, pesticides and chemicals are improving longevity and the quality of life. Neither need we fear anything from the genetic modification of organisms.

For a factual encyclopedia, the book has immense entertainment value, particularly in the way Lomborg traces the urban legends of the Green movement back to their sources. Consider the oft-repeated claim that 40,000 species go extinct every year. Such an annual loss of species, Lomborg points out, would be disaster for the future of life on earth, amounting perhaps to a loss of 25 to 50 percent of all species in the next half century. He manages, however, to locate the source of the story—an off-hand and completely unfounded guess made by a scientist in 1979. It's been repeated endlessly ever since—and in 1981 was increased by arch-doomsayer Paul Ehrlich to 250,000 species per year. (Ehrlich also predicted that half the planet's species would be extinct by 2000.)

Lomborg brings these unhinged forecasts back down to Earth by reminding us that the only actual scientific documentation for species loss is in United Nations figures, which show an actual loss of between a tenth of a percent and 1 percent of all species for all of the next 50 years. This includes beetles, ants, flies, worms, bacteria and fungi, which make up 99 percent of all species, plus a small but unknown number of mammals and birds. Extinction, Lomborg argues, is a problem to be realistically faced and solved, not a catastrophe to be bewailed.

Or consider deforestation. It's been claimed that the world has lost two-thirds of its forests since the dawn of agriculture. The real figure, Lomborg shows, is around 20 percent, and this figure has hardly changed since the World War II. Tropical forests are declining at a small annual rate of 0.46 percent, but this is offset by growth in commercial plantations, which should be encouraged, as their products take the pressure off the tropical forests. In fact, the world's wood and paper needs could be permanently satisfied by tree plantations amounting to just 5 percent of the world's forest cover.

Then there's waste disposal. Are we really running out of landfill space for our garbage? Lomborg shows how the entire trash-dumping requirements for the United States through the whole of the coming century (assuming the country doubles in population) could be met by a single landfill that measures 100 feet high and 18 miles square. That's a lot of trash, but as the total leavings of the increasing U.S. population over a hundred years, it is certainly not unmanageable, and if it's properly dealt with, it need pose no serious pollution threat to air or water.

Speaking of trash, Lomborg favors recycling, but only when it makes sense, and he gives a hilarious analysis of a scheme from Environment magazine to mail used toothbrushes to a plant where they could be recycled as outdoor furniture. This would cost $4 billion to implement for the U.S. population, and that's without taking into account the costs of the postal system handling a billion packages of new and used toothbrushes annually. The recycling cure can be worse than the consumption disease (though I can imagine the U.S. Postal Service might see this idea as a revenue opportunity).

Many well-intentioned environmental policies can have surprising outcomes: Suppose minute pesticide residues have the potential to cause cancer in a tiny number of cases—one estimate would have it around 20 cases per annum in the United States (not very many in a country where 300 people drown in bathtubs every year). So we ban the pesticides. This in turn, Lomborg points out, would sharply drive up the price of cancer-preventing fruits and vegetables. By reducing consumption, especially among the poor, the pesticide ban in the end would cause more cancer (perhaps 26,000 cases annually) than the pesticides would have caused in the first place. Sometimes, as with toothbrushes, the best thing to do about a "problem" is exactly nothing.

Lomborg enjoys placing what look to be serious environmental issues in a comparative context, which can often cause them to diminish considerably in scale. The Exxon Valdez oil spill was portrayed as a disaster of unparalleled magnitude: For example, it killed 250,000 birds. He shows how the long-term effects of the spill were far less damaging than environmentalists predicted, and also puts the avian mortality claim in perspective: Some 300,000 birds are killed by mammals, mostly cats, in Great Britain every 48 hours, and 250,000 birds die from striking plate glass in homes and offices in the United States every 24 hours. How could he know that? I wondered myself, so here as elsewhere, I followed Lomborg's claims back through the footnotes, traced the sources for myself, and found them to be sound. In fact, since The Skeptical Environmentalist was published last month in Britain, an army of angry environmentalists has been crawling all over the book, trying to refute it. Lomborg's claims have withstood the attack.

The book's longest, most detailed chapter is on global warming and the Kyoto Treaty. Lomborg agrees that a warming trend is real but says that the Intergovernmental Panel on Climate Change exaggerates the possible threats and present-day proportions of global warming, while neglecting the benefits of more carbon dioxide in the air and warmer nighttime temperatures. These changes would improve agricultural output in the U.S. and China, and make for vast increases in crop production for Canada and Russia. In any event, Lomborg is promoter of solar energy, which he believes will take over from oil as our major energy source in the next 50 years.

His most stunning conclusion: Even if the Kyoto treaty were fully implemented, it would stave off warming by only about six years—postponing it from 2100 to 2106. So what is the cost to the world economy of this almost invisible benefit we are to bestow on our great-great grandchildren? Anywhere from $80 to $350 billion per annum. Lomborg is very disturbed by these figures, since he sees health improvements as the greatest challenge now facing the human race—especially the enormous gains against disease and poverty that will come from increasing the supply of clean drinking water and the quality of sanitation in the developing world. The costs of Kyoto for one year could give clean water and sanitation to the whole of the developing world, saving 2 million lives, and keeping half a billion people from serious illness. For future, unknown and perhaps nonexistent benefits, Kyoto would squander money that should be applied right now to real, life-and-death human problems. Lomborg's calculations are meticulous, his argument compelling: Implementation of the Kyoto Treaty would be an unforgivable mistake.

Lomborg's original inspiration, the radical Julian Simon, was just a bit too far ahead of his time. This bald, vaguely right-wing economist was on the money, but in the late 20th century, with Green mythology ascendant, no one wanted to know. Paul Ehrlich, as reward for being wrong in all his scary predictions about population and the environment, was showered with prizes, including a MacArthur "genius" fellowship. As Simon cheerfully remarked, "I can't even get a McDonald's." This irrepressible scholar did, however, provoke a young Dane into trying to disprove his claims—a process that led to questioning the factual foundations of the environmental movement itself. Unlike Simon, Lomborg has the correct cultural aura: a young, left-wing European with the looks of a movie star. Simon, who died suddenly in 1998, would have loved to see how things are turning out.

Bjorn Lomborg's good news about the environment is bad news for Green ideologues. His richly informative, lucid book is now the place from which environmental policy decisions must be argued. In fact, *The Skeptical Environmentalist* is the most significant work on the environment since the appearance of its polar opposite, Rachel Carson's *Silent Spring,* in 1962. It's a magnificent achievement.

POSTSCRIPT

Is the Condition of the Environment Really as Bad as Environmentalists Claim?

You have just read two articles disputing the relative merits of Danish professor and statistician Bjorn Lomborg's book, *The Skeptical Environmentalist*. Regardless of which side of this debate you agree with, there seems to be no question that it is essential for us to have an accurate accounting of the state of world's environment if we are to utilize our scarce economic resources to best advantage. Most environmentalists argue that there is nothing wrong with maintaining an overly pessimistic view of the environmental situation because it tends to force governments and businesses to act from a preventative rather than from a reactive mindset. In other words, it is safer to be pessimistic. This view has dominated public discussion since the beginning of the modern environmental movement in the 1960s and is responsible for the numerous laws and regulations that affect virtually every aspect of our lives. But, as a growing number of critics have pointed out, in many instances, this view is much worse than a carelessly optimistic attitude where there are no environmental problems at all.

Consider the case of the corporate average fuel economy (CAFE) ratings for automobiles. A 1975 law subjected all cars to fuel-efficiency requirements; currently, new cars must meet a 27.5 mpg standard while larger vehicles such as SUVs must reach at least 20.7 mpg (Robert James Bidinotto, "Death by Environmentalism: What Happens When Humans Must Give Way to Nature," *The Navigator*, The Objectivist Center, March 2004, p. 4). The problem is that these standards have forced automakers to make smaller, lighter, less safe cars. How unsafe? Two reputable studies (1989 by Harvard University and the Brookings Institution; 2001 by the National Academy of Sciences) concluded that the CAFE standards result in 1,200–3,900 additional deaths every year. "In the trade-off between saving gasoline and saving lives, the government rules willingly sacrifice lives" (Bidinotto, p. 4). Given this, it is no surprise that large, safe SUVs are popular with the public; nor is it surprising that SUVs are viewed by environmentalists as major contributors to the depletion of fossil fuels and to global warming.

The point of the above example is that it is just as dangerous to error on the side of extreme pessimism about the environment as it is to be in a state of unfounded optimism. Clearly, then, what is needed is an accurate assessment of the real state of the world.

Suggested Readings

Readings supportive of *The Skeptical Environmentalist:*

Ronald Bailey, Debunking green myths. *Reason,* February 2002.

"Doomsday postponed." *The Economist,* September 6, 2001. http://
www.lomborg.com/files/Economist%20review%206-9-01.mht

Jim Peron, Maybe we can smile, the environment is looking pretty
good. *The Objectivist Center,* December 19, 2001. http://www.
objectivistcenter.org/articles/jperon_maybe-smile.asp

Readings critical of *The Skeptical Environmentalist:*

Paul R. Erlich, The brownlash rides again. *HMS Beagle,* issue 114,
November 9, 2001. http://www.lomborg.com/files/Erhlich%20
review.htm

Michael Grubb, Relying on manna from heaven? *Science,* vol. 294,
November 9, 2001. http://www.lomborg.com/files/Science%
20review%2012-11-01.pdf

Eric Newmayer, Picking holes in the litany of loss. *The Times Higher Education Supplement,* November 16, 2001. http://www.lomborg.com/
files/Times%20Higher%20Educational%20Supplement%2016-
11-01.mht

ISSUE 15

Can Economic Incentives Induce Top Management to Voluntarily Regulate Their Firm's Environmentally Harmful Behaviors?

YES: Raymond J. Patchak and William R. Smith, from *ISO 14000 Perspective: So Long! Command and Control . . . Hello! ISO 14000* (December 1998)

NO: Linda Greer and Christopher van Löben Sels, from "When Pollution Prevention Meets the Bottom Line," *Environmental Science and Technology* (vol. 31, no. 9, 1997)

ISSUE SUMMARY

YES: Hazard materials managers Raymond Patchak and William Smith believe that corporations, under the right set of circumstances, will willingly engage in self-regulatory environmental behavior.

NO: Environmental scholars Linda Greer and Christopher van Löben Sels present the results of a case study involving Dow Chemical in which expected cost savings were not enough incentive for Dow top management to adopt a voluntary pollution reduction plan.

Many environmental experts trace the beginnings of the modern environmental movement to the publication of Rachel Carson's seminal book *Silent Spring* in 1962. Her carefully documented text was one of the first to highlight the destructive effects unmonitored corporate behavior can have on the environment. Her report led to governmental investigation and the inevitable legislation designed to regulate those business activities deemed to be environment unfriendly. (In fact, it was Carson's book that ultimately led to the banning of DDT and other harmful pesticides in the early 1970s.) And in the social activist climate of the 1960s, the idea of slapping regulations onto presumably greedy, impersonal, corporations played to a receptive audience. Thomas Easton, professor of life sciences at Thomas College, notes that at least 22 distinct pieces of legislation or treaties involving environmental issues were implemented by the United States and the United Nations between the years 1967 and 2002 (*Taking*

Sides: Environmental Issues, pp. xviii–xix). This, of course, does not include the dozens of other governmental actions passed at the state and local levels in the United States during this time period.

Although it may be a bit simplistic, one might ask why corporations have to be regulated in order to get them to stop harming the environment in the first place. As members of society, wouldn't they want to avoid doing harm to the environment? While an affirmative answer to this question might seem obvious, classic economic theory gives us some insight as to why that is not necessarily the case. The traditional free-market view holds that corporations are in business first and foremost to increase shareholder wealth. This is usually accomplished by increasing revenues, decreasing costs, or, ideally, through a combination of both. Business activities that increase revenues and/or decrease costs will tend to be pursued, and those that do not will tend to be ignored. From the corporation's perspective, the problem with voluntarily restricting business activities that cause damage to the environment is that doing so usually results in lower revenues, reduced profits, and decreased shareholder wealth. In this way, it makes economic sense for corporations to refuse to voluntarily regulate their environmentally harmful business activities.

The history of business in America shows that it is fruitless to expect corporations to forego financial considerations and voluntarily address social problems out of altruistic concern for society. On the other hand, history confirms that social issues are very effectively addressed when doing so positively affects the bottom line. Thus, in instances when there are positive economic incentives for solving social questions, we can expect the power of free-market competition to provide us with viable answers. In instances where bottom line benefit is not likely to occur, however, securing corporate compliance usually requires governmental intervention. The tremendous increase in the number and scope of environmental legislation—since the publication of Carson's book attests to society's desire to reign in destructive corporate behavior.

So, can economic benefits induce top management decision makers to voluntarily regulate environmentally destructive corporate behavior? This is an important question because if the answer is "yes," then free-market advocates will have a strong weapon in their battle to reduce or eliminate what they view as destructive and unnecessary environmental regulation. If the answer is "no," then governmental interventionists will have support for their view that the only way big business will reign in its destructive behavior is if it is subject to coercive action in the form of environmental legislation.

Hazard materials managers Raymond Patchak and William Smith believe that corporations, under the right set of circumstances, will willingly engage in self-regulatory environmental behavior. In their article, the authors describe ISO 14000, an environmental regulatory volunteer program established by the International Organization for Standardization. They contend that voluntary corporate adherence to its guidelines will result in such organizationally desirable outcomes as increases in productivity and public image and declines in waste products.

In the second article, environmental scholars Linda Greer and Christopher van Löben Sels present the results of a case study involving Dow Chemical in which they found that expected cost savings were not enough incentive for Dow top management to adopt a voluntary pollution reduction plan.

Raymond J. Patchak and
William R. Smith

 **YES**

So Long! Command and Control . . . Hello! ISO 14000

The regulatory system currently in use by the United States Environmental Protection Agency (EPA), as well as other U.S. regulatory agencies, can be characterized as one of command and control. Developments in the regulatory approach taken by other industrialized nations and the advent of environmental management systems have ignited a process of critical review of our command and control system. Many new regulatory programs instituted in Europe seek to capitalize on the synergistic effect that can be obtained when you get both the regulated community and regulatory agencies working together to solve environmental problems. This idea is the basis for a new international environmental standard called ISO 14000. Let's take a quick look at both of these environmental systems.

Command and Control

The current system of environmental protection in the United States is, as a whole, the most advanced in the world. Environmental regulations have achieved a great deal in turning back the effects of toxic substances on the environment. Laws such as the Toxic Substances Control Act (TSCA) and the Resource Conservation and Recovery Act (RCRA) have been good control measures for the treatment and disposal of hazardous substances and wastes, while laws such as the Clean Air Act (CAA), the Safe Drinking Water Act (SDWA), and the Clean Water Act (CWA) have been instrumental in responding to and reducing toxic substance releases into the environment. One can easily argue that these regulations have contributed significantly to decreasing the proliferation of disasters like the ones at Love Canal, Times Beach and the burning of the Cuyahoga River in Ohio.

Two shortcomings exist in the current command and control approach to environmental protection. One is that regulations are often too rigid and complicated to allow innovation and common sense to play a role in environmental protection. Second, the current regulatory scheme does not foster a cooperative relationship between regulating agencies and industry. As a result, instead of working together to find common solutions to a problem, industry and the EPA all too often find themselves battling it out in the court system. Although these shortcomings have been reduced in recent years, the fact that the EPA is involved in some 600 lawsuits at any given time should be evidence enough to show that there is a fundamental conflict between business issues and regulatory constraints. The sad part about this situation is that valuable resources are being wasted in the courts rather than responding to the problem at hand.

Industry has made great progress in its efforts to learn how to protect the environment. They have spent hundreds of billions of dollars to decrease the release of toxic substances into the environment, while also developing technologies to reduce or eliminate hazardous waste generation. Many industry groups such as the Chemical Manufacturers Association have developed initiatives, which utilize pollution prevention programs as the cornerstone for their environmental protection efforts. These types of industry-led initiatives, coupled with advances in technology, are changing the way that many companies view and are responding to their environmental obligations.

The EPA Administrator, Carol M. Browner, has supported industry in furthering their environmental protection efforts by agreeing to look at beneficial ways to modify the current system. Ms. Browner's Common Sense Initiative (CSI) is a fundamentally different approach to environmental protection. In the development phase of CSI, the EPA worked with six pilot industries to look at the regulations that are impacting their businesses and to identify ways to change the ones that are complicated and inconsistent. The CSI program is attempting to promote creativity and encourage the development of innovative technologies by allowing industry more flexibility in meeting stronger environmental objectives. In this fashion, the goal of the CSI program is to develop a comprehensive strategy for environmental protection that will result in a cleaner environment at less cost.

What Is ISO 14000?

In the spirit of the Common Sense Initiative, ISO 14000 signifies a new generation in environmental protection. This standard is directed at establishing a link between business and environmental management for all companies no matter their size or purpose. ISO 14000 provides industry with a system to track, manage, and improve environmental performance without conflicting with the business priorities of an operation. Business considerations, flexibility, continual improvement and a simplistic approach to environmental protection are the main differences between ISO 14000 and the command and control system currently in place.

By design, ISO 14000 is a set of simplified environmental management standards that takes into account business and economic considerations while improving on already established environmental protection programs. In this context it should be pointed out that ISO 14000 standards are not intended to supersede current state and federal regulations. In fact, the ISO 14001 Specifications specifies the incorporation of these regulations as an integral part of a facility's EMS program.

In recent years there has been increasing interest and commitment to improve environmental management practices. This interest is demonstrated in collaborative international events such as the NAFTA Montreal Protocol and the mandates set during the 1992 Earth Summit in Rio de Janeiro. The birthplace of ISO 14000 can be traced back to the environmental goals established during the Earth Summit. At this Summit the United Nations convened representatives from the world's industrialized countries to discuss global environmental issues and to develop a means to meet their basic goal of "sustainable development."

At the conclusion of the Earth Summit, the International Organization for Standardization (ISO) set out to develop a group of international standards that meet the goals of the United Nations Conference. ISO established Technical Committee (TC) 207. Its mission, "to establish management tools and systems that organizations can voluntarily use for their own purposes which may, over time, improve their environmental performance levels." In this mission TC 207 created and is developing the ISO 14000 series of standards.

TC 207 is comprised of representatives from the ISO member nations. The United States's representative to TC 207 is the American National Standards Institute (ANSI). ANSI is responsible for fielding U.S. participation in the development of these international standards. They receive assistance within the U.S. through its Technical Advisory Group (TAG), which is administered by the American Society of Testing and Materials (ASTM). The TAG is further divided into Sub-TAGs, which are responsible for reviewing and commenting on progressive drafts of the individual policy documents that compose ISO 14000. Once completed the draft documents are voted on by the entire international membership of TC 207. Upon approval by the membership the documents become final standards.

ISO 14000 is the name for a family of environmental standards. This family is composed of five major components, each of which has one or more policy documents. The five major components are as follows:

- Environmental Management Systems (EMS)
- Environmental Auditing (EA)
- Environmental Performance Evaluation (EPE)
- Life-Cycle Assessment (LCA)
- Environmental Labeling (EL)

The **Environmental Management System (EMS)**, which incorporates policy documents numbered 14001 & 14004, were released as final standards in September of 1996. The EMS is the building block on which the other four components are incorporated. Through the EMS a company can identify its environmental goals and establish a program for monitoring their progress in reaching these goals.

Although individual EMS programs will differ from one organization to the next, they will all consist of seven core components. These include the following: Identification of the company's environmental policy, its objectives and targets, guidelines for identifying environmental concerns and applicable regulations, implementing procedures for controlling process and activities impacting the environment, a program for internal and external auditing of the system, clear assignment of responsibility and accountability, and a requirement for periodic review of the EMS by top level management.

The **Environmental Auditing (EA)** standards are composed of documents 14010 through 14012, and were released for publication as final standards in October 1996. These documents detail the requirements for the general principles of auditing. They include guidelines for conducting audits of EMS programs, and criteria for evaluating the qualifications of environmental auditors.

The **Environmental Performance Evaluation (EPE)** guidance is scheduled for publication in the second quarter of 1999. This standard includes document ISO 14031 as well as a technical report unofficially designated as TR 14032. EPE is an internal management process that uses indicators to provide management of an organization with reliable and verifiable information comparing the organization's past and present environmental performance with Management's environmental performance goals. ISO 14031 defines EPE as a "process to facilitate management decisions regarding an organization's environmental performance by selecting indicators, collecting and analyzing data, assessing information against environmental performance criteria, reporting and communicating, and periodic review and improvement of this process." These documents contain guidance for a process that identifies and quantifies the impact that a company has on the environment. These measurements are made against baseline levels, and the results are evaluated based on improvements from these levels.

The **Life Cycle Assessment (LCA)** guidance can be found in document numbers 14040 through 14043. Although no date has yet been set for final publication of ISO 14043, the ISO 14040 and ISO 14041 documents were released in late 1997 and 1998 respectively. These documents provide a means for determining what effects the products that are manufactured will have on today's environment, as well as that of future generations. This assessment looks at the impacts that are associated with the entire life of a product from raw material acquisition through production, use and disposal.

The **Environmental Labeling (EL)** standard is contained in documents 14020, ISO 14021, ISO 14024 and 14025. The ISO 14020 standard, published in late 1998, provides general principles of environmental labeling. The draft international standards ISO 14021 and ISO 14024 are expected for final release in early 1999. The overall goal of the environmental labeling standards is to provide manufacturers with a tool to assess and verify the accuracy of product environmental claims and to encourage the demand for those products that cause less stress on the environment. The intent of developing these EL standards is to stimulate the growth of market-driven continuous improvement of environmental performance.

In its development of ISO 14000, TC 207 was influenced by the British Standard BS 7750: "Environmental Management System" and the Global Environmental Management Initiative (GEMI). These systems utilize a consensus approach for determining their operational effectiveness. For example, GEMI is composed of 21 leading companies dedicated to fostering environmental excellence in businesses worldwide. It is intended to promote a worldwide business ethic for environmental management and sustainable development. The standard places an emphasis on individual companies and the incorporation of environmental goals into the company's overall corporate goals. These standards also set up a third party review process, to establish whether a company is working towards its goals.

How Will ISO 14000 Benefit an Organization?

ISO 14000 is not a rigid system of regulations, it is a flexible standard designed to fit any size and type of operation. Through this type of system a company can gain many benefits. These benefits can come in the form of improvements in public relations, improvements in management effectiveness, decreases in non-compliance fines, and improvements in marketing and customer relations.

The implementation of an effective ISO 14001 program can provide assurance to consumers that a company is committed to being not just environmentally friendly, but environmentally protective as well. In the same fashion, by maintaining conformance with the standard a company can make a much stronger case for their commitment to protecting the environment. ISO 14001 also makes regulatory compliance a more integral part of the business operation, and thus the likelihood of a violation can be minimized along with the stiff fines and penalties that normally accompany them.

Part of the ISO 14001 standard requires that a program for continuous improvement be developed and implemented throughout the company. The elements of a well orchestrated continuous improvement program can save even a small organization thousands of dollars per year in compliance and pollution control costs. These savings can come about as a part of improved compliance and in the form of reductions in fines and penalties, waste disposal costs, energy consumption and raw materials costs. For instance the implementation of an effective waste minimization program will not only decrease disposal costs, but can also reduce regulatory burden on the operation.

Other regulatory benefits related to implementing the ISO 14001 standard include reducing the number of audits by regulators. The EPA has already proposed, as part of their environmental auditing policy statement, that companies with internal self auditing programs, like ISO 14001, could be subject to less regulatory scrutiny and compliance audits.

Recent history has shown us that a company's market segment can also benefit by establishing a program like ISO 14000. This is exactly what happened when the International Quality Management Practices standard (ISO 9001) was released. As companies established and certified their ISO 9001/2 programs, they became strong believers in the importance of the program and in turn many required their major suppliers to become certified. This move is already underway with regard to ISO 14000, as many companies and government agencies in the U.S. and Europe are already posturing in this direction. Specific details about these companies are included in the next section.

One of the other business incentives for adopting and implementing ISO 14000 is that continuous improvement is crucial for maintaining prosperity and growth. As mentioned earlier in the article, ISO 14001 was developed in part from the United Kingdom BS 7750 Standard. Those companies that have already implemented the BS 7750 standard have reported improvements in the following areas:

- Productivity
- Waste reduction
- Paperwork declines, and
- Public relations

Industries' Acceptance of ISO 14000

As more and more companies have become familiar with the many benefits of ISO 14000 its acceptance has increased steadily. Companies within the U.S. are already lagging behind their European counterparts in taking the first step towards ISO 14000 certification. Many companies in Europe have established EMS programs and are certified to the draft ISO 14000 standards. The enthusiasm experienced in Europe has started to overflow into the U.S. This fact becomes apparent when you look at the SGS-Thompson Microelectronics facility in Rancho Bernardo, California. SGS-Thompson is the first U.S. manufacturer to have an EMS program certified; this occurred on January 3, 1996. SGS-Thompson, which is a corporation based in France, already has 5 facilities certified to the draft standards. Further, company representatives vow that all 16 SGS-Thompson facilities located in U.S., Europe, Southeast Asia, and North Africa will be certified by the end of 1997. As of December 1998 there have been over 5,000 facilities registered to the ISO 14001 standard worldwide.

According to a company official at SGS-Thompson, many of their major suppliers and contractors may find themselves forced to implement ISO 14000 standards by 1999 to maintain contractual preference. The official explains, "We assign an overall score to our suppliers based on many elements, including quality and environmental performance. . . . While an EMS program alone does not seem that important, [because of this scoring system] it may be the deciding factor when we decide who gets equipment and manufacturing supplier contracts."

Businesses are not the only ones that foresee the positive changes that can come about as a part of ISO 14000 implementation. Agencies with the United States government are also boarding the band wagon. Two of these agencies include the Department of Energy (DOE) and the Environmental Protection Agency (EPA). The DOE is encouraging all major contractors to implement an EMS program. Sources at the DOE have stated that specific contractors will be required to have ISO 14001 certification. The mood at the EPA can perhaps be best exemplified by the testimony of one of their representatives, who stated that "the old 'command and control' method of environmental regulation, so important in the first 25 years of the environmental movement, will occupy less time and fewer resources as companies start to use ISO 14000 and the next generation of environmental protection tools."

The EPA, which is studying how the ISO 14000 standards will influence and affect their operations, have already come out in support of them. This support has been heard at all levels including Carol M. Browner. Recently this support was testified to during the March 6, 1996 hearing in front of the Senate Environmental Resources & Energy Committee. During this hearing, James M. Seif, Secretary for the Pennsylvania Department of Environmental Protection, testified that ISO 14000 "represents the next generation of tools needed to more effectively achieve our environmental protection goals." Further, Mr. Seif said, "These new tools approach environmental protection in an entirely new way using performance-based environmental objectives, positive incentives to comply, external validation, a flexible approach to implementation and systems which constantly look for new opportunities to prevent pollution and reduce environmental compliance cost."

In the international arena, ISO 14000 is being seriously considered for adoption under NAFTA [North American Free Trade Agreement] and various GATT [General Agreement on Tariffs and Trade] trade agreements, to prevent the development of artificial trade barriers from country-specific environmental requirements. The standard is also viewed in Europe as meeting major components of the European Union's ECO-Management and Auditing Scheme (EMAS) regulations. And much like the proliferation of ISO 9000, it is expected that multi-national companies will require their suppliers to be ISO 14000 certified in order to do business in Europe.

In the U.S. a number of organizations that directly represent environmental and/or technical based members have already come out in support of ISO 14000. A partial list of these organizations includes:

- The American Society for Testing and Materials (ASTM),
- The American Society for Quality (ASQ),
- The Registration and Accreditation Board (RAB),
- The National Registry of Environmental Professionals (NREP),
- The American Forestry and Paper Association,
- The Academy of Certified Hazardous Materials Managers (ACHMM), and
- The American National Standards Institute (ANSI).

ISO 14000: A Business Decision

ISO 14000 is designed as a market driven approach to environmental protection. This system has the potential to be many times more effective in achieving significant environmental improvements than the current command and control approach.

Business success can be attributed partly to growth, strategic planning, and by maintaining a competitive edge in the market place. Organizations that fall in line behind the competition in market place developments often do not achieve a competitive advantage like the leaders in themarket. ISO 14000 is seen by many organizations not as a new environmental compliance burden, but as a market place trend, which can provide for a more productive operation. Only those organizations which look at ISO 14000 as a business decision will be able to utilize it to the fullest extent. These organizations will be able to capitalize on the long term cost savings while at the same time broaden their market and improve their customer relations.

NO

**Linda Greer and
Christopher van Löben Sels**

When Pollution Prevention
Meets the Bottom Line

What if a manufacturer learned that there were untapped opportunities to reduce waste and emissions within a plant that would also significantly cut costs? Conventional wisdom is that the company would seize on such opportunities and implement them.

But the reality is those opportunities are not always taken. A case study completed in 1996 at a Dow Chemical facility showed that certain pollution prevention strategies would save the company more than $1 million a year, approximately 10–20% of the existing environmental expenditures at the plant. Process changes would have eliminated 500,000 pounds (lb) of waste and allowed the company to shut down a hazardous waste incinerator. Surprisingly, these benefits were not enough of an incentive to outweigh other corporate priorities and the potential loss of future business that might have accompanied the incinerator's shutdown.

These findings came out of a collaborative study. In 1993, the pollution prevention pilot program (4P) was begun by the Natural Resources Defense Council (NRDC), an environmental advocacy group, and Dow Chemical, Monsanto, Amoco, and Rayonier Paper. Study participants, who were all interested in pollution prevention in a real-life industrial setting, wanted to know the reason for the lack of widespread reliance on promising pollution prevention techniques. Was it because there was not much to be gained environmentally or economically by using this environmental management technique? Was it because there were government regulations acting at cross purposes, incorporating barriers to implementation? If these factors did not explain the problem, what did?

Pollution prevention is conceptually quite different from pollution control, which relies on capturing emissions generated in processing before their release into the environment. Pollution prevention seeks opportunities to minimize reliance on toxic chemicals, increase efficiency, and decrease waste and emissions. Instead of focusing on changes required for environmental and health reasons, pollution prevention planners also identify opportunities to save money, making the process a potential "win-win" for industry and environmentalists.

From *Environmental Science and Technology*, Vol. 31, No. 9, September 1997, pp. 418–422.
Copyright © 1997 by American Chemical Society. Reprinted by permission.

This approach has failed, however, to take hold in the business world and at EPA and most state agencies. In fact, total waste production reported to the Toxics Release Inventory (TRI) in 1995 is up 6% from 1991, even though industry's TRI emissions have decreased. Some believe that, ironically, EPA'S regulations are responsible for this trend, because its highly prescriptive end-of-the-pipe nature discourages companies from implementing more holistic, innovative ideas at their plants. Others believe the more important obstacles to pollution prevention lie within the companies themselves. They suggest that the companies do not prioritize waste reduction initiatives in their business operations.

Texas Chemical Plant Selected

The study organizers picked a Dow Chemical Company facility in La Porte, Tex., as the primary site to evaluate. Located near the Houston ship channel, this relatively small, well-run chemical manufacturing operation produces methylene diamine diisocyanate (MDI), the major ingredient of foamed and thermoplastic polyurethane. Polyurethane foams appear in a variety of rigid foam products, from automobile parts to insulation in water heaters and picnic coolers. Polyurethane thermoplastic resins are used in tool handles and other clear plastics.

Dow sells most of the MDI from the plant as raw material to companies that combine it with various polyols to create foam and plastic; the rest is combined with polyols on site for some smaller volume Dow product lines. The La Porte facility's gross annual revenues are more than $350 million per year, and its estimated annual environmental expenditures are $5 million to $10 million.

Dow has several voluntary environmental improvement goals: reduction of dioxin emissions; decreased reliance on incinerators throughout the company; and, by 2005, a 50% decrease in the amount of waste generated prior to treatment. The La Porte facility's environmental staff are more interested in pollution prevention than most people in industry, making them good study participants. Because the La Porte facility's manufacturing operations are not especially unusual, study organizers thought that the results of this case study would be broadly applicable.

Dow La Porte's basic manufacturing process first combines formaldehyde and aniline to form methylenedianiline (MDA). The carbon atom from formaldehyde forms the methylene bridge between the two aniline molecules. MDA is then purified, placed in solution in monochlorobenzene (MCB), and reacted with phosgene (produced on site) to form monomeric and polymeric methylenebis(phenylisocyanate) (MDI and PMDI, respectively). In the final process step, MDI and PMDI are purified and then sold.

In 1993, La Porte's TRI releases for this process totaled 506,457 lb, well below the 1989 level of 1,137,300 lb (Table 1). Most of these releases were to air, followed by water. Because these emissions put the Dow La Porte facility in the top 4% of TRI facilities for total releases and transfers, its industrial operations were significant locally and nationally.

Table 1

Toxic Releases and Transfers, in Thousands of Pounds, From a Dow Chemical Facility

| Category | *Year* | | | | | | |
	1987	*1988*	*1989*	*1990*	*1991*	*1992*	*1993*
MCB air releases	712.0	980.0	1036.0	876.0	520.0	462.0	406.0
MDI transfers	620.0	426.0	630.4	181.0	230.0	182.6	227.0
Water releases	89.7	4.8	4.0	3.1	3.2	0.7	0.1
Other air releases	167.9	135.1	97.3	106.7	224.7	184.7	100.3
Other transfers	137.0	226.3	122.0	72.8	125.5	147.8	227.0
TOTALS	**1726.6**	**1772.2**	**1889.7**	**1239.6**	**1103.4**	**977.8**	**960.4**

Toxic releases from Dow Chemical's facility in La Porte, Tex., have declined steadily since 1989. Much of the decline has come from cutting monochlorobenzene (MCB) releases.

Source: Dow Chemical

At the time of the study, MCB was the leading chemical released annually from La Porte. In 1993, 406,000 lb of MCB (80% of the facility's total releases) were emitted (Table 1). In addition to being a toxic chemical, MCB is a volatile organic compound, emissions of which affect the region's ability to meet its ozone attainment levels. (After this study was completed, MCB emissions were substantially reduced; most are now captured and vented to the hazardous waste incinerator.)

La Porte treated about 1.5 million lb of TRI waste at the site in 1993, nearly three times as much as it released to the environment. Almost all of this treatment occurred in an on-site hazardous waste incinerator, covered by a Resource Conservation and Recovery Act (RCRA) permit. Phosgene and methanol provided the largest quantities of wastes burned, followed by 170,000 lb of MCB (see Table 2). (The amount of MCB burned today is greater than 170,000 lb, because additional quantities are now being captured.)

Table 2

TRI Wastes (in Pounds) Incinerated at Dow Chemical Facility in 1993

Ammonia	15,000
Aniline	6800
Chlorine	1400
Monochlorobenzene	170,000
Methanol	630,000
Phosgene	840,000
1,1,1 TCA	2575
TOTAL	**1,665,775**

Assessment of Pollution Prevention

La Porte already had a pollution prevention plan, as required by the state of Texas, and Dow was planning to capture most of the remaining MCB air emissions and incinerate them on site. However, this action was on hold pending a decision to upgrade the plant's section that produced these continuing emissions. All the other chemicals in Dow's existing pollution prevention plan were ozone depleters, required to be phased down under the Montreal Protocol.

Conventional wisdom suggests that good opportunities to reduce waste and emissions have already been identified by large, environmentally sensitive companies. In fact, when this study began, plant personnel said they believed no other "low-hanging fruit" remained at the plant; that is, no other opportunities to reduce wastes and emissions remained that could be readily implemented to the financial or environmental benefit of the facility.

Pollution prevention literature, however, suggests that conventional wisdom might be wrong, and that various barriers within companies *(1–3)* or in government regulations *(4)* keep many important opportunities from being identified or implemented. To find out whether this was the case at La Porte, the study team first examined its pollution issues, reviewed existing pollution prevention plans, and assessed further opportunities for prevention. Once the "fact pattern" was established, we identified various barriers to expanded use of pollution prevention and sought agreement on recommendations to further its use.

In the first phase of the project, to understand its environmental impact, the coverage of existing regulations, and the plant's view of opportunities and barriers to additional environmental improvement, we submitted written questions to the facility and obtained an extensive, documented response. We then toured the plant to clarify the written responses to our questions. From this work, we characterized the status of the plant before the project's pollution prevention assessment.

In the second phase of this 18-month project, a third-party pollution prevention assessor, Bill Bilkovich of Environmental Quality Consultants, Tallahassee, Fla., went to the plant to seek pollution prevention opportunities. Bilkovich spent about 300 hours at the plant, talking with the staff and investigating opportunities. Our group met many times with the consultant.

Pollution prevention assessments begin with an inventory of all wastes generated at a plant before treatment, recycling, or emission. They also require a chemical-use inventory for the site, which includes consumed chemicals that do not contribute to waste and emissions.

The inventory at La Porte required considerable work, as is common in a pollution prevention assessment. Even though major waste streams had been identified and tracked at the facility for pollution control (regulatory) purposes, data on their chemical composition were lacking. Such information is necessary for pollution prevention. For example, to continue the pollution prevention potential for one waste stream, we needed to know what components were present in the waste stream in less than 5% concentration. In another waste stream, a high degree of confidence in the distribution of minor constituents was required. Because this sort of information often is of no regulatory or process significance, it is not gathered. Much of the data could have been easily collected, however, if made a priority at the plant.

Following the waste and chemical-use inventory, we assessed opportunities for reduction through substitution, efficiency improvements in the process, recycling, and other options. Priorities can be set on the basis of financial considerations by working first on those projects that would deliver the highest rates of return. At La Porte, we set priorities primarily according to potential human health and environmental impact, which translated into high interest in MCB emissions to the air and the wastes burned in the hazardous waste incinerator.

For each chemical or waste being assessed for reduction opportunity, the team had to identify the reason the waste was generated. Answering this question required in-depth knowledge of the manufacturing process and basic plant chemistry as well as the conditions under which waste was generated (e.g., was it generated continuously or intermittently, under upset or normal conditions, etc.).

Because these critical pollution prevention issues are considered of little or no relevance in conventional assessments of a plant's environmental issues, it becomes critical to engage the production engineering personnel, especially the process chemistry experts, in pollution prevention planning. At La Porte, meetings with process engineers were key to developing a process flow diagram that showed material flow throughout the plant and indicated where each priority waste was generated.

Pollution Prevention Opportunities

After examining the process flow and waste information, project participants concluded that the site's single largest environmental opportunity would involve capturing and recycling MCB and ending the incineration of 500,000 lb of chlorinated hydrocarbons. If all of the other waste streams to the on-site RCRA incinerator (called a thermal oxidizer, or TOX) could also be reduced, recycled, or otherwise managed, the TOX could be closed altogether, a broader prospect with superb environmental and cost-savings benefits. (The cost saving from eliminating the TOX was determined to be substantial, in light of upcoming re-permitting requirements, soon-to-be-required upgrades in the unit, and operation costs.) Thus, we had found an option that would be good for the environment and save the company a lot of money.

To proceed on the TOX closure opportunity, six major waste streams that entered the TOX had to be examined: methanol contaminated with amines and ammonia, MCB air emissions captured by the pressure swing absorption/carbon adsorption system, other organic compounds captured on carbon, a phenyl isocyanate/MCB waste, phosgene manufacture vent gases (phosgene and carbon monoxide), and MCB from a groundwater pump-and-treat system that processed historical contamination from a previous owner. A pollution prevention assessment was undertaken for each of these waste streams. What follows is a consideration of options for the first two wastes, methanol and MCB, which offered the most interesting opportunities for reduction. We determined that the others were best addressed by using alternative treatment options.

Dealing With Waste Streams

At La Porte, options for conventional end-of-the-pipe alternative treatment of the methanol waste stream include processing in the wastewater treatment plant or sale as a product. Incineration, however, had been considered the best option because methanol is essentially a clean fuel, and its use reduced the need for TOX operations' supplementary fuels. The pollution prevention assessment started with a different set of questions about methanol, and it presented some interesting options.

First we asked, Where does the methanol originate? Although methanol is a major waste stream generated at the plant, a flow chart of the basic process chemistry does not show an obvious source. Interviews with plant personnel revealed that methanol enters the process in the formaldehyde-water solution (formalin) used to manufacture MDA. Formaldehyde is manufactured from methanol; and some residual methanol, in this case about 0.5%, is kept in the commercial product as a stabilizer. This methanol must be removed by La Porte before the phosgenation step. Because La Porte uses millions of pounds of formaldehyde each year, the amount of methanol waste being burned in the TOX reaches hundreds of thousands of pounds annually.

The next obvious question was, Can we substitute formaldehyde with a less toxic chemical that does not generate a waste stream? Formaldehyde is used in the plant to provide a carbon atom to connect two aniline molecules and form the intermediate MDA. Perhaps carbon dioxide (CO_2) could be used to achieve the same end. The assessor researched the use of CO_2 and found that, although there was a patent on the use of CO_2 in the manufacture of toluene diisocyanate (TDI), the process had never been commercialized and was not applicable to the manufacture of MDI. Other alternative sources of the carbon bridge atom were discussed with Dow research and development personnel, but we found no other good options and stopped this line of inquiry.

The next option was to look for ways to reduce or eliminate the methanol in the formalin. But conversations with a major formaldehyde manufacturer indicated that, under the temperature, humidity, and transit time conditions common in the Gulf Coast, at least 0.3% methanol is necessary to prevent the in-transit polymerization of formaldehyde. Thus, we could not decrease methanol waste to insignificant quantities by using this approach at this plant.

The identification of an alternative stabilizer, one that might be effective at part-per-million (ppm) levels, was not explored for La Porte; the driving force for developing an alternative would have to come more broadly from other formaldehyde users across the country. However, the assessment did raise interesting questions about the treatment and disposal costs incurred nationwide for the management of waste methanol at plants that use formaldehyde as a raw material. Approximately 8 billion lb of formaldehyde are used annually in U.S. manufacturing, and calculations show that 40 million lb of methanol are being handled or disposed of by the plants purchasing this chemical.

Full-cost accounting of the cost per pound of formaldehyde purchased as a raw material could reveal that the cost for residual waste methanol management is as high as or higher than the raw material cost—and open a market opportunity for higher priced, methanol-free formaldehyde.

Next we asked, If methanol is needed to stabilize the formaldehyde, might there be a way to remove the methanol as a clean waste stream before the formaldehyde enters production and comes in contact with aniline? Interest in this option was depressed by the low value of recovered methanol and the high cost of constructing and operating separation equipment to process millions of pounds of formaldehyde each year.

Because the trace quantities of aniline and other nitrogenous compounds make the waste methanol difficult to sell, we then asked whether the aniline could be removed from the methanol. Even though trace quantities of aniline could be removed and yield a salable methanol–water mix, the assessment team did not believe that aniline could be eliminated to levels considered safe for unrestricted commercial use of the methanol waste.

Project organizers then asked whether a customer could be found for methanol containing aniline. A cursory review of TRI data revealed no facility close to La Porte that had methanol and aniline emissions, and we did not pursue an in-depth review.

The final option we evaluated was returning the waste methanol to the formalin manufacturer for future processing into the formalin product Dow was interested in this option and would consider a "take back" provision in its purchase contract quite favorably, although this option has not been issued to date.

MCB Waste Stream

Analysis of MCB took the same initial path: identifying the use of MCB in processing (solvent carrier in the phosgenation step of the process) and seeking less toxic–chlorinated alternatives for this purpose. Finding no alternatives, we shifted our focus to recycling MCB instead of incinerating it. Plant personnel reported they had briefly considered this alternative when they decided to capture the MCB air emissions to reduce their air pollution, but they decided to incinerate the solvent because it was convenient and legal to do so, and they did not believe this practice would pose significant risk.

The plant personnel also believed that the presence of water in the used MCB would preclude recycling. The assessor researched this and found that water was not actually the principal barrier to recycling. To the contrary, the virgin MCB purchased by the plant is routinely treated on site to remove water introduction in a molecular sieve bed before introduction into the process. Production staff then raised a more important concern: If the waste MCB contained any impurities, they could build up in the system if MCB were recycled. Impurities were possible, but sufficient information was not available about the time course of their buildup. The uncertainty raised by this issue could be easily resolved by analysis of the actual level and identity of trace contaminants in this stream, however.

At the end, the assessment team's short-term recommendations included recycling the MCB waste stream that is currently incinerated; selling the methanol or burning it at an alternative, off-site incinerator; reducing levels of phosgene sent for treatment; and scrubbing the remaining waste phosgene instead of incinerating it.

If all these waste streams could thus be addressed, and several very minor waste streams were sent off site, Dow La Porte could conceivably shut down its on-site hazardous waste incinerator and avoid the cost of RCRA re-permitting. Dow personnel estimated the rate of return on investment for this project at 20–70%. The investment would pay for itself somewhere between 15 months and 5 years, depending on how the various projects were configured. Estimated savings are $1 million a year, derived from reduced raw material costs, incinerator operating costs, and re-permitting costs with regulatory authorities. Virgin solvent purchases alone might drop by 90%.

Barriers to Implementation

There were no significant regulatory barriers to adopting this plan. The problem lay within the company. Specifically, these opportunities were weak candidates in the capital investment process at Dow. The project was considered for implementation twice by the urethane business group within Dow Chemical and was put off both times because other, more financially attractive business opportunities were given higher priority.

Had EPA required that Dow reduce these waste streams, the 4P projects would have been mandatory, and the rate of return of the project would have been irrelevant to Dow's decision making. However, because these were voluntary opportunities, they were considered in the same way as other business opportunities would be. To succeed, these opportunities needed to do more than reduce waste and save money; they needed to be superior to other options for capital investment.

Although Dow hopes to implement the pollution prevention plan in the future, the La Porte pollution prevention project rests in an odd position: It is not required for the purposes of environmental compliance, and it is not of central interest to production engineers whose main priorities are in capacity building. Nor is the project highly compelling to business line personnel with profit-and-loss authority. They are more concerned with maximizing profit for their business among various Dow plant locations around the world.

Conventional wisdom says that most good opportunities to reduce waste and emissions have already been identified, but that belief was incorrect in this case: The 4P project found very promising opportunities that had not been identified by Dow. More significantly once pollution prevention opportunities were found, corporate business priorities and decision-making structures posed formidable barriers to implementing those opportunities.

Most environmental professionals outside of industry incorrectly assume that a pollution prevention plan that actually saves money and is good for the environment will be quickly seized upon by U.S. businesses. This work shows that at least in one firm, such opportunities may not be sufficiently compelling as a business matter to ensure their voluntary implementation.

References

1. Porter, M. E.; van der Linde, C. *Harvard Business Review* September-October 1995, 120–34.
2. New Jersey Department of Environmental Protection and Energy. *Industrial Pollution Prevention Planning: Meeting Requirements Under the New Jersey Pollution Prevention Act;* Office of Pollution Prevention, State of New Jersey: Trenton, July 1993.
3. Little, A. D. "Hitting the Green Wall," *Perspectives;* Arthur D. Little: Cambridge, MA, 1995.
4. Schmitt, R. E. *Natural Resources and Environment,* 1994, 9, 11–13, 51.

POSTSCRIPT

Can Economic Incentives Induce Top Management to Voluntarily Regulate Their Firm's Environmentally Harmful Behaviors?

Over the last three decades, industrial leaders have increasingly come to recognize the need to make voluntary, positive contributions toward the reduction of pollution and other environmentally damaging activities if they want to minimize government regulation. As a result, the idea of corporate self-regulation has started to gain momentum in both the U.S. and global business arenas. In the debate presented here, environmental experts Raymond Patchak and William Smith provide an account of a new, highly structured, global self-regulation initiative advocated by the International Organization for Standardization. One of the key elements of Patchak and Smith's argument that ISO 14000 can be an effective means of controlling environmental management practices is their belief that adherence to the programs policies will result in economically beneficial outcomes for participating organizations. In this sense, ISO 14000 is viewed not as a set of regulatory policies, but "a market driven approach to environmental protection. This system has the potential to be many times more effective in achieving significant environmental improvements than the current command and control approach [i.e., regulations]."

But are Patchak and Smith right that self-policing can be an effective alternative to governmental regulation? In order to answer this question, environmental scholars Andrew King and Michael Lenox examined the U.S. Chemical Manufacturers Association's adoption of a self-regulating code of conduct known as the Responsible Care Program (RCP). Participation in the program was voluntary, and there were no formal sanctions leveled against firms that violated the tenets of the RCP. One of the major reasons for the development of the RCP was the desire on the part of the industry to counteract decades of negative publicity about the environmental policies of chemical firms. After conducting a sophisticated analysis of the behaviors of member firms, the authors concluded that the RCP was unsuccessful in building, maintaining, or increasing a sense of adherence to environmentally desirable codes of conduct by participating organizations. This may well be due to the lack of sanctions for improper corporate behavior; nevertheless, their findings strike a blow at the view that corporations can successfully self-regulate their environmental management practices.

The Greer and van Löben Sels article also casts doubt on the possibility of self-regulation, although it must be remembered that their conclusions are based on the study of only one firm. Nevertheless, the decision-making process

Dow Chemical went through in ultimately rejecting the waste stream projects was based on standard capital investment analysis. The projects were "weak candidates" and thus low on the priority list. It is not hard to imagine that similar decisions would be reached by other companies in similar situations. As long as corporations require environmentally beneficial projects to also be superior financial-return projects, the argument that economic incentives are sufficient to induce environmental compliance will likely suffer from a lack of supporting evidence.

Suggested Readings

Magali A. Delmas, Barriers and incentives to the adoption of ISO 14001 by firms in the United States. *Duke Environmental Law and Policy Forum*, Fall 2000.

Andrew A. King and Michael J. Lenox, Industry self-regulation without sanctions: The chemical industry's responsible care program. *Academy of Management Journal*, vol. 43, no. 4, 2000, pp. 698–716.

Bjorn Lomborg, The skeptical environmentalist: Measuring the real state of the world. Cambridge University Press, 2001.

Paulette L. Stenzel, Can the ISO 14000 series environmental management standards provide a viable alternative to government regulation? *American Business Law Journal*, Winter 2000.

ISSUE 16

Is Economic Globalization Good for Humankind?

YES: Murray Weidenbaum, from "Globalization Is Not a Dirty Word: Dispelling the Myth About the Global Economy," *Vital Speeches of the Day* (March 1, 2001)

NO: Herman E. Daly, from "Globalization and Its Discontents," *Philosophy and Public Policy Quarterly* (Spring/Summer 2001)

ISSUE SUMMARY

YES: Foreign policy expert Murray Weidenbaum, in a reprint of a speech he delivered in 2001, promotes his "yes" response by systematically presenting, and then debunking, the most common "myths" surrounding globalization. He believes that globalization is a force for positive change.

NO: Professor Herman Daly feels that increasing globalization requires increases in political, social, and cultural integration across borders as well. The outcome is a loss of national identity for the countries involved as power is transferred from traditional domestic sources— i.e., governments, domestic businesses, local enterprises—to transnational corporations.

According to a leading textbook on international management, globalization is "global competition characterized by networks that bind countries, institutions, and people in an interdependent global economy" (Deresky, *International Management: Managing across Borders and Cultures*, 4th ed., Prentice Hall, 2003). Globalism is a phenomenon that has its roots in the rebuilding of Europe and Asia in the aftermath of World War II. As a measure of how powerful a phenomenon it has become, consider that the volume of international trade has increased over 3000 percent since 1960 (Griffin, *Management*, Houghton Mifflin, 2002)! Most of this tremendous growth has occurred in the TRIAD, a free-trade market consisting of three regional trading blocs: Western Europe in its current form as the Europe Union, North America, and Asia (including Australia). Increasingly, however, the developing nations of the world are contributing to the expansion in world trade. Foreign investment has grown at staggering rates as well: three times faster than the world output of goods (Deresky, 2003.) In the early part of the twenty-first century, it is not a stretch to say that virtually all businesses in industrialized nations are impacted to some degree by globalization.

It seems pretty clear that globalization will continue to grow as a dominant force in international relations among countries, particularly as more Second and Third World countries open their borders to international trade and investment. What may be less clear, however, is whether or not this is a positive development. In other words, as we ask in this topic, is economic globalization good for humankind? Foreign policy expert Murray Weidenbaum provides us with a positive response in a reprint of a speech he delivered in 2001. His is an interesting approach to this debate in that he promotes his view by systematically presenting, and then debunking, the most common "myths" surrounding globalization. What is left standing, he hopes, is the realization that globalization is a force for positive change, particularly in the case of poor nations. Weidenbaum believes that the main benefit of globalization is not material in nature; rather, it is the incredible opportunity it provides for the transfer and exchange of ideas between countries. He concludes his argument by asserting that for a country to choose isolationism over globalism is to cut themselves off from "the most powerful of all factors of production—new ideas." While considering Weidenbaum's argument, ask yourself if there are any "myths" he fails to take into account and, if so, consider how damaging they are to his stance.

Professor Herman Daly is strongly against globalization. The foundation for his position resides in his belief that a nation's economic, cultural, social, and political dimensions are intricately intertwined. He feels that increasing economic integration of large corporations across national borders—globalization—requires increases in political, social, and cultural integration across borders as well. The outcome is a loss of national identity for the countries involved as power is transferred from traditional domestic sources—i.e., governments, domestic businesses, local enterprises—to transnational corporations. If left unchecked, these huge, multinational corporate conglomerates will eventually replace national governments as the dominant forces in society. Taken to its logical conclusion, Daly's stance foresees a world where national borders, if they exist at all, are pointless since national identities have disappeared and domestic political structures no longer have meaning.

Daly presents four major negative outcomes he feels are associated with globalization. As you read each, compare it with the "myths" Weidenbaum discusses in his article. Does Weidenbaum address each of these points? If so, does he do so successfully? If not, how much of a threat do you feel Daly's points are to Weidenbaum's position?

Murray Weidenbaum

 **YES**

Globalization Is Not a Dirty Word

Delivered to the Economic Club of Detroit, Detroit, Michigan, January 22, 2001

Today I want to deal with a perplexing conundrum facing the United States: this is a time when the American business system is producing unparalleled levels of prosperity, yet private enterprise is under increasing attack. The critics are an unusual alliance of unions, environmentalists, and human rights groups and they are focusing on the overseas activities of business. In many circles, globalization has become a dirty word.

How can we respond in a constructive way? In my interaction with these interest groups, I find that very often their views arise from basic misunderstandings of the real world of competitive enterprise. I have identified ten myths about the global economy—dangerous myths—which need to be dispelled. Here they are:

1. Globalization costs jobs.
2. The United States is an island of free trade in a world of protectionism.
3. Americans are hurt by imports.
4. U.S. companies are running away, especially to low-cost areas overseas.
5. American companies doing business overseas take advantage of local people, especially in poor countries. They also pollute their environments.
6. The trade deficit is hurting our economy and we should eliminate it.
7. It's not fair to run such large trade deficits with China or Japan.
8. Sanctions work. So do export controls.
9. Trade agreements should be used to raise environmental and labor standards around the world.
10. America's manufacturing base is eroding in the face of unfair global competition.

That's an impressive array of frequently heard charges and they are polluting our political environment. Worse yet, these widely held myths fly in the face of the facts. I'd like to take up each of them and knock them down.

From *Vital Speeches of the Day*, March 1, 2001, City News Publishing.

1. Globalization Costs Jobs

This is a time when the American job miracle is the envy of the rest of the world, so it is hard to take that charge seriously. Yet some people do fall for it. The facts are clear: U.S. employment is at a record high and unemployment is at a 30 year low. Moreover, the United States created more than 20 million new jobs between 1993 and 2000, far more than Western Europe and Japan combined. Contrary to a widely held view, most of those new jobs pay well, often better than the average for existing jobs.

Of course, in the best of times, some people lose their jobs or their businesses fail, and that happens today. However, most researchers who have studied this question conclude that, in the typical case, technological progress, not international trade, is the main reason for making old jobs obsolete. Of course, at the same time far more new jobs are created to take their place.

2. The United States Is an Island of Free Trade in a World of Protectionism

Do other nations erect trade barriers? Of course they do—although the trend has been to cut back these obstacles to commerce. But our hands are not as clean as we like to think. There is no shortage of restrictions on importers trying to ship their products into this country. These exceptions to free trade come in all shapes, sizes, and varieties. They are imposed by federal, state, and local governments. U.S. import barriers include the following and more:

Buy-American laws give preference in government procurement to domestic producers. Many states and localities show similar favoritism. Here in Michigan, preference is given to in-state printing firms; the Jones Act prohibits foreign ships from engaging in waterborne commerce between U.S. ports; many statutes limit the import of specific agricultural and manufactured products, ranging from sugar to pillowcases; we impose selective high tariffs on specific items, notably textiles; and many state and local regulatory barriers, such as building codes, are aimed at protecting domestic producers.

It's strange that consumer groups and consumer activists are mute on this subject. After all, it is the American consumer who has to pay higher prices as a result of all of this special interest legislation. But these barriers to trade ultimately are disappointing. Nations open to trade grow faster than those that are closed.

3. Americans Are Hurt by Imports

The myth that imports are bad will be quickly recognized by students of economics as the mercantilist approach discredited by Adam Smith over two centuries ago. The fact is that we benefit from imports in many ways. Consumers get access to a wider array of goods and services. Domestic companies obtain lower cost components and thus are more competitive. We get access to vital metals and minerals that are just not found in the United States. Also, imports prod our own producers to improve productivity and invest in developing new technology.

I'll present a painful example. By the way, I have never bought a foreign car. But we all know how the quality of our domestic autos has improved because of foreign competition. More recently, we had a striking example of the broader benefits to imports. In 1997–98 the expanded flow of lower-cost products from Asia kept inflation low here at a time when otherwise the Fed could have been raising interest rates to fight inflation. The result would have been a weaker economy. Moreover, in a full employment economy, imports enable the American people to enjoy a higher living standard than would be possible if sales were limited to domestic production.

In our interconnected economy, the fact is that the jobs "lost" from imports are quickly replaced by jobs elsewhere in the economy—either in export industries or in companies selling domestically. The facts are fascinating: the sharp run-up in U.S. imports in recent years paralleled the rapid growth in total U.S. employment. Both trends, of course, reflected the underlying health of our business economy.

The special importance of imports was recently highlighted by the director of the Washington State Council on International Trade: "The people who benefit most critically are families at the lower end of the wage scale who have school-age children and those elderly who must live frugally." She goes on to conclude: "It is a cruel deception that an open system of the free trade is not good for working people."

4. U.S. Companies Are Running Away Especially to Low Cost Areas Overseas

Right off the bat, the critics have the direction wrong. The flow of money to buy and operate factories and other businesses is overwhelmingly into the United States. We haven't had a net outflow of investment since the 1960s. That's the flip side of our trade deficit. Financing large trade deficits means that far more investment capital comes into this country than is leaving.

But let us examine the overseas investments by American companies. The largest proportion goes not to poor countries, but to the most developed nations, those with high labor costs and also high environmental standards. The primary motive is to gain access to markets. That's not too surprising when we consider that the people in the most industrially advanced nations are the best customers for sophisticated American products. By the way, only one-third of the exports by the foreign branches of U.S. companies goes to the United States. About 70 percent goes to other markets, primarily to the industrialized nations.

Turning to American investments in Mexico, China, and other developing countries, the result often is to enhance U.S. domestic competitiveness and job opportunities. This is so because many of these overseas factories provide low-cost components and material to U.S.-based producers who are thus able to improve their international competitiveness.

In some cases, notably the pharmaceutical industry, the overseas investments are made in countries with more enlightened regulatory regimes, such as the Netherlands. "More enlightened" is not a euphemism for lower standards. The Dutch maintain a strong but more modern regulatory system than we do.

5. American Companies Doing Business Overseas Take Advantage of Local People and Pollute Their Environments

There are always exceptions. But by and large, American-owned and managed factories in foreign countries are top-of-the-line in terms of both better working conditions and higher environmental standards than locally-owned firms. This is why so many developing countries compete enthusiastically for the overseas location of U.S. business activities—and why so many local workers seek jobs at the American factories. After all, American companies manufacturing overseas frequently follow the same high operating standards that they do here at home.

I serve on a panel of Americans who investigate the conditions in some factories in China. I wish the critics could see for themselves the differences between the factories that produce for an American company under its worldwide standards and those that are not subject to our truly enlightened sense of social responsibility.

I'll give you a very personal example of the second category of facilities. While making an inspection tour, I tore my pants on an unguarded piece of equipment in one of those poorly-lit factories. An inch closer and that protruding part would have dug into my thigh. I also had to leave the factory floor every hour or so to breathe some fresh air. When I said that, in contrast, the American-owned factories were top-of-the-line, that wasn't poetry.

Yes, foreign investment is essential to the economic development of poor countries. By definition, they lack the capability to finance growth. The critics do those poor countries no favor when they try to discourage American firms from investing there. The critics forget that, during much of the nineteenth century, European investors financed many of our canals, railroads, steel mills, and other essentials for becoming an industrialized nation. It is sad to think where the United States would be today if Europe in the nineteenth century had had an array of powerful interest groups that were so suspicious of economic progress.

6. The Trade Deficit Is Hurting Our Economy and We Should Eliminate It

Yes, the U.S. trade deficit is at a record high. But it is part of a "virtuous circle" in our economy. The trade deficit mainly reflects the widespread prosperity in the United States, which is substantially greater than in most of the countries we trade with. After all, a strong economy, such as ours operating so close to full employment and full capacity, depends on a substantial amount of imports to satisfy our demands for goods and services. Our exports are lower primarily because the demand for imports by other nations is much weaker.

The acid test is that our trade deficit quickly declines in the years when our economy slows down and that deficit rises again when the economy perks up. Serious studies show that, if the United States had deliberately tried to curb the trade deficit in the 1990s, the result would have been a weak economy with high inflation and fewer jobs. The trade deficit is a byproduct of economic performance. It should not become a goal of economic policy.

There is a constructive way of reducing the trade deficit. To most economists, the persistence of our trade imbalance (and especially of the related and more comprehensive current account deficit) is due to the fact that we do not generate enough domestic saving to finance domestic investment. The gap between such saving and investment is equal to the current account deficit.

Nobel laureate Milton Friedman summed up this point very clearly: "The remarkable performance of the United States economy in the past few years would have been impossible without the inflow of foreign capital, which is a mirror image of large balance of payments deficits."

The positive solution is clear: increase the amount that Americans save. Easier said than done, of course. The shift from budget deficits (dissaving) to budget surpluses (government saving) helps. A further shift to a tax system that does not hit saving as hard as ours does would also help. The United States taxes saving more heavily than any other advanced industrialized nation. Replacing the income tax with a consumption tax, even a progressive one, would surely be in order—but that deserves to be the subject of another talk.

7. It's Not Fair to Run Such Large Trade Deficits With China or Japan

Putting the scary rhetoric aside, there really is no good reason for any two countries to have balanced trade between them. We don't have to search for sinister causes for our trade deficits with China or Japan. Bilateral trade imbalances exist for many benign reasons, such as differences in per capita incomes and in the relative size of the two economies. One of the best kept secrets of international trade is that the average Japanese buys more U.S. goods than the average American buys Japanese goods. Yes, Japan's per capita imports from the United States are larger than our per capita imports from Japan ($539 versus $432 in 1996). We have a large trade deficit with them because we have more "capita" (population).

8. Sanctions Work, So Do Export Controls

It is ironic that so many people who worry about the trade deficit simultaneously support sanctions and export controls. There is practically no evidence that unilateral sanctions are effective in getting other nations to change their policies or actions. Those restrictions on trade do, however, have an impact: they backfire. U.S. business, labor, and agriculture are harmed. We lost an overseas market for what is merely a symbolic gesture. Sanctions often are evaded. Shipping goods through third countries can disguise the ultimate recipient in the nation on which the sanctions are imposed. On balance, these sanctions reduced American exports in 1995 by an estimated $15–20 billion.

As for export controls, where American producers do not have a monopoly on a particular technology—which is frequent—producers in other nations can deliver the same technology or product without the handicap imposed on U.S. companies. A recent report at the Center for the Study of American Business showed that many business executives believe that sanctions and export controls are major obstacles to the expansion of U.S. foreign trade.

9. Trade Agreements Should Be Used to Raise Environmental and Labor Standards Around the World

At first blush, this sounds like such a nice and high-minded way of doing good. But, as a practical matter, it is counterproductive to try to impose such costly social regulations on developing countries as a requirement for doing business with them. The acid test is that most developing nations oppose these trade restrictions. They see them for what they really are—a disguised form of protectionism designed to keep their relatively low-priced goods out of the markets of the more advanced, developed nations. All that feeds the developing nations' sense of cynicism toward us.

In the case of labor standards, there is an existing organization, the International Labor Organization [ILO], which has been set up to deal specifically with these matters. Of all the international organizations, the ILO is unique in having equal representation from business, labor, and government. The United States and most other nations *are* members. The ILO is where issues of labor standards should be handled. To be taken more seriously, the United States should support the ILO more vigorously than it has.

As for environmental matters, we saw at the unsuccessful meetings on climate change at the Hague [recently] how difficult it is to get broad international agreement on environmental issues even in sympathetic meetings of an international environmental agency. To attempt to tie such controversial environmental matters to trade agreements arouses my suspicions about the intent of the sponsors. It is hard to avoid jumping to the conclusion that the basic motivation is to prevent progress on the trade front.

I still recall the signs carried by one of the protesters in Seattle, "Food is for people, not for export." Frankly, it's hard to deal with such an irrational position. After all, if the United States did not export a major part of its abundant farm output, millions of people overseas would be starving or malnourished. Also, thousands of our farmers would go broke.

The most effective way to help developing countries improve their working conditions and environmental protection is to trade with and invest in them. As for the charge that companies invest in poor, developing nations in order to minimize their environmental costs, studies of the issue show that environmental factors are not important influences in business location decisions. As I pointed out earlier, most U.S. overseas direct investment goes to developed nations with high labor costs and also high environmental standards.

10. America's Manufacturing Base Is Eroding in the Face of Unfair Global Competition

Unfortunately, some of our fellow citizens seem to feel that the only fair form of foreign competition is the kind that does not succeed in landing any of their goods on our shores. But to get to the heart of the issue, there is no factual basis for the charge that our manufacturing base is eroding—or even stagnant. The official statistics are reporting record highs in output year after year. Total industrial production in the United States today is 45 percent higher than in 1992—that's not in dollars, but in terms of real output.

Of course, not all industries or companies go up—or down—in unison. Some specific industries, especially low-tech, have had to cut back. But simultaneously, other industries, mainly high-tech, have been expanding rapidly. Such changes are natural and to be expected in an open, dynamic economy. By the way, the United States regularly runs a trade surplus in high-tech products.

It's important to understand the process at work here. Technological progress generates improved industrial productivity. In the United States, that means to some degree fewer blue-collar jobs and more while-collar jobs. That is hardly a recent development. The shift from physical labor to knowledge workers has been the trend since the beginning of the 20th century. On balance, as I noted earlier, total U.S. employment is at an all-time high.

If you have any doubt about the importance of rising productivity to our society, just consider where we would be if over the past century agriculture had not enjoyed rising productivity (that is, more output per worker/hour). Most of us would still be farmers.

It is vital that we correct the erroneous views of the anti-globalists. Contrary to their claims, our open economy has raised living standards and helped to contain inflation. International commerce is more important to our economy today than at any time in the past. By dollar value and volume, the United States is the world's largest trading nation. We are the largest importer, exporter, foreign investor, and host to foreign investment. Trying to stop the global economy is futile and contrary to America's self-interest.

Nevertheless, we must recognize that globalization, like any other major change, generates costs as well as benefits. It is essential to address these consequences. Otherwise, we will not be able to maintain a national consensus that responds to the challenges of the world marketplace by focusing on opening markets instead of closing them. The challenge to all of us is to urge courses of action that help those who are hurt without doing far more harm to the much larger number who benefit from the international marketplace.

We need to focus more attention on those who don't share the benefits of the rapid pace of economic change. Both private and public efforts should be increased to provide more effective adjustment assistance to those who lose their jobs. The focus of adjustment policy should not be on providing relief from economic change, but on positive approaches that help more of our people participate in economic prosperity.

As you may know, I recently chaired a bipartisan commission established by Congress to deal with the trade deficit. Our commission included leaders of business and labor, former senior government officials, and academics. We could not agree on all the issues that we dealt with. But we were unanimous in concluding that the most fundamental part of an effective long-run trade adjustment policy is to do a much better job of educating and training. More Americans should be given the opportunity to become productive and high-wage members of the nation's workforce.

No, I'm not building up to a plea to donate to the college of your choice, although that's a pretty good idea.

Even though I teach at major research universities—and strongly believe in their vital mission—let me make a plea for greater attention to our junior colleges. They are an overlooked part of the educational system. Junior colleges have a key role to play. Many of these community oriented institutions of learning are now organized to specially meet the needs of displaced workers, including those who need to brush up on their basic language and math skills. In some cases, these community colleges help people launch new businesses, especially in areas where traditional manufacturing is declining. A better trained and more productive workforce is the key to our long-term international competitiveness. That is the most effective way of resisting the calls for economic isolationism.

Let me leave you with a final thought. The most powerful benefit of the global economy is not economic at all, even though it involves important economic and business activities. By enabling more people to use modern technology to communicate across traditional national boundaries, the international marketplace makes possible more than an accelerated flow of data. The worldwide marketplace encourages a far greater exchange of the most powerful of all factors of production—new ideas. That process enriches and empowers the individual in ways never before possible.

As an educator, I take this as a challenge to educate the anti-globalists to the great harm that would result from a turn to economic isolationism. For the twenty-first century, the global flow of information is the endless frontier.

Herman E. Daly  **NO**

Globalization and Its Discontents

$\mathbf{E}$very day, newspaper articles and television reports insist that those who oppose globalization must be isolationists or—even worse—xenophobes. This judgment is nonsense. The relevant alternative to globalization is internation-alization, which is neither isolationist nor xenophobic. Yet it is impossible to recognize the cogency of this alternative if one does not properly distinguish these two terms.

"Internalization" refers to the increasing importance of relations among nations. Although the basic unit of community and policy remains the nation, increasingly trade, treaties, alliances, protocols, and other formal agreements and communications are necessary elements for nations to thrive. "Global-ization" refers to global economic integration of many formerly national economies into one global economy. Economic integration is made possible by free trade—especially by free capital mobility—and by easy or uncontrolled migration. In contrast to internationalization, which simply recognizes that nations increasingly rely on understandings among one another, globalization is the effective erasure of national boundaries for economic purposes. National boundaries become totally porous with respect to goods and capital, and ever more porous with respect to people, who are simply viewed as cheap labor—or in some cases as cheap human capital.

In short, globalization is the economic integration of the globe. But exactly what is "integration"? The word derives from *integer*, meaning one, complete, or whole. Integration means much more than "interdependence"— it is the act of combining separate although related units into a single whole. Since there can be only one whole, only one unity with reference to which parts are integrated, it follows that global economic integration logically implies national economic *dis*integration—parts are torn out of their national context (dis-integrated), in order to be re-integrated into the new whole, the globalized economy.

As the saying goes, to make an omelet you have to break some eggs. The disintegration of the national egg is necessary to integrate the global omelet. But this obvious logic, as well as the cost of disintegration, is frequently met with denial. This article argues that globalization is neither inevitable nor to be embraced, much less celebrated. Acceptance of globalization entails several

From *Philosophy & Public Policy Quarterly*, Spring/Summer 2001. Copyright © 2001 by Institute for Philosophy & Public Policy. Reprinted by permission.

serious consequences, namely, standards-lowering competition, an increased tolerance of mergers and monopoly power, intense national specialization, and the excessive monopolization of knowledge as "intellectual property." This article discusses these likely consequences, and concludes by advocating the adoption of internationalization, and not globalization.

The Inevitability of Globalization?

Some accept the inevitability of globalization and encourage others in the faith. With admirable clarity, honesty, and brevity, Renato Ruggiero, former director-general of the World Trade Organization, insists that "We are no longer writing the rules of interaction among separate national economies. We are writing the constitution of a single global economy." His sentiments clearly affirm globalization and reject internationalization as above defined. Further, those who hold Ruggiero's view also subvert the charter of the Bretton Woods institutions. Named after a New Hampshire resort where representatives of forty-four nations met in 1944 to design the world's post–World War II economic order, the institutions conceived at the Bretton Woods International Monetary Conference include the World Bank and the International Monetary Fund. The World Trade Organization evolved later, but functions as a third sister to the World Bank and the International Monetary Fund. The nations at the conference considered proposals by the U.S., U.K., and Canadian governments, and developed the "Bretton Woods system," which established a stable international environment through such policies as fixed exchange rates, currency convertibility, and provision for orderly exchange rate adjustments. The Bretton Woods Institutions were designed to facilitate *internationalization, not globalization,* a point ignored by director-general Ruggiero.

The World Bank, along with its sister institutions, seems to have lost sight of its mission. After the disruption of its meetings in Washington, D.C. in April 2000, the World Bank sponsored an Internet discussion on globalization. The closest the World Bank came to offering a definition of the subject under discussion was the following: "The most common core sense of economic globalization . . . surely refers to the observation that in recent years a quickly rising share of economic activity in the world seems to be taking place between people who live in different countries (rather than in the same country)." This ambiguous description was not improved upon by Mr. Wolfensohn, president of the World Bank, who told the audience at a subsequent Aspen Institute Conference that "Globalization is a practical methodology for empowering the poor to improve their lives." That is neither a definition nor a description—it is a wish. Further, this wish also flies in the face of the real consequences of global economic integration. One could only sympathize with demonstrators protesting Mr. Wolfensohn's speech some fifty yards from the Aspen conference facility. The reaction of the Aspen elite was to accept as truth the title of Mr. Wolfensohn's speech, "Making Globalization Work for the Poor," and then ask in grieved tones, "How could anyone demonstrate against *that?*"

Serious consequences flow from the World Banks' lack of precision in defining globalization but lauding it nonetheless. For one thing, the so-called definition of globalization conflates the concept with that of internalization. As a result, one cannot reasonably address a crucial question: Should these increasing transactions between people living in different countries take place *across national boundaries* that are economically significant, or *within an integrated world* in which national boundaries are economically meaningless?

The ambiguous understanding of globalization deprives citizens of the opportunity to decide whether they are willing to abandon national monetary and fiscal policy, as well as the minimum wage. One also fails to carefully consider whether economic integration entails political and cultural integration. In short, will political communities and cultural traditions wither away, subsumed under some monolithic economic imperative? Although one might suspect economic integration would lead to political integration, it is hard to decide which would be worse—an economically integrated world *with*, or *without*, political integration. Everyone recognizes the desirability of community for the world as a whole—but one can conceive of two very different models of world community: (1) a federated community of real national communities (internationalization), versus (2) a cosmopolitan direct membership in a single abstract global community (globalization). However, at present our confused conversations about globalization deprive us of the opportunity to reflect deeply on these very different possibilities.

This article has suggested that at present organizations such as the International Monetary Fund and the World Bank (and, by extension, the World Trade Organization) no longer serve the interests of their member nations as defined in their charters. Yet if one asks whose interests are served, we are told they service the interests of the integrated "global economy." If one tries to glimpse a concrete reality behind that grand abstraction, however, one can find no individual workers, peasants, or small businessmen represented, but only giant fictitious individuals, the transnational corporations. In globalization, power is drained away from national communities and local enterprises, and aggregates in transnational corporations.

The Consequences of Globalization

Globalization—the erasure of national boundaries for economic purposes—risks serious consequences. Briefly, they include, first of all, standards-lowering competition to externalize social and environmental costs with the goal of achievement of a competitive advantage. This results, in effect, in a race to the bottom so far as efficiency in cost accounting and equity in income distribution are concerned. Globalization also risks increased tolerance of mergers and monopoly power in domestic markets in order that corporations become big enough to compete internationally. Third, globalization risks more intense national specialization according to the dictates of competitive advantage. Such specialization reduces the range of choice of ways to earn a livelihood, and increases dependence on other countries. Finally, worldwide enforcement of a muddled and self-serving doctrine of "trade-related intellectual property rights" is a direct contradiction of the Jeffersonian dictum that "knowledge is the common property of mankind."

Each of these risks of globalization deserves closer scrutiny.

1. Standards-lowering competition Globalization undercuts the ability of nations to internalize environmental and social costs into prices. Instead, economic integration under free market conditions promotes standards-lowering competition—a race to the bottom, in short. The country that does the poorest job of internalizing all social and environmental costs of production into its prices gets a competitive advantage in international trade. The external social and environmental costs are left to be borne by the population at large. Further, more of world production shifts to countries that do the poorest job of counting costs—a sure recipe for reducing the efficiency of global production. As uncounted, externalized costs increase, the positive correlation between gross domestic product (GDP) growth and welfare disappears, or even becomes negative. We enter a world foreseen by the nineteenth-century social critic John Ruskin, who observed that "that which seems to be wealth is in verity but a gilded index of far-reaching ruin."

Another dimension of the race to the bottom is that globalization fosters increasing inequality in the distribution of income in high-wage countries, such as the U.S. Historically, in the U.S. there has been an implicit social contract established to ameliorate industrial strife between labor and capital. As a consequence, the distribution of income between labor and capital has been considered more equal and just in the U.S. compared to the world as a whole. However, global integration of markets necessarily abrogates that social contract. U.S. wages would fall drastically because labor is relatively more abundant globally than nationally. Further, returns to capital in the U.S. would increase because capital is relatively more scarce globally than nationally. Although one could make the theoretical argument that wages would be *bid up* in the rest of the world, the increase would be so small as to be insignificant. Making such an argument from the relative numbers would be analogous to insisting that, theoretically, when I jump off a ladder gravity not only pulls me to the earth, but also moves the earth towards me. This technical point offers cold comfort to anyone seeking a softer landing.

2. Increased tolerance of mergers and monopoly power Fostering global competitive advantage is used as an excuse for tolerance of corporate mergers and monopoly in national markets. Chicago School economist and Nobel laureate Ronald Coase, in his classic article on the theory of the firm, suggests that corporate entities are "islands of central planning in a sea of market relationships." The islands of central planning become larger and larger relative to the remaining sea of market relationships as a result of merger. More and more resources are allocated by within-firm central planning, and less by between-firm market relationships. Corporations are the victor, and the market principle is the loser, as governments lose the strength to regulate corporate capital and maintain competitive markets in the public interest. Of the hundred largest economic organizations, fifty-two are corporations and forty-eight are nations. The distribution of income within these centrally-planned corporations has become much more concentrated. The ratio of the salary of the Chief Executive Officer to the average employee has passed 400 (as one would expect, since chief central planners set their own salaries).

3. Intense national specialization   Free trade and free capital mobility increase pressures for specialization in order to gain or maintain a competitive advantage. As a consequence, globalization demands that workers accept an ever-narrowing range of ways to earn a livelihood. In Uruguay, for example, everyone would have to be either a shepherd or a cowboy to conform to the dictates of competitive advantage in the global market. Everything else should be imported in exchange for beef, mutton, wool, and leather. Any Uruguayan who wants to play in a symphony orchestra or be an airline pilot should emigrate.

Of course, most people derive as much satisfaction from how they earn their income as from how they spend it. Narrowing that range of choice is a welfare loss uncounted by trade theorists. Globalization assumes either that emigration and immigration are costless, or that narrowing the range of occupational choice within a nation is costless. Both assumptions are false.

While trade theorists ignore the range of choice in *earning* one's income, they at the same time exaggerate the welfare effects of range of choice in *spending* that income. For example, the U.S. imports Danish butter cookies and Denmark imports U.S. butter cookies. Although the gains from trading such similar commodities cannot be great, trade theorists insist that the welfare of cookie connoisseurs is increased by expanding the range of consumer choice to the limit.

Perhaps, but one wonders whether those gains might be realized more cheaply by simply trading recipes? Although one would think so, *recipes—* trade-related intellectual property rights—are the one thing that free traders really want to protect.

4. Intellectual property rights   Of all things, knowledge is that which should be most freely shared, since in sharing, knowledge is multiplied rather than divided. Yet trade theorists have rejected Thomas Jefferson's dictum that "Knowledge is the common property of mankind" and instead have accepted a muddled doctrine of "trade-related intellectual property rights." This notion of rights grants private corporations monopoly ownership of the very basis of life itself—patents to seeds (including the patent-protecting, life-denying terminator gene) and to knowledge of basic genetic structures.

The argument offered to support this grab is that, without the economic incentive of monopoly ownership, little new knowledge and innovation will be forthcoming. Yet, so far as I know, James Watson and Francis Crick, co-discoverers of the structure of DNA, do not share in the patent royalties reaped by their successors. Nor of course did Gregor Mendel get any royalties—but then he was a monk motivated by mere curiosity about how Creation works!

Once knowledge exists, its proper price is the marginal opportunity cost of sharing it, which is close to zero, since nothing is lost by sharing knowledge. Of course, one does lose the *monopoly* on that knowledge, but then economists have traditionally argued that monopoly is inefficient as well as unjust because it creates an artificial scarcity of the monopolized item.

Certainly, the cost of production of new knowledge is not zero, even though the cost of sharing it is. This allows biotech corporations to claim that they deserve a fifteen- or twenty-year monopoly for the expenses incurred in research and development. Although corporations deserve to profit from their efforts, they are not entitled to monopolize on Watson and Crick's contribution—without which they could do nothing—or on the contributions of Gregor Mendel and all the great scientists of the past who made fundamental discoveries. As early twentieth-century economist Joseph Schumpeter emphasized, being the first with an innovation already gives one the advantage of novelty, a natural temporary monopoly, which in his view was the major source of profit in a competitive economy.

As the great Swiss economist, Jean Sismondi, argued over two centuries ago, not all new knowledge is of benefit to humankind. We need a sieve to select beneficial knowledge. Perhaps the worse selective principle is hope for private monetary gain. A much better selective motive for knowledge is a search in hopes of benefit to our fellows. This is not to say that we should abolish all intellectual property rights—that would create more problems than it would solve. But we should certainly begin restricting the domain and length of patent monopolies rather than increasing them so rapidly and recklessly. We should also become much more willing to share knowledge. Shared knowledge increases the productivity of all labor, capital, and resources. Further, international development aid should consist far more of freely-shared knowledge, and far less of foreign investment and interest-bearing loans.

Let me close with my favorite quote from John Maynard Keynes, one of the founders of the recently subverted Bretton Woods Institutions:

> I sympathize therefore, with those who would minimize, rather than those who would maximize, economic entanglement between nations. Ideas, knowledge, art, hospitality, travel—these are the things which should of their nature be international. But let goods be homespun whenever it is reasonably and conveniently possible; and, above all, let finance be primarily national.

POSTSCRIPT

Is Economic Globalization Good for Humankind?

According to Freedom House, a non-partisian think tank that monitors the progress of freedom and democracy around the world, the rise in globalization and free trade over the last 30 years has been accompanied by an increase in the percentage of countries whose population enjoys civil and political freedom (Griswold, 2003). Since 1972, the share of those countries where these rights are denied has dropped from 47 percent to 35 percent, whereas the share of those countries enjoying these rights has increased from 34 percent to 45 percent. Freedom House also reports that the most economically open—that is, receptive to the idea of globalization—are three times more likely to enjoy full civil and political liberties than are economically closed countries. Further, numerous studies indicate that nations that are receptive to free trade grow faster and have higher levels of per capita income than nations that resist economic openness.

Facts such as these seem to provide considerable support for Murray Weidenbaum's pro-globalization stance presented here. But recall that Daly doesn't necessarily deny that economically open nations will benefit materially from globalization. His argument is that a country's national and cultural identity will be swept away in the wake of rapid economic growth. And in case you think his fears unfounded, consider the existence of the European Union (EU). There is strength in size, and joining a unified collection of European nations allows each country to better compete in the global marketplace. However, membership in the EU has come at a price: Member countries have to agree to dissolve its currency and adopt a new, single currency, the euro. Across Europe, the history and cultural identity of many countries is intimately tied to its currency, and the decision to disband it for economic reasons was the source of much social unrest. Many critics of the EU agree with Daly and fear that this is merely an early example of the destructive effects globalization—in the form of the EU—has on the national sovereignty of those countries that embrace it.

Suggested Readings

Cato Center for Trade Study Analysis, The benefits of globalization. *Cato Institute*, 2003. http://www.freetrade.org/issues/globalization.html

Vic George and Paul Wilding, *Globalization and Human Welfare*. Palgrave, 2002.

Robert Gilpen, *The Challenge of Global Capitalism*. The Princeton University Press, 2000.

Dan Griswold, Trading tyranny for freedom: How open markets till the soil for democracy. *Trade Policy Analysis, Cato Institute,* January 6, 2003.

Richard Langhome, *The Coming of Globalization: Its Evolution and Contempary Consequences.* St. Martin's Press, 2001.

Edwin A. Locke, Anti-globalization: The Left's violent assault on prosperity. *The Ayn Rand Institute,* September 5, 2003.

William K. Tabb, The amoral elephant: Globalization and the struggle for social justice in the twenty-first century. *Monthly Review Press,* 2001.

ISSUE 17

Are Global Sweatshops Exploitative?

YES: Richard Appelbaum and Peter Dreier, from "The Campus Anti-Sweatshop Movement," *The American Prospect* (September–October 1999)

NO: Radley Balko, from "Sweatshops and Globalization," *A World Connected Web Site* (2004)

ISSUE SUMMARY

YES: The first article, written by scholars Richard Appelbaum and Peter Dreier, chronicles the rise of the grassroots, college campus, anti-global sweatshops movement in the late 1990s.

NO: Columnist and social commentator Radley Balko argues that sweatshops are not exploitative. His article presents several additional points frequently offered in defense of globalization in general, and sweatshops in particular.

Historically, the word "sweatshop" is usually linked with the tremendous industrial growth of the American economy during the mid-nineteenth century. Originally associated with the apparel and garment industries, the use of the term eventually grew to describe any factory position in which employees—frequently, women and children—worked excessively long hours, often in unsanitary or unsafe working conditions, for barely subsistence-level wages. The massive influx of immigrants into the country during this time period resulted in low wage rates and provided corporations with little incentive to improve working conditions in their plants and factories (Matt Zwolinski, "Sweatshops," *Social Issues Encyclopedia*, Entry 167, 2004). Social commentators and union activists at the turn of the century argued that sweatshops were exploitative and called for their abolition. Their efforts resulted in a series of successful labor strikes and legislative actions that helped to dramatically improve worker conditions in the United States. As a result, by the end of the second decade of the twentieth century, sweatshops had become the exception rather than the norm in the manufacturing sector of the U.S. economy.

Recently, the topic of sweatshops has re-emerged as an important social and political issue, this time at the global level. Much of the recent attention on "global sweatshops" is attributed to a series of high-profile investigations into the overseas labor practices of major American and European firms during the 1990s. Newspaper and television news programs reported abusive labor practices and sweatshop working conditions in overseas factories like those owned by contractors hired by Nike, The Gap, and Wal-Mart (through its association with Kathie Lee Gifford). In addition, the Clinton administration pursued several legal lines of attack against firms and industries accused of using sweatshops, and anti-sweatshop activist organizations sprang up on college campuses across America, most calling for boycotts of products made in sweatshop factories. In several instances, campus organizations such as the United Students Against Sweatshops (USAS), buoyed by public outrage and moral indignation, forced multinational firms to close their operations in countries where sweatshops were being employed.

In their current manifestation, sweatshops are portrayed as an inevitable outcome of economic globalization (see issue 16 in this text for more on the subject of globalization) (Zwolinski, 2004). Critics of globalization argue that sweatshops are inherently exploitative since multinational corporations take advantage of the low wages and poor working conditions characteristic of developing countries. The developing countries must compete with each other in order to attract foreign firms; they do this by decreasing their labor standards. Thus, according to critics of globalization, multinational firms use the poverty and desperation of the developing countries to their advantage. Critics also point out that it is not just the workers in the sweatshops who are exploited—jobs in western countries are lost when global firms decide to locate their operations overseas in order to take advantage of the low labor costs.

Proponents of globalization note that most anti-sweatshop efforts actually hurt the very people they intend to help. The reason is simple: workers in developing countries usually have no other alternatives; like it or not, sweatshops represent the best of a bad situation. Shutting down sweatshops takes money out of their hands and sends the workers onto the street where, in many instances, they starve to death or turn to illegal activities, such as prostitution, in order to survive (Radley Balko, "Third World Workers Need Western Jobs," Foxnews.com, May 6, 2004). Proponents of globalization also note that virtually every industrialized first world economy capitalized on cheap labor early in its economic development. For example, consider that the rapid growth of Hong Kong and Singapore over the last quarter of the twentieth century was due in large measure to their willingness to exploit the comparative advantage of cheap labor early in their economic development.

The following articles address the question, are global sweatshops exploitative? The first article, written by scholars Richard Appelbaum and Peter Dreier, chronicles the rise of the college campus, anti-global sweatshops movement in the late 1990s. Columnist and social commentator Radley Balko argues that sweatshops are not exploitative. In addition to those mentioned above, his article presents several additional points frequently offered in defense of globalization in general, and sweatshops in particular.

Richard Appelbaum
and Peter Dreier

 **YES**

The Campus Anti-Sweatshop Movement

If University of Arizona activist Arne Ekstrom was aware of today's widely reported student apathy, he certainly was not deterred when he helped lead his campus anti-sweatshop sit-in. Nor, for that matter, were any of the other thousands of students across the United States who participated in anti-sweatshop activities during the past academic year, coordinating their activities on the United Students Against Sweatshops (USAS) listserv (a listserv is an online mailing list for the purpose of group discussion) and Web site.

Last year's student anti-sweatshop movement gained momentum as it swept westward, eventually encompassing more than 100 campuses across the country. Sparked by a sit-in at Duke University, students organized teach-ins, led demonstrations, and occupied buildings—first at Georgetown, then northeast to the Ivy League, then west to the Big Ten. After militant actions at Notre Dame, Wisconsin, and Michigan made the *New York Times, Business Week, Time,* National Public Radio, and almost every major daily newspaper, the growing student movement reached California, where schools from tiny Occidental College to the giant ten-campus University of California system agreed to limit the use of their names and logos to sweatshop-free apparel. Now the practical challenge is to devise a regime of monitoring and compliance.

The anti-sweatshop movement is the largest wave of student activism to hit campuses since students rallied to free Nelson Mandela by calling for a halt to university investments in South Africa more than a decade ago. This time around, the movement is electronically connected. Student activists bring their laptops and cell phones with them when they occupy administration buildings, sharing ideas and strategies with fellow activists from Boston to Berkeley. On the USAS listserv, victorious students from Wisconsin counsel neophytes from Arizona and Kentucky, and professors at Berkeley and Harvard explain how to calculate a living wage and guarantee independent monitoring in Honduras.

The target of this renewed activism is the $2.5 billion collegiate licensing industry—led by major companies like Nike, Gear, Champion, and Fruit of the

Loom—which pays colleges and universities sizable royalties in exchange for the right to use the campus logo on caps, sweatshirts, jackets, and other items. Students are demanding that the workers who make these goods be paid a living wage, no matter where in the world industry operates. Students are also calling for an end to discrimination against women workers, public disclosure of the names and addresses of all factories involved in production, and independent monitoring in order to verify compliance.

These demands are opposed by the apparel industry, the White House, and most universities. Yet so far students have made significant progress in putting the industry on the defensive. A growing number of colleges and clothing companies have adopted "codes of conduct"—something unthinkable a decade ago—although student activists consider many of these standards inadequate.

In a world economy increasingly dominated by giant retailers and manufacturers who control global networks of independently owned factories, organizing consumers may prove to be a precondition for organizing production workers. And students are a potent group of consumers. If students next year succeed in building on this year's momentum, the collegiate licensing industry will be forced to change the way it does business. These changes, in turn, could affect the organization of the world's most globalized and exploitative industry—apparel manufacturing—along with the growing number of industries that, like apparel, outsource production in order to lower labor costs and blunt worker organizing.

The Global Sweatshop

In the apparel industry, so-called manufacturers—in reality, design and marketing firms—outsource the fabrication of clothing to independent contractors around the world. In this labor-intensive industry where capital requirements are minimal, it is relatively easy to open a clothing factory. This has contributed to a global race to the bottom, in which there is always someplace, somewhere, where clothing can be made still more cheaply. Low wages reflect not low productivity, but low bargaining power. A recent analysis in *Business Week* found that although Mexican apparel workers are 70 percent as productive as U.S. workers, they earn only 11 percent as much as their U.S. counterparts; Indonesian workers, who are 50 percent as productive, earn less than 2 percent as much.

The explosion of imports has proven devastating to once well-paid, unionized U.S. garment workers. The number of American garment workers has declined from peak levels of 1.4 million in the early 1970s to 800,000 today. The one exception to these trends is the expansion of garment employment, largely among immigrant and undocumented workers, in Los Angeles, which has more than 160,000 sweatshop workers. Recent U.S. Department of Labor surveys found that more than nine out of ten such firms violate legal health and safety standards, with more than half troubled by serious violations that could lead to severe injuries or death. Working conditions in New York City, the other major domestic garment center, are similar.

The very word "sweatshop" comes from the apparel industry, where profits were "sweated" out of workers by forcing them to work longer and faster at their sewing machines. Although significant advances have been made in such aspects of production as computer-assisted design, computerized marking, and computerized cutting, the industry still remains low-tech in its core production process, the sewing of garments. The basic unit of production continues to be a worker, usually a woman, sitting or standing at a sewing machine and sewing together pieces of limp cloth.

The structure of the garment industry fosters sweatshop production. During the past decade, retailing in the United States has become increasingly concentrated. Today, the four largest U.S. retailers—Wal-Mart, Kmart, Sears, and Dayton Hudson (owner of Target and Mervyns)—account for nearly two-thirds of U.S. retail sales. Retailers squeeze manufacturers, who in turn squeeze the contractors who actually make their products. Retailers and manufacturers preserve the fiction of being completely separate from contractors because they do not want to be held legally responsible for workplace violations of labor, health, and safety laws. Retailers and manufacturers alike insist that what happens in contractor factories is not their responsibility—even though their production managers and quality control officers are constantly checking up on the sewing shops that make their clothing.

The contracting system also allows retailers and manufacturers to eliminate much uncertainty and risk. When business is slow, the contract is simply not renewed; manufacturers need not worry about paying unemployment benefits or dealing with idle workers who might go on strike or otherwise make trouble. If a particular contractor becomes a problem, there are countless others to be found who will be only too happy to get their business. Workers, however, experience the flip side of the enormous flexibility enjoyed by retailers and manufacturers. They become contingent labor, employed and paid only when their work is needed.

Since profits are taken out at each level of the supply chain, labor costs are reduced to a tiny fraction of the retail price. Consider the economics of a dress that is sewn in Los Angeles and retails for $100. Half goes to the department store and half to the manufacturer, who keeps $12.50 to cover expenses and profit, spends $22.50 on textiles, and pays $15 to the contractor. The contractor keeps $9 to cover expenses and profits. That leaves just $6 of the $100 retail price for the workers who actually make the dress. Even if the cost of direct production labor were to increase by half, the dress would still only cost $103—a small increment that would make a world of difference to the seamstress in Los Angeles, whose $7,000 to $8,000 in annual wages are roughly two-thirds of the poverty level. A garment worker in Mexico would be lucky to earn $1,000 during a year of 48 to 60 hour workweeks; in China, $500.

At the other end of the apparel production chain, the heads of the 60 publicly traded U.S. apparel retailers earn an average $1.5 million a year. The heads of the 35 publicly traded apparel manufacturers average $2 million. In 1997, according to the *Los Angeles Business Journal,* five of the six highest-paid apparel executives in Los Angeles all came from a single firm: Guess?, Inc. They took home nearly $12.6 million—enough to double the yearly wages of 1,700 L.A. apparel workers.

Organizing workers at the point of production, the century-old strategy that built the power of labor in Europe and North America, is best suited to production processes where most of the work goes on in-house. In industries whose production can easily be shifted almost anywhere on the planet, organizing is extremely difficult. Someday, perhaps, a truly international labor movement will confront global manufacturers. But in the meantime, organized consumers may well be labor's best ally. Consumers, after all, are not as readily moved as factories. And among American consumers, college students represent an especially potent force.

Kathie Lee and Robert Reich

During the early 1990s, American human rights and labor groups protested the proliferation of sweatshops at home and abroad—with major campaigns focusing on Nike and Gap. These efforts largely fizzled. But then two exposés of sweatshop conditions captured public attention. In August 1995, state and federal officials raided a garment factory in El Monte, California—a Los Angeles suburb—where 71 Thai immigrants had been held for several years in virtual slavery in an apartment complex ringed with barbed wire and spiked fences. They worked an average of 84 hours a week for $1.60 an hour, living eight to ten persons in a room. The garments they sewed ended up in major retail chains, including Macy's, Filene's and Robinsons-May, and for brand-name labels like B.U.M., Tomato, and High Sierra. Major daily papers and TV networks picked up on the story, leading to a flood of outraged editorials and columns calling for a clampdown on domestic sweatshops. Then in April 1996, TV celebrity Kathie Lee Gifford tearfully acknowledged on national television that the Wal-Mart line of clothing that bore her name was made by children in Honduran sweatshops, even though tags on the garments promised that part of the profits would go to help children. Embarrassed by the publicity, Gifford soon became a crusader against sweatshop abuses.

For several years, then—Labor Secretary Robert Reich (now the *Prospect's* senior editor) had been trying to inject the sweatshop issue onto the nation's agenda. The mounting publicity surrounding the El Monte and Kathie Lee scandals gave Reich new leverage. After all, what the apparel industry primarily sells is image, and the image of some of its major labels was getting a drubbing. He began pressing apparel executives, threatening to issue a report card on firms' behavior unless they agreed to help establish industry-wide standards.

In August 1996, the Clinton administration brought together representatives from the garment industry, labor unions, and consumer and human rights groups to grapple with sweatshops. The members of what they called the White House Apparel Industry Partnership (AIP) included apparel firms (Liz Claiborne, Reebok, L.L. Bean, Nike, Patagonia, Phillips-Van Heusen, Wal-Mart's Kathie Lee Gifford brand, and Nicole Miller), several nonprofit organizations (including the National Consumers League, Interfaith Center on Corporate Responsibility, International Labor Rights Fund, Lawyers Committee for Human Rights, Robert F. Kennedy Memorial Center for Human Rights, and Business for Social Responsibility), as well as the Union of Needletrades, Industrial and Textile Employees (UNITE), the Retail, Wholesale, and Department Store Union, and the AFL-CIO.

After intense negotiations, the Department of Labor issued an interim AIP report in April 1997 and the White House released the final 40-page report in November 1998, which included a proposed workplace code of conduct and a set of monitoring guidelines. By then, Reich had left the Clinton administration, replaced by Alexis Herman. The two labor representatives on the AIP, as well as the Interfaith Center on Corporate Responsibility, quit the group to protest the feeble recommendations, which had been crafted primarily by the garment industry delegates and which called, essentially, for the industry to police itself. This maneuvering would not have generated much attention except that a new factor—college activism—had been added to the equation.

A "Sweat-Free" Campus

The campus movement began in the fall of 1997 at Duke when a group called Students Against Sweatshops persuaded the university to require manufacturers of items with the Duke lable to sign a pledge that they would not use sweatshop labor. Duke has 700 licensees (including Nike and other major labels) that make apparel at hundreds of plants in the U.S. and in more than 10 other countries, generating almost $25 million annually in sales. Following months of negotiations, in March 1998 Duke President Nannerl Keohane and the student activists jointly announced a detailed "code of conduct" that bars Duke licensees from using child labor, requires them to maintain safe workplaces, to pay the minimum wage, to recognize the right of workers to unionize, to disclose the locations of all factories making products with Duke's name, and to allow visits by independent monitors to inspect the factories.

The Duke victory quickly inspired students on other campuses. The level of activity on campuses accelerated, with students finding creative ways to dramatize the issue. At Yale, student activists staged a "knit-in" to draw attention to sweatshop abuses. At Holy Cross and the University of California at Santa Barbara, students sponsored mock fashion shows where they discussed the working conditions under which the garments were manufactured. Duke students published a coloring book explaining how (and where) the campus mascot, the Blue Devil, is stitched onto clothing by workers in sweatshops. Activists at the University of Wisconsin infiltrated a homecoming parade and, dressed like sweatshop workers in Indonesia, carried a giant Reebok shoe. They also held a press conference in front of the chancellor's office and presented him with an oversized check for 16 cents—the hourly wage paid to workers in China making Nike athletic shoes. At Georgetown, Wisconsin, Michigan, Arizona, and Duke, students occupied administration buildings to pressure their institutions to adopt (or, in Duke's case, strengthen) anti-sweatshop codes.

●◆◉◆●

In the summer of 1998, disparate campus groups formed United Students Against Sweatshops (USAS). The USAS has weekly conference calls to discuss their negotiations with Nike, the Department of Labor, and others. It has sponsored training sessions for student leaders and conferences at several campuses where the sweatshop issue is only part of an agenda that also includes helping to build the labor movement, NAFTA, the World Trade Organization, women's rights, and other issues.

Last year, anti-sweatshop activists employed the USAS listserv to exchange ideas on negotiating tactics, discuss media strategies, swap songs to sing during rallies, and debate the technicalities of defining a "living wage" to incorporate in their campus codes of conduct. In May, the USAS listserv heated up after the popular Fox television series *Party of Five* included a scene in which one of the show's characters, Sarah (played by Jennifer Love Hewitt), helps organize a Students Against Sweatshops sit-in on her campus. A few real-life activists worried that the mainstream media was trivializing the movement by skirting the key issues ("the importance of unionized labor, the globalization of the economy, etc.") as well as focusing most of that episode on the characters' love life. University of Michigan student Rachel Paster responded:

> Let's not forget that we ARE a student movement, and students do complain about boyfriends and fashion problems. One of the biggest reasons why USAS and local student groups opposing sweatshops have been as successful as we have been is that opposition to sweatshops ISN'T that radical. Although I'm sure lots of us are all for overthrowing the corporate power structure, the human rights issues involved are what make a lot of people get involved and put their energies into rallies, sit-ins, et cetera. If we were a 'radical' group, university administrations would have brushed us off. . . . The fact that they don't is testament to the fact that we have support, not just from students on the far left, but from students in the middle ground who don't consider themselves radicals. Without those people we would NEVER have gotten as far as we have.

Indeed, the anti-sweatshop movement has been able to mobilize wide support because it strikes several nerves among today's college students, including women's rights (most sweatshop workers are women and some factories have required women to use birth control pills as a condition of employment), immigrant rights, environmental concerns, and human rights. After University of Wisconsin administrators brushed aside anti-sweatshop protestors, claiming they didn't represent student opinion, the activists ran a slate of candidates for student government. Eric Brakken, a sociology major and anti-sweatshop leader, was elected student body president and last year used the organization's substantial resources to promote the activists' agenda. And Duke's student government unanimously passed a resolution supporting the anti-sweatshop group, calling for full public disclosure of the locations of companies that manufacture Duke clothing.

The Labor Connection

At the core of the movement is a strong bond with organized labor. The movement is an important by-product of the labor movement's recent efforts, under President John Sweeney, to repair the rift between students and unions that dates to the Vietnam War. Since 1996, the AFL-CIO's Union Summer has placed almost 2,000 college students in internships with local unions around the country, most of whom work on grassroots organizing campaigns with low-wage workers in hotels, agriculture, food processing, janitorial service, and other industries. The program has its own staff, mostly young organizers only a few years out of college themselves, who actively recruit on campuses, looking for the next generation of union organizers and researchers, particularly minorities, immigrants, and women. Union Summer graduates are among the key leadership of the campus anti-sweatshop movement.

UNITE has one full-time staff person assigned to work on sweatshop issues, which includes helping student groups. A number of small human rights watchdog organizations that operate on shoestring budgets—Global Exchange, Sweatshop Watch, and the National Labor Committee [NLC]—give student activists technical advice. (It was NLC's Charles Kernaghan, an energetic researcher and publicist, who exposed the Kathie Lee Gifford connection to sweatshops in testimony before Congress.) These groups have helped bring sweatshop workers on speaking tours of American campuses, and have organized delegations of student activists to investigate firsthand the conditions in Honduras, Guatemala, El Salvador, Mexico, and elsewhere under which workers produce their college's clothing.

Unions and several liberal foundations have provided modest funding for student anti-sweatshop groups. Until this summer USAS had no staff, nor did any of its local campus affiliates. In contrast, corporate-sponsored conservative foundations have, over the past two decades, funded dozens of conservative student publications, subsidized student organizations and conferences, and recruited conservative students for internships and jobs in right-wing think tanks and publications as well as positions in the Reagan and Bush administrations and Congress, seeking to groom the next generation of conservative activists. The Intercollegiate Studies Institute, the leading right-wing campus umbrella group, has an annual budget over $5 million. In comparison, the Center for Campus Organizing, a Boston-based group that works closely with anti-sweatshop groups and other progressive campus organizations, operates on a budget under $200,000.

This student movement even has some sympathizers among university administrators. "Thank God students are getting passionate about something other than basketball and bonfires," John Burness, a Duke administrator who helped negotiate the end of the 31-hour sit-in, told the *Boston Globe*. "But the tone is definitely different. In the old days, we used to have to scramble to cut off phone lines when they took over the president's office, but we didn't have to worry about that here. They just bring their laptops and they do work."

At every university where students organized a sit-in (Duke, Georgetown, Arizona, Michigan, and Wisconsin) they have wrested agreements to require licensees to disclose the specific location of their factory sites, which is necessary for independent monitoring. Students elsewhere (including Harvard, Illinois, Brown, the University of California, Princeton, Middlebury, and Occidental) won a public disclosure requirement without resorting to civil disobedience. A few institutions have agreed to require manufacturers to pay their employees a "living wage." Wisconsin agreed to organize an academic conference this fall to discuss how to calculate living-wage formulas for countries with widely disparate costs of living, and then to implement its own policy recommendations. [See Richard Rothstein, "The Global Hiring Hall: Why We Need Worldwide Labor Standards," *TAP*, Spring 1994.]

The Industry's New Clothes

Last November, the White House-initiated Apparel Industry Partnership created a monitoring arm, the Fair Labor Association (FLA), and a few months later invited universities to join. Colleges, however, have just one seat on FLA's 14-member board. Under the group's bylaws the garment firms control the board's decisionmaking. The bylaws require a "supermajority" to approve all key questions, thus any three companies can veto a proposal they don't like.

At this writing, FLA member companies agree to ban child and prison labor, to prohibit physical abuse by supervisors, and to allow workers the freedom to organize unions in their foreign factories, though independent enforcement has not yet been specified. FLA wants to assign this monitoring task to corporate accounting firms like PricewaterhouseCoopers and Ernst & Young, to allow companies to select which facilities will be inspected, and to keep factory locations and the monitoring reports secret. Student activists want human rights and labor groups to do the monitoring.

This is only a bare beginning, but it establishes the crucial moral precedent of companies taking responsibility for labor conditions beyond their shores. Seeing this foot in the door, several companies have bowed out because they consider these standards too tough. The FLA expects that by 2001, after its monitoring program has been in place for a year, participating firms will be able to use the FLA logo on their labels and advertising as evidence of their ethical corporate practices. [See Richard Rothstein, "The Starbucks Solution: Can Voluntary Codes Raise Global Living Standards?" *TAP*, July–August 1996.]

The original list of 17 FLA-affiliated universities grew to more than 100 by mid-summer of this year. And yet, some campus groups have dissuaded college administrations (including the Universities of Michigan, Minnesota, Oregon, Toronto, and California, as well as Oberlin, Bucknell, and Earlham Colleges) from joining FLA, while others have persuaded their institutions (including Brown, Wisconsin, North Carolina, and Georgetown) to join only if the FLA adopts stronger standards. While FLA members are supposed to abide by each country's minimum-wage standards, these are typically far below the poverty level. In fact, no company has made a commitment to pay a living wage.

⋅◈⋅

The campus movement has succeeded in raising awareness (both on campus and among the general public) about sweatshops as well as the global economy. It has contributed to industry acceptance of extraterritorial labor standards, something hitherto considered utopian. It has also given thousands of students experience in the nuts and bolts of social activism, many of whom are likely to carry their idealism and organizing experiences with them into jobs with unions, community and environmental groups, and other public interest crusades.

So far, however, the movement has had only minimal impact on the daily lives of sweatshop workers at home and abroad. Nike and Reebok, largely because of student protests, have raised wages and benefits in their Indonesian footwear factories—which employ more than 100,000 workers—to 43 percent above the minimum wage. But this translates to only 20 cents an hour in U.S. dollars, far below a "living wage" to raise a family and even below the 27 cents Nike paid before Indonesia's currency devaluation. Last spring Nike announced its willingness to disclose the location of its overseas plants that produce clothing for universities. This created an important split in industry ranks, since industry leaders have argued that disclosure would undermine each firm's competitive position. But Nike has opened itself up to the charge of having a double standard, since it still refuses to disclose the location of its non-university production sites.

Within a year, when FLA's monitoring system is fully operational, students at several large schools with major licensing contracts—including Duke, Wisconsin, Michigan, North Carolina, and Georgetown—will have lists of factories in the U.S. and overseas that produce university clothing and equipment. This information will be very useful to civic and labor organizations at home and abroad, providing more opportunities to expose working conditions. Student activists at each university will be able to visit these sites—bringing media and public officials with them—to expose working conditions (and, if necessary, challenge the findings of the FLA's own monitors) and support organizing efforts by local unions and women's groups.

If the student activists can help force a small but visible "ethical" niche of the apparel industry to adopt higher standards, it will divide the industry and give unions and consumer groups more leverage to challenge the sweatshop practices of the rest of the industry. The campus anti-sweatshop crusade is part of what might be called a "conscience constituency" among consumers who are willing to incorporate ethical principles into their buying habits, even if it means slightly higher prices. Environmentalists have done the same thing with the "buy green" campaign, as have various "socially responsible" investment firms.

Beyond Consumer Awareness

In a global production system characterized by powerful retailers and invisible contractors, consumer action has an important role to play. But ultimately it must be combined with worker organizing and legislative and regulatory remedies. Unionizing the global apparel industry is an organizer's nightmare. With globalization and the contracting system, any apparel factory with a union risks losing its business.

Domestically, UNITE represents fewer than 300,000 textile and garment industry workers, down from the 800,000 represented by its two predecessor unions in the late 1960s. In the low-income countries where most U.S. apparel is now made, the prospects for unionization are dimmer still. In Mexico, labor unions are controlled by the government. China outlaws independent unions, punishing organizers with prison terms. Building the capacity for unfettered union organizing must necessarily be a long-term strategy for union organizers throughout the world. Here, the student anti-sweatshop movement can help. The independent verification of anti-sweatshop standards that students want can also serve the goal of union organizing.

Public policy could also help. As part of our trade policy, Congress could require public disclosure of manufacturing sites and independent monitoring of firms that sell goods in the American market. It could enact legislation that requires U.S. companies to follow U.S. health and safety standards globally and to bar the import of clothing made in sweatshops or made by workers who are denied the basic right to organize unions. In addition, legislation sponsored by Representative William Clay could make retailers and manufacturers legally liable for the working conditions behind the goods they design and sell, thereby ending the fiction that contractors are completely independent of the manufacturers and retailers that hire them. Last spring the California Assembly passed a state version of this legislation. Student and union activists hope that the Democrat-controlled state senate and Democratic Governor Gray Davis—whose lopsided victory last November was largely attributed to organized labor's get-out-the-vote effort—will support the bill.

◆

Thanks to the student movement, public opinion may be changing. And last spring, speaking both to the International Labor Organization in Geneva and at the commencement ceremonies at the University of Chicago (an institution founded by John D. Rockefeller and a stronghold of free market economics, but also a center of student anti-sweatshop activism), President Clinton called for an international campaign against child labor, including restrictions on government purchases of goods made by children.

A shift of much apparel production to developing countries may well be inevitable in a global economy. But when companies do move their production abroad, student activists are warning "you can run but you can't hide," demanding that they be held responsible for conditions in contractor factories no matter where they are. Students can't accomplish this on their own, but in a very short period of time they have made many Americans aware that they don't have to leave their consciences at home when they shop for clothes.

Radley Balko  **NO**

Sweatshops and Globalization

"In a village in the Mekong delta in Vietnam a woman and her twelve-year old daughter sit all day in the shade from five in the morning until five in the evening making straw beach mats. For their labour they receive $1 a day."

"In China, workers at Wellco Factory making shoes for Nike are paid 16 cents/ hour (living wage for a small family is about 87 cents), 11–12 hour shifts, 7 days a week, 77–84 hours per week; workers are fined if they refuse overtime, and they're not paid an extra rate for overtime hours."

Stories like these are common when we hear talk about "sweatshop" plants in the developing world. We hear worse, too—terrible stories about women and children tricked into bondage, of union organizers getting beaten or killed, of terrible working conditions, long hours, and no bathroom breaks.

And yet American companies still operate low-wage factories—"sweat-shops"—in developing countries. And there's still a copious source of labor in those countries eager to take the low-paying jobs western factories offer them.

So what's the story on sweatshops? Are they as bad as globalization critics claim they are? Should we boycott companies that operate them? Can they be stopped? Should they be stopped?

The Race to the Bottom

Globalization critics often cite sweatshops as a prime example of the "race to the bottom" phenomenon. A "race to the bottom" is what happens, they say, when world markets are opened to free, unfettered trade. Without transnational labor guidelines and regulations, big corporations will look to place factories and manufacturing plants in countries with the most relaxed environmental and—for our purposes—labor standards.

Developing countries then compete for the patronage of these companies by lowering labor standards—minimum wages and workplace safety requirements, for example. The result: horrendous working conditions like those described above, and no state oversight to make the factories change them.

Critics of free trade say in some countries it's gotten so bad that companies have begun using slave labor, workers compelled to work unpaid by totalitarian governments eager to entertain western businesses.

In the book *The Race to the Bottom,* author Alan Tonelson describes the process while discussing the 1999 World Trade Organization protests in Seattle:

> Internationally, WTO boosters faced an equally knotty dilemma. Most of the organization's third world members—or at least their governments—opposed including any labor rights and environmental protections in trade agreements. They viewed low wages and lax pollution control laws as major assets they could offer to international investors—prime lures for job-creating factories and the capital they so desperately needed for other development-related purposes. Indeed, they observed, most rich countries ignored the environment and limited workers' power (to put it kindly) early in their economic histories. Why should today's developing countries be held to higher standards?

Tonelson goes on to say that it is workers, then, who must shoulder globalization's burdens, while western companies win cheap labor, western consumers win cheap sneakers and straw hats, and corporate CEOs win eight-figure salaries. And, Tonelson and his supporters argue, it's not just third-world workers. Western workers lose when factories in the U.S. close down, and migrate overseas in search of laborers willing to work for poverty wages.

Critics say sweatshops are a way for corporations to exploit the poverty and desperation of the third world, while allowing them to circumvent the living wages, organization rights, and workplace safety regulations labor activists have fought long and hard for in the west.

What of Sweatshop Workers?

When *New York Times* journalists Nicholas Kristof and Sheryl Wudunn went to Asia to live, they were outraged when they first arrived at the sweatshop conditions Asian factory workers worked under. Like most westerners, the thought of 14+ hour shifts six or seven days a week with no overtime pay seemed unconscionable.

After spending some time in the region, however, Kristof and Wudunn slowly came to the conclusion that, while regrettable, sweatshops are an important part of a developing nation's journey to prosperity. The two later documented the role of sweatshops in emerging economies in their book *Thunder from the East.* Kristof and Wudunn relay one anecdote that helped them reach their conclusion *in the New York Times*:

> One of the half-dozen men and women sitting on a bench eating was a sinewy, bare-chested laborer in his late 30's named Mongkol Latlakorn. It was a hot, lazy day, and so we started chatting idly about the food and, eventually, our families. Mongkol mentioned that his daughter, Darin, was 15, and his voice softened as he spoke of her. She was beautiful and smart, and her father's hopes rested on her.
> "Is she in school?" we asked.

"Oh, no," Mongkol said, his eyes sparkling with amusement. "She's working in a factory in Bangkok. She's making clothing for export to America." He explained that she was paid $2 a day for a nine-hour shift, six days a week.

"It's dangerous work," Mongkol added. "Twice the needles went right through her hands. But the managers bandaged up her hands, and both times she got better again and went back to work."

"How terrible," we murmured sympathetically.

Mongkol looked up, puzzled. "It's good pay," he said. "I hope she can keep that job. There's all this talk about factories closing now, and she said there are rumors that her factory might close. I hope that doesn't happen. I don't know what she would do then."

Globalization's proponents argue that sweatshops, for all their unseemliness, often present developing laborers the best-paid jobs with the best working environment they've ever had; often their other options are begging, prostitution, or primitive agriculture.

Removing the best of a series of bad options, they say, does nothing to better the plight of the world's poor.

Boycotts and Bans

Anti-sweatshop organizations have achieved an impressive level of organization and influence in the last several years. Campus groups have persuaded university administrators at dozens of colleges around the country to refuse to buy school apparel from companies who use sweatshop labor. The activists demand that corporations pay a "living wage" and agree to international monitoring, or face the loss of collegiate licensing privileges—which amount to some $2.5 billion in annual revenue for the likes of Nike, Reebok and Fruit of the Loom.

So far, evidence has shown that boycotts and public pressure do get results, but perhaps not the kinds of results that are in the best interests of sweatshop workers.

Free traders argue that instead of providing better working conditions or higher wages, which had until then offset the costs of relocating overseas, western companies respond to public pressure by simply closing down their third world plants, or by ceasing to do business with contractors who operate sweatshops.

The result: thousands of people already in a bad situation then find themselves in a worse one.

In 2000, for example, the BBC did an expose on sweatshop factories in Cambodia with ties to both Nike and the Gap. The BBC uncovered unsavory working conditions, and found several examples of children under 15 years of age working 12 or more hour shifts.

After the BBC expose aired, both Nike and the Gap pulled out of Cambodia, costing the country $10 million in contracts, and costing hundreds of Cambodians their jobs.

There are lots more examples like that one.

- In the early 1990s, the United States Congress considered a piece of legislation called the "Child Labor Deterrence Act," which would have taken punitive action against companies benefiting from child labor. The Act never passed, but the public debate it triggered put enormous pressure on a number of multinational corporations. One German garment maker that would have been hit with trade repercussions if the Act had passed laid off 50,000 child workers in Bangladesh. The British charity organization Oxfam later conducted a study which found that thousands of those laid-off children later became prostitutes, turned to crime, or starved to death.
- The United Nations organization UNICEF *reports* that an international boycott of the Nepalese carpet industry in the mid-1990s caused several plants to shut down, and forced thousands of Nepalese girls into prostitution.
- In 1995, a consortium of anti-sweatshop groups threw the spotlight on football (soccer) stitching plants in Pakistan. In particular, the effort targeted enforcing a ban on sweatshop soccer balls by the time the 1998 World Cup began in France. In response, Nike and Reebok shut down their plants in Pakistan and several other companies followed suit. The result: tens of thousands of Pakistanis were again unemployed. According to UPI, mean family income in Pakistan fell by more than 20%.

In his book *Race to the Top,* journalist Tomas Larsson discussed the Pakistani soccer ball case with Keith E. Maskus, an economist at the University of Colorado:

> "The celebrated French ban on soccer balls sewn in Pakistan for the World Cup in 1998 resulted in significant dislocation of children from employment. Those who tracked them found that a large proportion ended up begging and/or in prostitution."

In response, several activist groups have stopped calling for boycotts, and have since started calling for pressure from the governments in whose countries the multinational corporations call home. Still, free traders argue, companies make decisions that are in the best interests of their shareholders and investors, and so if locating overseas isn't offset enough by cheap labor to make the investment worthwhile, companies will merely chose not to invest, costing poor countries thousands of jobs.

Are Sweatshops a Stop on the Road to Prosperity?

In his book, Larsson also argues that poor labor standards are usually symptomatic of other problems in a developing country, and that in the long run, they are in fact a *disadvantage* to that country's ability to compete in the international economy. "It is not . . . countries with the worst human rights records that top the annual rankings of national competitiveness," Larsson writes, "and it is certainly not the countries with the lowest wages and least protection for workers that dominate export markets, or attract the lion's share of foreign direct investment."

Every prosperous country today was once mired in "developing" status. And every prosperous country today once employed child labor in its economic adolescence that would today be considered "sweatshop" working conditions. That includes Britain, France, Sweden, Germany and the United States. Only with the prosperity brought by international trade, globalization's adherents say, can a country then afford to demand better working conditions for its workers.

The economist and syndicated columnist Thomas Sowell writes:

> Half a century ago, public opinion in Britain caused British firms in colonial West Africa to pay higher wages than local economic conditions would have warranted. Net result? Vastly more job applicants than jobs.
>
> Not only did great numbers of frustrated Africans not get jobs. They did not get the work experience that would have allowed them to upgrade their skills and become more valuable and higher-paid workers later on.

Today of course, West Africa is still mired in poverty. Contrast Africa to Hong Kong, or to Taiwan, two countries that embraced an influx of foreign investment, and made a leap to prosperity in just 25 years that took most European countries nearly a century.

Kristof and Wudunn likewise point out that fifty years ago, countries like India resisted allowing foreign investment, while countries like Taiwan and South Korea accepted it—including the poor working conditions that came with it. Today, Taiwan and South Korea boast modern, well-educated, first-world economies. India has become more amenable to investment in the last several years—and its economy has shown promise in response. But for decades, India's refusal to accept foreign "exploitation" wrought wide scale poverty and devastation.

In his book *In Defense of Global Capitalism*, Swedish public policy expert Johan Norberg notes that although India still battles poverty, its improving economy has shrunk its proportion of child laborers from 35% in the 1950s to just 12% in the last few years. Norberg further writes that the burgeoning economies in East and Southeast Asia may enable most of the countries in that region to eliminate child labor altogether by 2010.

Globalists also point out that the modern world economy and its interconnectivity makes it possible for a country to make the transition from an economy where child labor is a necessity to an economy that can afford to ban it in a period of time never before contemplated.

Kristof notes that from the onset of the Industrial Revolution, it took Great Britain 58 years to double its per capita income. In China—where sweatshops are prevalent—per capita income doubles every 10 years. In the sweatshop-dotted southern providence of Dongguan, China wages have increased fivefold in the last few years. "A private housing market has appeared," Kristof writes of Dongguan, "and video arcades and computer school have opened to cater to workers with rising incomes. . . . a hint of a middle class has appeared."

The anti-sweatshop activists response to these arguments says that because the west has wealth and prosperity, it is the west's responsibility to bring the developing world into modernization without exploiting its laborers. Multinational corporations can still secure comfortable profit margins without paying miniscule wages, forbidding union organization, and forcing long hours with overtime. As Kevin Danaher of the activist group Global Exchange writes, "Should trade agreements be designed largely to benefit corporations, or should they instead put social and environmental concerns first?"

But free trade advocates say that cheap labor is the one commodity developing nations can offer that first world countries can't. Force corporations to pay artificially high wages in those countries, they say, and there's no incentive for a company to endure the costs of shipping, construction, and risk that come with installing plants overseas. If corporations don't invest, those third world laborers again get forced back into the fields, the alleys, the brothels, and the black market. Better to endure the discomfort of poor working conditions in the short run, so that these countries can begin to build the economies that will enable them to demand better working conditions in the long run.

Common Ground?

In the end, there are at least a few areas in which both free traders and anti-sweatshop crusaders can agree. Most free trade advocates agree, for example, that benefiting from slave labor is no better than theft. Sweatshop workers are often the envy of their communities—they make more money than the farmhands or beggars, for example. But it's important that they're working in factories of their own free will. The key to building prosperity is choice, and if workers don't have the option to quit, or to take a job with a factory across town offering better wages, the "free" in "free trade" is a misnomer, and the benefits of globalization are tainted.

Likewise, free traders and anti-globalization activists usually agree that human rights violations should be documented, and that perpetrators of such violations should be publicized and embarrassed. If in its desire to attract foreign investment a government refuses to police a sweatshop factory where women are being forced into sexual favors, or where union organizers get beaten, it's certainly acceptable—in fact it's imperative—that that government be held accountable in the international community.

The fundamental disagreement in the sweatshop debate seems to be whether or not it's fair for big western companies to benefit from cheap labor in the developing world. Globalists say that menial manufacturing labor is the historical first step in a developing economy's first steps toward prosperity. Sweatshop activists say western corporations can afford to pay artificial "living" wages, and that anything less reeks of exploitation. They further argue that if corporations aren't willing to offer better working conditions on their own, western governments should penalize them, and consumers should refrain from buying their products. Globalists argue that if that happens, corporations would have no incentive to invest in the third world in the first place.

As trade barriers continue to fall, developing countries will continue to chose one track or the other—to embrace foreign investment, or to demand wages not proportional to what their national labor market would naturally allow. Which track delivers prosperity and which track produces continued poverty will lend clues as to who's winning the debate.

Further Reading

Global Exchange—An advocacy group that promotes "fair trade" in lieu of "free trade."

Nicholas Kristof—*New York Times* columnist who regularly writes on globalization issues.

Sweatshops.org—Co-op guide to ending America's sweatshops and encouraging "fair trade."

National Labor Committee—is supported by American labor unions to oppose sweatshops in the developing world

United Students Against Sweatshops—Clearinghouse website for campus anti-sweatshop activists.

www.free-market.net-Free-Market.Net's Globalization Directory—Hosts a litany of articles related to sweatshops and other globalization issues.

David R. Henderson—A Hoover Institution scholar and economist who frequently opposes movements to end sweatshops in the developing world.

Between a Rock and a Hard Place—A Smithsonian Institution history of American sweatshops.

POSTSCRIPT

Are Global Sweatshops Exploitative?

Opponents of global sweatshops argue that they are exploitative in two ways. First, as noted in the introduction to this debate, exploitation occurs when multinational corporations systematically single out countries with favorable labor conditions to produce their products at considerably lower expense than they could in their home country. In addition to this practical position, opponents of sweatshops argue from a moral perspective. In this view, derived from Immanuel Kant's categorical imperative, people are entitled to respect because they are moral beings possessed of dignity. Ethics scholars Denis Arnold and Norman Bowie quote Kant: "In Kant's words, 'Humanity itself is a dignity; for a man cannot be used merely as a means by any man . . . but must always be used at the same time as an end. It is just in this that his dignity . . . consists . . .'" (Arnold and Bowie, "Sweatshops and Respect for Persons," *Business Ethics Quarterly*, vol. 13, no. 2, 2003, p. 222). According to Arnold and Bowie, global sweatshops are inhumane and exploitative because they treat workers as means to an end and not as ends in and of themselves. The below-subsistence wage rates and dangerous, abusive working conditions in sweatshops more than testify to the truth of this assertion.

The standard defense of sweatshops consists primarily of practical observations and arguments, most of which were covered in the article you just read by Radley Balko. But there is a philosophical justification as well. This line of defense argues that workers have a right to do what they want with their labor. Granted, in most developing countries, workers have few options available in terms of deciding how to spend their labor; nevertheless, as long as they decide to work on their own volition, the sweatshops are not guilty of exploiting the workers. Indeed, it is the opponents of sweatshops who are guilty of immoral behavior since they want to take away—through the shutting down of sweatshops and the punishment of multinational firms that use them—the local worker's right to decide how to use his labor. This leads to a difficult question for the sweatshop critics: What right do you (the critic) have to go into another country and tell its people where they can and cannot work?

Suggested Readings

Articles against sweatshops:

> Denis Arnold and Norman Bowie, Sweatshops and respect for persons. *Business Ethics Quarterly*, vol. 13, no. 2, April 2003.

> Liza Featherstone and United Students Against Sweatshops, *Students Against Sweatshops*. Verso, 2002.

William Greider, No to global sweatshops. *The Nation,* May 7, 2001.

Matt Zwolinski, Sweatshops, Entry 167. *Social Issues Encyclopedia,* 2004.

Articles supportive of sweatshops:

Radley Balko, Third world workers need western jobs. Foxnews.com, May 6, 2004. http://www.foxnews.com/story/0,2933,119125,00.html

Allen R. Myerson, Sweatshops often benefit the economies of developing nations, in *Child Labor and Sweatshops,* Mary E. Williams, ed. Greenhaven Press, 1999.

Thomas Sowell, Third world sweatshops: Multinational opportunity vs. nihilistic indignation. *Capitalism Magazine,* January 28, 2004. http://www.capmag.com/article.asp?ID=3489

Stephen Spath, The virtues of 'sweatshops.' *Capitalism Magazine,* January 18, 2001. http://www.capmag.com/article.asp?ID=151

Contributors to This Volume

EDITOR

DR. MARC STREET is currently an assistant professor of management at the University of South Florida, St. Petersburg. He received his BA (economics) from the University of Maryland, College Park (1983); his MBA from the University of Baltimore (1993); and his PhD (organizational behavior) from The Florida State University (1998). Prior to his current position, Dr. Street spent five years on faculty at the University of Tulsa. His primary research interests include business ethics and corporate social responsibility. To date, Dr. Street has published a total of 29 refereed conference papers, book chapters, and publications in journals such as *Organizational Behavior and Human Decision Processes, Journal of Business Ethics, Journal of World Business, Small Group Research,* and *Journal of Social Behavior and Personality,* among others. Prior to entering academia, Dr. Street spent 10 years in the private sector, the last four as a financial consultant for Merrill Lynch in Baltimore, MD.

STAFF

Larry Loeppke	Managing Editor
Jill Peter	Senior Developmental Editor
Nichole Altman	Developmental Editor
Beth Kundert	Production Manager
Jane Mohr	Project Manager
Tara McDermott	Design Coordinator
Bonnie Coakley	Editorial Assistant
Lenny Behnke	Permissions Coordinator Lead

AUTHORS

FRITZ ALLHOFF is currently a philosophy doctoral candidate at the University of California, Santa Barbara. He has published numerous journal articles on a wide range of topics including philosophy, history of philosophy, and business ethics.

SARAH ANDERSON is a director of the Global Economy project at the Institute for Policy Studies, a progressive think tank dedicated to a variety of issues.

RICHARD APPELBAUM is a professor of sociology and global and international studies at the University of California, Santa Barbara. He currently serves as director of the Institute for Social, Behavioral, and Economic Research (ISBER) and as codirector of the ISBER's Center for Global Studies. He is the founding editor of *Competition and Change: The Journal of Global Business and Political Economy,* and he is currently engaged in a multidisciplinary study of the apparel industry in Los Angeles and the Asian-Pacific Rim.

STEPHEN BAINBRIDGE is professor of law at the UCLA School of Law, where he teaches corporate and securities law. He writes the `ProfessorBainbridge` `.com` blog.

RADLEY BALKO is a freelance writer living in Arlington, Virginia. Balko publishes his own blog, The Agitator, and writes occassionally for Tech Central Station and `Foxnews.com`, where he has a regular column.

KATERINA BEZRUKOVA is an affiliated faculty member at the Wharton School of the University of Pennsylvania. Her research focuses on workplace diversity, organizational conflict, and group productivity. Her most recent work investigates the effects of demographic faultlines in diverse workgroups.

SISSELA BOK is a faculty member of the Center for Advanced Study in the Behavioral Sciences in Stanford, California, and a former associate professor of philosophy at Brandeis University in Waltham, Massachusetts. Her publications include *Lying: Moral Choice in Public and Private Life* (Random House, 1979); *Secrets: On the Ethics of Concealment and Revelation* (Vintage Books, 1983); and *A Strategy for Peace: Human Values and the Threat of War* (Pantheon Books, 1989).

JANICE BROWN is an associate justice of the Supreme Court of the State of California. She earned her J.D. from the University of California, Los Angeles, Law School, and, prior to her appointment to the bench, served as legal affairs secretary to Governor Pete Wilson. In 1994 Governor Wilson appointed her to a state appeals court, and two years later he elevated her to the state's supreme court.

JOHN CAVANAGH has been director of the Institute for Policy Studies since 1998. He is the co-author of 11 books on the global economy, most recently *Alternatives to Economic Globalization: A Better World Is Possible.* He is a graduate of both Princeton University and Dartmouth College.

HERMAN E. DALY is a professor in the School of Public Affairs at the University of Maryland and the author of a classic on the subject of environmental economics, *Steady-State Economics: The Economics of Biophysical Equilibrium and*

Moral Growth (W. H. Freeman, 1977). Recently he authored *Beyond Growth: The Economics of Sustainable Development* (Beacon Press, 1996) and *Ecological Economics and the Ecology of Economics: Essays in Criticism* (Edward Elgar, 1999).

PETER DREIER is the Dr. E. P. Clapp Distinguished Professor of Politics and director of the Urban & Environmental Policy Program of the Urban & Environmental Policy Institute at Occidental College in Los Angeles, California. Prior to joining the Occidental faculty in 1993, he served nine years as director of housing at the Boston Redevelopment Authority and as senior policy adviser to Mayor Ray Flynn of Boston, Massachusetts. He has also taught at Tufts University.

DANIEL W. DREZNER is assistant professor of political science at the University of Chicago and the author of *The Sanctions Paradox*. He keeps a weblog at www.danieldrezner.com/blog.

DENIS DUTTON is a professor of philosophy who lectures on the dangers of pseudoscience at the science faculties of the University of Canterbury in New Zealand. He is also editor of the website Arts & Letters Daily (http://www.aldaily.com).

ROBIN ELY is an associate professor of organizational behavior at the Harvard Business School. Her research focuses on how organizations can better manage their race and gender relations while at the same time increasing their effectiveness. She is currently exploring learning—the process of improving performance through interactions that advance knowledge and understanding—as a key mechanism through which diversity enhances work group functioning.

DR. JOSEPH T. GILBERT teaches strategy and management ethics at the graduate level, and his research has been published in a number of journals.

EDMUND R. GRAY is professor and chair of the department of management at Loyola Marymount University. He has authored or coauthored five books and over 70 articles and other scholarly publications.

LINDA GREER, a senior scientist with the Natural Resources Defense Council, has worked for more than 15 years on the regulation of toxic chemicals and hazardous waste.

LARRY GROSS, CPCU, is an account executive with Insurance Services Office, Inc. (ISO) and has been with ISO for 15 years. He was chair of the Research Committee for the CPCU Society's Philadelphia Chapter at the time of this publication.

HEIDI I. HARTMANN is president of the Institute for Women's Policy Research and a contributing author to the organization's propriety publications.

ROBERT D. HAY is a professor of management at the University of Arkansas. He retired in 1990 after 41 years of teaching, research, and service. He is the author of 11 books as well as numerous articles and cases.

SUSAN JACKSON is professor of human resource management and director of the doctoral program in Industrial Relations and Human Resources at the School of Management and Labor Relations, Rutgers University. Her research interests include human resource management systems, work team functioning, and workforce diversity. For more information about this work, visit her Web site at www.rci.rutgers.edu/~sjacksox.

KAREN JEHN is professor of management at the Wharton School of the University of Pennsylvania. Her research focuses on the effects of diversity on group processes and on the effects of conflict on group performance.

WILBERT JENKINS is associate professor of history at Temple University and the author of *Climbing Up to Glory: A Short History of African Americans During the Civil War and Reconstruction* (Scholarly Resources, 2002).

APARNA JOSHI is assistant professor at the Institute of Labor and Industrial Relations, University of Illinois at Urbana–Champaign. She conducts research in the area of diversity in teams and organizations and in the area of management of global teams. She currently teaches courses on Managing Workforce Diversity and Training and Development.

IRA T. KAY is the practice director in charge of Watson Wyatt Worldwide's compensation practice. He has written and spoken widely on executive compensation issues. He is also the author of several books on the subject.

JOYCE L. KENNARD is an associate justice of the Supreme Court of the State of California. She earned her J.D. from the University of Southern California School of Law in 1974, served as a judge in several lower courts during the 1980s, and was appointed to the state's supreme court by Governor George Deukmejian in 1989.

THOMAS KOCHAN is the George M. Bunker Professor of Management at the MIT Sloan School of Management. His research focuses on the changing nature of work and employment relationships and their implications for organizational governance and public policies.

ROBERT A. LARMER is an associate professor of philosophy at the University of New Brunswick in Fredericton, New Brunswick, Canada. His research interests focus on the philosophy of religion, the philosophy of the mind, and business ethics. He has written numerous articles in these fields, and he is the author of *Water Into Wine? An Investigation of the Concept of Miracle* (McGill-Queen's University Press, 1996). He received his PhD from the University of Ottawa.

JONATHAN LEONARD is professor of economics at the Haas School of Business at the University of California, Berkeley. His research focuses on the effects of affirmative action on employment and on the effects of industrial relations practices and activities on performance.

DAVID LEVINE is a professor at the Haas School of Business at the University of California, Berkeley, where he is also editor of the journal *Industrial Relations* and associate director of the Institute of Industrial Relations. His research focuses on labor markets and workplaces. His recent books are *Reinventing the Workplace* (1995); *The American Workplace: Skills, Pay and Employee Involvement* (1999); and *Changes in Careers and Wage Structures at Large American Employers* (2002).

NAOMI LOPEZ is director of the Center for Enterprise and Opportunity at the Pacific Research Institute in San Francisco. She has written extensively on issues of gender discrimination.

ALEXEI M. MARCOUX is assistant professor of management at Loyola University in Chicago and sometime contributor to the Cato Institute.

JENNIFER MOORE, a former assistant professor of philosophy at the University of Delaware in Newark, Delaware, has done teaching and research in business ethics and business law. She is the author of *Math Bridge* (Rainbow Bridge, 1999) and coauthor, with Karen Musalo and Richard A. Boswell, of *Refugee Law and Policy: Selected Statutes, Regulations and International Materials* (Carolina Academic Press, 1998).

LISA H. NEWTON is a professor of philosophy and director of the Program in Applied Ethics at Fairfield University in Fairfield, Connecticut. She is coauthor, with Catherine K. Dillingham, of *Watersheds 3: Ten Cases in Environmental Ethics*, 3rd ed. (Wadsworth, 2001) and coauthor, with David A. Schmidt, of *Wake-up Calls: Classic Cases in Business Ethics* (Wadsworth, 1996). She is also the author of numerous articles in journals of business and health care ethics.

RAYMOND J. PATCHAK, a certified hazardous materials manager, has over 10 years of environmental regulatory compliance experience, during which time he has been responsible for auditing and developing compliance programs at many different types of manufacturing and waste-handling facilities. An active member of the Academy of Certified Hazardous Materials Managers (ACHMM), he is a founding member of the ACHMM's ISO 14000 Committee as well as president of the Michigan chapter of the ACHMM.

DAVID PIMENTEL, a professor at Cornell University in Ithaca, New York, holds a joint appointment in the Department of Entomology and the Section of Ecology and Systematics. He has served as consultant to the Executive Office of the President, Office of Science and Technology, and as chairman of various panels, boards (including the Environmental Studies Board), and committees at the National Academy of Sciences, the United States Department of Energy, and the United States Congress.

CHRIS PROVIS studied and taught philosophy and now is associate professor in the School of International Business at the University of South Australia. His work has appeared in numerous journals including the *Australian Journal of Labour Law* and the *Negotiation Journal*.

ALAN REYNOLDS is a senior fellow at the Cato Institute. A former columnist with *Forbes* and *Reason*, Reynolds has been a frequent contributor to such publications as *The Wall Street Journal*, *American Spectator*, *National Review*, and *Harvard Business Review*.

STEPHEN J. ROSE, formerly a senior economist at the Educational Testing Service, is now with ORC Macro.

STEVEN E. RUSHBROOK is a senior consultant in the compensation practice in Waston Wyatt Worldwide's New York office. He has degrees from Trinity College and Vanderbelt University's Owen Graduate School of Management.

DR. JOAN M. SCHORK is a chemical engineer specializing in gas separations and process technology. With almost 20 years of industrial experience, she has worked in gas and chemical plant operations, fundamental and applied research, process design, and numerical modeling. She currently manages the Fluorine Technology Center and the Reference Standards Lab within the electronics division of Air Products and Chemicals Inc.

WILLIAM R. SMITH, a certified hazardous materials manager and an ISO 14001 Environmental Management Systems (EMS) auditor, is a principal at Competitive Edge Environmental Management Systems, Inc. He has served on the Registrar Accreditation Board's Auditor Certification Board, which governs the ISO 14000 EMS auditor certification program in the United States, and he is a board member of the Academy of Certified Hazardous Materials Managers. He is also the founding chairman of the ISO 14000 Committee.

DAVID THOMAS is the H. Naylor Fitzhugh Professor of Business Administration at the Harvard Business School. His research focuses on the influence of cultural diversity on organizational and individual effectiveness, minority executive development, and strategic human resource management. His most recent book (with John Gabarro), *Breaking Through: The Making of Minority Executives in Corporate America,* was the 2001 Academy of Management George R. Terry Book Award winner for outstanding contribution to management theory and practice.

ROBERT B. THOMPSON is the George Alexander Madill Professor of Law at Washington University, St. Louis, Missouri. His work has been published in numerous law journals across the country including the *Case Western Reserve Law Review.*

CHRISTOPHER VAN LÖBEN SELS is a senior project analyst for the Natural Resources Defense Council in San Francisco, California.

MICHAEL A. VERESPEJ is a writer for *Industry Week.*

MURRAY WEIDENBAUM is the chairman of the Weidenbaum Center at Washington University in St. Louis. He is also the author of *Business and Government in the Global Marketplace,* 6th ed. (Prentice Hall, 1999) and *Looking for Common Ground on U.S. Trade Policy* (Center for Strategic and International Studies, 2001).

WALTER E. WILLIAMS is the John M. Olin Distinguished Professor of Economics at George Mason University.

Index